BEYOND
POLITICAL
CORRECTNESS

To David —

Thanks for the marvelous
job you are doing with
the library!   Best wishes,
                    Mike

Transformations in Politics and Society
Series Editor: Theodore Becker

BEYOND POLITICAL CORRECTNESS

Social Transformation in the United States

Michael S. Cummings

LYNNE
RIENNER
PUBLISHERS

BOULDER
LONDON

Published in the United States of America in 2001 by
Lynne Rienner Publishers, Inc.
1800 30th Street, Boulder, Colorado 80301
www.rienner.com

and in the United Kingdom by
Lynne Rienner Publishers, Inc.
3 Henrietta Street, Covent Garden, London WC2E 8LU

Library of Congress Cataloging-in-Publication Data
Cummings, Michael S., 1943–
    Beyond political correctness: social transformation in the United States/
Michael S. Cummings.
    (Transformations in politics and society)
    Includes bibliographical references and index.
    ISBN 1-55587-863-6 (alk. paper)
    ISBN 1-58826-006-2 (pb)
    1. Liberalism—United States. 2. Communitarianism—United States.
3. Political correctness—United States. 4. United States—Social policy—1993–
5. United States—Politics and government—1993–   I. Title. II. Series.
JC574.2.U6 C85   2001
320.51'3'0973—dc21   00-053326

British Cataloguing in Publication Data
A Cataloguing in Publication record for this book
is available from the British Library.

Printed and bound in the United States of America

       The paper used in this publication meets the requirements
 ∞   of the American National Standard for Permanence of
       Paper for Printed Library Materials Z39.48-1984.

       5 4 3 2 1

*For Petra, Anthony, and Eliza
and in memory of Libbus and Jocko*

Contents

Preface

This book is about political correctness, or PC. It is also about social transformation. It is especially about how political correctness impedes the kind of social change that could greatly improve our country. It is written for students and scholars of politics, for social activists, and for concerned citizens. In the glossary at the end of the book, you will find definitions of key terms such as "political correctness," "progressive," "liberal," and "conservative." These definitions are neither right nor wrong, but are simply the ones I have found most useful in my own thinking. You will notice that particular people you know may fit the generic definitions imperfectly, because few people fit into a single definitional box.

A particular term, for instance "adultism," may push your buttons, perhaps because it feels too PC or anti-PC. Please don't throw the book across the room, as a student of mine did recently with a book I had assigned, but intellectually gird your loins to engage my argument. As I make my "progressive" case against PC, I will take positions that may surprise you. My purpose is not to create a new set of politically correct proposals, but to bring out of the closet and into the light of day some provocative ideas that have been shortchanged by PC. I'd be happy to engage you further at <mcumming@carbon.cudenver.edu>. I enjoy passionate, conscientious disagreement more than casual or unconsidered agreement.

* * *

The ideas in this book have been inspired by many thinkers, from Plato and Marx to W.E.B. Du Bois, and Betty Friedan to Christopher Lasch and Jeanne Bethke Elshtain. They have been enriched by the work of many public servants, including my distant relative Blue Jacket, Cesar Chavez, Ina May Gaskin, Clarence Jordan, Ralph Nader, Nellie Story, Norman Thomas, Harriet Tubman, and George Wiley. They also have benefited from my engagement with a generation of students, colleagues, and political activists.

The following people read all or parts of the manuscript: Leanne Anderson, Steve Barr, Ted Becker, Molly Boone, Zach Boone, Karen Breslin, Susan Cummings, Ken Dolbeare, Dan Eades, Larry Hanks, Patrizia Longo, Bill Patrick, Mike Robinson, Ed Schwerin, Christa Slaton, Peter Stillman, Thad Tecza, Petra Ulrych, Scott Vickers, Mike Woontner, Regina Woontner, and Betty Zisk. Their reactions, critiques, and suggestions have been invaluable, and I am deeply beholden to them. I owe a special debt of thanks to Ted Becker for soliciting and encouraging me in this lengthy project, to Jerry Jacks for helping me with the research, and to Dan Eades of Lynne Rienner Publishers for supporting it at every stage.

Finally, a number of friends have made special contributions, both direct and indirect, to my work on the book, including Albert Bates, Harv Bishop, Bob Clifton, Joel Edelstein, Vasek Hlavaty, Cheng Liang Lee, Ken Gordon, Jan Lapetino, Scott Logan, Patty McMurray, Russell Means, Glenn Morris, Karla Haas Moskowitz, Ken Newman, Zdenka Pilna, Don Pitzer, John Rensenbrink, Tony Robinson, Giuseppa Saccaro del Buffa, Lyman Tower Sargent, Steve Thomas, Ray Tillman, and Stacey Winslow. Most of these contributors have provided transformative examples, or helped me think outside of my box, or both.

—*M.S.C.*

BEYOND POLITICAL CORRECTNESS

Introduction:
Political Correctness as
Antitransformational

"This is no time to engage in the luxury of cooling off, to take the tranquilizing drug of gradualism . . . Now is the time. . . . I have a dream. . . .
Let freedom ring."
                                        —Martin Luther King, Jr., August 28, 1963

"But the hushing of the criticism of honest opponents is a dangerous
thing."
                                        —W.E.B. Du Bois[1]

This is a book about how left-wing political correctness, or PC, unintentionally undermines progressive causes such as social justice, children's
rights, ecology, economic democracy, and the building of strong communities. PC's silencing of dissent and chilling of debate, I shall argue, does
more damage to the cause of social transformation than to the cause of conservatism. Left-wing ideological closure obscures many promising ideas
and insights; the chapters that follow take some of them out of the closet
and put them on the table for frank discussion. These ideas promise to
transform affirmative action, shift our shared values from win-lose to win-
win, enfranchise youth, empower families, preserve the balance of nature,
restore communities beset by crime, and democratize the economy.

No one smirks or protests when a mathematician claims that a math
problem has a single correct solution and that all other answers are simply
wrong. Politics, on the other hand, is a matter of opinion, and it makes less
sense to speak of a "politically correct" solution to a social problem. "Just
so," say political conservatives. "Yet some people act as if they had the single correct political solution." For more than a decade, conservatives have
charged their leftist foes with claiming political correctness, for themselves
and their liberal or radical beliefs. The term "political correctness" was created in the 1920s and 1930s by communist groups, and notably used without apology by Chinese leader Mao Zedong for over four decades, to depict
their own political views as objectively, scientifically valid.[2] In the 1980s

the term was rediscovered and given a satirical twist by conservatives to debunk the narrow-mindedness of their left-wing opponents.

Today, criticisms of political correctness come mostly from conservatives fed up with liberalism, radicalism, socialism, feminism, multiculturalism, environmentalism, egalitarianism, and other left-wingisms.[3] These right-wing critics of PC charge their leftist opponents with acting unfairly, even oppressively, toward conservative principles, policies, and people. In 1999 an anti-PC Princeton professor quoted a colleague's complaint that academic freedom had come to mean "the moral right to be as far to the moral left as you please."[4] As a result, charge such anti-PC groups as the American Council of Trustees and Alumni (ACTA), nonleftists don't get a fair shake on college campuses.[5] Both Lynne Cheney, wife of Vice President Dick Cheney, and 2000 Democratic VP nominee Joseph Lieberman play prominent roles in ACTA.

Many conservatives believe that were it not for the successful interventions of the politically correct left, the conservative vision for America would naturally prevail. In this book, I fault leftist PC for the opposite reason: that it unintentionally helps to perpetuate the status quo. It does so by keeping vital but troubling issues in the closet, by silencing dissent, by distorting reality, by miring progressives in sterile ideological conflicts of the partisan left and right, and thus, most importantly, by obscuring real transformational alternatives. Most notably, PC has weakened the progressive agenda in the areas mentioned above as well as in its slighting of the fundamental issue of personal and social values. In areas such as affirmative action, family values, and criminal justice, PC practitioners on the left have tried to quarantine truth in a futile attempt to keep it from infecting their ideologies and their followers.

As I argue in subsequent chapters, the conservative vision suffers not from the ravages of left-wing PC but from its own arbitrary elitism, entropic values, contradictory blend of Christianity and capitalism, pecuniary sacrifice of families and communities, and undemocratic, ecocidal political economy. Burdened by a vision that a majority will never knowingly accept and that the earth cannot long tolerate, conservatives can nevertheless offer insightful critiques of left-wing follies. When they do, progressives would do well to listen and learn rather than retreat myopically behind a veil of political correctness. This book explores vital alternatives for social transformation that have been short-circuited by the strictures of PC.

PC and Anti-PC Are Still the Rage

After more than a decade of pro- and anti-PC furor, charges and defenses of political correctness show no signs of abating. Indeed, the rhetorical use of the term "political correctness" has spread far beyond its original domain. For instance, sexual conversation and behavior is often normed for political correctness. "Reading about new sexual harassment suits," writes Professor Mary Karr, "I used to be spring-loaded on 'You go, girl,' certain in the feminist marrow of my bones that some deep wrong was being righted. Then I found myself threatened with such a suit, and my worldview wheeled around."[6] Karr reports the Byzantine events, including potential lawsuits, that she lived through, adding, "On the battleground of political correctness, it's not the possibility of a lawsuit that's scary. It's the silence."[7] PC makes people afraid to speak their minds. This book is intended to break some of the silences that Karr fears.

Artistic and literary awards are now subject to PC screens. Some previously unknown, white Australian writers and artists have recently won acclaim after adopting aboriginal personas, because, claims one writer, "politically correct publishers and awards judges discriminate against white men in favor of female, Aboriginal, and immigrant-descended writers."[8] In 1998, the Association for Asian American Studies (AAAS) rescinded the award it had given Japanese-American writer Lois-Ann Yamanaka for her novel *Blu's Hanging,* called "powerful," "arresting," and "brilliant" by critics. Yamanaka had won previous awards "for her searing depictions of poverty, violence and racism in her native Hawaii." But because some Filipinos took offense at her depiction of a minor Filipino character in the novel, the AAAS reconsidered, determined that the book was "racist," and canceled the award. Poet David Mura blasted the AAAS's belated PC screening as equivalent to its "functioning like the thought police." He added: "The purpose of writers is not to produce idealized portraits of the community."[9]

The Motion Picture Academy moved in the opposite direction in March 1999, when it gave an honorary, lifetime-achievement Oscar to director Elia Kazan despite objections by many film-industry professionals that Kazan had cooperated with the House Un-American Activities Committee's blacklisting of suspected communists in the 1950s. *Boston Globe* commentator Martin Nolan wrote: "When the Motion Picture Academy approved an honorary Oscar for Elia Kazan, their historic decision hastened the demise of the 'politically correct' instinct in America."[10] As we shall see, PC's demise is far less imminent than Nolan implies. In mid-2000, former George Bush speechwriter Tony Snow complained that each day brings "fresh spasms" of PC: for instance, "The Director's Guild of America abandons the D.W. Griffith award for reasons of political correctness."[11]

In 1999, the Walt Disney Corporation came out with yet another version of "Tarzan," to mostly favorable reviews. Some critics, however, noted that Disney's animated "Tarzan" is set in Africa but has nary an African character. The many previous versions that did have African characters tended to portray them in a traditional European or American racial stereotype. Critic

Peter Rainer wrote that "perhaps Disney thought the best way to get around the ooga-booga stereotype was to eliminate blacks altogether. It's the neutron bomb version of political correctness."[12]

Even science has come in for its share of PC disputes. Herrnstein and Murray's (1994) *The Bell Curve* continues to ignite political reaction to its contention that African Americans suffer from lower average innate intelligence than white Americans. The authors conclude that programs to compensate blacks for their social disadvantages are useless and ill-advised—a merciless inference even if their IQ findings were valid. William Julius Wilson has pointed out that Herrnstein and Murray's methodology cannot account for the subtly cumulative effects of historical racism, which tarnish role models, reduce self-confidence, stunt ambition, and eliminate informal support networks. Faulting their scientific methods, biologist Stephen Jay Gould responds: "Like so many conservative ideologues who rail against the largely bogus ogre of suffocating political correctness, Herrnstein and Murray claim that they only want a hearing for unpopular views so that truth will out."[13] Wilson and Gould believe that their criticisms of *The Bell Curve* are both politically and scientifically correct.

Archaeologist Gary Matlock and anthropologist Stephen LeBlanc tell of the PC pressure against studying violence among indigenous puebloans of the U.S. Southwest. "Mainstream anthropology has, until recently, been loathe [*sic*] to recognize warfare as a major force in social evolution," says LeBlanc. "Searching for warfare has been widely considered politically incorrect, plain and simple."[14] Zoologists Robert Pitman and Susan Chivers complain about popular and media negativity toward their discovery of two different types of killer whales, a "docile" type and a "wilder" type that ravages sperm whales by hunting in packs. "The forces of political correctness and media marketing seem bent on projecting an image of a more benign form (the *Free Willy* or Shamu model), and some people urge exclusive use of the name 'orca' for the species, instead of what is perceived as the more sinister label of 'killer whale.'"[15] In 2000, a team of UCLA psychologists reported physiological and behavioral differences between men and women in responding to stress. Noting the finding's political incorrectness, lead researcher Shelley Taylor said, "I hope women don't find it offensive."[16]

A medical finding by France's leading obstetrician, Dr. Emile Papiernik, has led to political criticisms or media blackouts of his study by left-wing French periodicals like *Le Monde* and *Liberation*. His data show that, on average, the fetuses of black women reach full term a week sooner than those of white women. "Recognizing that difference," he argues, "allows doctors to begin monitoring African mothers one week earlier. This can cut in half prenatal deaths, fetal distress during delivery and the neonatal damage associated with post-term births." Having lost his father to a Nazi concentration camp in World War II, the Jewish Papiernik says he knows firsthand about the dangers of racial classification, but that acknowledging racial differences is a necessary step toward achieving equal medical care. "As a doctor, I can tell you in numbers of lives lost about the stupidity of political correctness."[17] Psychiatrist Sally Satel labels as "indoctrinologists" ("their diagnosis is oppression and their prescription is social reform") those of her medical colleagues who criticize U.S. medical care for being racist and sexist: "The critics are beginning to fashion a world of politically correct medicine."[18]

I hope that Chapter 2's criticisms of affirmative action do not lead to mysterious disappearances of my book, as happened to Professor Jay Bergman's postings of anti-affirmative-action fliers around his Central Connecticut State University campus. When he finally spotted forty-year-old student Dawn Bliesener taking one from a bulletin board, "he began screaming so loudly that nearby professors came out to quiet him." After the university sided with the student, Bergman's case became a cause célèbre for conservative academics "as an example of how colleges will tolerate the suppression of unpopular views while cracking down on those who are not considered 'politically correct.'" Bergman was aided by the National Association of Scholars, which investigates PC improprieties on college campuses.[19]

In 1998, the tobacco industry began to shift its marketing tactics when R.J. Reynolds developed ads that satirized antismoking groups as puritanical prudes and killjoys. The ads portray smoking as a forbidden fruit that a courageous, rebellious person might want to explore rather than cravenly kowtow to nay-sayers such as parents or the surgeon general. New Camel ads feature mock warnings headlined "Viewer Discretion Advised" along with the legally required health warning. A Winston billboard declares, "At least you can still smoke in your own car." "Judge me all you want, just keep the verdict to yourself," says another. Ever true to the tobacco-industry approach, Reynolds spokeswoman Fran Creighton denied any satirical intent in the ads. "We would never make fun of the cigarette health warning," she said. "This is maybe more about the P.C. (politically correct) world we live in. The world has an authoritarian view on everything."[20] After the U.S. government filed a massive suit against the tobacco industry in 1999, Phillip Morris lawyer Greg Little promised, "We will not succumb to politically correct extortion."[21]

In early 2000, the gun industry and its supporters protested Citibank's policy of refusing to do business with customers involved in manufacturing or selling arms. Former U.S. attorney and gun-club spokesman James Winchester accused Citibank of unfair discrimination and "political correctness run amok."[22] Under threat of boycott, Citibank soon reversed itself. Complaining about the arbitrary racial classifications of the 2000 U.S. Census, news editor Vincent Carroll says, "Welcome to America: where even the Census form is politically correct."[23]

Even military critics of NATO's 1999 bombing campaign in Yugoslavia drew insight from the PC wars. One of the world's top defense institutes, the London-based International Institute for Strategic Studies, charged that NATO's strategy had violated basic principles of warfare by failing to make sufficiently credible threats of force and by "desperately trying to avoid casualties." The institute's director, John Chapman, said that the alliance had been guilty of "strategic correctness," by which he meant an excessively humanitarian approach to warfare intended to soothe the sensibilities of the leaders' own political constituencies.[24]

In "Hobby Not Always Politically Correct," chess grand master Larry Evans reports that in some quarters chess is frowned upon for being too warlike and competitive. One of his readers wrote: "Last year my kid's intermediate school principal forbade holding chess tournaments on the school's premises on the grounds that it was 'too competitive and does not foster the appropriate spirit commensurate with the school's principles.'" The father noted with irony that the same school has two baseball stadiums. Evans replies, "Chess too competitive but not baseball? Give me a break."[25]

In 1997, a long-brewing conflict over political correctness in Denver led to the termination of the National Western Stock Show's black-white team of Leon Coffee, an African-American rodeo "clown," and his white sidekick, good friend and rodeo announcer Hadley Barrett. I put "clown" in quotes because Coffee's job—"bullfighter," in rodeo lingo—entails not only entertaining the crowd but saving the lives of thrown bull riders by distracting angry bulls. This case illustrates, not only in black and white but in suggestive detail, some legitimate pros and cons of PC. Over the years, Barrett and Coffee's raw humor has gotten many laughs but has also rankled some rodeo fans, including women and ethnic minorities.

Here is a typical exchange between the two: "Coffee joshes a rodeo spectator about his bald spot. Barrett's voice booms out through the arena in the spectator's defense, telling Coffee to take off his silly hat. 'See that?' Barrett says, pointing to the clown's tightly curled black hair. 'That's the original Velcro right there.'"[26] Coffee and Barrett defend their equal-opportunity jokes, which they say are aimed at everyone, including themselves. But the NAACP and other groups have taken offense at their political incorrectness. "Politically correct," fumes Coffee. "I hate those words. You can't be politically correct and be funny." Rather than avoid sensitive issues such as race, he prefers to tackle them head-on, as reflected in one of his favorite jokes. "He shouts up to Barrett in the announcer's booth that when white people are born, they're pink. When they get mad, they're red. When they get cold, they're blue. When they get sick, they're green. And they call me colored!"

Coffee maintains that the rodeo is run on merit, not race or privilege, as exemplified by recent African-American champion cowboys such as Chris Littlejohn. Coffee believes that he has earned his own "bullfighting" job on merit too: "There isn't a cowboy out there with a bull on his butt that says, 'Don't send the black guy to save me, send the white guy.'" Defending his equal-opportunity insults, Coffee argues that "I don't pick on any-body—I pick on everybody. I take no prisoners." The problem with this argument, PC supporters might reply, is that being picked on equally does not mean being affected equally by being picked on. White people being told that they turn different colors are less likely to feel hurt than obese women hearing the clowns tell Barrett that "their girlfriends lost 45 pounds overnight, just by shaving their legs. Had to use a Weed-Eater" and that "one girlfriend was so fat, she enjoyed watching the rodeo from Section HH, Seats 5, 6, and 7." Although Barrett and Coffee defend their right to poke fun in good humor, Barrett did apologize in 1997 for thoughtlessly joking about "jewing down" someone, saying that he had intended no offense to Jews.

Justifiable Ambivalence About PC

Andrew Hudson, a spokesman for the black liberal mayor of Denver, Wellington Webb, reported that his office had gotten frequent complaints about Coffee and Barrett. Hudson said he regarded many of them as valid. "Our biggest concern," he said, "is that you have a very diverse crowd, ethnicities and backgrounds, who were bringing their family and children to an event, and being exposed to these types of comments. People bringing kids to a rodeo shouldn't have to expect this kind of thing."[27] By contrast, conservative columnist Linda Chavez defended the television show *Seinfeld* for the very reason that Hudson, Webb, and stock show officials agreed on Coffee and Barrett's termination in 1997: "Where most comedy shows eschew offending any liberal interest groups," she wrote, "*Seinfeld* was an equal opportunity insulter, with homosexuals, handicapped persons and minorities fair game for parody." She added that the show's humor "was never cruel or malicious." What Chavez liked best about *Seinfeld* was that it was funny "because it exaggerated the worst aspects of our narcissistic, materialistic, politically correct culture."[28]

A civilization's history of racism, sexism, and other forms of arbitrary discrimination makes it hard to draw a "correct" line in social interactions between, on the one hand, an apt sensitivity to past injuries and, on the other, a hypersensitivity that can make people humorless and even speechless. Despite the criticisms I launch at PC in this book, I can hardly join Joseph Stromberg in viewing concerns about personal dignity and indignities as "some egregiously goofy manifestation such as 'political correctness.'"[29] For both good and bad, political correctness is far more than a goofy manifestation. A young American Indian woman writes, "For Native Americans, political correctness and multicultural programs are important steps toward self-determination, political power, and resistance to a history of federal policies of cultural genocide."[30] Historian Patricia Limerick believes that "what we call the politically correct more often than not turns out to be the factually correct."[31] Richard Rorty (1998: p. 81) defends liberal political correctness: "The adoption of attitudes which the Right sneers at as 'politically correct' has made America a far more civilized society than it was thirty years ago." And Paul Peterson (1995: p. 3) asserts that "the politically correct answer in a pluralist democracy is also likely to be ethically correct."

In a 1999 PC episode in Washington, D.C., David Howard, a white staffer for black mayor Anthony Williams, used "niggardly" in a meeting, accidentally offending a black staffer who mistook this synonym for "miserly" as an ethnic slur. Under pressure to fire Howard by blacks who already regarded the Ivy League mayor as insufficiently black, Williams accepted his friend's resignation, prompting a critical retort by Cynthia Tucker, African-American editor of the *Atlanta Constitution*. In her article "The Blacker Than Thou Thing," she opined that Mayor Williams "might have brought this dumb little drama to a close by handing out vocabulary books" rather than accepting Howard's resignation.[32] She quotes Julian Bond, "the literate chairman of the board" of the National Association for the Advancement of Colored People, as saying, "You hate to think you have to censor your language to meet other people's lack of understanding." *New York Times* columnist Maureen Dowd wrote that "even if the mayor is having a teensy-weensy identity crisis, he should never have sided with ignorance or succumbed to P.C. poisoning."[33]

Jesse Jackson's compromise position on this racially loaded episode reflects the hard-to-define correct-sensitivity line I referred to earlier. He proposed that Williams rehire Howard (which he did, but to a different position) while suggesting that Howard—and the rest of us—try to avoid such words as "niggardly" that can easily be misinterpreted. I am concerned that many of the parties who expend energy on such PC brouhahas share an underlying concern for bettering society that gets lost in the shuffle. The critique of PC developed in this book seeks above all to reverse PC's dissipation of progressive energies and its stunting of transformational visions.

The proposals I make in Chapters 2 through 9 are frankly transformational, even utopian, intended to change U.S. society fundamentally. Indeed, my critique of political correctness is incidental to a greater purpose threatened by PC: the building of societies that better nurture their people and the planet on which we all depend. Transcending the limits and blinders of the partisan left and right does not mean seeking a "moderate" center touted—and courted—by U.S. politicians in general elections. Indeed, the arguments made in this book show just how immoderate the center of U.S. politics can be. By internationally shared criteria for the well-being of human beings and the earth, mainstream U.S. policy is in many areas quite "extreme."[34]

As this book was nearing completion, a tragic incident brought home once again the ways in which political correctness can obscure the causes of social problems and confound their solutions. Traveling with my family through the Czech and Slovak Republics in the spring of 1999, I learned of the massacre at Columbine High School in Littleton, Colorado, a suburb of Denver, where we live. Teenagers Eric Harris and Dylan Klebold had killed twelve of their fellow students and teacher Dave Sanders, and wounded thirteen other students before killing themselves. Coming on the heels of a rash of other school shootings in Mississippi, Kentucky, Arkansas, Pennsylvania, Tennessee, and Oregon, the Columbine slaughter has prompted much soul-searching by Americans about what is wrong with U.S. society. It has also spawned a great deal of pontificating by political and religious pundits as well as panderers of special interests. But as I shall argue in the book, neither the soul-searching nor the pontificating has gotten to the roots of the social pathologies besetting Americans young and old.

Former U.S. House Speaker Newt Gingrich blamed liberalism for the Columbine massacre, citing thirty-five years of cultural contamination by "the political and intellectual elites and political correctness" for undermining American values.[35] Vice President Al Gore countered that it is the lack of gun control that best explains such incidents, and President Clinton charged that the Republican leadership in the House "seems intent on ignoring the lessons of Littleton" by defeating the administration's gun-control proposals.[36] When some left-leaning activists criticized the memorial service for Columbine victims as "too evangelical and too white," columnist Kathleen Parker charged that "political correctness has no shame."[37] Christians seized on victim Cassie Bernall's alleged affirmation of her belief in God—when asked about it by one of the gunmen just before he killed her—to promote their recruitment efforts and their religious beliefs, one of which is presumably that God works in mysterious ways.

Housing and Urban Development Secretary Andrew Cuomo came closer to basic causes when he cited intolerance, youth alienation and fear, division, and lack of community as breeding grounds for youth violence. Except for noting the privileged status of high school athletes, targeted by the Columbine killers, few if any leading voices cited the harshly competitive winner-loser values of U.S. culture as a fertile ground for revenge by socially marginalized people like Harris and Klebold. After Columbine we might have expected criticisms of this entropic culture from political progressives—until we consider that left-wing PC has cast "the values thing" as a red herring of the right, used by conservatives to distract us from the true, structural causes of our societal ills. The Marxian tradition of reducing values to an "epiphenomenon" of underlying economic causes has seduced many progressives into ceding a wide range of values issues, including family values, to the right. But a society that celebrates Coach Vince Lombardi's dictum that "winning is the only thing" will continue to produce Dylan Klebolds who rage against their loserhood and refuse to go quietly "into that good night."[38]

What Exactly Are
Political Correctness and Social Transformation?

Until we define our terms, we may be unclear about whether we approve or disapprove of either PC or transformation; about the importance of PC for transformation; about whether PC is a recent or long-standing phenomenon and whether it occurs only on the left or all across the ideological spectrum; and about the connection between PC and such vital concepts as ideology, commitment, loyalty, and political effectiveness. The examples we have explored give us a practical context within which to grasp, judge, and use the definitions that follow.

The essence of political correctness is not the specific beliefs and ideologies disliked by conservatives. It is, rather, the way in which (conservatives allege) liberals and radicals hold and act on their beliefs: namely, narrowly, dogmatically, unfairly, intolerantly, self-righteously, and oppressively. Indeed, the satiric bite achieved by conservatives' clever appropriation of the Marxist term "political correctness" stems first and foremost from the irony that liberals (and, by extension, humanistic radicals)—who are supposed to be broad-minded—have come to speak and act in narrow-minded, illiberal, antihumanistic ways.[39] Thus for a "liberal" to favor or require "political correctness" is an ironic contradiction in terms, recalling Jerry Rubin's yippie dictum "Scratch a liberal; find a fascist."[40]

It is this ironic contradiction that host Bill Maher of *Politically Incorrect* exploits so well in his late-night television show. Maher skewers the political correctness of his guests both left and right, as well as those who are in between or completely off the chart. What is politically incorrect about his show is that its humorous and heated, free-flowing dialogues and diatribes tend to defy all claims to self-righteous correctness in political, philosophical, religious, and social matters. As suggested by Maher's approach, I define political correctness as *an ideological narrowing, intolerance, and silencing of dissent, commonly attributed to the left by the right.* As such, PC resembles "an ideological fanaticism, which cannot tolerate ambiguity and which must immediately assign a stamp of blessing or damnation to everything and everyone coming to its attention."[41] This attitude of closure leads to a cumulative distortion of reality. So defined, political correctness spans the political spectrum, applying to the left, right, and center, as well as locations off the traditional ideological continuum, such as anarchism and postmodernism. And so conceived, it tends to undermine the long-term success of its practitioners.

This approach may help us understand why "the left has a penchant for grasping defeat from the jaws of victory."[42] Indeed, each chapter of this book explores one or more areas in which the left has a natural political advantage that it has squandered, benefiting the right. Ironically, the political correctness of conservatives sometimes allows the forces of change to prevail in spite of

themselves. The rigidity and short-sightedness of ancient regimes has hastened their demise. By contrast, the flexibility and far-sightedness of liberal
capitalists—those willing to challenge the free-market dogmas of right-
wing PC—have been the key to capitalism's health and survival. Consequently, progressives would do well to leave right-wing PC alone, other
than to satirize it, because it often benefits the cause of change. On the
other hand, they desperately need to address PC within their own ranks, because it has served to cripple "The Movement,"[43] if indeed there is any
such thing left to injure further.[44] As Alan Wolfe (1996: p. 238) notes, when
"posturing substitutes for persuasion, . . . social criticism is unlikely to be
either inventive or interesting."

I am most concerned, then, about PC closure and distortion among political progressives: those who typically support feminism, multiculturalism, the rights of historically disadvantaged groups (especially ethnic minorities), environmentalism, the welfare state, Keynesian and/or socialistic
regulation of markets, abstract preference for the common good over individual liberties but concrete advocacy of minority group rights over majoritarian conformity, sociological as opposed to biological or psychological explanations of behavior, opposition to Eurocentric tradition and the
"Western canon," resistance to imperialism and the New World Order of
global capitalism, participatory rather than passive democracy, and a wide
range of more specific programs such as affirmative action.[45]

These and related beliefs comprise the core "politically correct" ideology that, conservatives charge, leftists dogmatically defend and intolerantly
try to impose. As we shall see, "politically correct" positions on the left are
seldom identified as such by their proponents, who wish to skirt the negative
connotations intended in the PC charges of conservatives. Once again, the
key to political correctness is not the mere holding of any of these positions
but the doing so in a way that precludes open discussion of alternatives. The
point of this book is certainly not that these positions are "wrong." Indeed,
I agree with many of them. The point is to rescue progressive causes from a
kind of closure and distortion that culminate in their advocates' shooting
themselves in the foot and trumping the transformation of society. In *The
Devil's Dictionary,* Ambrose Bierce (1911) highlighted self-contradictory
tendencies on the left when he defined radicalism as "the conservatism of tomorrow injected into the affairs of today" (p. 100), and political revolution
as "an abrupt change in the form of misgovernment" (p. 107).

I am not the first to note the dangers of the kind of narrow-mindedness
that political correctness has come to symbolize. "For every complicated
problem," said H. L. Mencken, "there is an answer that is short, simple, and
wrong." John Stuart Mill warned, "He who knows only his own side of the
case, knows little of that." George Santayana, perhaps best-known for his
warning that those who ignore history are condemned to repeat it, also
commented, "Fanaticism consists in redoubling your efforts when you have

forgotten your aim." Winston Churchill targeted the defense against reality inherent in political correctness when he declared, "Men occasionally stumble on the truth, but most of them pick themselves up and hurry off as if nothing had happened." Each of these four captured a key dimension of PC: (1) its black-and-white oversimplification of the world in terms of right and wrong; (2) its discouragement of self-insight and perspective; (3) its substitution of ideological fervor for philosophical clarity; and (4) its flight from uncomfortable truths.

Chapter 2 illustrates these four dimensions by examining affirmative action, a program invented and implemented by white male elites to contain the dangers they saw spreading in the urban riots of the 1960s. For three decades, affirmative action has been defended by progressives even as it has helped to divide and conquer the very groups it nominally benefits. As later chapters reveal, the politically correct narrowing of progressive ideology can work in apparently opposite ways. For instance, in the areas of values, crime, and family empowerment, the politically correct left rejects valid arguments by virtue of their guilt by association with conservative advocates. In the areas of adultism and ecology, by contrast, the left has listened too well to conservatives, who have so convinced the left of its permissiveness and greenness that progressives bask in their politically correct enlightenment rather than confront their own adultism and complicity with ecocide. What is identical in all of these areas, however, is the cumulative distortion of reality that the PC lens has wrought in progressive thought and practice.

Chapter 2 also shows why affirmative action is antitransformational. By social transformation I mean fundamental changes in the values, consciousness, and institutions of society, especially along such dimensions as (1) which groups exercise effective institutional power, (2) who benefits or suffers from these institutions, and (3) how they affect the ecological fabric on which humans ultimately depend. In a dynamic system such as liberal capitalism, transformation is ongoing whether we like it or not. But we can all help to shape it. A purpose of this book is to mobilize and tailor political activism that favors certain kinds of transformation: namely, those culminating in social institutions that better nurture our people, strengthen our communities, and steward our environment.

PC and Anti-PC on the U.S. Left

This book does not indict any particular segment of the ideological spectrum for any particular degree of political correctness. Such an indictment, let alone a conviction, would require a large-scale empirical study beyond the scope of this book. Rather, I argue that, disclaimers to the contrary notwithstanding,[46] political correctness is broadly evident among progressives in the United States, that it stymies the progressive transformation of

U.S. society, and that progressives for whom the PC shoe fits would be wise to welcome this critique.

In Chapter 1, I take a sampling of both PC and opposition to PC among the four major self-described progressive segments of the U.S. ideological spectrum: Clinton-Gore centrist liberals (or New Democrats), left liberals (or New Majority), left radicals, and socialists.[47] Many individuals and interest groups overlap the categories. For instance, feminists, environmentalists, multiculturalists, and unionists span the gamut of these four progressive locations along the continuum. Readers more interested in my own new proposals on affirmative action, values, children, families, ecology, crime, and political economy, rather than in the existing positions of leading progressives, may wish to skip Chapter 1 and go directly to Chapter 2. In Chapter 1, I criticize the four leftist contenders according to the transformational criteria I develop in Chapters 2 through 8. The faults I find most frequently are opportunism, especially among the Clinton-Gore liberals; incompleteness and self-contradiction, particularly among the left liberals; a lack of cohesive or unifying vision, notably among the left radicals; and an ideological malaise bordering on paralysis among socialists. In different ways, these faults all bear the telltale markings of political correctness.

It is significant that even the least radical of the four segments, the centrist liberals, describes its program as "transformational." True or false, this claim testifies to the seriousness of the problems facing a prosperous U.S. society at the turn of the century. "Miringoff's social-health index—which combines 16 social indicators, including child poverty, infant mortality, crime, access to health care and affordable housing—plummeted from a rating of 77 out of a possible 100 in 1973 to 38 in 1993," before recovering modestly to 46 by 1997.[48] In the face of continuing environmental destruction and planetary unsustainability, dangerous international anarchy, unprecedented citizen disaffiliation from politics, persistent poverty of "the other America," a growing crisis in health care, the weakening of the family, violent crime unparalleled elsewhere in the industrialized world, and relentless indicators of social pathology, even liberals have given up on incremental muddling-through to something better. Basic changes that are needed are threatened both by political opportunism, most common among liberals, and by political correctness, most evident among radicals and socialists.

Indicators of the transformative nature of our times crop up almost daily. As the cult of high modernism (Scott 1998) eliminates family farms, farmers mask suicides so that their families will receive full death benefits.[49] A ten-year project on public-interest polling reveals that on issue after issue, governmental and media elites are out of touch with the preferences of ordinary citizens, notably in the areas of health care, environmental protection, campaign-finance reform, governmental accountability to citizens, and peaceful approaches to international conflict resolution (Kay 1998). A meeting of the World Trade Organization in Seattle in 1999 is disrupted and virtually scuttled by massive street protests of labor unionists, environmentalists, advocates for the poor, and populist critics of the New Global Order of corporate capitalism. The protests prompt the ever opportunistic Bill Clinton, the world's premier ringleader of free trade, to side with the protesters.

In response to these mounting symptoms of popular malaise, some progressive activists are jump-starting themselves in new directions. Pioneer mainstream feminist Betty Friedan (1997: p. 2) declares, "What I sense is a need for a paradigm shift beyond feminism, beyond sexual politics, beyond identity politics altogether. A new paradigm for women and men." In honor of the 150th anniversary of *The Communist Manifesto,* progressive activists hold a "Manifestivity" at Cooper Union in New York City, at which they speak of breaking free of the left-wing shibboleths of old. At this lively gathering, Cornel West criticizes the left for failing to develop a compelling, cohesive strategy for change, and labor unionist Brenda Stokely proclaims, "It is necessary to stop debating endlessly about what is the correct line, to learn to speak to the people/workers, and to participate in local struggles."[50]

Many left liberals and radicals in the United States have long pointed to Western European, and especially Scandinavian, social democracy as the best feasible model for reforming U.S. public policy. But this model is seriously creaking at the joints, with persistently high levels of unemployment and its own partisans struggling to break free from their own social-democratic version of political correctness. In November 1999, leftist leaders from the eleven European countries they govern met in Paris for the 21st Congress of the Socialist International. The leaders' ambivalence toward social-democratic principles was captured by British Laborite prime minister Tony Blair, who said at a press conference that social democracies such as his own must "jettison outdated doctrine and dogma that stands in our way." For instance, "the German left is in the midst of its most profound identity crisis since 1968."[51] The governing German Social Democrat–Greens alliance presides over "a malaise [that] is rooted in a welfare state that has become so elaborate and expensive that enterprises say they can no longer afford to hire new workers."[52] Beyond economic uncertainty, "many [German] people talk of a kind of moral void, a bleak 'elbow society' where elbows thrust as advancement is restlessly sought but values of community have been lost."[53] Responding to market pressures while fighting PC resistance from social-democratic voters, "center-left parties in European countries like Britain, the Netherlands, France and Spain have cut government subsidies and encouraged private business."[54]

It is noteworthy that the most widely revered model of social democracy, Sweden, is now experiencing the greatest economic and fiscal problems. Sweden's welfare state consumes almost half of the gross national product, and taxes its working middle-class citizens at a 60 percent rate. As in Germany, businesses in Sweden complain that high taxes and government regulations make them inefficient at home and uncompetitive abroad. For decades, Sweden "was the renowned Middle Way that sought to provide a humane passage between controlling totalitarianism and uncaring capitalism." But now, the Swedish "model of rationality, tolerance, cradle-to-grave care of citizens and generosity to people in less advantaged countries" has become tarnished, with stagnant incomes, rising unemployment, and foreign workers living in segregated suburbs. Politicians have become afraid to raise taxes or cut bloated programs. In short, Sweden has become "just another normal nation."[55] In early 2000, Austria, the most social-democratic country south of Scandinavia, shocked the rest of the European Union by forming a right-wing coalition government including the anti-immigration Freedom Party, whose then-leader, Joerg Haider, has Nazi sympathies and ties.

There is some evidence that these recent problems of Europe's social democracies have spurred increased citizen activism, including massive demonstrations against Haider's Freedom Party. While polls show European citizens' reduced confidence in state institutions and greater dissatisfaction with the way their democracies work, they also find a greater citizen interest in politics, more political discussions among friends, more petition signing, and increased support for boycotts, demonstrations, and other forms of direct action.[56] What remains unclear is where the pressures for change will lead the European social democracies in the future. Like the United States, Japan, and Israel, these countries are facing new competitive challenges from the increasingly global economy.

If Tony Blair's intellectual guru, Anthony Giddens, is any indication, European social democracy is strategically adrift. In *The Third Way: The Renewal of Social Democracy,* Giddens (1998) states, "In spite of their electoral successes social democrats have not yet created a new and integrated political outlook" (p. 24). And the Third Way Giddens proposes, for example, barely touches on the world's impending ecological crisis, doing so in the palest of green tones: Given the ecological dangers of economic growth, he timidly recommends "in the environmental arena, an adoption of the precautionary principle where feasible" (p. 68). If former President Clinton's New Democrats are any indication, it seems that even the most mainstream of U.S. progressives are harking back to the advice of Martin Luther King a quarter of a century ago: "This is no time to engage in the luxury of cooling off, to take the tranquilizing drug of gradualism." I agree with the New Democrats and other progressives that the problems besetting Americans at the turn of the century require a transformative response. But this response must be one that is self-reflective enough to correct its own inevitable errors. Transformationalists must also heed the words of King's brilliant predecessor W.E.B. Du Bois: "The hushing of the criticism of honest opponents is a dangerous thing."

An Overview of the Rest of the Book

Chapter 2, "Affirmative Action: Hanging Separately While the Gentry Feast," illustrates a classic example of progressive political correctness that undermines social transformation. It credits affirmative action for creating a less unjust demography of winners and losers in the U.S. version of Hobbes's "war of all against all," but criticizes it for logical and moral inconsistency and for perpetuating the entropic system of conquest itself. Affirmative action now serves primarily to divide and conquer the very people—disadvantaged citizens—who most need relief from the excesses and injustices of corporate capitalism. I present a transformational alternative to affirmative action that would substitute fullness of opportunity for equality of opportunity as the proper goal of compensatory programs for the disadvantaged. This transformation depends upon a values shift in U.S. society.

Chapter 3, "Transformative Values: Synergy, Entropy, and Social Change," questions PC progressives' coolness to values issues and advocates a shift from zero-sum, entropic values such as power, status, and wealth to synergistic values such as family, friendship, knowledge, craftsmanship, art, and simple daily pleasures. Entropic, or zero-sum, values divide a society into winners and losers, thus sacrificing community and patriotism while riddling society with social pathologies. Synergistic values are goods whose pursuit by one person increases the likelihood of other people's achieving them as well. They do not require, although they may benefit from, superhuman rationality, pure altruism, or other rare qualities of human nature. Unlike the Christian or Marxist millennium, value synergism does not require heroic exhortations to self-sacrifice. Synergistic value choices can resolve otherwise intractable conflicts between liberty and equality that have plagued modern Western philosophers from Mill to Rawls.

Chapter 4, "Beyond Liberalism and Communitarianism: The Invisible Hand of Synergy," credits Adam Smith for his Invisible Hand of the free market but argues that it cannot bear the burden assigned it by classical liberals. Synergistic values comprise a second Invisible Hand, reducing zero-sum and increasing positive-sum interactions in social and market life. By pursuing synergistic values, even if self-interestedly, citizens increase available social value. Fostering synergistic values promotes social justice, which in turn serves to protect synergistic values from perverse transformation into their opposites. Synergism is a more compelling basis for the good society than either liberalism or communitarianism, the two prime ideological contenders, now that state socialism has waned.

Chapter 5, "The Missing Child in Transformational Politics," notes the absence of young people's voices in the analyses and programs of the left. In fact, by adultist presumption "the left" has meant "the adult left," whose political concern for young people has been almost entirely paternalistic. PC adults generally ignore the disempowerment of the young. A rich array of real-world cases undermines the "KRRESI" (pronounced "cr-razy") assumptions used to justify the disfranchisement of the young: namely, that adults are inherently more knowledgeable, rational, responsible, experienced, selfless, and intelligent than children. In fact, many young people are more politically competent than many adults. Children are, on average, more progressive than adults on a wide range of political issues.

Chapter 6, "Beyond Adultism: Political Empowerment for Young People," documents the fact that children are the largest severely disadvantaged class in the world, suffering disproportionately from poverty, hunger and malnutrition, sickness and inadequate health care, crime and violence, war and physical displacement, psychological trauma, personal belittlement, and arbitrary curtailment of their liberties and opportunities. Adult paternalism has failed. Children would likely be treated better if their votes had to be considered. I refute the most common objections to enfranchising the young, including the "Tiny Tot," "Big Family," "Manipulated Child," "Unlimited Candy and Recess," "Dumbing Down," and "Disappearing Childhood" objections. Empowering young people would strengthen, not weaken, families.

Chapter 7, "Family Empowerment in Social Transformation: The Politics of Birthing, Nursing, and Parenting," dissents from the politically correct critique of the family as inherently patriarchal, conservative, and oppressive. Families can become a progressive force for social transformation. To play this transformative role, families need to reconsider their patterns of consumption, production, reproduction and child rearing, networking with other families, and self-conscious activity in the public sphere. Family-empowering choices in childbirth, child feeding, and child rearing can increase the independence of families from corporations, government, and the helping professions and thereby prepare them to forge an alliance of families to demand a more family- and child-friendly society.

Chapter 8, "Missing Synergies in Ecology, Crime, and Political Economy," examines PC assumptions that keep progressives from grasping linkages among these three vital areas—an unawareness that promotes "solutions" that in fact undermine one another and miss potential problem-solving synergies. Not only is the left soft on crime; it is soft on ecocide and political economy as well. The left excuses criminals of all sorts, because "the system made them do it"; prides itself on being greener than the right while in fact selling out the environment to growth and consumerism; and remains allergic to both free markets and strong leadership as keys to social transformation. Transformative solutions obscured by PC include restorative justice, the outlawing of ecocide, and economic democracy. Ecocidal and criminal behavior could be alleviated by a fully democratic economy. Together, synergistic values, mandatory ecological stewardship, and economic democracy could eliminate the main excesses of corporate capitalism while retaining the advantages of free markets.

My "Conclusion: Ideology as Friend and Foe of Transformation" retrieves ideology as a key element of social transformation. The purpose of the book is not to debunk ideology or proclaim its end but to harness ideological passion by correcting the excesses of political correctness that are derailing the efforts of progressive forces to transform U.S. society. In a future United States, citizens might enjoy fuller opportunities to realize their own unique potentials, win-win values might prevail, young people might have equal rights and families be healthy and empowered, poisoning the earth might be prohibited, first-time offenders rehabilitated and their communities restored, and people's material needs met by an economy controlled by decent, ordinary citizens. Though utopian, the society envisioned is far from perfect. Indeed, the perfectionist view of ideals, visions, and utopias is a straw theory used to justify an oppressive status quo.

Notes

1. W.E.B. Du Bois, *The Souls of Black Folk* (Chicago: A.C. McClurg, 1903), excerpted in Dolbeare (1998: p. 388).

2. Before Mao (1927), Lenin had warned that "to deviate from [socialist ideology] in the slightest degree means strengthening bourgeois ideology." A similar sentiment was expressed by the high-modernist city planner Le Corbusier, who had tried to sell the Soviets his plan for Moscow: "The despot is not a man. It is the Plan. The correct, realistic, exact plan." Both quoted in Scott (1998: p. 112). Notwithstanding Engels's and other socialists' efforts to distance their own correct, "scientific" socialism from the incorrect utopian socialism of Owen, Saint-Simon, and Fourier, utopian scholars such as Kitwood (1978) and Geogheghan (1989) have made a strong case that Marxists are in fact moralistic utopians, not politicized scientists.

3. A good current example is John Leo, *Incorrect Thoughts: Notes on Our Wayward Culture* (New Brunswick, NJ: Transaction, 2001).

4. Robert P. George, "Viewpoint: On the Debate About Peter Singer's Appointment," *Princeton Alumni Weekly*, January 27, 1999, p. 10.

5. For a critique of campus speech codes and their arguably left-wing bias, see Alan Charles Kors and Harvey A. Silvergate, *The Shadow University* (New York: Simon and Schuster, 1998).

6. This quote could apply to me. Luckily, my accuser turned out to be an outpatient from a psychiatric hospital who had been diagnosed as a paranoid-schizophrenic and had previously made equally unfounded charges against three other faculty members.

7. Mary Karr, "A Witch Reports, Post-Witch Hunt," *Civilization*, February-March 1999, p. 42.

8. Peter James Spielmann, "White Man Admits He Wrote Aboriginal Book," Associated Press, March 14, 1997.

9. Donna Foote, "Trouble in Paradise: A Hawaiian Novelist Sparks a PC Protest," *Newsweek*, August 17, 1998.

10. Quoted in *The International Herald Tribune*, "Politically Correct No More," March 24, 1999.

11. Tony Snow, "Should We Stick with Standards or Pacify the Malcontents?" *Detroit News,* June 16, 2000.

12. I·efluto have called the neutron bomb the ultimate capitalist weapon, killing people but leaving property relatively intact. *New York* magazine's Rainer is quoted by Lewis Beale, "Moviegoers Note Blacks' Absence in Disney's 'Tarzan,'" Knight Ridder News Service, June 28, 1999.

13. Stephen Jay Gould, "Mismeasure by Any Measure," in Russell Jacoby and Naomi Glauberman, eds., *The Bell Curve Debate* (New York: Random House, 1995), p. 12.

14. Electa Draper, "Terror Scarred Anasazi Culture: Grisly Finds Suggest Warfare, Cannibalism," *Denver Post,* December 31, 2000.

15. Robert Pitman and Susan Chivers, "Terror in Black and White," *Natural History,* December 1998-January 1999, p. 29.

16. Curt Suplee, "When Stressed, Women Tend to Befriend," *Washington Post,* May 19, 2000.

17. Marilyn August, "Doctor's Gestation Theory Spurs Racism Concern," Associated Press, November 21, 1998.

18. Sally Satel, "The Indoctrinologists Are Coming," *Atlantic Monthly,* January 2001, p. 59.

19. Jonathan Rabinovitz, "Professor, University War over Free Speech," *New York Times,* January 1996.

20. Scott Shane, "New Tobacco Ads Rebel Against Smoking Foes," *Baltimore Sun,* July 13, 1998.

21. Lorraine Adams and David A. Vise, "Business Interest Groups Wary of U.S. Tobacco Suit," *Washington Post,* September 23, 1999.

22. Jason Blevins, "Gun Dealers Voice Outrage over Bank Rule," *Denver Post,* February 19, 2000.

23. Vincent Carroll, "The Census' Odd Definition of Race," *Rocky Mountain News,* March 19, 2000.

24. Agence France Presse, "NATO Conduct of War Is Inept, Institute Finds," *International Herald Tribune,* May 5, 1999.

25. Larry Evans, "Hobby Not Always Politically Correct," *Denver Post,* February 21, 1999.

26. Michael Booth, "Politically Incorrect: Can't You Take a Joke?—Stock Show Clown Defends His Off-Color Humor," *Denver Post,* January 19, 1996.

27. "Rodeo Announcer and Clown Out in Humor Hubbub," *Denver Post,* December 17, 1997.

28. Linda Chavez, "Seinfeld: A Tory's Secret Vice," syndicated column, December 31, 1997.

29. Joseph R. Stromberg, book review of Dario Fernandez-Morera, *American Academia and the Survival of Marxist Ideas,* in *The Independent Review: A Journal of Political Economy* II, no. 4, spring 1998, p. 597.

30. Melissa Dineen Ortiz, "An Argument for Politically Correct Speech and Multicultural Programs," term paper, Denver, Colorado, April 17, 1998.

31. Patricia Nelson Limerick, "A Hard Look at Heroes: Measure by Heroic Moments," *Denver Post,* June 7, 1998.

32. Cynthia Tucker, "The Blacker Than Thou Thing," *Atlanta Constitution,* February 2, 1999.

33. Maureen Dowd, "Niggardly City," *New York Times,* February 1, 1999.

34. Green activist John Rensenbrink (1999: p. 66) charges that "the corporate, laissez faire movement of capital has almost always meant a radical, exteme disruption

of the lives of people." In Chapter 8, I analyze the extremist ideology of growth that dominates U.S. political economy.

35. Chuck Raasch, "Gingrich: Liberalism Led to Colorado Massacre," *USA Today,* May 14, 1999.

36. Susan Greene, "Mayors Focusing on Violence," *Denver Post,* June 15, 1999.

37. Kathleen Parker, "Protests in Poor Taste," *Orlando Sentinel,* May 1, 1999.

38. Klebold's namesake, Welsh poet Dylan Thomas, wrote: "Go not quietly into that good night./ But rage, rage against the dying of the light."

39. In "A Short History of the Term *Politically Correct,*" PC apologist Ruth Perry's (Aufderheide 1992: p. 78) stylistic medium, denial, is also the message: the dogmatism of PC thinking. She calls the conservative anti-PC campaign "ludicrous" in "pretending to expose some narrow-minded doctrinaire position."

40. The anarchistic Youth International Party (Y.I.P.), or yippies, of the late 1960s and 1970s were in effect politicized hippies, as well as linguistic forerunners (but ideological opponents) of today's yuppies.

41. Peter Berger, Brigitte Berger, and Hansfried Kellner, *The Homeless Mind* (New York: Vintage, 1974), p. 231.

42. Michael Albert in South End Press Collective (1998: p. 7).

43. "The Movement" is a term popularized by activists during the 1960s and 1970s to imply, wishfully, that progressives were united in a movement to transform U.S. society.

44. "It is often said that we Americans, at the end of the twentieth century, no longer have a Left," says Richard Rorty (1998: p. 91). Moreover: "When the Right proclaims that socialism has failed, that capitalism is the only alternative, the cultural Left has little to say in reply" (p. 79). G. William Domhoff (1998: p. 301) adds: "A fragmented leftist movement at war with itself has little chance of attracting many activists who stay around for very long."

45. Some conservatives might add postmodernism to the list of PC positions, and many of them attack it mercilessly (if often ignorantly). But many leftists also attack postmodernism for its relativism, which, taken to the extreme, eliminates any moral basis on which to criticize the status quo. For instance, in "Maoism, the New Left in the United States, and the Rise of Postmodernism," Greg DeLaurier comments on the antitransformational character of postmodernism. *New Political Science,* no. 36-37, summer-fall 1996, p. 152. Darryl Jarvis faults postmodernism because "the cult of political correctness accompanying it has stigmatized postmodernism's detractors," in "Postmodernism: A Critical Typology," *Politics and Society* 26, no. 1, March 1998, p. 131.

46. E. J. Dionne asserts: "We live in a time when socialists say they're pro-business, when liberals say they're tough on crime and when faithful friends of the welfare state say they're for work and 'personal responsibility.'" The superficiality of this depiction is hinted at a paragraph later when Dionne characterizes these symptoms as "the movement of the left toward the center"—in a word, opportunism. E. J. Dionne, "The German Clinton," *Washington Post,* March 5, 1998. He continued this line of thought in a column entitled "The End of Ideology" on June 18, 1999.

47. European-style social democrats, not an organized segment of the U.S. political spectrum, overlap left liberals, radicals, and socialists.

48. Alexander Stille, "Indices Measure Nation's Level of Contentment," *New York Times,* May 25, 2000.

49. Barry Bedlan, "Some Farmers Masking Suicides So Families Get Death Benefits," Associated Press, November 27, 1998.

50. Joseph A. Buttigieg, "Marking the Anniversary of *The Communist Manifesto*," *Chronicle of Higher Education* 45, no. 16, November 1998, p. B9

51. Andrei S. Markovito, "The Identity Crisis of the German Left: A Report from Berlin," *Dissent*, summer 1999, p. 17.

52. William Drozdiak, "Pressure on Schroeder for Sweeping Changes: Business Chiefs Demand Economic Reforms," *International Herald Tribune*, March 24, 1999.

53. Roger Cohen, "Young Politician Part of Creating a 'New Germany,'" *New York Times*, December 3, 1998.

54. Warren Hoge, "Sweden Seeks Solution to Socio-Economic Decline," *New York Times*, September 24, 1998.

55. Ibid.

56. Ronald Inglehart, *Modernization and Postmodernization: Cultural, Economic, and Political Change in 43 Societies* (Princeton: Princeton University Press, 1997).

I

PC, Opportunism, and Transformative Deficit on the Left

Centrist Liberalism

How comprehensive, cohesive, and inspiring are the visions of U.S. leftists today? In *Building the Bridge* (Marshall 1997), fifteen influential New Democrats, affiliated with both the Democratic Leadership Council (DLC) and the Progressive Policy Institute (PPI), offer "10 Big Ideas to Transform America." Their standard-bearer, former President Clinton, "distanced himself from liberal orthodoxy" and thereby won reelection in 1996. The DLC/PPI concludes, "The big losers in 1996 were the extreme partisans of the left and right." But the "Bridge Builders" hasten to reject the notion that they and Bill Clinton have opportunistically headed to the ideological middle simply to win votes. "1996 was no mandate for moderation. The answers to our problems won't be found in the mushy middle of the tired, left-right debate." Contrasting with moderation in the mushy middle is the New Democrats' staked-out claim: the "vital center" of American politics, referred to by Clinton in his 2000 State of the Union address (p. 1).

Unfortunately, after 223 pages of big ideas, the distinction between mushy middle and vital center, between opportunism and principle, remains unclear. Indeed, in the afterword, former Democratic vice presidential candidate Senator Joseph Lieberman combines the book's often florid rhetoric with a familiar bottom line. The book's big ideas are "the stuff of which peaceful revolutions are made," comprise "nothing less than a transcendent reform of our national polity," and prepare us to be "architects of a modern brand of governance that is suited for the third millennium." But the bottom line is that all of this idealism pays off: "The election results make clear that those who govern from the vital center will hold the balance of power in the Congress" (p. 223). This juxtaposition of transcendent politics with election results recalls Ambrose Bierce's (1911: p. 95) definition of politics as "a strife of interests masquerading as a contest of principles."

The centrist Democrats appeal directly to Republicans, whose ideas, especially on market economics, are well represented in the book. Republican president George W. Bush praised the centrist Democratic Leadership Council during his 2000 presidential campaign."The two parties," writes Lieberman, "can build the bridge to the twenty-first century together if they follow the blueprint outlined in this book. That is because," as JFK had argued forty years earlier, "it is based not so much on ideology as on what works"—a pragmatic claim that always begs the question, Works for what and for whom? Taking a page from Iroquois history, but watering it down by six-sevenths, Lieberman praises the foresightfulness of the centrist blueprint because "it was designed not with the next election in mind, but the next generation" (Marshall 1997: p. 223).[1] As we shall see, the left liberals are considerably more skeptical of the DLC/PPI blueprint than is the centrist Democratic minority leader, Senator Tom Daschle, who is quoted on the cover: "*Building the Bridge* proves that bold ideas are perfectly consistent with the philosophy of the center." Like other progressives, I have been unable to determine exactly what this center, or its philosophy, ultimately is.

On the other hand, some of the book's authors offer proposals, verbally endorsed by Clinton and Gore, that could become part of a truly transformational vision. In doing so, they have tapped the political pulse of the electorate in ways radical transformationalists have often resisted, in part for reasons of political correctness. The centrist liberals are ready to shift the focus of affirmative action from racial and gender group preferences to universal help for the urban poor, although the rural and suburban poor receive little attention (the latter being less PC than the urban poor). No longer soft on crime, they favor vigorous community self-defense by community policing and prosecution culminating in a "restorative justice"—an approach that has shown promise of cutting crime and restoring community in a number of U.S. cities in the 1990s (cf. my Chapter 8).

These New Democrats are willing to oppose feminist criticism of the family as a locus of patriarchy and conservatism: they make strengthening the besieged family one of their top priorities. The family they hope to strengthen, however, is not entirely the so-called traditional one of male breadwinner plus stay-at-home mom and kids,[2] because "for the foreseeable future, most families will need two adults with wage-earning capacities to remain securely in the middle class" (p. 151). Thus they set themselves up for a conservative charge of "no one at home on the left." They do make a vague reference (p. 155) to recognizing the efforts of stay-at-home parents of young children. When advocating public policies that favor the two-parent family as the most beneficial for children, they anticipate criticism from feminists, gays and lesbians, and advocates for black and single-parent families. The less-than-transformational quality of their blueprint is nowhere more evident than in their brief and laudatory reference to Clinton's Family and Medical Leave Act of 1994, whose benefits pale in comparison with the far more family-friendly provisions of European law. The left liberals take the Clinton centrists to task for making "exaggerated claims about [this] primarily symbolic regulatory measure," which are bound to appear fraudulent to most working families (Greenberg and Skocpol 1997: p. 128).

Perhaps the most politically incorrect stance of the Clinton Democrats, which earns them strong criticism from New Majority left liberals, is the centrist liberals' shift to market solutions for problems typically addressed by governmental bureaucracies and affiliated experts from the helping professions. Despite the good intentions of social welfarism, "the government's social safety net became a snare for many poor citizens, a final destination rather than a way station back to family, work, and self-reliant citizenship" (Marshall 1997: p. 28). The centrist liberals recommend greater reliance on private charity, nonprofit community development corporations, tax incentives for small business and for companies that hire former welfare recipients, tradable pollution allowances, and domestic and international free markets—all of which, they believe, will work better than government programs. These solutions rely, however, on an assumption of strongly progrowth economic policies whose crux is ever-increasing productivity.

Although this DLC/PPI tract omits any mention of political correctness per se, its authors clearly see themselves as courageously biting the bullet of political incorrectness in defying some traditional liberal positions and in risking the wrath of various left-wing interest groups. What is less than bold about their blueprint is its silence on the contribution of corporate capitalism to social pathology and ecocide, on the miserable record of the United States regarding young people, on families as a potential locus of political empowerment, on the right of all citizens to the basic requirements for a dignified life, and on the continuing contradiction between the ideal of democratic equality and the reality that wealth buys votes and influence.[3] Fundamentally, this vision is one that preserves U.S. class society and its zero-sum culture of power, status, and wealth; its perpetuation of extreme wealth and poverty; and its subversion of participatory democracy.

This conservatism is evident in the centrist liberals' redefinition of "progressive" to mean anyone whose votes they might get: "We welcome progressive-minded citizens of all stripes to this discussion: Democrats, Republicans, independents, liberals, conservatives, and moderates" (p. 35). What is most obviously lacking in their demand for "sweeping changes in the basic structure of government" (p. 19) is democracy itself, in the rigorous sense of Jefferson and Lincoln, according to which popular government means "government of the people, by the people, and for the people." The centrist liberals' key to restoring the American Dream is neither democracy nor a decent life for all, but "accelerating economic growth, expanding opportunity, and enhancing security" (p. 25). When they argue for environmental protection, the authors fail to grasp the implications of their own proviso that "markets do not create the right to do harm to others, their property, or the community at large" (p. 180). A "willingness to think hard about the dynamics of taming capitalism as a system," charges the social-democratic liberal Robert Kuttner, is "something all too rare among liberals" (Burnham 1995: p. 54).

The values vacuum at the center of this materialist blueprint is underscored by an unfortunate choice of inspirational role models, coming just prior to the Monica Lewinsky revelations. Taking tougher divorce laws as symbolic of responsible values, the Clinton Democrats believe that "the moral authority of the presidency (and the example of the first family, which has remained intact despite hard times) could be deployed to great effect" (Marshall 1997: p. 157). Polls show otherwise. Values notably missing from the market-growth blueprint are values of social solidarity, in the sense of "an ethic based on the treatment of people as citizens with equal rights and entitlements, rather than as consumers purchasing commodities in a marketplace based on their private incomes" (Kuttner, in Burnham 1995: p. 55).

The centrist liberals offer no evidence for their claim that at present "no ideology rivals liberal democracy as a system of universal appeal" (Marshall 1997: p. 204). European social democrats, despite their own problems, might take exception to this claim. It is also likely that environmentalism, or ecologism, already has more adherents worldwide than liberal democracy, and is steadily extending its lead.[4]

Left Liberalism

In *The New Majority: Toward a Popular Progressive Politics* (Greenberg and Skocpol 1997), sixteen left liberals, or U.S.-style social democrats, take issue with the centrist liberalism of the Democratic Leadership Council and the Progressive Policy Institute. They are especially critical of centrist Democrats' increasing focus on free markets to solve social problems. They do, however, agree with the DLC/PPI that the appropriate instrument for progressive change in the United States is the Democratic Party. And like the centrist liberals, they place great rhetorical emphasis on the family, although "nonworking" families—e.g., welfare recipients, the disabled, the retired, stay-at-home single parents—seem to be excluded from the New Majority team, which seeks to unite "middle-class and less-privileged working families in a broad, winning electoral alliance. This is what we mean by popular progressive politics" (p. 6). As in the case of *Building the Bridge, The New Majority* avoids reference to the term "political correctness" while both engaging in it and purporting to courageously transcend it.

Coeditor and left-liberal pollster Stanley Greenberg might think twice before polling Americans on the book's claim that "Democrats can become the moral voice of all American families" (p. 2). No polling data indicate that Americans think of either major party as a moral voice of anything.[5] In fact, "approval ratings for both parties now rank at the lowest levels in three decades of such record keeping" (p. 279). Moreover, "the current period seems to reflect the exhaustion of political forces that have battled to an inclusive and ugly draw" (p. 4)—a characterization that is even more apt in the aftermath of the Clinton impeachment proceedings and the no-mandate presidential election of 2000.

After working families, the second-most-important player for left liberals is unions, arguably revitalized by "bold new leaders" like John Sweeney (p. 8), the reform president of the AFL-CIO. Sweeney is cast in the tradition of Walter Reuther, long-time leader of the United Auto Workers and one of "the most farsighted leaders of the civil rights era" (p. 17). No longer "failing to organize new workplaces and acquiescing in undemocratic internal procedures," Sweeney's New Directions movement and specific individual unions "are turning these trends around" (p. 210). This New Majority view is expressed in Jo-Ann Mort's (1998) *Not Your Father's Movement: Inside the AFL-CIO,* a collection of essays written mostly by AFL-CIO insiders praising themselves for their reforms. By contrast, in *The Transformation of U.S. Unions: Voices, Visions, and Strategies from the Grassroots* (Tillman and Cummings 1999), nineteen union-democracy reformers and advocates, while crediting New Directions for its greater openness and new efforts at recruiting, document how little progress the new leadership has made in correcting the AFL-CIO's prevailing undemocratic internal procedures, for which the "far-sighted" Reuther was notorious.

In opposition to the centrist liberals' call for a leaner, meaner government, the left liberals buck the smaller-government trend and argue: "The modern Democratic Party has rightly used the powers of government to regulate the economy, promote economic growth, and further social justice" (Greenberg and Skocpol 1997: p. 18). They fault Clinton for succumbing to Republicans' message to struggling families that "You're on your own." They go beyond the centrists by insisting that every American has basic rights to a job and to health care. They specify key economic functions that the private sector cannot reliably carry out, such as the maintenance of infrastructure and the educating of the work force. But the materialistic core-value premise of the left liberals is hardly distinguishable from that of the centrists: "Expanding economic opportunity is at the core of most Americans' conception of the good society. . . . We vary by ethnicity and religion, but we are united by our faith in the American dream—the hope that, through hard work, we can do better for us and our families" (p. 23). Indeed, the two liberal camps try to outdo each other in chanting the mantra of "More Is Better, Growth Is Good," thereby joining conservatives in mistaking the problem for the solution (cf. my Chapter 8).

The left liberals are willing to buck the affirmative-action lobby by recommending that group preferences be substantially replaced by a policy of "affirmative opportunity," undergirded by new race-neutral social rights for all Americans, including jobs and job training, improved public education, better child and health care, and protection from crime and drug abuse. Not targeted at ethnic minorities or women per se, these programs would still "disproportionately benefit the most disadvantaged segments of the population, especially poor minorities" (p. 73).

The New Majoritarians are also willing to break with leftist strictures against playing the conservatives' values game: "The cultural conservatives are right to worry about the coarsening effects of popular entertainment, which, taken together with the advertising that drives it, induces a passion for consumption and a passivity toward politics that are at odds with civic virtue." But unlike conservatives and centrist liberals, the left liberals indict market forces for the degradation of values: "[Cultural conservatives] are wrong to ignore the most potent force of all—the corrosive power of an unfettered market economy" (p. 147). The left liberals are aware that this corrosion affects the political process and the Democratic Party: "Nothing undermines the sense that the Democratic Party is the party of the people more than the realization that it, too, along with the Republicans, is waist-deep in the muck of private-interest financing in politics" (p. 203). Accordingly, the New Majority supports campaign-finance reform along the lines of Maine's voluntary program that passed in 1996. Far from being visionary, however, this proposal already enjoys more than two-to-one support among Americans while falling far short of full public funding of political campaigns (Kay 1998).

Moreover, any third-party challenges to the mucked-up, lucre-corrupted Democrats and Republicans exceed the left liberals' bounds of tolerance for diversity. Despite their advocacy of "tolerance and openness" (Greenberg and Skocpol 1997: p. 260), they reject the notion of progressives who might feel that independent or third-party challenges such as those of the Green Party, the New Party, the Labor Party, the Natural Law Party, or the Reform Party could be a healthy tonic for a stagnant political system: "What is so bizarre about such third-party efforts is that the Democratic Party itself is so open to reform and innovation" (p. 234). In other words, the progressive New Majoritarians plan to take over the Democratic Party, and then things can safely be left to them. Indeed "the image of the reformer as outsider is obsolete" (p. 235). Any attempt at a progressive multiparty democracy would become a cacophony of voices, an "indiscriminate postmodernism of the left" (p. 237). The New Majority Democrats unintentionally invoke overtones of Russia's new majority party of 1917, the Bolsheviks ("Bolshevik" being Russian for "majority"). Because progressives must "know that their causes are hopeless if the Democratic Party shrivels to secondary status," it follows that "the party itself must become a cause" (p. 235). In short, unless we join the vanguard party, all is lost.

Of greater concern than the latent Bolshevism of liberal intellectuals is what is omitted from "this bold and visionary book."[6] Democrats must be tough on crime, but the authors don't say how and in fact say almost nothing about crime, which Americans consistently place high on their list of public concerns (Kay 1998: p. 272). Universal medical coverage is proclaimed a vital right of all Americans, but no plan for national health insurance is set forth. Ambitious campaign-finance reform is advocated, but no mandatory proposals are advanced. Nothing is said about the implications of a high-growth economy for environmental protection and sustainability. In fact, despite recognizing the environment as a traditional Democratic theme, the New Majoritarians, unlike the American people, seem to have lost interest in it (p. 144).

Most disappointing in the end is the book's treatment of its ideological frontispiece, the beleaguered American family. "Democrats can build a new majority in national politics," the book opens, "by championing the needs and values of American families striving for a better life in the face of unsettling changes" (Greenberg and Skocpol 1997: p. 1). But the narrowness of the left liberals' familism soon becomes apparent. The authors tell us that the families most deserving of attention are those in which the parents are earning incomes in the cash economy. "The people who most require—and deserve—extra support are working parents" because, unlike welfare recipients, the retired, the disadvantaged, or stay-at-home parents, "they are doing vital service on which all of us depend, today and tomorrow" (p. 120). In short, work that pays and spurs growth, counts; effort that merely fulfills needs, including much "emotional labor," does not.[7]

The left liberals recognize the importance of "fashioning a more family-friendly economy and society," including opportunities for parental leave from cash jobs. But the authors offer only the vaguest proposal: "There must be rights to family leave on terms that make it truly available to all employees" (p. 121). Any social-democratic readers from Europe, where greatly expanded and fully paid parental leave is common, must wonder about the crimped vision of their left-liberal American compatriots. In addition, to help families, "we progressives support tough crime laws and active measures to make neighborhoods safe, clean, and orderly" (p. 121). But what kind of laws and measures, we can only guess. Help is also needed by gay families, unmentioned by either liberal group, perhaps from fear that homosexuality might alienate the "vital center" of the electorate. Gay partners and parents face serious social and legal discrimination, and, as a left-radical source points out, "we have families as gay people that include children, parents, extended families in very many of the same ways that heterosexual people have families."[8]

The left liberals withhold criticism of careerist parents who relegate their very young children to nannies or day care in order to maintain a high standard of living. Indeed, the fact "that both parents now work as a matter of course, even when they have young children, is just a mundane part of the problem" (p. 291). As we shall see in Chapter 7, much evidence implicates this "mundane" choice in serious problems children experience as children, as well as later in life. In addition, "One-half of marriages now end in divorce, and only one-half of divorced men make the payments that are due to their children and former wives" (p. 291). The left liberals basically accept this situation as something that divorced parents and their children will just have to adjust to. They propose no transformational alternatives that might address the ongoing plague of family dysfunction. Nor do they examine any possibilities for families, whether functional or dysfunctional, to work together for community betterment or for a family-empowerment movement to demand a family-friendly economy and polity—a grass-roots effort that could alleviate the problems themselves (see my Chapter 7).

What, finally, do the left liberals have to offer America's most vulnerable citizens, its children? What they offer is another case study of *The Missing Child in Liberal Theory* (O'Neill 1994). For purposes of public policy, children disappear into their families. Not only are children, as usual, not to be a primary concern of public policy, but neither are any parents who might opt to stay at home to care for them. "There are strong social, economic, and political reasons why popular progressives should put *working parents* at the center of the new family politics" (Greenberg and Skocpol 1997: p. 118, emphasis in the original). The political reasons are especially telling. After all, "working fathers and most especially working mothers find themselves under extraordinary pressures today" (p. 119). Even where children's needs are most acute, as in health care, "how wise is it for progressives to concentrate on expanding health coverage just for kids . . . ?" Naked politics answers this rhetorical question: "Adults, after all, are the ones who vote." Therefore, it is "more understandable to average voters" if any benefits granted children are matched by benefits given to adults (p. 127).

In short, these progressive, majoritarian adults do not foresee any transfer of benefits, let alone power, from adults to children. This stance will take on extra meaning when we see, in Chapter 6, "Beyond Adultism," that children comprise the largest severely disadvantaged class in U.S. society. In the left-liberal vision of *The New Majority,* when children do take on importance, it is a crassly utilitarian one: "In a high-tech, fast-changing economy, the rearing of children and young people into productive workers and participating community members demands much greater reserves of parental and institutional support than ever before" (pp. 119–120). What happened to the concept of a child as a beautiful, magical creation, to be valued as a unique being in his or her own right? In its instrumentalist concern for children, the New Majority's generational imagination, like that of the centrist liberals, falls six generations short of the Iroquois standard that helped inspire our own Founding Fathers.[9]

Left Radicalism

In the post–Cold War era, many American left radicals who were also socialists have lost confidence in the state ownership of the means of production while still favoring fundamental change in the institutions and culture of U.S. political economy. Economically, some favor market socialism, as variously represented in Yugoslavia and post-Maoist China; others prefer economic democracy, with popular ownership and control of both public and private sectors; and yet others support Scandinavian-style social democracy. Politically, left radicals in the United States prefer direct, participatory democracy over indirect, representative democracy in which politics is primarily carried out by elites. Culturally, they seek to wrest control of mass media and public schools from the hegemony of corporate capitalist ideology and its associated values of power, status, and wealth, as well as its historical association with racism and patriarchy. A good sampling of current left radicalism is South End Press Collective's 1998 book *Talking About a Revolution: Interviews with Manning Marable, Winona LaDuke, Michael Albert, Howard Zinn, bell hooks, Urvashi Vaid, Peter Kwong, Noam Chomsky, and Barbara Ehrenreich.*

Unlike the authors of *Building the Bridge* and *The New Majority,* these nine radical activist-scholars make no effort to reconcile their positions to create a collective one. With "The Left" or "The Movement" somewhere between disarray and disappearance, these partisans are considerably more self-critical than their two liberal counterparts. The interviews give little of the sense of self-importance and vanguardism of the two camps of Democrats. These radicals share a realization that vanguard radicalism has culminated in "the alienation of the self-conscious left from its potential participants and allies" (South End Press Collective 1998: p. xi). Unlike the centrist and left liberals' insistence on the Democratic Party as the proper focus of political action, the consensus of the left radicals, as expressed by Noam Chomsky, is just the opposite: "Where is the place to organize? Just about anywhere" (p. xi).

The left radicals oppose elitism of all sorts. Unlike the centrist and left liberals, whose paternalistic catering to "working-class families" fairly leaps off their texts, the radicals openly fess up to a kind of unintended elitism: "The left is . . . often far more identified with and oriented toward the life views, values, and aims of the [expert] coordinator class than it is toward working people," offers Michael Albert (p. 5). Hoping to correct this left-wing incongruity, virtually all of the radicals have involved themselves in the active struggles of working and disadvantaged people. Unlike the insider New Democrats and the would-be-insider New Majoritarians, the radicals reject the notion that outsider-reformers are "obsolete." They seem far more aware than the liberals that many of the reforms of the liberal state—including the abolition of slavery, voting rights for women, workers' right to organize, Social Security, and citizens' right to initiative, referendum, and recall—originated in the radical proposals of outsiders such as the Abolitionists, suffragists, utopian Bellamy Clubs, Progressives, the Socialist Party, and the Congress of Industrial Organizations.

The solutions entertained by the radicals are far more transformational than the "bold" and "visionary" ideas of the centrist and left liberals. For this reason, evidence of political correctness among the radicals becomes all the more important to examine. Several of them criticize the radicals' own tendency to enumerate ills rather than develop solutions. "Most people on the left can't answer the question, 'What are you for?' beyond very vague and unconvincing generalities," points out Albert (p. 9). Lack of vision is costly: "What is the solution? What is your vision? It is hard to get people to change if they can't articulate or see where we're going," emphasizes Winona LaDuke (p. 77).

The radicals also acknowledge that many radicals' resistance to liberal reforms, such as increases in the minimum wage, ignores the urgent need of the severely disadvantaged for some relief. On the one hand, reformist feminism should be opposed because, as bell hooks says, it "gets incorporated by the existing state structure to reinscribe its own values, as opposed to actually engaging in any type of radical, transformational questioning" (p. 49). On the other hand, argues Albert, "It won't do to say that everyone will be better after the revolution. People need better conditions now, on moral grounds, and also to have any faith in future prospects" (p. 8).

The radicals solidly reject the formerly PC view of orthodox Marxists that everything is determined by economic forces and their "inevitable" path of development. Determinism serves, Noam Chomsky believes, "to make people feel helpless, as if there is some kind of mysterious economic law that forces things to happen in a particular way, like the law of gravitation or whatever. That is just nonsense" (pp. 24–25). Rejecting inevitability also means rejecting the illusion that the majority of the populace will inevitably accept radicals' ideas. To gradually persuade nonradicals without taking an elitist posture implies two-way communication in which radical partisans acknowledge the possibility that they will end up being the ones who are persuaded to change their views—a posture consistent with zeal but directly opposite to political correctness, which seeks to shut out discordant views. When activist Peter Kwong (p. 56) found that "Chinatown residents were not interested in socialist ideas," he reflected critically on his own political practice rather than debunking the "false consciousness" of the residents.

Running counter to the traditional macrostructuralism of socialists, these leftists emphasize the importance of social movements, including ethnic-identity politics, and of decentralized, grass-roots action. "I believe in the 'small is beautiful' idea, and I believe that one of the important things about native communities is that we have been 'intentional communities' for thousands of years," emphasizes Native American LaDuke (p. 79). When identity politics ends up separatist, these radicals demur, as in the words of Peter Kwong: "I have no problem with identity politics, if identity politics gives us strength to mobilize. Identity only matters in contact and struggle with others. Otherwise, it is nothing but an empty self-indulgence" (p. 66). Ethnic resistance movements are necessary, argues Manning Marable (p. 92), "but there is no Black strategy for health care that can be addressed solely by working within the Black community." The left should not, he believes, perpetuate divisions based on the unjust history of our country.

Native American activist Winona LaDuke embodies the strategy of reaching out to allies in her multiple political roles—from tribal concerns among her own Ojibwe people, to Greenpeace activism, to serving as Ralph Nader's running mate on the Green Party's 2000 presidential ticket. Lesbian scholar-activist Urvashi Vaid thinks that "one of the failures of our identity-based movements is that we let go of the project of developing the common politics." Despite "speaking about the world and the issues from my perspective as a lesbian, . . . I very much believe I can link up and find common ground with a heterosexual mother who lives in the suburbs. I think I can link up and find common ground with a straight white businessman" (p. 102).

With the collapse of Soviet-style socialism, some former state socialists, such as Marable, have redefined their position to emphasize "socialism as a project of radical participatory democracy" (p. 90). Some have gone even further from socialist orthodoxy. "We have to come together as the progressive populist movement of the 21st century," says Urvashi Vaid (p. 106), who has come all the way over to supporting a socially responsible capitalism, because "I don't believe we are going to overthrow capitalism" (p. 108). All of the radicals agree with Howard Zinn's proposition that "so long as the society is dominated by wealth, wealth will dominate politics" (p. 120). While still critical of free markets, the left radicals in general support a system of participatory economics, which Albert says emphasizes "remuneration according to effort and sacrifice, not power or property or even contribution to the social product (which is favored by many other progressives)" (p. 11). Among many former Marxists, pay according to work is no longer regarded as a temporary, socialist way station to true communist justice, according to which people would be paid in relation to their needs while working according to their abilities. As I will argue in future chapters, this politically incorrect revision of the Marxist canon implicitly reflects a changed, and more realistic, view of human nature.

The left must not imagine, emphasizes Barbara Ehrenreich, that it has all the answers or that it already "somehow represents the majority of people" (p. 29). Examples of ways in which the left has typically diverged from majority tendencies include its traditional stance against religion (Marx's "opiate of the masses") and against involvement in mainstream activities such as sports. "One of the greatest difficulties the left faces in reaching out to masses of people in America is its profound disrespect of spirituality and religious life," theorizes Ehrenreich (p. 43). Many activities can be passionate experiences, from political organizing to going to a baseball game. The difference between these two is that "you don't get anything out of [the baseball game] . . . it is just the sheer excitement of the crowd without any content." Then Ehrenreich catches herself in the anti–popular-culture PC of the radical left: "Well, maybe I say that because I'm not a baseball fan" (p. 33).

The left-wing puritanism that Ehrenreich self-corrects is also criticized by Howard Zinn regarding art. "I think of art as having a double function, of giving pleasure and enhancing social consciousness. To accomplish the first alone is not something to be scorned." He points out that socialist authorities such as Stalin would not allow pure art. But in Zinn's view, "we should always be acting out those delights of the good life—humor, music, poetry, excitement, adventure—that we hope will be available to large numbers of people in the world when freed from sickness, war, and suffocating work conditions" (p. 117). Similarly, the element of sexual puritanism among feminists such as Andrea Dworkin (for whom heterosexual intercourse is inherently an act of rape) has come under criticism from other feminists, including propornography feminists.[10]

Urvashi Vaid criticizes the "old guard of the New Left" for its dogmatism. "What I challenge is their unquestioned assumption that they've got it right and everybody else has it wrong. . . . You've got to look at what's wrong with what you're doing, no matter who you are" (p. 105). Having occasionally suffered from other radicals' political correctness, these left radicals bluntly espouse intellectual openness: "Dogmatism doesn't belong on the left," declares Ehrenreich, including the dogmatic-left rejection of all biological explanations of human differences, problems, and possibilities (p. 33).[11] Another example is prochoice leftists who refuse to work with antichoice groups such as Catholic bishops on issues of common concern, like the reduction of poverty. Single-issue fanatics, like some animal-rights activists, can undermine the larger cause of transformation. "The depressing thing at many left gatherings I've been to is this sort of purism," notes Ehrenreich. "I was speaking on a panel recently, and somebody mentioned Ben and Jerry's as an example of socially responsible business. Some guy in the audience jumps up at question time to talk about how they exploit cows or something. Please!" (p. 38).

Manning Marable (pp. 87–88), a black progressive critic of affirmative action, argues that capitalism has fostered "a growing class stratification within the Black community and [has] bought off a social layer, a privileged, middle-class group of African Americans, to go along with the system."[12] He has pointed out that Richard Nixon supported affirmative action precisely for the purpose of dividing the black community within itself and from other communities of color. A number of other radicals also see the need for going beyond the racial and gender preferences of affirmative action. "An issue that takes us beyond affirmative action, an issue, which, if dealt with, would make affirmative action less necessary, . . . is the distribution of wealth, the economic system," suggests Zinn. "In other words," Zinn goes on, "we need to make such fundamental changes in our economic arrangements that Blacks and whites, and men and women, would not have to compete for resources (jobs, college positions) made scarce by capitalism" (p. 116). Such politically incorrect questioning of affirmative action has begun to spread throughout not only the U.S. legal system but all four leftist segments of the ideological spectrum.

Unlike some leftists and Marxists who have looked to charismatic leaders for inspiration, these radicals seem aware of the dangers of depending on individual leaders, even when fawning adulation is politically correct. For instance, unless leftist leaders have prepared others to take over for them, their movements are vulnerable to their leaders' assassination, as in the cases of Gandhi, Martin Luther King, Malcolm X, John and Robert Kennedy, Che Guevara, and Leon Trotsky. In retrospect, only the personality cult of Mao Zedong seemed capable of propping up the increasingly inefficient Chinese system of state socialism, which has been fundamentally transformed since his death in 1976. "The major weakness of the Rainbow Coalition was its failure to consolidate a democratic, membership-based organization, with elected leadership accountable to all members," notes Marable. The problem was overdependence on a single leader: "[Jesse] Jackson favored a charismatic, populist style of Black leadership, which inevitably destroyed his own organization after 1989" (p. 89). Many radicals, like Vaid, now see a connection between leader worship and ideological dogmatism. "We can't spend our time waiting for The Perfect Vision, The One and Only Answer, The Charismatic Leader Who Will Lead Us Into Salvation. It's nirvana. It ain't gonna happen" (p. 109).

When a charismatic, popular, and politically correct radical leader goes astray, do these radicals think it appropriate to buck the tide and openly criticize such a leader? They do. Black Muslim leader Louis Farrakhan, arguably the most popular radical black leader in the United States in the wake of his Million Man March on Washington in 1995, is "essentially the late 20th-century version of Booker T. Washington," having "no program to challenge racism and . . . no program to advance the movement." He serves to divide and conquer the left because "he's homophobic, he's anti-Semitic, and he's deeply conservative and patriarchal; he's opposed to women's reproductive rights. . . . He represents a kind of Black authoritarianism that can't be tolerated," says Marable (p. 92).

What about the situation when a highly respected radical scholar goes wrong? "By and large, most Black male thinkers don't show any interest in dialoguing with Black women," charges bell hooks (p. 45), "and I don't think it's any accident that as Cornel West has become more firmly situated within a mainstream, patriarchal, white institution like Harvard, he has been less interested in dialoguing across boundaries with myself and other progressive thinkers." Thus hooks essentially accuses West of political dogmatism, or PC, when she suggests that it is specifically those "progressive thinkers who don't agree with a lot of the positions that he now takes" with whom he no longer wants to dialogue.

Notwithstanding these left radicals' honesty, self-criticism, and willingness to innovate, they fail to address critical aspects of social transformation. The key topics that are "missing in action," partly for reasons of political correctness, are the typical lacunae of the radical left.

First, these leftists, like the radical left in general, express no detailed consensus on even the basic outlines of an economic vision for the future. They find themselves between the rock of failed socialism and the hard place of the cruel market.[13] Unwilling to embrace the failed models of state socialism, they seem unable to incorporate market freedoms or supply and demand into an alternative to corporate capitalism. Their brief comments on political economy vary from remnants of state socialism, through economic democracy, to reformed capitalism. Even if economics is not as determinative as Marx and Engels thought, surely it is a vital topic deserving more than desultory attention. Michael Albert, who (with Robin Hahnel) has written important books on socialist economics, makes the least-abbreviated comments (about a page) but seems reticent either to defend or to transcend his earlier visions of socialism, or "participatory economics." He singles out economics as the area in which the radical left's typical vagueness about the future is most pronounced. What technical work there is in radical political economy is mostly ignored by radical thinkers and activists.[14] Since the best radical political economists are now incorporating markets into their analyses, it appears to be the traditional, PC Marxian aversion to markets that is quashing most left radicals' confrontation of this critical issue.

Second, the left radicals present no general model of the participatory political system they all favor. Most importantly, what institutional features of governance will engage ordinary citizens in public decisionmaking on a regular basis? The radicals give suggestive examples, often based on personal experience, of ways activists can engage in protest and resistance, but they offer no cohesive vision for citizen empowerment in the government of the future. Third, they offer no set of alternative values that might underpin a liberatory political economy of the future. The reader infers that left radicals disapprove of the winner-take-all mentality of capitalist society, but the authors offer neither a clear set of alternative values nor a strategy for the resocialization of citizens in the present or the future.

Third, it is probably a residue of Marxism that today's left radicals resist as utopian any clear vision of a more humane society of the future. To avoid the politically incorrect tab of "utopian," post-Marxist radicals continue to defer to the citizen-proletarians of the future all decisions about the kind of institutions and values that should define the future society. To do otherwise, and actually envision the future society, is viewed by most left radicals as either unscientific, coercive, or both. The radical left has consequently ignored the richly suggestive literature of utopias and dystopias that has flourished in the United States for the last twenty years.[15] These utopias have provided detailed proposals for the political, economic, and sociocultural institutions of the future, proposals that could provide the basis for creative and constructive discussion and experimentation on the left.

Fourth, the left radicals virtually ignore the subject of families, parents, and children—a topic defaulted to a netherworld somewhere between civil society and "the individual." Thanks to research in child development, we now know that this netherworld of the family is the most important thing that will ever happen to most people. Despite second-wave feminists' giving the family long-overdue critical attention, these left radicals, including several radical feminists, say almost nothing about the vital role families play in the well-being of their members or about the role a federation or movement of empowered families might play in social transformation. As for children, these adult radicals omit them entirely, as reflected in the familiar adultist oversight of Michael Albert (p. 2) when he lists "winning universal suffrage" as one of the achievements of the left that give him the most hope for the future. The third-graders I once taught weren't buying this claim for a minute. My opening line of "Well, let's begin with the fact that in this country, everybody gets to vote, right?" was met with a chorus of "NO, NO, NO!—we don't get to vote!"[16] Radicals are supposed to get to the root of things, beginning with the recognition that a thing exists. Most adult radicals literally do not recognize the disfranchisement of children—nor their own complicity in the political silencing of young people's voices.

Fifth, the left radicals say next to nothing about crime, an issue of high priority to most Americans. Most important, they offer no program to fight crime, other than making politically correct references to "sentences [that] are way too long" (Ehrenreich, p. 30) and "exploitative prison labor" (Zinn, p. 123). Presumably, crime will go away when our unjust society is transformed, and in the meantime we all just need to watch out for ourselves. Sixth, it is hardly a coincidence that only the Native American radical Winona LaDuke has much to say about the environment. Despite a recent upsurge in red-green linkages among progressive thinkers and activists,[17] most radical greens are not very red and most reds are not very green.

Finally, the radical left continues to suffer from factionalism, a problem reflected in many comments made by the interviewees of *Talking About a Revolution*. Typical is the tendency of each radical-left group to claim that it is the most progressive. For instance, hooks claims: "We have to recognize that to the degree that revolutionary feminism critiques and intervenes on racism, class elitism, and sexism, which includes homophobia, it is the most left movement that we have in our nation" (p. 46). Nothing is more divisive than claims that one's own group is the most politically correct.

PC is also reflected in internal bickering that cannot be resolved: "[LaDuke] was also part of a huge political battle that ensued at Greenpeace last year, that ended with a bunch of us being forced out" (p. 73). Internal squabbling also occurs between radicals and liberals in particular organizations, as LaDuke also notes: "I think that if the debate in the Sierra Club over immigration is any indicator, we have some real problems in the politics of the environmental movement" (p. 76). "The New Left splintered because of ego problems, ego wars between its leaders," says Vaid (p. 104). Repeated experiences of internal conflict have made many activists cynical toward progressive leaders and the movement as a whole.

Socialism

"'Real socialism' in theory and practice has been declared by nonsocialists and many ex-socialists to be 'dead on arrival,'" reports eco-socialist James O'Connor (1998: p. 269). "It is not *a la mode* these days to advocate socialism of any sort," complains market socialist David Schweickart (1998: p. 7). "Socialism is dead. . . . It is not fashionable to defend socialism these days." Schweickart's pessimism is purposefully exaggerated, but a large kernel of truth lurks within his hyperbole. The overlap between left radicals and socialists, a subspecies of left radicals, reflects many activists' uncertainty about exactly where they stand on economic issues.

Let us identify, first, the positions commonly endorsed by U.S. socialists; second, the traditional, politically correct assumptions among socialists that many socialists are now questioning; and, third, the PC remnants of socialism that continue to dog the radical and socialist left. Texts representative of widely held views among rank-and-file socialists include Steve Shalom, ed. (1983), *Socialist Visions,* a South End Press Collective point-counterpoint among twenty-three socialists; Samuel Bowles and Herbert Gintis (1987), *Capitalism and Democracy;* Michael Harrington (1992), *Socialism: Past and Future;* Bertell Ollman, ed. (1998), *Market Socialism: The Debate Among Socialists,* a point-counterpoint among Ollman, Hillel Ticktin, James Lawler, and David Schweickart; and James O'Connor (1998), *Natural Causes: Essays in Ecological Marxism,* which presents and critiques an array of radical and socialist perspectives.

First and foremost, U.S. socialists of the 1980s and 1990s reject capitalism as unjust and inefficient. Second, they reject Soviet-style state socialism as undemocratic and oppressive. Third, whatever forms of economic ownership and planning replace capitalist forms, they must be democratic and participatory. Fourth, noneconomic forms of oppression that have accompanied capitalism must be resisted in their own right, especially sexism and racism. Fifth, socialism should not suppress but should accommodate cultural diversity; indeed, socialist transformation will require the participation of diverse groups and social movements, not just the industrial proletariat. Sixth, the socialist transformation should be nonviolent, either because violence is immoral, or because any attempt at the violent overthrow of U.S. capitalism would be self-defeating. These positions constitute a revision of Marx based on a century of experience with capitalism and socialism after Marx's death, and on the special conditions of U.S. society.

A number of traditionally unexamined PC assumptions are still evident, although increasingly subject to criticism, among socialists. Historical materialism assumes that economics, and especially relations of ownership and production, are the basic moving force of history. Politics, religion, culture, individual psychology, and social institutions such as the family all purportedly derive from underlying material causes. From the early 1980s (Hayden 1983: p. 95) to the late 1990s (James O'Connor 1998: pp. 29–47), socialists have continued to propound the materialist conception of history. By contrast, like Gramsci, Frankfurt School critical theorists, socialist feminists, and Freudo-Marxian cultural critics such as Lasch and Zaretsky, many rank-and-file socialists now accord these "superstructural" factors an importance of their own. "Socialism is a necessary but *insufficient* condition to the liberation of women and gender" (Helmbold and Hollibaugh: p. 213). "Marxism is weakened by unsustainable attempts to treat distinct spheres of social life as passive reflections of others" (Bowles and Gintis 1987: p. 18).

The scientific claims of Marxism have always been challenged by idealistic, moralistic, and utopian socialists, but these groups have generally occupied the fringes of the socialist tradition in the United States. Because the historical evidence has not consistently supported Marxian hypotheses, or "laws," Marxian socialists have in many cases creatively interpreted the data to fit their hypotheses. For instance, the workability of communistic ownership in U.S. intentional communities such as the Shakers, as well as cooperative forms of living among indigenous peoples such as the Iroquois, have been used by Marx, Engels, and other Marxians as evidence that such patterns would be equally workable in large, industrialized societies. Unfortunately, as Erasmus (1985), Scott (1998), and others have shown, when social groupings get larger and more anonymous, the common good gets provisioned less by spontaneous cooperation and more by some combination of differential pay, centralized planning, and legal coercion.

In a current example of data spinning, market socialist David Schweickart (1998: pp. 7–9) uses China as a successful example of market socialism, despite admitting its oppressive features. What he does not admit is the increasingly capitalistic nature of the Chinese economy, underscored by the Chinese government's announcement in January 2000 that "all obstacles to the development of the private sector should be scrapped."[18] China officially accelerated the free-market approach in October 2000. Emphasizing the socialistic aspect of the Chinese economy, Schweickart notes that "as of 1990, only 5.1 percent of China's GNP was generated by the 'private' sector" (p. 8)—a figure that only dramatizes China's headlong rush into capitalism when other sources report that "by the mid-1990s more than half of China's economic output came from the non-state sector."[19] "China's real accomplishments have been stunning," remarks Schweickart. Perhaps, but with state-owned firms increasingly disciplined by market standards and the private sector by far the most dynamic, are these accomplishments socialist or capitalist? One symptom of political correctness is the ignoring or explaining away of politically incorrect evidence.

Related to Marxist scientism is a belief in the inevitability of proletarian revolution. In Marx's words: "What the bourgeoisie, therefore, produces, above all, is its own grave diggers. Its fall and the victory of the proletariat are equally inevitable."[20] Michael Harrington (1992: p. 211) believed not only that the transformation of work over the next half century would undermine cherished injustices of capitalism, but also that "we can confidently predict this future." Officially, scientific Marxism was opposed to utopian models of the socialist or communist future society, although Marx and Engels both engaged in a fair share of highly utopian speculation.[21]

Granted, a detailed vision of the future, if slavishly followed, would constitute a form of political correctness. But socialists' more typical avoidance of anything "that can be projected beforehand in 'correct form'" (Brecher 1983: p. 173) has become its own brand of antiutopian PC. Scientific Marxists see no need to develop and agitate for a new system of values, because they believe that such values will inevitably develop from workers' struggle against capital.[22] Some socialists do believe that a vision of the future is necessary to inspire prospective partisans of socialist struggle,[23] and today many socialists flatly reject Marxian inevitability.[24] Indeed, many socialists now see Marxism as one part social science and one part ideology, or moral philosophy.

Despite official opposition to utopian speculation, the transparently utopian communist society of the future relies on a heroically cooperative conception of human nature, whether altruistic, rationalistic, or both. Under communism, people would contribute according to their abilities but receive according to their needs, as exemplified in small Shaker communes and indigenous Inuit communities. Albert and Hahnel (1983) beg the reader's agreement with their rationalistic-altruistic vision of workers and consumers under socialism: "As a worker under socialism would you hold back your energies, or try to honestly commit your capabilities to meeting society's needs? Everyone has an interest, and understands their interest, in the overall well-being of the community." But good socialist citizens, they assume, will go beyond enlightened self-interest in their communitarian ethic:

under socialism, "consumers recognize when work is painful and try to moderate their requests accordingly while the character of worklife has changed dramatically. In these circumstances we believe workers will seek to ensure that *everyone* benefits from their efforts to the greatest possible extent" (p. 271).

But as Erasmus (1985) and others have shown, reciprocal altruism in face-to-face groups of close neighbors and relatives cannot be extrapolated to large, anonymous societies that lack strong, informal social incentives for compliance with reciprocity. Many socialists now accept the permanent need for rewards that are proportionate to one's work or contribution to society. Responding directly to Albert and Hahnel, Sirianni (1983: p. 284) says, "An economic system cannot be built on the basis of the presumed honesty and good intentions of all the participants and freely interactive units." As Harrington (1992: p. 234) notes, "Ironically, during the next period, socialists may come to be the champions of a traditional 'Protestant ethic' that links rewards to work done in the real world." Bowles and Gintis (1987: p. 207) "doubt that any society will dispense with the need to motivate work." In short, many socialists now accept as permanent a socialist standard of justice, which Marx viewed as a transitional compromise to be replaced eventually by true justice under communism.

Closely related to optimistic assumptions about human behavior and justice is the Marxian-socialist denigration of free markets.[25] Socialists have traditionally attributed a great deal of the harm of capitalism, especially its creation of a class society of rich and poor, to the individualistic, selfish, competitive, and acquisitive nature of market behavior. "Antisocial priorities are imposed by the market upon the workers even when [as in Employee Stock Ownership Programs] they do have the vote on the Board of Directors" (Harrington 1992: p. 226). An aversion to markets has led some socialists to wishful thinking: "The market is utopian and its day is over" (Ticktin 1998: p. 78).

On the contrary, cross-cultural evidence shows that "market economy continues to spread everywhere" (Erasmus 1985: p. v), transforming peasant societies, engulfing formerly socialist countries, even changing the socialist kibbutz communities of Israel.[26] The accelerating triumph of the market has impressed Marxist economists as well: "Everywhere market economy and liberal democratic ideas on the right, and radical democratic ideas on the left, seem to be defeating socialism and socialist ideas" (James O'Connor 1998: p. 269). Traditionally, socialists have argued that the incentives and Invisible-Hand benefits of free-market supply and demand could be replaced by the rational and altruistic cooperation of socialist citizens. But in fact, "nowhere do we find a collective good maintained without self-interest" (Erasmus 1985: p. 330).

Many socialists no longer want to sacrifice all of the freedoms and efficiencies of the market. "Only under socialism and democratic planning will it be possible for markets to serve the common good as Adam Smith thought they did under capitalism. . . . Markets can be an instrument of free choice rather than of perverse maldistribution" (Harrington 1992: pp. 245–246).[27] Schweickart (1998), Lawler (1998), and others have recently developed detailed rationales for more fully incorporating markets into a socialist system. But even many market socialists, like Lawler (p. 146), still hold out the hope that eventually Marx will be proved right and markets will vanish: "Ollman and I, as Marxists, will argue forcefully that the market, even the socially regulated market of the transitional society, will eventually have to go."

From a traditional socialist perspective, markets are bad but growth is good. In fitting with their materialist conception of history, socialists did not fault capitalism for its maximization of material growth and wealth. Rather, the proletariat was expected to expropriate the capitalist means of production in order to pursue growth even more effectively. "When machines make machines and technology can ensure an abundance of sources of power and raw materials, costs are reduced to zero" (Ticktin 1998: p. 75). Accordingly, socialists paid little attention to the environmental costs of unchecked economic growth or the limits of natural resources. Indeed, the ecological idea of steady-state economics, or zero growth, is a "dangerous utopia" (Harrington 1992: p. 291). "All of the innovations in social ownership will work only if there is growth and full employment" (p. 229). Unlike capitalism, socialism does not compel growth, but "this is not to say socialist economies will not *choose* growth that is both desirable and ecologically balanced" (Albert and Hahnel 1983: p. 272). Bowles and Gintis (1987) believe that workers' technological conservatism is problematic for a healthy level of economic growth under a system of worker-controlled economic democracy.

Today, however, some socialists question the "growth is good" equation and entertain ecological considerations.[28] Indeed, eco-socialist James O'Connor (1998: p. 43) believes that "historical materialism is also not materialistic enough. Marx wrote before the age of ecology." O'Connor urges progressive groups to work together and listen to one another, especially "socialists (including Marxists), anarchists, oppressed minorities, bioregionalists, and ecological feminists" (p. 289). Marxists must pay "as much attention to the questions of land and community, of race and ethnicity, and of gender and ecology, as to the workplace, labor, and economy."[29] As reflected in the journal he edits, *Capitalism, Nature, Socialism,* O'Connor believes that "'Reds' have increasingly adopted one or another of the 'Green' discourses, and 'Greens' have tended to lean more to the left" (p. 300). He advocates a Preservation First! ethic to replace the traditional progrowth ethic of socialism (p. 318).

In a pitch against the remnants of PC that continue to plague the left, O'Connor concludes that this political holism "means giving what used to be called 'orthodox Marxism' final rites, and making the turn to a cultural and ecological Marxism." He notes approvingly the attitude of New Zealand's progressive alliance: "We don't have any answers, only questions." In a clear departure from political correctness, he suggests that "this caution and willingness to challenge basic assumptions about the world may be the very definition of a 'progressive' today" (p. 292).

In the end, though, O'Connor cannot resist trying to recapture the normative struggles of progressives for Marxist "science": "Ecosocialism is not, strictly speaking, a normative position but rather a positive analysis of socioeconomic conditions and *imminence*." Progressive groups today "are, in fact, struggling to subordinate exchange value to use value and the production for profit to production for need" (p. 332). His retreat from moral struggle, of course, begs the question of what activists should do if progressive groups "in fact" falter in their struggle.

Socialists have tended to avoid developing programs to combat the pathologies of key institutions under capitalism, especially the institutions of the family, criminal justice, and government. Socialists have believed that these pathologies would naturally be cured when the working class finally assumed ownership and control of the means of production. Socialism would deconstruct the family and its possessive tendencies under capitalism, in part by socializing child care; it would remove the need for criminals to break the law, because it would replace unjust capitalist laws with just socialist laws; and it would make the transitional socialist government fully accountable to the proletariat while paving the way for a "withering away of the state" under communism. Following the lead of feminist theorists, Bowles and Gintis (1987: p. 107) further the deconstruction of the family by "reject[ing] the view of the family as a unit, or as a homogeneous actor with common objectives." While intended to free wives from oppressive husbands, and perhaps children from oppressive parents, this politically correct, though ironically individualistic, view vitiates the family as a progressive political force and hands its members over to the paternal state and its affiliated helping professions—a topic of Chapter 7.

But some socialists have become leery of the automatically therapeutic consequences of new, socialized patterns of ownership and care for curing social pathology. Regarding socialized child care, for instance, Martin Bierbaum (1983) warns, "I have already witnessed situations among 'progressive people' where 'a woman's place is in the home' has been abruptly supplanted by 'no one's place is in the home' to the detriment of all involved." He cautions, "People, both men and women, who wish to have children, may have to modify career plans and share responsibility, not abnegate it" (p. 92). An occasional socialist has even noted the existence of adultist oppression of young people, which will not automatically disappear when capitalism disappears. Family caring is "perverted by the power that men have over women, adults over children, younger adults over our elders, whites over people of color, and heterosexuals over gay members of families"

(Helmbold and Hollibaugh 1983: p. 194). Indeed, "legally and morally most children are powerless and trivialized" (p. 203).

Transcending PC:
From Making History to Transformational Politics

In *Making History: The American Left and the American Mind,* Richard Flacks (1988) touched on many of the themes I have explored among the four current leftist camps. He noted the disorganization and infighting among U.S. leftists—qualities that impede their effectiveness as agents of social change. He argued that the rebellious nature of leftists makes them resistant to political organization and discipline, especially given the historical perception that *"left parties reduced members' freedom without increasing commensurately their capacities to be politically effective"* (p. 196, emphasis in the original). In other words, the relatively undogmatic and antiauthoritarian individuals most likely to become critics of U.S. society and to seek social change have been put off by a politically correct narrowing of viewpoint and behavior among activists.[30] When activists' own experience runs counter to the group's politically correct line, the group is less likely to welcome dissent, respond dialectically, and thus improve its own praxis, than to silence or ostracize the dissenter. This tempting option for premature closure serves both to warp the group's analysis and to undermine its long-term solidarity. "All of the American left organizations were thus undermined by tendencies to enforce certain kinds of ideological conformity at the expense of members' direct experience" (p. 205).

Flacks makes it clear that such PC narrowing is not a tendency peculiar to the left. "Active organizational membership restricts freedom of thought. The loyal member must be something of an apologist for the organization, something of a romantic about its potential achievements, something of a chauvinist vis-à-vis competing groups, something of a factionalist in organizational disputes." The goal-orientedness of an ideologue makes excessive tolerance costly: "Just as a salesperson cannot afford to be openminded about the virtues of competing products or the flaws in what he is selling, so the party member cannot readily be objective about his or her commitments and is inclined to suppress rather than entertain negative evidence and private doubts" (p. 197). In this book I explore some of the serious costs of this suppression of evidence and doubt, and suggest ways in which intellectual openness can actually serve the cause of political commitment in the long run.

The analogy of the salesperson suggests the way in which short-term dissent can serve long-term solidarity and effectiveness. An obvious exception to Flacks's generalization about salespersons is the one who is truly selling a superior product. That seller alone can afford to tell the whole truth about the product being offered as compared with its competitors. In ideological terms, the "superior product" is the theory and program that best serve the needs and goals of the target audience. The only way to develop the best theory and program in the long run is to subject it to criticism and improvement in the short run. Political correctness serves to minimize criticism and thereby stymies theoretical and programmatic improvement.

Flacks provides a bridge to Woolpert, Slaton, and Schwerin's (1998) *Transformational Politics: Theory, Study, and Practice,* a book written by fifteen scholar-activists from the Ecological and Transformational Politics section of the American Political Science Association. Unlike liberals, these writers advocate fundamental change in U.S. social, political, and economic values and institutions. Unlike much of the socialist and radical left (from which most of them came), they seek to transcend the limitations inherited from a mechanistic, Eurocentric, patriarchal, materialist, and industrial tradition without succumbing to either opportunism or political correctness. Their book is an initial collective foray into asking new questions about social transformation rather than an attempt to provide answers in the form of a political program. Flacks emphasizes "everyday life as a terrain for history making" (1988: p. 238), and the transformationalists (who formed in 1987, just as his book was going to press) appear to pick up where he left off.

Theoretically, they begin with (1) the obsolescence of prevailing conservative, liberal, and radical paradigms of how we view the world and what a good society entails; (2) a systemic and ecological perspective on human values, behavior, and institutions; (3) the intimate relationship between the personal and the political; and (4) a purposive or spiritual transcendence of the materialism of both Marxism and liberal capitalism. Substantively, they appraise the praxis of Green politics, both appreciatively and critically, paying close attention to psychological elements that can either strengthen or weaken partisan effectiveness; explore innovative methods of implementing direct democracy; examine the challenges and promise of transformational leadership; propose transformational alternatives for overcoming social inequality and injustice; and discuss a rich array of transformative approaches to teaching and doing research about the fundamental problems and prospects of contemporary society.

I propose to pursue these issues further in the following chapters, with special attention to developing fundamental critiques and transformational alternatives that have been ignored by progressives, in part because of the strictures and seductions of political correctness.

Notes

1. The Iroquois Confederacy's constitution required leaders to consider the effects of their policies on the next seven generations.

2. Lasch (1997) makes a good case that this so-called traditional family, targeted by Betty Friedan (1983) in *The Feminine Mystique,* was mostly a creation of the postwar suburbs. In the nineteenth and early twentieth centuries, Lasch points out, women played many important roles outside the home, including economic, civic, and philanthropic roles essential to the development of urban amenities we now take for granted.

3. Cf. Charles Lindblom, *Politics and Markets: The World's Political-Economic Systems* (New York: Basic Books, 1977).

4. Evidence of the spread of environmentalism includes the worldwide proliferation of proecology groups and Green parties, the ever-stronger environmentalism of the world's youth (Temple 1993), and ever-increasing proenvironmental polling results, notably in the United States. Cf. Kay (1998); Richard J. Ellis and Fred Thompson, "Culture and the Environment in the Pacific Northwest," *American Political Science Review* 91, no. 4, December 1997, p. 885.

5. Kay (1998).

6. From the book's jacket.

7. See Ronnie J. Steinberg and Deborah M. Figart, eds., *Emotional Labor in the Service Economy,* special edition of *The Annals of the American Academy of Political and Social Science,* no. 561, January 1999.

8. Urvashi Vaid, in South End Press Collective (1998, p. 97).

9. See Donald A. Grinde Jr. and Bruce E. Johansen, *Exemplar of Liberty: Native America and the Evolution of Democracy* (Los Angeles: University of California, 1991).

10. Women of Kerista, the former Haight-Ashbury "polyfidelity" commune, described themselves as propornography feminists, a philosophy reflected in the commune's frequent self-publications. These women were critical of antisexual tendencies of some feminists. See also Nadine Strossen, *Defending Pornography: Free Speech, Sex, and the Fight for Women's Rights* (New York: Anchor, 1995).

11. Partly out of fear of the allegedly conservative implications of biologism, many Marxists and Marxian leftists ignore or reject the very concept of a uniquely human nature. "The dominant view (including much of the left, Marxists particularly) is that there is no human nature but only culture, history, environment, and so on. This is about as sensible a view as the view that the embryo becomes a human or a bird depending on the nutritional input; in short, it is an idea that is completely off the wall." Noam Chomsky, letter to James O'Connor (1998: p. 47, fn 7).

12. As we shall see in Chapter 2, it is this group of privileged blacks, along with middle-class white women, who have primarily benefited from affirmative-action programs.

13. The most socialist of these nine radicals, Michael Albert, stipulates that his envisioned system of "participatory economics . . . rejects markets as antithetical to justice and self-management" (South End Press Collective 1998: p. 11).

14. Cf. Przeworski (1991); Martin O'Connor (1994); James O'Connor (1998); and the journals *Review of Radical Political Economics, Capitalism, Nature, Socialism*, and *Dollars and Sense: What's Left in Economics.*

15. See the journal *Utopian Studies* and its predecessor *Alternative Futures*, as well as the four collections of essays entitled *Utopian Studies I–IV,* which bridged the chronological gap between the two journals in the mid-1980s.

16. The thirty students were split on whether young people like themselves should have the right to vote. A boy asked, "How would we know what we were voting for or against, since we don't read newspapers or anything?" A girl replied, "But if we had the right to vote, we'd want to start reading newspapers!"

17. See especially the journals *Democracy and Nature* and *Capitalism, Nature, Socialism.*

18. John Pomfre, "China Pushes Private Enterprise," *Washington Post,* January 5, 2000.

19. Ibid

20. Marx (1988 [1848]: p. 66).

21. For instance, Engels, the more hardheadedly economistic of the two, wrote in "The Principles of Communism": "Finally, when all capital, all production, and all exchange are concentrated in the hands of the nation, private ownership will already have ceased to exist, money will have become superfluous, and production will have so increased and men will be so much changed that the last forms of the old social relations will also be able to fall away." Karl Marx and Max Engels, *Collected Works* (Moscow: Progress Publishers, 1976), vol. 6, p. 351.

22. "For the Marxist, social labour is not a moral good but an objective necessity" (Ticktin 1998: p. 75).

23. William Connolly criticizes Marxism for "placing agency at the level of structure and displacing the idea of the subject, [thereby] bypass[ing] the issue of securing personal freedom in a socialist polity." *Appearance and Reality in Politics* (Cambridge: Cambridge University Press, 1981), p. 175.

24. "We seek to avoid both the individualism of choice theories and the presumption of a pregiven logic of either stability or crisis in structural theories" (Bowles and Gintis 1987: p. 96). "I try to steer clear of the fake scientific claims of Stalinist 'dialectical materialism,' on the one hand, and the chaos of postmodern relativism, on the other" (James O'Connor 1998: p. xi).

25. "Social and economic inequality, unemployment, idle machines and factories, ecological destruction, widespread corruption and exaggerated forms of greed . . . are the inevitable byproducts of market economies" (Ollman 1998: p. 81).

26. The best source on the rapidly changing conditions of kibbutz economy and society is the Israeli journal *Kibbutz Trends,* published by scholars who live in kibbutz communities.

27. Yugoslav Marxist Svetozar Stojanovic argues that "self-management is not only threatened by statism, but also by a utopian image of human nature, which leads to the naive expectation that self-managed groups produce rationally, without being challenged by competition. In a system without competition, solidarity turns into its opposite, into parasitism." Quoted in Harrington (1992: p. 272).

28. "How does society discipline nationalized—and all other—industries to respect the environment? By measures that are, at a minimum, national in scope. . . . to guard against the 'collective egoism' of social property" (Harrington 1992: p. 224).

29. As usual, people suffering from the effects of ageism, notably children, are ignored in this envisioned alliance.

30. A great deal of evidence supports the correlation between open-mindedness and antiauthoritarianism, on the the one hand, and support for social change, on the other. See my (1975) *Dogmatism, Ideology, and Political Behavior.*

2

Affirmative Action: Hanging Separately While the Gentry Feast

"We must all hang together or, most assuredly, we will all hang separately."
—Benjamin Franklin[1]

"The militant peasants can be counted upon to start squabbling among themselves long before they reach the castle gates."
—Michael Lind[2]

Originally signifying affirmative efforts to root out illegal discrimination, after 1965 affirmative action came to be identified with group-preferential treatment on the basis of race and gender. The policy of compensatory group preferences, focusing initially on blacks, was devised in a haphazard, reactive fashion by white male elites in the Johnson administration who were alarmed by the spreading urban violence of 1963 to 1968. Tactically, the policy was continued by the Nixon administration in an effort to embarrass and divide the Democrats by pitting against each other their two biggest allies, the civil-rights movement and organized labor. Strategically, Democrats and Republicans alike hoped that affirmative action would promote "black capitalism," foster a growing black middle class as a buffer between white society and the black underclass, and discourage the formation of multiracial alliances of poor and working people across the United States. All of these hopes have been borne out in the subsequent thirty-five years.

Ironies of Affirmative Action

In *The Ironies of Affirmative Action,* the most detailed study of the early history of affirmative action, John Skrentny (1996) documents the political considerations that led Presidents Johnson and Nixon to support racial preferences in a variety of public programs. Skrentny, who neither favors nor opposes affirmative action, reveals a series of ironies that are all but forgotten today but that shed light on the unintended consequences of a program

49

that most progressives have supported for the last three decades. To hundreds of ghetto riots leading to thousands of injuries and arrests, almost two hundred killed, and millions of dollars in property damage, "government and business elites responded with race-conscious policies and programs, understood and now more safely advocated as tools of social control and hedges against further disorder" (p. 68). Thus affirmative action was "largely the construction of white male elites who traditionally have dominated government and business" (p. 5). President Johnson's idealized explanation for group preferences, as a way to restore a level playing field for disadvantaged groups, struck a respondent chord among many Americans, although never a majority (pp. 4–5).

Because such civil-rights leaders as Martin Luther King and Bayard Rustin opposed racial preferences as divisive, affirmative action "became a political possibility *without* the benefit of any organized lobbying for the policy" (p. 5, emphasis in the original). These leaders "sensed that affirmative action would be counterproductive to the long-range goals of civil rights groups. Whites could not be left out of 'compensatory' programs" (p. 231). In Rustin's view, the poorest of the poor, especially blacks, needed fundamental change in the U.S. political economy, which could universally ensure such essentials as good jobs, decent housing, and adequate medical care. "Preferential treatment cannot help them," he believed.[3] King wrote: "It is my opinion that many white workers whose economic condition is not too far removed from the economic condition of his black brother, will find it difficult to accept a 'Negro Bill of Rights,' which seeks to give special consideration to the Negro."[4] Indeed, "in a great irony of affirmative action, the Nixon administration planned to lobby the civil rights leaders to support affirmative action" (p. 205).

On one thing King and Nixon agreed: "Liberal Martin Luther King and conservative Richard Nixon both knew that affirmative action for blacks would disrupt the liberal coalition" (p. 232). Civil-rights groups "did not begin to demand affirmative action until after the government constructed it" (p. 231). Favoritism for blacks and women soon brought demands for favoritism toward other disadvantaged groups. Despite chronic bickering among themselves for affirmative-action benefits, these groups became a formidable affirmative-action lobby. For obvious political reasons, these lobbyists have claimed that the government-enforced racial and gender "set-asides," "proportional representation," and "numerical goals" they sought were fundamentally different from "strict or rigid quotas." But Nixon speechwriter William Safire later admitted that the pioneering Philadelphia Plan that the Republican administration was pushing through Congress in 1969 "waddled and quacked enough like a quota for it to be so adjudged."[5]

Not only did most civil rights groups initially oppose race-conscious remedies for historical discrimination, but "the Right did virtually nothing to stop affirmative action" (p. 6). What about business groups, who traditionally oppose governmental regulations and "should presumably have had an interest in protecting their rights to hire, promote, and fire as they pleased? . . . To the surprise of regulators, business groups were almost completely absent as opponents of affirmative action. In fact, as crisis managers, some business leaders were *advocates* of affirmative action" (p. 232, emphasis in the original). Nixon administration internal documents now confirm the view of AFL-CIO president George Meany, an opponent of Nixon's Philadelphia Plan of preferential hiring for blacks in construction. Meany charged that Nixon was trying to embarrass labor, and indeed Nixon did accuse unions of racial exclusion. With little support from civil-rights leaders and heavy opposition from labor, the Philadelphia Plan nonetheless passed Congress in 1969 with most Republicans supporting it and most Democrats opposing it.[6]

After the vote, White House insiders were giddy with victory. In White House notes, presidential aide John Ehrlichman wrote "Beaten the unions" and Nixon caricatured George Meany's blue-collar speech thus: "When I was a plumber, it never occoid [*sic*] to me to have niggers in the union" (p. 208). Ehrlichman later recalled: "The NAACP wanted a tougher requirement; the unions hated the whole thing. Before long, the AFL-CIO and the NAACP were locked in combat over one of the passionate issues of the day and the Nixon Administration was located in the sweet and reasonable middle."[7] Several black observers saw through Nixon's strategy. For instance, Clarence Mitchell called the affirmative-action plan a "calculated attempt coming right from the President's desk to break up the coalition between Negroes and labor unions." Congressman Augustus Hawkins said, "Nixon's people are forcing employers to lay off workers and then telling them to put in a certain quota of blacks into these vacancies. It is a strategy designed to increase friction between labor and Negroes" (p. 210).

Regarding the new affirmative-action law, Ehrlichman wrote to Nixon: "In due time, if we administer it without undue zeal, it can become a 'slow and reasonable' approach to civil rights such as Scammon describes in his advice for Republicans" (p. 214). Two months later, "plans were made to split the black community, targeting the 'black silent majority,' or the 'probably 30% who are potentially on our side.'" An internal memo described this "politics of preemption," to which Nixon scribbled, "OK." Soon, hard-hat unionists came to the defense of Nixon's policies in Vietnam, he no longer needed black allies, and "slow and reasonable" support for preferential hiring "faded into ambiguity" (p. 215).

Nixon administration support for black capitalism through the Office of Minority Business Enterprise tied individual grants to political contributions for Republicans. These doubly preferential fruits were not known to most Americans. Gallup polls showed—and continue to show—that most Americans oppose racial preferences (pp. 4–5). Indeed, Sniderman and Piazza (1993) found that the mere mention of affirmative action made respondents' attitudes toward blacks more negative. As more Americans became aware of affirmative action, they became more negative to whomever they saw as supporting it. Yet "as if on cue, the Democrats clumsily embraced the quota concept at their 1972 convention. . . . All that remained was for America to forget that it was the Republican Nixon who pushed racial quotas through a formerly reluctant Congress" (Skrentny 1996: p. 217).

In general, ordinary Americans, while sometimes supporting "affirmative action" in the abstract, have opposed preferential treatment, primarily on the moral grounds that it rewards or penalizes a person on the basis of qualities, such as race and gender, over which the individual has no control.[8] Indeed, cross-cultural data show that gender-preferential affirmative action is "massively unpopular" not only in the United States but in Australia, England, Germany, and Italy, even among women, who would benefit from it. Sniderman and Piazza (1993: p. 134) suggest the reason why: "Proposing to privilege some people rather than others, on the basis of a characteristic they were born with, violates a nearly universal norm of fairness." On the other hand, "many of the most powerful people in the [United States]," who are personally unaffected by affirmative action, "began to see specifically hiring black Americans as a sensible and appropriate thing to do" (p. 223). In the words of A. Barry Rand, a vice-president at Xerox, "Diversity is good for business."[9] This sentiment is echoed by the Women's Legal Defense Fund: "Affirmative action also improves businesses' bottom line."[10]

Why It Is Politically Incorrect
to Criticize Affirmative Action

The idealized purpose of affirmative action was to enable historically disadvantaged groups to compete successfully with white males. Despite the political maneuvering of interest groups described earlier, the most vocal opponents of affirmative action since 1970 have been conservatives, often racist and sexist. The intended beneficiaries came from groups that had suffered unspeakable discrimination. These two facts have so colored the debate over affirmative action that most progressives with qualms about the fairness or effectiveness of group-preferential treatment have muffled their doubts. Until the mid-1990s, the left generally viewed white male critics of affirmative action as presumptively racist or sexist, and female and minority critics as "sell-outs." Guilt and self-righteousness became the two sides of the common currency of political discourse on affirmative action.

In recent years many progressives—including women and people of color—have begun to question affirmative action. Leftists, including multiculturalists, have roundly attacked them for doing so. As a result, most progressives still hesitate to criticize affirmative action publicly, and thus help to perpetuate an appearance of progressive harmony on this issue. We saw in Chapter 1 that leading liberals, without criticizing affirmative action, are now favoring the extension of preferential treatment to poor people generally. But most progressives hesitate to fault affirmative action for logical or moral inconsistency, or for spreading enmity within the working class. To do so is still politically incorrect.

In fact, most progressives have serious doubts about affirmative action, but few will express them publicly. Indeed, using Kuklinski's "List" experimental procedure, Sniderman and Carmines (1997: p. 468) were able to measure respondents' true feelings about affirmative action and discovered that "liberals are just as likely to be angry and upset over affirmative action as conservatives." Moreover, "those who are most committed to achieving equality for blacks are just as likely [as those who oppose racial equality] to be angry and upset over affirmative action." But as Sniderman and Piazza (1993: p. 66) had reported earlier, the charge of racism or Uncle Tomism against critics of affirmative action "has had a chilling effect on intellectual discussion of the place of race in American life." Black critics of affirmative action have been attacked as "race traitors" (Carter 1991: pp. 99–123).

Jean Bethke Elshtain (1998: p. 262) faults "the Left's general inability to tolerate diversity in the ranks of minority groups—presumably they should all think alike and have identical needs that whites can minister to." PC blacks are far from alone in trying to silence critics of affirmative action. White liberals and radicals often join the attack with zeal. When Georgetown University law student Timothy Maguire published an article critical of affirmative action, the university tried to confiscate every copy it could find (Lind 1996: pp. 166–167). In 1998, the University of Michigan returned a $10,000 gift intended to name a new reading room of the Residential College after scholar Carl Cohen, a college founder, because of Cohen's well-known criticisms of affirmative action, which bothered some ethnic minorities.[11]

Progressive voices speaking out against both affirmative action and left-wing PC are growing in number, and find resonance among most Americans.[12] In rejecting the bean-counting approach to diversity, journalist Michelle Malkin writes, "I am not a brown jelly bean. . . . I want my readers to know me for my ideas, ideology and idiosyncrasies—not for my Filipino heritage."[13] In Oakland, California, after many years of mostly black governance, Hispanic, Asian-American, and black officials now share power with recently elected white mayor Jerry Brown. City council president Ignacio de la Fuente and utilities-board member Danny Wan agree with the sentiment expressed by Shannon Reeves, a black Republican who heads the Oakland NAACP: "I think we make a mistake when we go out saying this candidate has to be black. I think we have to find good candidates."[14]

When such sentiments are seen as encroaching on affirmative action, however, they are still typically condemned on the left. Even if reluctantly, most progressives still side with NAACP national president Kweisi Mfume, who asserted in 1998 that racism still dominates life in the United States and dismisses as "house Negroes" African-American opponents of affirmative action.[15] Democratic congresswoman Maxine Waters, who co-chaired President Clinton's 1992 presidential campaign, three years later threatened the president for waffling on affirmative action: "No President is so important that we will belong to him if he undermines us on this issue."[16]

Affirmative Action as a
Program of Division and Conquest

In the harsh glare of PC, most progressives shy away from confronting the contradictions and self-defeating aspects of affirmative action, especially its group preferences. The "backlash" noted by reporter Susan Faludi (1991) continues unabated, but it is pitting not only men and sexists against women and feminists, but white against black, Latino against Asian, poor against poor, the "more qualified" against the "less qualified," and protected classes against the unprotected. Pressing for more affirmative action for itself, each demographic interest group zealously curries favor with the controlling elites while envying other groups' successes. As Robert L. Woodson, Sr., black president of the National Center for Neighborhood Enterprise, points out, "In essence, an underlying premise of race-preferential policies is that the destiny of the black community lies in what others do— or fail to do."[17] He stresses that by the mid-1990s almost half of blacks polled opposed affirmative-action policies.

Black feminist bell hooks argues that affirmative action has encouraged a kind of competitive victimization, with which different groups try to outdo one another "in the competition for favors and reparations from the white male power structure."[18] Radical psychologist Michael Lerner believes that "the transformative and spiritual dimension of the civil rights movement was lost amid a flurry of claims for the 'right' to compete on better terms."[19] Conservative columnist Linda Chavez adds, "An ugly power struggle among racial groups competing to establish their claims to victimhood is the inevitable result."[20] It is no surprise, then, that "inter-ethnic tension between communities of color intensified dramatically during the 1980s and 1990s."[21] Stated mathematically, the people's solidarity in struggle against privileged elites varies inversely with the length and intensity of group-preference programs. Stated politically, the disadvantaged are fighting one another over crumbs while the gentry feast.

By conferring group benefits on some and denying them to others, affirmative action has often pitted different ethnic groups against each other. For instance, "A federal judge yesterday reversed himself on a prior ruling that [had] promoted five Hispanic Denver deputy sheriffs after black deputies objected to the move."[22] In an irony related to this ruling, the previous mayor of Denver (also the former U.S. Secretary of Energy) Federico Peña, was accused of giving his own Latino ethnic group an unfair hiring advantage over blacks, whereas his black successor, Wellington Webb, was criticized for favoring blacks over Latinos. Webb's subsequent efforts to reach out to his nonblack constituents has brought him criticism from black political opponents who charge that he has done too little to help blacks.[23] Such disputes are unfortunate in a city that has elected a minority mayor for four straight terms despite having a white-majority electorate. Similarly, when whites helped St. Louis's popular black police chief Clarence Harmon unseat black mayor Freeman Bosley, Jr., Harmon's harshest critics were blacks who charged him with being "simply a front man for a white establishment eager to retake the reins of power."[24]

As William A. Henry III reports, "Mamie Grant, who heads the organization representing black city workers in Los Angeles, protests about Hispanics: 'They're trying to siphon off all our gains.'" Her counterpart at the county level, Clyde Johnson, adds that affirmative action was originally intended for blacks, and "all the others are latecomers and bandwagon jumpers." [25] Yvonne Gonzalez, Latina superintendent of the Dallas school district, was hounded out of office after only eight months by blacks who criticized her "as another example of powerful Anglos and Hispanics shutting blacks out."[26]

In multicultural America, argues Michael Lind (1996: p. 183), "the majority is fragmented while the elite is unified. The bipartisan white overclass can pursue its goals with little opposition, as long as racial preference policies, the ideology of diversity, and culture-war politics encourage potential opponents to battle among themselves." In the important case *Poberesky v. Kirwin,* a federal appeals court in 1995 ruled in favor of Hispanic applicant Daniel Podberesky, who had been denied a scholarship set aside for African-American students by the University of Maryland. To receive a Banneker scholarship, black applicants needed only a 3.0 GPA in high school and a combined SAT score of only 900, compared with Poberesky's GPA of 4.0 and SAT score of 1,340 (Malman 1996: p. 152).

In a sad irony, recent surveys indicate that "minorities are more likely than whites to agree to negative stereotypes about other minority groups," including religious minorities.[27] For instance, 33 percent of Hispanics, 22 percent of Asians, but only 12 percent of whites agreed with the statement, "Even if given a chance, [African Americans] aren't capable of getting ahead." Regarding stereotypes about Jews, 54 percent of blacks, 43 percent of Hispanics, 35 percent of Asians, but only 27 percent of non-Jewish whites agree with the statement: "When it comes to choosing between people and money, Jews will choose money." In the mid-1990s, San Jose, California, black councilwoman Kathy Cole gained notoriety for her caricatures of Hispanics, Asians, and gays, all of whom, she believed, unfairly got preferential treatment from city hall. According to David Hayes-Bautista, director of the Center of Latino Health at UCLA, "some of the things black councilmen [in Los Angeles] say about the Latino population sound like the kinds of things Southern whites would have said about blacks in the '50s: 'We were here first. We're being pushed out. These are our jobs; how dare you take them away?'"[28]

Author bell hooks (1995) believes that Native, Asian, and Hispanic Americans "consistently seek to distance themselves from blackness" because they are "jockeying for white approval and reward" (p. 199). She warns, "Until racist anti-black sentiments are let go by other people of color, no transformation of white supremacy will take place" (p. 201). As Chavez (1994: p. 177) notes, "though few black or Hispanic leaders are willing to discuss it publicly, tensions between blacks and Hispanics have risen recently, fueled by competition over affirmative action programs and jobs." In 1999, ethnic conflict between Hispanic and black high-school students in Los Angeles became so serious that Inglewood High School scrapped celebrations of Black History Month and Cinco de Mayo out of a fear of ethnic violence. Each side resented what it saw as favoritism given to the other.[29] In the words of Viet Dinh (1994: p. 280), ". . . affirmative action can fan the flames of racial animosity. Each racial and ethnic group looks on the others as competitors rather than allies in the fight for a share of the American pie."

Gender animosity fomented by some feminists has had a similar effect of dividing and conquering supporters of gender equality. Just as many U.S. women as men oppose abortion rights today, and Gallup polls show that in the 1970s slightly *more* women than men opposed the failed Equal Rights Amendment. "On many so-called 'women's issues,' there is no gender gap," and the problem remains sexism, not men per se.[30] Many white females identify more strongly with their race than with their gender, and resent special privileges being accorded to blacks, Latinos, and other non-whites with whom they must compete. Even women who do not particularly identify with their own race may understandably resent racial favoritism that works against them. Their resentment is not simply a matter of white-female racism. Similarly, many black and Hispanic males resent favoritism shown toward women with whom they are contending for positions or promotions. Again, this antipathy does not necessarily reflect black and Latino sexism. Minority contractors have opposed extending preferential status to women-owned firms in affirmative-action programs involving government contracting. "My feeling is that although white, female-owned businesses historically have had disadvantages, it's very difficult to absorb them into that program without having a negative impact on minority businesses because the overall amount of resources has not been increased," says Sam Carradine, executive director of the National Association of Minority Contractors.[31]

Careful statistical analysis suggests that after more than thirty years of interest-group squabbling, the affirmative-action employment benefits to protected classes have been "generally positive and statistically significant, though small."[32] In short, what amounts to preferential crumbs offered by Lind's "white overclass" encourages dependence of potential recipients on elites as well as antagonism toward one another. The main beneficiaries of affirmative action—especially in business promotions, academia, and government contracting—have been middle-class blacks and middle-class white women, although observers differ on which of these two groups has benefited more.[33] During the heyday of affirmative action, from 1975 to 1995, white men's real incomes declined as those of women and middle-class blacks increased, but it is unclear how much of this divergence is due to affirmative action.[34]

In the early 1990s, in a discussion of divide-and-conquer tactics used by U.S. authorities, Green Party activist and scholar John Rensenbrink (1992: p. 81) argued that

> the affirmative action mechanism has been used to alienate those from one another who could, and need to, help each other: African Americans and Euro-Americans who have the insight and strength to be friends. By keeping them absorbed in the minutiae of affirmative action legislation and litigation, the powers-that-be have sought, often successfully, to undercut the intent and impact of affirmative action. They have stymied the overall efforts of the creative spirits to join forces to fight for real alternatives.

More recently, Rensenbrink (1999: p. 144) made a more pointed charge against elites' cunning use of divide-and-conquer tactics against the masses: "[The oligarchy's] propaganda engines work tirelessly to keep the semantics of deprivation and minorities and upward mobility alive, to keep the particularistic 'rights' pot boiling." The purpose, he asserts, is "to play one 'rights' group off against the others . . . [and] against the 'white middle class.'"

Theda Skocpol (1994: p. 291) fears that future historians "will chronicle the inability of American progressives in the 1990s to overcome mutual recriminations." And she agrees with black liberal sociologist William Julius Wilson (1994) that the racial and gender preferences of affirmative action have played into the hands of conservative Republicans, who "would like nothing better than for liberals during the 1990s to become committed to fighting repeated legislative battles to defend affirmative action quotas against court reversals" (Skocpol 1994: p. 296).

But, a skeptic might ask, if affirmative action serves elite interests, why don't the elites support it? The answer is that many of them do, despite its intrusion into traditional elite domains. Many of the same corporations that rail—and lobby—against government intervention, have welcomed official support for affirmative action. Typically, it is "the largest firms [that] have been supportive of a government role, saying it simply complements efforts they are making on their own."[35] Dupont, for instance, decided in the early 1980s "to make half of its new hires for professional and management positions women or minorities" (Thernstrom and Thernstrom

1997: p. 452). In 1995, the chairman of Mobil said, "I have never felt a burden from affirmative action, because it is a business imperative for us." The fact that affirmative action does not threaten corporate power but can boost profits explains "why many companies . . . go well beyond what the law requires."

Typical of the pro–affirmative-action trend among large corporations is the position of DaimlerChrysler, a new megacorporation formed by the recent merger of two corporate giants. "NO MORE BUSINESS AS USUAL" proclaims DaimlerChrysler in a special 1999 advertising section in *Working Woman*.[36] The ad touts "Diversity as Strategic Advantage in Business Today," and reports that in the United States the company's workforce is 20 percent women and 27 percent people of color. In the ad, corporate-speak meets PC: "Leveraging America's diversity is a top business priority as companies discover that organizational cultures modeled on homogeneity and sameness are out of step with today's dynamic market conditions." Lest the tough-minded readers of *Working Woman* think that the world's biggest maker of commercial vehicles has gone mushy with humanitarianism, the ad explains that a diverse work force is better able to "read" customers of color. And: "In the U.S. today, African-Americans, Hispanics, and Asian Americans have an estimated combined spending power of almost $650 billion." Companies are wise to avoid discrimination suits, the ad points out, because "a corporate image is expensive to build and costly to maintain." In short, reports the American Civil Liberties Union, "Corporate America is for affirmative action" because diversity "is good for dollars."[37]

"There is irony in this diversity, however," warns G. William Domhoff (1998: p. 43), "because the social class and educational backgrounds of the women and minorities tend to be similar to those of their white male counterparts. They also share the Christian religion and Republican politics with most of the white males. . . . There is also evidence that women and minority directors usually share the same perspectives on business and government as other directors." Racial and gender "set-asides" (quotas by another name) "allow the large corporations that currently monopolize the building trades to continue to do so provided they make the minor concession of hiring a few minority subcontractors." Far from being transformational, "the arrangement keeps profits returning to banks and outside corporate investors, and does nothing to redistribute wealth."[38] Referring to required numerical goals or targets of government-mandated affirmative action, Eleanor Holmes Norton (1996: p. 41) points out: "Ironically, goals can also help employers to avoid culpability."

Affirmative action helps to create a buffer class to reduce class consciousness. "By means of college-to-Congress racial preference policies," charges Lind (1996: p. 101), "the white overclass, over the past thirty years, has attempted to create and maintain small, artificial black and Hispanic overclasses. It has done so, not out of charity, but in order to co-opt the potential leaders of black and Hispanic dissent." But doesn't increasing racial and gender diversity undermine the power and privileges of the white male power structure? "We can be certain that, if racial preferences threatened the jobs or incomes of overclass Americans, those preferences would be abolished tomorrow" (p. 102). But the jobs and incomes threatened are those of ordinary Americans who remain unprotected, or insufficiently protected, by the limited and arbitrary classifications of affirmative action.

In an Ashleigh Brilliant "Pot-Shots" cartoon, a well-dressed patrician is scratching his chin next to the caption "The problem is: How can we promote equality . . . while still retaining our advantage?" The tokenism of group preferences, in Lind's words, "provides a suitably 'progressive' camouflage for a system of divide-and-rule politics in which the homogeneous American social and economic elite—the white overclass—benefits from divisions among the American majority" (pp. 13–14). In the United States, "racial divisions ensure that the lower-half Americans waste their energies in zero-sum struggles between races" (p. 255). Regarding remedies for inequality, progressives seem to have forgotten Ben Franklin's advice that "we must all hang together or, most assuredly, we will all hang separately."

What Is Wrong With Affirmative Action?

Despite these considerations, if affirmative action is simply the right thing to do, perhaps we should do it despite its serving the interests of the powers-that-be. Perhaps the divisive and elite-friendly consequences of group preferences are an unfortunate cost that progressives, at least in the short run, must simply grin and bear. But is affirmative action legally, logically, and morally sound?

Inconsistencies of Law and Policy

Some scholars, such as Manning Marable, date affirmative action from the Civil Rights Acts of 1866 and 1875, which granted a variety of equal rights for whites and blacks. Others trace its beginnings to executive orders issued by Presidents Truman or Kennedy (Nicoleus Mills 1994). "The phrase affirmative action first appeared as part of the 1935 National Labor Relations Act. Here, it meant that an employer who was found to be discriminating against union members or union organizers would have to stop discriminating, and also take affirmative action to place those victims where they would have been without the discrimination" (Skrentny 1996: p. 6). But these earlier moves by government to "act affirmatively" to end discrimination explicitly forbade government to consider race or other job-irrelevant factors in hiring practices. In banning federal employment discrimination on the basis of race, color, religion, sex, or national origin, supporters of the

Civil Rights Act of 1964 pointed out that these protections did not grant "preferential treatment to any group because of race, color, religion, sex, or national origin" (Nicoleus Mills 1994: p. 6).

But no sooner had the Civil Rights Act become law than President Johnson, faced with consecutive hot summers of ghetto rioting, dramatically redefined "affirmative action" from its traditional opposition to group preferences in the executive orders of Presidents Truman in 1953 and Kennedy in 1961 and in the 1964 civil-rights law. "Freedom is not enough," said LBJ, in a ringing speech at Howard University in 1965. "You do not take a person who, for years, has been hobbled by chains and liberate him, bring him to the starting line of a race and then say, 'You are free to compete with all others' and still justly believe you have been completely fair." The president argued that "not just legal equity" but "equality of result" were required for those who had been denied equal opportunity in the past (quoted in Mills, p. 7). Johnson used Executive Orders 11246 and 11375 to implement the new definition of affirmative action, characterized by black Harvard law professor Randall Kennedy as "policies that provide preferences based explicitly on membership in a designated group" (quoted in Mills, p. 3). In short, almost from the beginning of the new, group-preference approach to affirmative action, administrative policies came into direct conflict with the intent and wording of national law on civil rights.

The United States Supreme Court's tortured ruling of 1978 in *University of California Regents v Bakke* has both reflected and encouraged the inconsistent laws, applications, and rulings on affirmative action throughout the country. In essence, the Court said that whites must be allowed to compete for admission to all available slots in law school but that it would be permissible to partially hobble them with the chains of their race in order to compensate for the historical hobbling of black applicants. In *Bakke,* four justices supported the University of California's racial quotas (or set-asides) in medical-school admissions, four opposed them, and one, Justice Lewis Powell, "broke the deadlock between the two blocs by splitting the difference: he prohibited racial quotas, but nevertheless allowed race to be taken into account as one factor in university admissions" (Bybee 1999: p. 1). Powell announced the Court's judgment and wrote the majority opinion "even though no other justice actually joined his opinion." In effect, Powell brokered a political compromise that "returned affirmative action to the people in a form that was politically acceptable and amenable to further debate" (p. 4).[39]

As *Bakke* supporter Keith Bybee concedes, "Without a well-specified justification, setting forth general rules that transcend its immediate outcome, Bakke defies conventions of principled judicial decision-making" (1999: p. 2). While both supporters and opponents of affirmative action claimed victory, constitutional lawyers noted the illogic of the Court's position, an anomaly cited in a 1999 suit against the affirmative-action policy of the University of Michigan.[40] "Indeed, during this same period, Powell had trouble persuading his own law clerks that racial quotas failed his ju dioial test while racial preferences did not" (Bybee 1999: p. 2). In "A Politically Correct Solution to Affirmative Action," Paul Peterson (1995) embraces Powell's politically convenient, though morally inconsistent, approach. Peterson concedes that in approving Harvard's implicit racial favoritism in admissions (with race okayed as one factor) while rejecting the University of California's explicit favoritism (with racial set-asides), "Powell came very close to giving constitutional sanction to public hypocrisy as a policy" (p. 7)—a criticism made by dissenting justice Harry Blackmun. In fact, writes Peterson, despite efforts to give *Bakke* credibility, "its only defense is its political acceptability" (p. 8). He argues, however, that *Bakke*'s very ambiguity is a strength: "Politically correct solutions are likely to be imprecise, inconsistent, pragmatic, logically indefensible. That does not make them any less ethical" (p. 6). This political opportunism appealed to presidential candidate Bill Clinton as well, who "campaigned in favor of affirmative action but against quotas, . . . adopt[ing] a position as ambiguous—but politically correct—as the one taken by Powell" (p. 7).

A key sponsor of the Civil Rights Act of 1964, Senator Hubert Humphrey, had sought to calm fears of his colleagues that it would entail reverse discrimination: "Title VII prohibits discrimination," he said. "In effect, it says that race, religion, and national origin are not to be used as the basis for hiring and firing. Title VII is designed to encourage hiring on the basis of ability and qualification, not race or religion" (Skrentny 1996: p. 3). Seminal contradictions such as that between President Johnson and his own Civil Rights Act of 1964, and the one within the Supreme Court's *Bakke* decision, have spawned a plethora of later ambiguities and contradictions. "After more than twenty years of debate and judicial decisions, the ambiguities of Bakke remain" (Bybee 1999: p. 3), a fact that helps explain why in recent years the very kind of group preferences hypothetically approved in *Bakke* have been outlawed in Texas, California, Georgia, Louisiana, Michigan, and Washington. Because the Fifth and North Circuit Courts of Appeal have rendered contrary opinions on *Bakke*'s applicability, the U.S. Supreme Court may finally reconsider its controversial 1978 ruling. In addition, many cities, including Miami, Houston, Los Angeles, Philadelphia, and Denver, have had their affirmative-action programs in contracting ruled illegal by the courts, and the Clinton administration quietly scaled back its own programs of group preference in federal contracting.[41]

In recent years, courts have increasingly ruled against racial preferences in hiring and firing, as well as in school admissions. For instance, a white New Jersey schoolteacher won a reverse-discrimination case after she was replaced solely to promote racial diversity among the faculty. Shortly before the case was to be tried by the U.S. Supreme Court, national civil-rights groups urged the school board to settle out of court because they feared that "an adverse ruling in this case could gut the infrastructure of affirmative action across the country." About 70 percent of the $433,500 settlement was paid for by the civil-rights groups. "The surprise settlement was further evidence, said lawyers and policy specialists, of a shifting political and legal consensus in America away from affirmative action and toward policies that are neutral in addressing race and gender."[42] In 1999, the San Francisco school system, faced with a suit by Chinese Americans, agreed to stop discriminating against them in applications to the flagship magnet school, Lowell High, whose preferential policies had favored blacks, whites, Hispanics, and non-Chinese Asians. In March 2000, a federal appeals court ruled against Maryland's use of race as a factor in public-school admissions or reassignments.

It should not be surprising that at some universities gays and lesbians are a protected class, but not at others; that a povertied background wins preferential treatment in faculty searches at some campuses but not at others; that prior to California's Proposition 209, which banned group preferences, Filipino Americans were a protected class at UC-Berkeley but Italian Americans were not, while the reverse was true at the City University of New York. Such inconsistencies in affirmative action, already noted by Mezey in the early 1990s, intensified throughout the decade.[43] As the century came to a close, Americans faced a patchwork of inconsistent and unsatisfying solutions to inequality.

Treating All Members of Groups As If They Were Identical

The variations in competitive advantage within groups such as "all blacks," "all whites," "all men," and "all women" are far greater than the average competitive differences among these groups. Many blacks are more competitive for many jobs, contracts, and university admissions than many whites, just as many women are more competitive than many men. The reason is that race and gender are but two of many factors that confer advantage or disadvantage. Accordingly, even many supporters of affirmative action concede that it should be more complexly defined and more narrowly honed. For instance, General and Secretary of State Colin Powell, the first African American with a credible chance to win the presidency, has generally supported affirmative action but says, "I don't believe that anyone with money or connections should be helped by affirmative action."[44] Preferences given such people would constitute a form of "reverse discrimination" especially difficult to defend.

In response to charges of reverse discrimination, supporters of affirmative action have added to President Johnson's athletic metaphor of justification. University of Wisconsin labor-law professor James E. Jones, Jr., equates rejection of affirmative action with saying, "We stopped poisoning the lakes and we don't have to do anything to reverse what we've done."[45]

Others argue, analogously, that the caboose of a train will never catch up with the engine unless it is placed on a separate track and given an extra puoh. In the past, say supporters of affirmative action, society has relegated women to the kitchen and blacks to the back of the bus. Now it is time to give them seats in the corporate boardroom and at the front of the bus. Turnabout is fair play.

But is it? Who are the "we" who committed the original injustices, and to whom? An honest assessment of these questions reveals the unfortunate truths:

1. That historical injustices cannot be cleanly or fully righted in any case (as African American Shelby Steele [1990: p. 43] puts it, "It is impossible to repay blacks living today for the historical suffering of the race");

2. That—as affirmative-action proponents charge—ignoring the present effects of history perpetuates old injustices (as black playwright Saundra Smokes said in 1997, "there has been a centuries-old affirmative action program in place to benefit whites");

3. That—as affirmative-action opponents reply—mitigating these effects creates new injustices; and that, consequently,

4. President Johnson's intimation notwithstanding, there is no "completely fair" cure for our history of racial and gender oppression.

Believing otherwise is to believe that we can retroactively right all the bad things that have happened as a result of unjust discrimination. Refusing to give special consideration to women and nonwhites *is* unfair. But so is requiring innocent white males—especially those suffering from other disadvantages not of their own making—to sacrifice for the sins of their ancestors. And as we shall see, it is not only white males who are unfairly injured by group preferences.

This dilemma amounts to a "choice of evils" created by an evil history. It is a serious problem made worse by those who refuse to recognize it. Conservatives may deny the dilemma by positing, with Henry Ford, that "history is bunk," in the sense of believing that the living should not be blamed for the sins of the dead. Progressives deny the dilemma by viewing all of today's white males as benefiting from racism and sexism, even if they did not cause them, and thus owing a helping hand to all of today's women and nonwhites. Both sides tout their views as ethically pure, but simple logic says otherwise.

Arbitrary, Political Bestowal of Preferential Classification

Under affirmative action, what is the logic of privileging one disadvantaged group, for instance African Americans, but not another, for instance people battered in childhood? Both conditions are oppressive and confer serious disadvantages. Neither is a matter of choice. In both cases, a more powerful group—whites and adults, respectively—have abused a less powerful group, blacks and children. In both cases, unusually blessed individuals within the oppressed group can sometimes surmount their disadvantages, while typical members of the deprived group continue to lag behind their nondeprived peers. Both blacks and the previously battered suffer an average deficit in opportunity, self-esteem, and quality of life compared to other ethnic groups and compared to people who have been nurtured rather than brutalized in childhood. In both cases, membership in the advantaged or disadvantaged group is unearned—a matter of pure chance. Contributing to both groups' suffering are biological facts—skin color and youth—poisoned by social conditions—white racism and adult cruelty. Government policies of omission and commission, supported by whites and adults, respectively, have further contributed to the plight of blacks and abused children. The parallels between these two groups, as well as with other disadvantaged groups, are powerful and should be decisive in terms of the need for affirmative action. But blacks get preferential treatment ("protection") under affirmative action while those suffering from childhood abuse do not.[46]

There is no good reason why one such group should be protected and the other neglected by affirmative action. The list of anomalous comparisons could go on, matching the few protected classes against a much larger number of deserving but unprotected ones. Needy but generally unprotected groups include those who grew up in poverty, broken homes, orphanages, polluted environments, rural settings, or substandard educational districts, as well as those disabled by current poverty, chronic bad health, addiction, anxiety, depression, physical abnormalities, and, indeed, a wide variety of developmental impediments to effective physical and mental functioning. Admittedly, some of these disadvantages, unlike skin color or gender per se, affect academic or job performance, but so do many historically inherited disadvantages associated with skin color or gender. The purpose of a logically consistent affirmative-action program would be to help all such disadvantaged persons overcome their performance-relevant impairments. Affirmative-action programs sometimes—but inconsistently—recognize physical handicap or disability as worthy of preferential treatment. But why not consistently? And why are emotional, psychological, and cognitive disabilities not so favored? Such an impairment may or may not be job-relevant, and may or may not be remediable.

It is probable, of course, that a disproportionate percentage of women and nonwhites suffer from some of these additional categories of disadvantage. But why should women and nonwhites who are unusually *advantaged* in these other respects automatically get preferential treatment over whites and men who are unusually disadvantaged? This anomaly of affirmative action means that many people who already enjoy a net competitive advantage are, by government policy, further advantaged, while many of the already disadvantaged are further disadvantaged. By the mid-1990s, an increasing number of observers on the left had noted this anomaly, including white liberals such as the late syndicated columnist Mike Royko[47] and Alice Kessler-Harris (1994); social democrats such as Theda Skocpol (1994) and Michael Lerner (1996); black liberals such as Stephen Carter (1991) and Carol Swain (1995); and black radicals such as bell hooks (1995) and Manning Marable (1995). Scholarly sources have documented the anomaly as well.[48] Of course, many on the right agree with this assessment, including black Republican Tony Brown (1995: p. 268), who charges affirmative-action programs with "a quarter century of ignoring disadvantaged Blacks and redirecting an estimated 80 percent of affirmative action preferences to middle-class White women as well as middle-class Blacks and Hispanics."

"The truly disadvantaged," as William Julius Wilson (1987) calls the poorest of the poor, have seldom benefited from affirmative action because they rarely have the wherewithal to take advantage of the opportunities afforded by it. Black Yale law professor Stephen Carter (1991: pp. 71–72) argues:

> What has happened in black America in the era of affirmative action is this: middle-class black people are better off and lower-class black people are worse off. Income stratification . . . in the black community has increased sharply, even as it has softened in the white community. . . . And at the elite educational institutions . . . the [affirmative action] programs are increasingly dominated by the children of the middle class. One need not argue that affirmative action is the *cause* of increasing income inequality in black America to understand that it is not a solution.

This perverse illogic of affirmative action plays into the hands of conservatives, giving them a strong card to play against the left. In 1987, then-chairman of the Civil Rights Commission Clarence Thomas (1994: p. 99) argued: "Any preferences given should be directly related to the obstacles that have been unfairly placed in those individuals' paths, rather than on the basis of race or gender or on any other characteristics that are often poor proxies for true disadvantage." Dinesh d'Souza finds "no justification for giving a university admissions preference to the government official's son who attends a private school in Washington, D.C., just because he belongs to an underrepresented group, over the daughter of an Appalachian coal miner or a Vietnamese refugee." More generally, "those who are not disadvantaged should not get preferences."[49] Notwithstanding other, dubious positions such conservatives may have taken, they happen to be right on this score.[50]

Not only disadvantaged white men are hurt by affirmative action's limited classifications. A woman or person of color who suffers from additional, unrecognized disadvantages gets credit for only one or two of her or his many disadvantages. For instance, a poor, chronically anxious, uneducated, rural Latina from a dysfunctional family can seldom compete on an equal basis with a middle-class, suburban Latina who comes from a supportive family and is well-educated and self-confident. Affirmative action seeks to compensate these two women for one or perhaps both of their shared disadvantages—race and gender—and then assumes they are competing on a level playing field. In arguing against the "bean counting" of affirmative action, journalist Robyn Blumner says, "I probably have more in common with any given middle-class, college-educated, African-American male from suburban New York than I do with a white, female, high school dropout from rural Alabama, although the bean counters would see me and the Alabamian as interchangeable."[51]

Ironically, the concern to help women achieve a level playing field for college admissions has given way to alarm over the rapidly dwindling number of men now in college, who comprise a steadily decreasing minority of most student bodies. According to a 1999 report, "Schools say they stop short of offering 'affirmative action for men,' but some confide that giving male applicants a slight break is becoming a standard, albeit unspoken, practice." According to the president of the American Association for Higher Education, "Colleges and universities are dipping down deeper into their male pool than their female pool."[52] Some of the startling shift in the gender demography of college students can reasonably be attributed to the many years of reverse discrimination against males dramatized in Frederick Lynch's (1991) *Invisible Victims: White Males and the Crisis of Affirmative Action.* Prominent feminists such as Betty Friedan (1997) and Susan Faludi (1999) have recently transcended PC by stressing the wide range of problems and concerns shared by men and women.

The fact that the arbitrary classifications of affirmative action discriminate against tens of millions of people who are neither white nor male helps explain why by the mid-1990s an increasing number of women and people of color had become critical of affirmative action (Thomas 1987; Wilson 1987, 1994; Steele 1990; Carter 1991; Skocpol 1992; Chavez 1994; Njeri 1993; Dinh 1994; Kessler-Harris 1994; Sowell 1994; Tony Brown 1995; Marable 1995; Swain 1995; Loury 1996). A majority of these recent critics of affirmative action are progressives, and do not necessarily agree with the criticisms of conservatives such as Chavez and Sowell.[53] Affirmative action offers nothing to the disappointed applicant—man or woman, white or nonwhite—who says, "I tried as hard as I could, but my opponents used their nonrural background, superior health, supportive families, and emotional stability to beat me out." In essence, affirmative action replies, "Tough luck. Your disadvantages don't count." Each time an additional group, e.g., veterans or gays or dyslexics, wins protected status, the members of disadvantaged but still unprotected groups suffer yet another competitive setback. As Kessler-Harris points out in "Feminism and Affirmative Action" (1994: p. 77), "expanding opportunities for one group limits the opportunities of unprotected individuals."

Most Americans, like most people everywhere, present a rich mixture of competitive assets and liabilities. Fairness and logic require at the very least that affirmative action consider all of a person's major sources of unearned advantage and disadvantage, not just some small number that have found political favor. In Carl Cohen's (1995: p. 31) words: "Compensatory affirmative action, if undertaken at all, must be undertaken for every person who qualifies on some reasonably objective standard." But the main factor determining who wins protected classification is not logic or fairness but political clout.

Blacks have beaten other ethnic minorities, including American Indians, to the punch by organizing sooner and better than others. For obvious reasons, those with physical handicaps, though disabled, have been politically more effective in advancing their cause than those with mental disabilities. Homosexual activists can take part of the credit for President Clinton's addition of sexual preference to the list of federally protected classes in 1998. A Johns Hopkins University study published in 1999 "found that diseases with strong political lobbies—especially AIDS—got more money according to the DALY [disability-adjusted life-years] measure than diseases with less-vocal advocates, such as emphysema and depression."[54]

Some conditions calling for protection make it difficult for their sufferers to organize and agitate politically. In this respect, it is not surprising that children have fought ageism less effectively than senior citizens have. Veterans have also organized politically to win preferential treatment, but on what grounds, we might ask, should veterans be a protected class? If the rationale is that veterans have been inadequately compensated for their dangerous and thankless work, why not also recognize migrant farm workers, firefighters, inner-city teachers, and social workers? Blacks, women, seniors, and veterans—especially the best-positioned of them—enjoy protected status because they have been able to organize politically and agitate more effectively than, for example, those suffering from dysfunctional families, anxiety, low self-esteem, addiction, phobias, childhood abuse, or youth itself. There is little justice to this division of affirmative-action winners and losers, unless we revert to a crass criterion of political market power presumably rejected by advocates of affirmative action. While admiring the political savvy of groups that have won preferential status, we may still question the arbitrariness of the classifications.

Doubts About Competence

An increasing chorus of nonwhites has joined white commentators such as Charles Murray in arguing against what they see as affirmative action's demeaning implication that nonwhites cannot compete with whites on their own merits. In his 1984 *New Republic* article "Affirmative Racism," Murray (1994: p. 207) says that a greater evil of preferential treatment than its unfairness to the unpreferred is the fact that "it perpetuates an impression of inferiority." As African-American writer Shelby Steele (1990: 41) puts it: "Under affirmative action, the quality that earns us preferential treatment is an implied inferiority." In *Reflections of an Affirmative Action Baby,* black Yale law professor Stephen Carter (1991: chapter 3) refers to "the best black" syndrome that haunts blacks who have benefited from affirmative action but are perceived, or perceive themselves, as succeeding not because they were the best candidate but because they were the best black candidate. Black economist Glenn Loury (1996) writes, "Affirmative action creates doubt about the qualification of the blacks who benefit from it." This doubt may have nothing to do with racism. As Loury underscores, "When it is common knowledge that a lower threshold is used for the selection of black than of white workers, and if job performance is related to the criteria of selection, then it is rational to expect lower average job performance from people in the group that has been preferentially favored" (pp. 53–54).

Defenders of affirmative action point out that whites and males who received preferential treatment in the good old days of rip-roaring racism and sexism did not appear bothered by such self-doubts. While true, this argument misses the point that white-male favoritism occurred in a sociohistorical context of assumed white-male superiority: "We're superior, so we deserve advantages." Today, preferential treatment of women and nonwhites occurs in a context of assumed competitive *inferiority* of women and nonwhites: "We admit we can't compete on our merits, so we *need* advantages." The psychological difference is profound. Are the recipients of preferential treatment inferior and therefore unable to compete on an equal basis, or are they not inferior and therefore undeserving of preferential treatment? They cannot have it both ways. Either an evil history of racism and sexism has damaged today's descendants of the original victims, or it has not and its evils are no longer with us. To accept preferential treatment, in other than an opportunistic way, is to accept that one is history's damaged goods. (That one may be discriminated against unfairly is another matter, requiring forceful and immediate redress.)

One partial escape from this dilemma merits attention. Some argue that the justification for preferential treatment is not to boost an inferior candidate but to repair an inferior institution suffering from a lack of cultural diversity, perhaps because it defines its job qualifications too narrowly. Whether the institution is a business, a public agency, or a university, it will benefit in many ways (so goes the argument) by recruiting a more diverse work force or student body, and affirmative action will help it become more diverse. All members of the institution should benefit from its increased diversity. Indeed, as the 1990s wore on, President Clinton's own defense of affirmative action "focused more on the value in having diverse workplaces and classrooms than on the need to correct past discrimination."[55]

This is a strong argument, but it deflects rather than refutes the criticism of "I'm inferior but I'm still equal" inconsistency spelled out above.

An institution that needs (for example) more women, nonwhites, or gays should straightforwardly go after them, soliciting and taking the best woman, nonwhite, or gay candidate available. It should not, however, go through a charade of soliciting all candidates when what it is really wants— and needs—is a woman, a Latino, or a gay. A fear of legal challenges may chill most institutions' willingness to exchange hypocrisy for straightforwardness. The reasons for needing more veterans, or indigenous people, or the physically challenged can be as compelling as the reasons for needing more legal secretaries or violinists or engineers. But this rationale should be frankly spelled out. Diversity-enhancing candidates recruited because they are the best persons to improve a flawed institution will have no reason to feel inferior or ambivalent about their selection. There is no "superior" white male candidate who can bring the experience, or role model, of a black woman into a classroom, boardroom, or public agency.

To shed any aura of implied inferiority, many candidates from disadvantaged groups prefer to compete on an equal, rather than a preferential, basis even if doing so means having to work harder to succeed. Of course, it should always be the role of affirmative action to affirmatively root out any process that discriminates, for instance, against a black candidate who is the best applicant for a position in nuclear physics, linguistics, or music theory.

PC's pretense of respect for diversity is no substitute for the respect one earns by the Three P's: Problem-solving, Perseverance, and Performance. A dramatic example is the Tuskegee Airmen of the 99th Fighter Squadron, black pilots trained in the segregated Army Air Corps of World War II. Despite the discriminatory conditions of their training, "the black pilots created a distinguished record in combat, flying 1,578 missions escorting bombers flown by their white counterparts through enemy territory. While 66 of the Tuskegee graduates were killed in action and 32 more were taken prisoner, the 99th Squadron attained legendary stature by not losing a single bomber that they escorted to enemy aircraft." It was their performance that typically got them chosen as escorts over less accomplished white fighter pilots: "Flying in the face of the pervasive racism in America and especially in the military, white bomber crews routinely requested the black pilots of the 99th as escorts to their targets."[56]

The three P's, rather than preferential treatment, loom large in recent, noted accomplishments of members of protected classes. When the impeached President Clinton was fighting for his political life in 1999, he and his advisors presumably chose counsels Cheryl Mills, a young black woman, and the late Charles Ruff, a paraplegic, to defend him because of their exceptional legal and oratorical skills, not because they enjoyed protected status under affirmative action. Even Senate Republicans were impressed by Mills and Ruff's brilliant and successful defense of their embattled chief. Likewise, Cynthia Trudell, a Ph.D. in physical chemistry and the first woman to head an automaker's car division, was chosen by Saturn not because of her gender but because, unlike many of her male predecessors, she had excelled in spending "most of the past 19 years in factories, mainly transmission and engine factories and a foundry, some of the grittiest, dirtiest, most macho and most dangerous workplaces in the auto industry."[57]

NASA rocket scientist and inventor Lonnie Johnson not only has helped design three NASA space probes but has patented forty-nine inventions, including the renowned Super Soaker water gun, of which 250 million were sold in its first eight years of production—"not bad for a black kid who was told while growing up in the South that he didn't have what it took to be an engineer."[58]

Former beauty queen and nurse Angelle Seeling "is widely regarded as the fastest human on two wheels" not because of her gender or good looks but because of her motorcycle-racing skills.[59] The strongest role models are those about whom there is no doubt how they earned their laurels.

Complicity in the War of All Against All

In one obvious respect, affirmative action has done more good than bad. On balance, it has tended to level the playing field and thus to correct an unjust demography of winners and losers in the American war of all against all. But, as pointed out by Iris Marion Young, it does nothing to challenge the underlying system of winning and losing per se.[60] Indeed, it serves to rationalize that system by cleansing it of a degree of racial and sexual injustice. In this respect, far from being too liberal or too radical, affirmative action is too conservative in that it helps to perpetuate the political economy of corporate capitalism. "Affirmative action can and should be criticized from the left," argues black radical scholar Manning Marable (1995: p. 87), "because it was 'too conservative.' It sought to increase representative numbers of minorities and women within the existing structure and arrangements of power, rather than challenging or redefining the institutions of authority and privilege."

Even strong supporters of affirmative action such as Luke Harris and Uma Narayan (1994: p. 12) admit that "affirmative action initiatives do not do anything to redress the problems that arise from a hierarchical division of labor." But the PC blinders on both left and right have generally prevented either side from identifying this system-maintaining character of affirmative action. Indeed, it is PC on the right that has prevented many conservatives from grasping affirmative action's own conservatism. If they were as clever as Richard Nixon was, they might well join the many corporate and governmental officials who already support affirmative action.

But perhaps some of today's conservatives are even more clever than Nixon. By railing against group preferences, they win plaudits from most Americans and a knee-jerk defense of affirmative action by many progressives.

As we have seen, a sizeable majority of Americans, though opposing arbitrary discrimination against women and nonwhites, also oppose giving preference to these groups. Americans especially oppose set-asides, "proportional representation" according to race or gender, and numerical quotas. With our history of severe historical discrimination, preferential group treatment may sound compassionate and reasonable to those who value fairness and equality. But "the idea that places should be, explicitly or implicitly, 'set aside' for minority (or women) applicants has never been accepted by a majority of Americans" (Skocpol 1994: p. 296).

The stereotyped notion that women and people of color must be either supporters of affirmative action or "sell-outs" of their race or gender is promoted by leaders increasingly out of touch with those they purport to represent. As mentioned earlier, recent surveys show that in Australia, Germany, Italy, the United Kingdom, and the United States, "giving preferential treatment for jobs and promotions is massively unpopular," even among women (Sniderman and Piazza 1993: pp. 133–134). African-American scholar Carol Swain (1996: p. 12) reports on a survey comparing the opinions of black interest-group leaders with those of the black public: "Seventy-seven percent of black leaders supported preferential treatment of minorities, yet only 23 percent of the black public did."

While proponents continue to defend affirmative action, the number of vocal, enthusiastic supporters is dwindling all across the ideological spectrum, including the left. I conclude by offering three alternatives to affirmative action: one meritocratic, one liberal, and one transformational—but all more defensible than the status quo. The first seeks to embrace the war of all against all but tries to make it more fully meritocratic. The second seeks to humanize this war by guaranteeing everyone the basics of a dignified life. The third incorporates the second, but replaces affirmative action's unrealistic goal of equal opportunity with the more practical, yet also more radical, prospect of fuller opportunity.

Meritocratic, Liberal, and Transformational Alternatives to the Status Quo

In *In Defense of Affirmative Action,* Barbara Bergmann (1996) avoids most of the difficult issues raised in this chapter. She prefers instead to argue that because other sorts of arbitrary favoritism are common (such as admissions preferences for alumni children), racial and gender group preferences ought to be acceptable as well. She also warns that it would be difficult to measure sources of disadvantage other than race and gender. Moreover, like other liberal defenders of affirmative action, she is committed to corporate-capitalist institutions and therefore poses no objections to its role in perpetuating them by dividing and conquering the citizenry. By contrast, the three alternatives I present below are all more defensible on logical and moral grounds than the group-preference-based affirmative action of the last thirty years.

Solution 1: A Logically Defensible and Just Affirmative Action

A number of analysts, mostly on the left, have recently suggested changing or expanding the factors to be considered in affirmative action. African-American scholar Cornel West (1994: p. 85) advocates a "more wide-ranging affirmative action policy." Black journalist Clarence Page, a supporter of affirmative action, concedes the "excesses of affirmative action . . . that . . . decline to take need as well as race into consideration."[61] John K. Wilson (1995), a liberal, agrees with Dinesh d'Souza, a conservative, that a class-based affirmative action would come closer to benefiting the truly needy than a primarily or exclusively race- and gender-based affirmative action. In *Race Versus Class: The New Affirmative Action Debate,* black political scientist Carol Swain (1996: p. 37) writes, "The best course of action for those who want to assist the 'truly disadvantaged' among America's minority poor may well be class-based affirmative action rather than race-based." Feminist Betty Friedan (1997: p. 52) supports affirmative action but believes that "the new paradigm has to go beyond it: alternatives to downsizing that would provide more jobs for everybody, not women versus men, or blacks versus whites."

Conservative Republican Jack Kemp and moderate Republican Colin Powell, both potential presidential candidates in 2000, support class-based affirmative action. As Reagan's secretary of housing and urban development, Kemp emerged from his celebrated visit to Chicago housing projects saying, "I've gone into places where no Republican has ever been, and I've seen things that no Republican has ever seen."[62] Subsequently he came to advocate not only affirmative action for the poor but resident ownership of the predominantly black housing projects. Powell, the first African-American chairman of the Joint Chiefs of Staff and presently Secretary of State, says that he was helped by affirmative action but opposes quotas and "reverse discrimination" and thinks that only the neediest, most powerless minorities should benefit from it.

If fairness is defined as equal opportunity, then fairness requires that affirmative action go much further than it presently does in addressing inequality and disadvantage. Roughly speaking, justice would require that each American be assigned a net Inequality of Opportunity, or Unearned Advantage/Disadvantage, score, reflecting *all* of his or her significant unearned competitive advantages or disadvantages—i.e., those resulting from something other than personal effort and sacrifice. The national average Inequality of Opportunity score would be set at 0. Maximum net-advantage and net-disadvantage scores might be set at +10 and −10. All citizens with a net-advantage score of (say) +1 or higher could then be required to enact an affirmative-action program for all citizens scoring −1 or lower. The only neutral observers would be that small percentage of the populace at or very near the median, i.e., those between +.99 and −.99.[63]

In effect, then, except for these few unusually average citizens, the privileged half of the nation would carry out an affirmative action program for the underprivileged half. Under the status quo, by contrast, "nearly 80 percent of the U.S. labor force enjoy protected minority status," including women (who are in fact a majority).[64] Polls consistently show that most of this protected 80 percent, including most women, reject the very concept of group preferences as unjust to individual members of groups (Sniderman and Carmines 1997). Let us recall that official recognition for a single disadvantage may err in either direction, either (a) privileging those whose advantages already outweigh their disadvantages or (b) falling short of leveling the playing field for those with additional, unrecognized disadvantages.

Under the proposed system, the degree of protection, or compensatory aid, given or received by a particular person would be a function of his or her distance from the median, i.e., his or her degree of net advantage or disadvantage. To attain the even playing field intended by affirmative action, a person suffering a net disadvantage of −1 or −2 would get only a little relief, whereas someone scoring −9 would need massive help. Likewise, those modestly above the median would have less obligation to help their fellows achieve equal opportunity than would those well above it.

An unintended consequence lurks within this less arbitrary, fuller system of affirmative action: the resulting distribution of winners and losers would be meritocratic and thus far less assailable by the new class of deserving losers. Competitive justice would reign supreme. Jefferson's natural aristocracy, in the classical sense of the rule of the best, would be free to emerge, effortlessly. In theory, "affirmative action is not anti-elitist," says William Henry III in his book *In Defense of Elitism.* The problem, he says, is "the ham-handed practice" of affirmative action.[65] Tony Brown (1995: p. 70) attributes many other middle-class blacks' support of affirmative action to an "elitist vision."

The problem with this logical, meritocratic extension of affirmative action is its cost and intrusiveness. Its implementation would exhaust and virtually bankrupt the nation. The technology, bureaucracy, and sheer energy required to carry out such a program would need to become the central focus of public life. Indeed, much of what we now consider private life would have to become public in order for the people collectively, or its delegated authorities, to ascertain just how advantaged or disadvantaged each of us really was, and then to correct each of us, upward or downward.[66]

The urge to expand protection under affirmative action makes good sense, both logically and ethically. But while each previously unprotected group winning preference would cheer, most taxpayers, civil libertarians, and disadvantaged-but-still-unprotected groups would jeer. Any group's *loss* of preferential status would have the reverse effect, with the opposite choruses of fans and critics. On the continuum of affirmative-action trade-offs, each step toward greater fairness is costlier and more intrusive while each step to cut costs and resist intrusion thereby increases injustice. In short, affirmative action as equal opportunity secured by group preferences will forever be caught between the Scylla of unfairness and the Charybdis of unworkability.

Solution 2: Entitlement to Dignity

Some recent thinkers, notably William Julius Wilson and Theda Skocpol, have grasped the tragic dilemma of our evil history as well as the contradictory quality of affirmative action's attempt to correct the evil consequences. They have proposed programs intended not so much to equalize opportunities—an elusive goal at best—but to secure absolute equality in one vital sense. They believe that a rich society has an obligation to provide every citizen with the minimum requisites for a dignified life.

In "Race-Neutral Programs and the Democratic Coalition," Wilson (1994: pp. 167–168) credits affirmative action with having brought about "a sharp increase in the number of blacks entering higher education and gaining professional and managerial positions." But, he adds, "neither policies based on the principle of equality of individual opportunity, nor policies that call for preferential group treatment, such as affirmative action, will do much for less advantaged blacks because of the combined effects of past discrimination and current structural changes in the economy. Now more than ever we need broader solutions than those we have employed in the past." The essence of these new solutions is a set of mostly race-neutral programs and a reinvigorated coalition politics led by the Democratic Party, for which Wilson has served as a key adviser on problems of race and poverty. The programs Wilson has advocated would go a long way toward satisfying citizens' basic needs according to Maslow's (1943) hierarchy of human needs: survival, security, affection, and respect. "Full employment policies, job skills training, comprehensive health-care legislation, educational reforms in the public schools, child care legislation, and crime and drug abuse prevention programs—these are the race-neutral policies likely to begin making a difference for the poor, black and white" (Wilson 1994: p. 168).

For both moral and political reasons, Theda Skocpol (1994: pp. 297–298) favors replacing affirmative action with a set of universal social policies. "To help less privileged minorities through government programs, the first step is to establish a baseline of broad benefits and services that span classes and races (and that can be supplemented by targeted services for the elderly, children, and other vulnerable people)." For example, to address the needs of single-parent families headed by minority mothers, Skocpol proposes "a Family Security Program that would encompass four policies:

assured child support for all single custodial parents; universal health coverage; paid maternity leaves and benefits to help all working parents afford child care; and employment training and assistance in obtaining employment at a living wage." Although this program would disproportionately benefit minority mothers, it would also help poor fathers who head households as well as poor whites. She believes that the nondivisive nature of such programs would help unite and revitalize a progressive coalition for social change.

In effect, this approach to helping the disadvantaged promotes the kind of political development James Davies (1986) recommended based on the universality and validity of Maslow's hierarchy of human needs, as revised by Davies. A more highly developed political system, according to Davies, is not one that maximizes economic or technological development, but one that creates the conditions under which all citizens have an opportunity to develop their higher needs of self-actualization. By late 1997, a *New York Times*/CBS News poll found that the majority of Americans disapproved of racial preferences but that "the majority of blacks and whites [said] they favored policies giving preferential treatment in college admissions and employment to poor people over wealthier citizens."[67] At this point, a defender of affirmative action might ask whether Wilson's and Skocpol's alternative of universal social policies would not permit racial and gender inequities to persist, so that even with citizens' basic needs fulfilled, many white males would still have historically inherited advantages in the quest for self-actualization. This question brings us to a final, transformational alternative to affirmative action.

Solution 3: From Equal Opportunity to Full Opportunity

The truth is that inherited, unfair advantages will never completely disappear, especially if we include genetic, developmental, and other fortuitous sources of unearned advantage and disadvantage. Some people will always "do better" than others, partly because their life opportunities will never be equal. When society—media, schools, business, families—teaches us to value ourselves primarily according to how well we stack up against others, society gets itself stuck in a losing game, one that divides it against itself. For every winner, there will have to be one or more losers. If, being advantaged, we yearn primarily to stay on top, then we won't concede anything that might allow our inferiors to catch up. If, disadvantaged, we long for parity, then we will envy those blessed by genes, environment, history, or dumb luck who are surpassing us. As we glance or lash out at our nemeses, we get mired in dependency on *the other,* and thus on outcomes we cannot control. Let us recall Woodson's warning African Americans (1996: p. 115) against the dependency on others that is implicit in affirmative action: "an underlying premise of race-preferential policies is that the destiny of the black community lies in what others do—or fail to do."

For over two centuries, the struggle for equality of various kinds has served as a useful weapon against arbitrary power and privilege. Gaining equality was a victory for the underclass and a defeat for the ruling class. I agree with Wilson and Skocpol's calls for society to ensure all citizens an equal right to life's basics. But once this goal is achieved and the grossest of purposeful inequalities are overcome, the banner of "Equality!" runs the risk of becoming a tar baby of invidious comparison, a beguiling trap rather than a shining beacon.[68] Like superiority, equality as a competitive goal focuses our attention on, and thus gives power to, *the other,* and to our need to live up to, or exceed, the other, rather than on our desire to develop ourselves. Stressing self-realization, Tony Brown (1995: p. 265) urges other blacks "to psychologically let White people go."

As we shall see in Chapters 3 and 4, whether we are trying to win equality with or superiority over the other, the very emphasis on winning can just as easily breed mediocrity as excellence. As the bookmakers can attest, most competitions are not equal, and the outcomes are typically predictable. So long as I can attain equality, or beat out my inferiors, why should I care about any further improvement in my performance? Or, on the other hand, when my competitors are clearly superior, only luck will allow me to win, so why should I give my best effort? If, however, my main concern is self-betterment, then others can serve as inspirational examples rather than as excuses to slack off. As Lerner (1996) has argued, seeking preferential status under affirmative action's clarion call for "equal opportunity" has translated into an unspoken plea to "give me an advantage so I can win." The collective result is perpetual squabbling in a sea of mediocrity.

What is the alternative to demanding equal opportunity to—in Olympic skater Tonya Harding's words—"kick butt"? The alternative is for society to temper the inevitable comparisons and competitions of life with a commitment to provide all citizens, especially its youngest, with optimal conditions for the realization of their own unique potentials. Indeed, the rest of this book urges progressives to cast off the blinders of political correctness and help transform society to achieve some of these conditions: synergistic values, a political voice for youth, empowered families, radical stewardship of the earth, restorative criminal justice, and a democratic political economy.

The transformational alternative to affirmative action is to devote resources—in our schools, media, families, workplaces, governments, and communities—to the nurturing of our futures rather than the rectifying of our pasts. This approach does not deny the need to rectify current squalor and indignity—of needless poverty, ignorance, illness, ecocide, and prejudice—which forestall our individual and collective self-realization. The fullness of opportunity implicit in this vision is, on the one hand, worthier than that of equal opportunity to "kick butt" and, on the other, more practical than any attempt to homogenize our disparate, complex lives.

It is ironic that President Johnson, in the same 1965 speech in which he redefined affirmative action as preferential treatment to achieve equal opportunity, also glimpsed the higher standard of full opportunity. He envisioned a time when every American "could become whatever his qualities of mind and spirit would permit—to survive, to seek, and, if he could, to find his happiness" (Curry 1996: p. 23). The United Nations' Declaration of the Rights of the Child includes two rights that conjure up a similar goal of self-actualization: "the right to full opportunity for play and recreation" and "the right to be a useful member of society and to develop individual abilities." In 1993, the Parliament of the World's Religions attempted to fuse equality and fullness of opportunity by defining a just social and economic order as one "in which everyone has an equal chance of reaching his or her full potential."[69]

Conclusion:
From Affirmative Action to Transformative Action

At best, affirmative action counteracts an oppressive history and shifts the demography of winners and losers so as to lessen net injustice. People whom it unfairly injures are sacrificed for the greater number who benefit—a utilitarian trade-off uneasily justified by the criterion of the greatest happiness of the greatest number. I say "uneasily" because of the cloud of inferiority that hangs over the beneficiaries of group preferences. If the victims of affirmative action are filled with resentment while its beneficiaries are plagued by self-doubt, the net benefit remains uncertain. In fact, fewer and fewer people seem in any sense "happy" about affirmative action.

Least happy about it should be the radical critics and would-be transformers of corporate capitalism. To dedicate ourselves to purifying the competitive process so that every blessed one of us—black and white, man and woman, gay and straight, short and tall—has an equal opportunity to defeat our fellows is to sell our souls for a mess of pottage. The pottage is the inherently entropic pursuit of power, status, wealth, and privilege that only a few can win. I hope that the losers in this futile game of conquest will not stand and cheer "Ah, Fortune, I am conquered but fairly so!" when the ranks of their oppressors finally include the proper percentage of men and women, white and nonwhite.

Arbitrary discrimination, including racism and sexism, is an evil that progressives must always oppose. But so is every system of domination in which the advantaged—which there will always be—use their advantages to diminish the opportunities of others. How, we must ask, might things be otherwise? How might one person's advantage benefit rather than harm another? We assume that the "advantages" parents have over their newborn—of strength, quickness, knowledge, wealth, and power—will be used to benefit rather than harm the growing child. But we also assume that parents love their children, a bond we cannot count on among members of a large, anonymous society.

John Stuart Mill struggled with this question in his various, unsuccessful attempts to reconcile (1) the greatest good of the greatest number, (2) the self-interest of the market, and (3) individual liberty balanced against social harm (Cummings 1989). For all his brilliance, Mill missed the same underlying secret overlooked by proponents of equal opportunity today. Mill's nineteenth-century liberal concern was to render liberty relatively harmless by appropriate, minimal state intervention. Affirmative action's twentieth-century liberal goal was to render inequality (difference, diversity, advantage) relatively harmless by appropriate, minimal state intervention.

Both Mill and today's left fail to ask the critical question: Under what conditions do people use their liberties or advantages in ways harmful, or helpful, to others? The answer to this question is the crux of progressive transformation of a society that now sacrifices both liberty and equality to the bottom line of profit, market control, power, and privilege. What this transformation requires most fundamentally is a shift in the values instilled by the socializing institutions of family, school, media, workplace, and government. In the next chapter, we turn to a values shift that points us toward fullness of opportunity as a more inspiring and practical goal than equal opportunity.

Notes

An earlier version of this chapter was published as "Transforming Public Policy: Beyond Affirmative Action," Chapter 9 in Stephen Woolpert, Christa Daryl Slaton, and Edward W. Schwerin, eds., *Transformational Politics: Theory, Study, and Practice* (Albany: SUNY Press, 1998), pp. 215–231.

1. The People's Bicentennial Commission, *First Principles: The Platform of '76* (Washington, DC: The People's Bicentennial Commission).

2. Lind (1996: p. 256).

3. Bayard Rustin, "From Protest to Politics: The Future of the Civil Rights Movement," *Commentary,* February 1965, p. 28, quoted in Lind (1996: p. 177).

4. Quoted in David J. Garrow, *Bearing the Cross: Martin Luther King, Jr., and the Southern Christian Leadership Conference* (New York: Vintage, 1986), p. 312.

5. William Safire, *Before the Fall* (New York: Da Capo Press, 1975), p. 571, quoted in Skrentny (1996: p. 202).

6. Tapes recently made public leave little doubt that Nixon's motives in promoting affirmative action had nothing to do with sympathy for disadvantaged groups. Women, he thought, were "a pain in the neck, very difficult to handle," while "with blacks, you look the other way. The same with Mexicans, you've got to look the other way. You've got to find one who's honest." George Lardner, Jr., "Tapes Reveal an Outrageous Nixon," *Washington Post,* December 28, 1998.

7. John Ehrlichman, *Witness to Power: The Nixon Years* (New York: Simon and Schuster, 1982), p. 228.

8. Because group-preferential treatment has never been popular among Americans, some defenders of affirmative action have cast protected classes as something other than preferred groups. See, e.g. Harris and Narayan 1994.

9. A. Barry Rand, "Diversity in Corporate America," in Curry (1996: p. 75).

10. Judy Lichtman, Jocelyn Frye, and Helen Norton, "Why Women Need Affirmative Action," in Curry (1996: p. 181).

11. "UM Withdraws Honor for Opponent of Affirmative Action," *Campus* 10, no. 2, winter 1999, p. 11.

12. By the mid-1990s, and ever since, about three-quarters of the U.S. public has opposed racial and gender preferences. "Poll: 75% Oppose Affirmative Action," *Washington Post*/ABC News poll, March 23, 1995; Mortiner B. Zuckerman, "Piling on the Preferences," *U.S. News & World Report,* June 28, 1999.

13. Michelle Malkin, "Diversity—Not Unanimity," *Seattle Times,* July 25, 1999.

14. Zachary Coile, "Oakland in Midst of Shift in Power," *San Francisco Examiner,* April 4, 1999.

15. Michael Fletcher, "Mfume Vows to Fight: NAACP to Back Affirmative Action," *Washington Post,* July 14, 1998.

16. Steven A. Holmes, "Programs Based on Race and Sex Are Under Attack," *New York Times,* March 16, 1995.

17. Robert L. Woodson Sr., "Personal Responsibility," in Curry (1996: p. 115).

18. bell hooks (1995: p. 55).

19. Michael Lerner (1996: p. 114).

20. Linda Chavez, "Promoting Racial Harmony," in Curry (1996: p. 314).

21. Edward Yuen, "Social Movements, Identity Politics and the Genealogy of the Term 'People of Color,'" *New Political Science,* no. 38-39, winter-spring 1997, p. 106.

22. *Denver Post,* November 19, 1993.

23. Susan Greene, "Webb Blasted on Black Issues," *Denver Post,* April 11, 1999.

24. Charles Mahtesian, "Clarence Harmon: Race Reversal," *Governing,* November 1997, p. 72.

25. William A. Henry III, *In Defense of Elitism* (New York: Anchor Books, 1994), p. 74.

26. Chris Newton, "Latest Dallas School Chief Falls Victim to Racial Turmoil," Associated Press, September 18, 1997.

27. National Conference of Christians and Jews, *Taking America's Pulse: Summary Report* (Washington, DC: LH Research, 1994), p. 5. A 1998 survey by the Anti-Defamation League also found anti-Semitism high among blacks.

28. Sam Roberts, "Hispanics Largest Minority in Four of 10 Biggest Cities," *New York Times,* October 30, 1994.

29. "Ethnic Celebrations Canceled at School," Associated Press, February 15, 1999.

30. Richard Morin and Claudia Deane, "Misrepresenting the Gender Gap," *Washington Post,* April 17, 2000, p. 21.

31. Steven A. Holmes, "Affirmative Action Change to Aid Whites," *New York Times,* August 15, 1997.

32. Heidi Hartmann, "Who Has Benefited from Affirmative Action in Employment?" in Curry (1996: pp. 91–92).

33. While Manning Marable (1996: p. 9) asserts that "white women have been overwhelmingly the primary beneficiaries of affirmative action," Glenn Loury (1996: p. 53) claims that "it is now beyond dispute that the principal beneficiaries of affirmative action are relatively well-off blacks." No respectable scholar claims that affirmative action has primarily benefited society's neediest citizens.

34. The most methodologically sophisticated empirical study of the effects of affirmative action on the incomes of protected versus unprotected classes is Martin J. Sweet (1999).

35. John F. Harris and Kevin Merida, "Affirmative Action Under Fire," *Washington Post,* April 24–30, 1995, p. 6.

36. *Working Woman,* March 1999, p. 68.

37. ACLU, "Briefing Paper: Affirmative Action," 1999.

38. Mari Matsuda and Charles Lawrence, *We Won't Go Back* (Boston: Houghton-Mifflin, 1996), p. 190.

39. Constitutional analysts such as Cass Sunstein and Keith Bybee, who admire the U.S. system of interest-group politics, have praised such judicial compromise, or "minimalism," by arguing that "on the whole, judges serve the cause of democratic deliberation best by refusing to pronounce comprehensive judgments, thereby encouraging political actors to resolve controversies on their own" (Bybee 1999: p. 6).

40. Peter Schrag, "The Diversity Defense," *The American Prospect,* no. 46, September-October 1999, p. 59.

41. Steven A. Holmes, "Administration Cuts Affirmative Action While Defending It," *New York Times,* March 16, 1998.

42. John Aloysius Farrell, "Rights Suit Settled on Fear of Loss: White Teacher Claimed Reverse Discrimination," *Boston Globe,* November 22, 1997.

43. Susan G. Mezey, *In Pursuit of Equality: Women, Public Policy, and the Federal Courts* (New York: St. Martin's, 1992).

44. *Newsweek,* June 6, 1996, p. 21.

45. Joye Mercer, "Assault on Affirmative Action," *Chronicle of Higher Education,* March 16, 1994.

46. Some reject this comparison by saying that children will grow out of childhood, whereas blacks cannot grow out of blackness. But many children do not survive childhood because of their treatment by adults, and many more of those who do survive their childhoods remain deeply scarred by it.

47. Quoted in Tony Brown (1995: p. 29). "Where's mine?", not social justice, has become the driving force of affirmative action and other high-sounding pleas, according to Royko.

48. See, for instance, W. Avon Drake and Robert D. Holsworth, *Affirmative Action and the Stalled Quest for Black Progress* (Urbana: University of Illinois Press, 1996); Thernstrom and Thernstrom (1997); and Helene Slessarev, *The Betrayal of the Urban Poor* (Philadelphia: Temple University Press, 1997).

49. Dinesh d'Souza, *The End of Racism* (New York: Free Press, 1995), p. 540.

50. For instance: "But what blacks need to do is to 'act white' . . . and embrace mainstream cultural norms" (d'Souza, *The End of Racism,* p. 556). Contrast Tony Brown (1995: p. 219): "Acting White is not the same as proving competence."

51. Robyn Blumner, "Diversity by the Sword Wounds Us All," *St. Petersburg Times,* July 3, 1998.

52. Brendan Koerner, "Where the Boys Aren't," *U.S. News and World Report,* February 8, 1999, p. 54.

53. Most of these critics, along with supporters, of affirmative action appear in Nicoleus Mills (1994) or Curry (1996).

54. *New England Journal of Medicine,* June 17, 1999, reported by the Associated Press, "Disparities Found in Research Funding," June 17, 1999.

55. Peter Baker, "Answers Elusive in Dialogue on Race," *Washington Post,* July 9, 1998.

56. Jim Kirksey, "Col. Rice, a Tuskegee Airman, Dies," *Denver Post,* February 27, 1999.

57. Keith Bradsher, "Saturn Chief Ready to Roll: First Woman to Head Division Knows Cars from Trannie Up," *New York Times,* December 28, 1998,

58. Patricia J, Mayn. "NASA Awuuh In Toy's Success," Associated Press, January 21, 1999.

59. Mike Chambers, "Fastest Human on Two Wheels: Seeling Rode to Top of Biker World," *Denver Post*, July 16, 1999.

60. Iris Marion Young, *Justice and the Politics of Difference* (Princeton: Princeton University Press, 1990), p. 200.

61. Clarence Page, *Showing My Color* (New York: HarperCollins, 1996), p. 234.

62. Lars Erik-Nelson, " HUD Don Quixote Kemp Faces a Long Ride," *New York Daily News,* October 19, 1989.

63. Jonathan Goldman (in Swain 1996) develops a "Fresh Start matrix" that, though adding only socioeconomic class to race and gender, could be expanded "to account for an infinite number of different types of discrimination if society finds such expansions necessary" (p. 195).

64. Gregory Rodriguez, "Is Today's Civil Rights Movement Too Inclusive?", originally published in the *Los Angeles Times,* republished in the *Denver Post,* March 15, 1998.

65. Henry III, *In Defense of Elitism*, p. 74.

66. Kurt Vonnegut satirizes an even more extreme reductio ad absurdum of affirmative action in his dystopian short story "Harrison Bergeron."

67. "Diversity Backed But Not Methods," Associated Press, December 15, 1997.

68. In Joel Chandler Harris's *Tales of Uncle Remus,* the tar baby trapped all who pursued him.

69. Craig Stoltz, "A New Global Ethic? Seeking Unity, Religious Leaders Find Common Ground," *USA Weekend,* December 17-19, 1993, p. 11.

3

Transformative Values:
Synergy, Entropy, and Social Change

"Winning isn't everything. It's the only thing."
　　　　　　—NFL-champion football coach Vince Lombardi

"I have a sickness with achievement. I have a sickness with pressure. I have a sickness of trying to be successful."
　　　　　　—NFL-champion football coach Alex Gibbs[1]

"Always beating everybody isn't the most important thing."
　　　　　　—Arthur Reed, to schoolyard bully Binky Barnes[2]

A transformational alternative to affirmative action must do more than adjust the demography of society's winners and losers. It must reject society's choice of fostering winner-loser values that make enemies of citizens, necessarily dividing society against itself. Unfortunately, the left suffers from a politically correct tendency to ignore values as a vital force for social change, rather than embracing win-win, or synergistic, values, while rejecting win-lose, or entropic, values.

Values, not Saintliness,
as a Crux of Social Transformation

The issue is not the "materialism" versus "postmaterialism" of the values pursued but their inherently competitive, "win-lose" nature.[3] By contrast, "synergistic" values—whether material, ethereal, or (like art) both—are ones whose pursuit by one person tends to benefit others, even if unintentionally, while rejecting win-lose, or entropic, ones. Such values can fertilize the bumpy, imperfectly level playing field of life so that all players can thrive, enjoying the game without fretting excessively over their relative stats or the game scores. Values are critical to the game of life and to the institutions—from family to government—that shape the game. Unfortunately,

83

the left has tended to avoid values questions, for two reasons. First, values, being personal, are held by individuals but shaped by institutions, and the left believes it is wiser to try to change a few key institutions than 270 million individuals. Second, the left believes that conservatives use the issue of values—family, godliness, patriotism—to distract citizens from structural evils such as corporate capitalism, political oligarchy, and institutional religion.

But this dichotomy is false, because values and institutions shape each other, daily and perpetually. Transforming personal values is a key to transforming institutions, and vice versa. A strategy aimed at changing one of these two factors while ignoring the other is a formula for failure. In particular, synergistic values are a key to transforming not only affirmative action but, as we shall see, families, communities, criminal justice, political economy, and the conflict between growth and ecology. These values alone make possible a society no longer divided against itself, a society less beset by the social pathologies of crime, addiction, mental disorder, and splintered families. In May 2000, Chief Justice William Rehnquist advised young lawyers that aspiration to greatness is fine but urged them to "develop a capacity to enjoy pastimes and occupations that many can enjoy simultaneously—love for another, being a good parent to a child, service to your community."[4] Such values are neither rare nor arcane, and pursuing them can benefit society without requiring saintliness. Fostering synergy does not require preaching morality, because achieving a synergistic value—for instance, knowledge—can help others achieve it even when we pursue it self-interestedly.[5]

Changing the system without changing our values is a shell without substance, doomed to betray its transformative purposes. A "democratic" society whose citizens passively defer to authority is a sham democracy, just as a "socialist" society whose citizens pursue capitalist values soon gives way to state capitalism. Synergistic values are a vital part of any progressive transformation of U.S. society. A few concrete examples will pave the way for the formal definition that follows.

Synergistic Values That Have Stood the Test of Time

The pursuit of synergistic values is evident even in societies such as the United States, which promote antisynergistic values like power, status, and wealth. Pessimists such as Hobbes and Freud exaggerate the irrational and violent side of human nature, whereas optimists such as Marx and Proudhon exaggerate the rational and cooperative side. In fact, our biology is compatible with a wide range of motives and values, both synergistic and antisynergistic. Which direction we take depends on many things, including the socialization choices made by authorities, especially parents, teachers, employers, leaders, and the mass media. Both in our personal lives and as cultural authorities, we can make alternative value choices that could help transform the quality of our lives and our communities. The "green" philosophy I explore in Chapter 8 accepts both competitive and cooperative sides of our natures more readily than do conventional ideologies of the left and right (Rensenbrink 1999: p. 138).

Family Ties

"Social science surveys have universally concluded that people claim to be most happy with friends and family, or just in the company of others."[6] National polls show that although "the family unit is on the decline, . . . the desire for family satisfaction is on the rise."[7] Asked to rate the quality of their lives over diverse domains, Americans rated experiences with their children and in marriage the highest—8.7 and 8.1 out of a possible 10.[8] Parents who love and nurture their children are not simply altruistic; they typically enjoy the family experience they help create.[9] The most common regret of many parents, especially fathers, is that they allowed their careers to rob them of precious time with their children.

A 1997 Roper Starch Worldwide poll of a thousand *Newsweek* readers found that their second most important value was to have a good family life, rated as very important by 89 percent of the sample, second only to freedom of choice in how to live their lives (94 percent). By comparison, 57 percent judged helping others, and only 29 percent becoming wealthy, as very important.[10] That many of the respondents sacrifice family well-being in the pursuit of wealth and career reflects the pressures of the U.S. political economy. A *USA Weekend* scientific poll in 1997 found that 86 percent of Americans believe that "despite our mobile society, family ties are more important than ever."[11] For millennia, parental genes have survived and reproduced to the degree that parents nurtured and protected their offspring.

Recent experimental research in psychology has confirmed the growing belief of biologists that humans, while selfish, also "evolved to be altruistic because groups in which members help each other fare better than those in which each member stands alone."[12] The selective advantage enjoyed by genes so lucky as to be hosted by strongly committed families is great when compared to genes so unfortunate as to be carried by the possessive individualists of liberal theory. Genes' long-term survival depends on far more than the individual survival strategies of their present carriers (Mansbridge 1990). Psychologist Mary Pipher (1996: p. 226) judges that "family affection is the glue that holds lives together."

Friendship, Love, and Fraternity

As with parenthood, many people discover late in life that friendship deserved more than they gave it, and for some friendships the discovery comes too late. Family members may or may not become friends as well. Aristotle's three levels of friendship encompass all the many intra- and extrafamilial varieties. The lowest level is based on exchanges of benefits, as in the case of business friendships. The middle level is based on a genuine pleasure the friends take in each other's company. The highest level is based on friends valuing each other simply for who they are, irrespective of any benefit or pleasure they expect from the other person. These "true" friends will make sacrifices merely to help their loved ones.

As important as these distinctions are, reflecting differences in trust, caring, and depth of the friendly relationship, all three types of friendship are synergistic. In all three cases, a quality absent in the separate individuals emerges through their interaction, and the building of a friendship entails no necessary loss of friendship by others. Furthermore, the associated personality trait of friendliness breeds more of itself, thus helping others fulfill their own quest for friendship. Actual friendships often overlap Aristotle's three categories, or change from one to the other, as, for example, when we come to care genuinely for someone who has paid us well or given us pleasure.

Love is a special case of level-three, intense friendship with an altruistic component. It may or may not include erotic, romantic, familial, or humanitarian aspects. Folk wisdom holds that "a friend in need is a friend indeed" and that "love makes the world go 'round." As Juliet tells Romeo, "The more love I give you, the more I have, for it is infinite." Religious tradition, literary imagination, folk music, and scientific psychology agree that loveless and friendless humans face a desperate plight, comparable to that of children who grow up without family support.[13] Not only do such people suffer in their own lives, but they visit their sufferings on others.

Fraternity is a special case of friendship, writ large and politicized as a basis of community solidarity. Communitarian advocates (Glendon and Blankenhorn 1995; Etzioni 1998) are reasserting the importance of "the ties that bind" by reemphasizing qualities like fraternity, long ignored by liberal democrats fixated on the liberty and equality of individuals. Citizens whose "habits of the heart"[14] transcend individualism and make them feel they are "in it together" achieve mutual benefits better than citizens resigned to Durkheimian anomie or Hobbesian conflict. Retreats into privacy and reliance on public coercion reflect the victory of entropy over synergy (Jacobs 1961).

"We are living in a market-driven culture, where hedonism, narcissism and short-term gains reign," says Cornel West, making a case for friendship writ large. "We have to reclaim non-market values, such as love, kindness, sweetness, fidelity. . . . We are in this ship together: We go up together and we go down together." Olympic track champion Jesse Owens once put competition and friendship in perspective. "Friendships born on the field of athletic strife," he said, "are the real gold of competition. Awards become corroded. Friends gather no dust."[15] Hard-headed scientists are putting these notions into an evolutionary perspective. Robert Wright notes a recent trend among social biologists and evolutionary psychologists: "Oddly, Darwinian success in a dog-eat-dog social world turns out to involve lots of mushy feelings. Swoons of romance, love of kin, devotion to friends and pity for the needy could be useful tools in the social jungle. Even conscience and the sense of justice are now said to have roots in our genes."[16]

Exploration, Awareness, Knowledge, Truth, Wisdom

Throughout the ages, people have risked their lives exploring the world and the heavens in order to know. In part, they have wanted to know because they needed something that knowledge could bring them: food, safety, a shorter route, a mate. But partly they got a kick out of just "getting it": Who am I? Who are we? What is our purpose? What do the heavens contain? What is at the bottom of the deep, blue sea? Unlike politicians, they do not seek knowledge to gain power. Unlike bankers, they do not seek it to make money. Unlike academics, they do not publish it to gain tenure. The knowledge that lay philosophers acquire rubs off on others even when they do not consciously teach or share it. The more any of them knows, the more others are likely to learn. Unlike in the case of gaining money or public office, when you take knowledge from me, I do not lose it. When we share it, it is not divided up like a pie; rather, it multiplies and undergoes creative transformations. For the seeker of knowledge, the path leads from curiosity to exploration to awareness to understanding—and sometimes even to wisdom. If it makes sense to find ways of fulfilling ourselves without combating others, then choosing the path to wisdom may be a wise choice indeed.

High Art, Mundane Beauty

Humans enjoy beauty and like to create it. "Five thousand years ago, unimaginably poor Stone Age women living in Swiss swamps were weaving intricate, multicolored patterns into their textiles and using fruit pits to create beaded cloth. Even in the most difficult of subsistence economies, mere utility—in this case, plain, undecorated cloth—does not satisfy human imaginations."[17] In more recent centuries, European culture has esteemed art but relegated its creation to the few. At least, posited arts critic Jeff Bradley, "Europeans respect culture and try to make music, art and theatre part of their everyday lives. In America, everything is driven by the bottom line."[18] Balinese and Ituri-pygmy cultures, on the other hand, have traditionally encouraged their members to express their spirituality artistically.[19] When the Ituri pygmies "are not hunting or improving their villages, they sing, dance, play musical instruments, or tell stories to each other."[20] Before or after a day's labor, the Balinese have traditionally honed their skills in painting, sculpture, woodcarving, dancing, instrumental playing, landscaping, and architecture. The synergism of art is reflected by European and Balinese artists, especially painters and musicians, who have profoundly influenced each other—as have English rock musicians and their Caribbean reggae counterparts.[21] As "elite" European artists have incorporated "folk" influences from Bali or Jamaica, so have their Balinese and Jamaican counterparts blended European techniques with their own, justifiably gaining world renown.

Americans who stroll through Dutch neighborhoods are surprised to discover the artistry of Dutch interior design beckoning them from the living rooms of the homes they pass—with curtains drawn back from plateglass windows to invite the appreciation of passers-by. In many U.S. cities, certain blocks are known for spectacular Christmas displays that provide weeks of delight to both creators and viewers. On a year-round basis, amateur landscape architects beautify their yards and thus their neighborhoods and cities, sometimes forming gardening cooperatives. In arid states of the U.S. Southwest, residential and commercial xeriscapers enhance their environs while also conserving water.

Even where art is widely considered an elite enterprise, as in Euro-America, many people fulfill their creative impulses in the art of daily living. From singing a song or writing a poem to viewing or sketching a sunset, from photographing wildlife to acting in community theatre, from arranging flowers to "dressing to kill," many people make each day an esthetic experience, often inspiring others. Some citizen esthetes derive insight from visiting a Jamaican festival, a Japanese tea garden, a Balinese temple, or a Dutch neighborhood, but many do just fine without ever leaving their native shores. The production and consumption of art, both "high" and "low," are a classic case of synergistic values in action.

Craftsmanship

Work takes up half, or more, of most people's lives. As the price we pay for needing to consume, work is the classic means to an end. But work can take on value in itself. As President Nixon said on Labor Day, 1971, "The 'work ethic' holds that labor is good in itself; that a man or woman becomes a better person by virtue of the act of working." Christopher Lasch (1997: p. 126) asserts that "the only escape from the polarity of egoism and altruism lies in the selflessness experienced by those who lose themselves in their work, in the effort to master a craft or a body of knowledge, or in the acceptance of a formidable challenge that calls on all their resources."

Respect for one's craft, and for those who perform it well, can rise above the most intense competition. In a 1998 telephone conversation with Bob Herbert of the *New York Times,* 67-year-old baseball Hall-of-Famer Willie Mays reported playing in the 1951 World Series against his idol, Joe

DiMaggio: "I never told this to anybody, but Joe hit a home run at the Polo Grounds in that Series, and I knew that was his last year, so I was happy for him even though I was playing against him. So what I did was, I started clapping. And you just didn't do that in New York. But there I was, standing in the outfield for the Giants clapping for Joe as he's rounding the bases."[22]

A similar reaction occurred at the 1972 world chess championship, in which Bobby Fischer of the United States defeated Boris Spassky of the Soviet Union. "It was much more than a chess match," reports grandmaster Larry Evans. "The Soviets used supremacy at chess as a potent propaganda tool to prove the superiority of communism and regarded the crown as theirs by right." Fischer responded in kind: "I've been chosen to teach the commies a lesson." Privately, the Soviets feared that Spassky could not beat Fischer and pressured their ace to claim victory by default when Fischer, protesting the playing conditions, failed to show up for the opening ceremony. Spassky refused to win by default, and when Fischer eventually defeated him with brilliant play, the Soviet "remained on stage and joined in the general applause. In the car on the way back to his hotel, Fischer was incredulous. 'Did you see what Spassky did?' he asked over and over. 'Did you see him applaud? That's real sportsmanship. That shows he's a true sportsman.'"[23] In respect of their craft, the two champions had checkmated the forces of political correctness.

In May 2000, U.S. Tae Kwon Do competitor Esther Kim forfeited her place on the U.S. Olympic team rather than fight her injured best friend, Kay Poe. While Poe recovered and went on to the Olympics thanks to Kim's generosity, Kim won her first U.S. national championship shortly thereafter.

We may get a sense of the power of craftsmanship as a synergistic value from humbler sources as well. Stonemason Carl Murray Bates tells author Studs Terkel (1972: pp. 17–22):

> Stone's my life. I daydream all the time, most times it's on stone. . . .
> There's not a house in this country that I [have] built that I don't look at every time I go by. (Laughs.) . . . If there's one stone in there crooked, I know where it's at and I'll never forget it. . . . I can't imagine a job where you go home and maybe go by a year later and you don't know what you've done.

Ralph Waldo Emerson may have had someone like Bates in mind when he wrote, "We put our love where we have put our labor."[24] Or perhaps he was thinking of a worker like firefighter Tom Patrick, whose story to Terkel (p. 762) testifies to the synergism of personal example:

> Last month there was a second alarm. I was off duty. I ran over there. I'm a bystander. I see these firemen on the roof, with the smoke pouring out around them, and the flames, and they go in. It fascinated me. Jesus

Christ, that's what *I* do. I was fascinated by the people's faces. You could
see the pride they were seein'. . . . You see them put out a fire. You see
them come out with babies in their hands. You see them give mouth-to-
mouth when a guy's dying. . . . I can look back and say, "I helped put out
a fire. I helped save somebody." It shows something I did on this earth.

Charles Derber (1996: p. 9) gives two examples of synergistic craftsmanship: "A doctor who works hard to perfect her medical skills may advance her own career, but she also saves lives," and, "If I strive to be the
best writer I can be—an individualistic aspiration—I am educating others
while fulfilling myself." For those who care how well and to what end they
labor, there is plenty of value to go around.

Pure Pleasures

"Pure pleasures" is an umbrella for a wide range of specific synergistic values, as distinguished from the meaningless circularity that "all values reduce to pleasure because if they didn't bring pleasure, we wouldn't pursue
them."[25] On the contrary, many of our value pursuits are difficult, unpleas-
ant, or dangerous. The argument here is that our big, curious, creative
brains make us capable not only of stoic value pursuits but also of a wide
range of activity for the sheer fun of it. Many of these activities do not de-
tract from anyone else's enjoyments, in fact often enhance them, and thus
function synergistically.

Popular pleasures include cooking and eating good food; sampling va-
rietal wines, microbrewed beers, and international coffees and teas; sharing
humor, telling jokes, and performing magic tricks; playing card games such
as bridge and poker, board games such as Monopoly and chess, or sports
such as softball and tennis; going hiking, climbing, camping, backpacking,
fishing, hunting, and bird watching; dancing; sharing massages; taking
whirlpool baths; and engaging in sex. In addition to the pure pleasure of
these activities, they may also fulfill values of knowledge, beauty, friendship, and love. Experiencing the pleasure these values afford need not cause
pain for others and in fact often increases their pleasure. The endless fasci-
nations of game playing, like the manifold joys of lovemaking, cannot be
achieved or understood by adding up the capacities and experiences of the
separate individuals. Pure pleasures requiring two or more participants are
synergistic values par excellence if they cause no pain to others.

For centuries, the Protestant ethic and its economic partner, capitalism,
militated against pleasure. "The roots of this feeling are deep; the American
ethic of work before pleasure is as old as Calvinism." But times have
changed. "In 1998, for the fourth year running, the pollsters asked 2,500
Americans what their top priorities were for the coming year. And, for the
fourth year running, the No. 1 answer was: 'Have more fun.'"[26] This Yankelovich poll found that roughly half of Americans suspect that life's simple

pleasures are passing them by, despite a consumerist plethora of packaged indulgences.

Other Synergistic Values

The synergistic value clusters I have mentioned are but a few of those pursued by diverse individuals, families, and communities in many cultures and nations. A veritable showcase of others can be examined by watching but a few episodes of *Mr. Rogers' Neighborhood,* ordained minister Fred Rogers's secular but inspired television show for children and adults. The show's title underscores the importance of the value of community, exhibited in each episode of the program's unparalleled thirty-year run. Also prominent in this friendly neighborhood are the values of expressing one's feelings, of communicating honestly with others, and of fully developing one's talents. Many episodes also illustrate the values of achieving dignity no matter what the circumstances, for instance by transcending limitations as serious as blindness or paralysis. Mr. Rogers elevates qualities such as courage, empathy, and humility from intermittent human tendencies to goals of lasting value. For example, his character Daniel the Striped Tiger struggles with his fears to achieve a kind of courage akin to Hemingway's "grace under pressure."

Many people value consistency and integrity—the achievement of congruence among their beliefs, habits, and actions. Others pursue respect and self-respect, honor and faithfulness, inner harmony or spiritual faith, and piety. Balance and moderation, security and stability, social responsibility, and community are paramount for yet others. Some people want mostly to be trusted or well-liked by their peers. Achieving such values need not hurt anyone else.[27] Indeed, in many cases, one person's success spreads to others. Of course, pejoratives can be added to any of these values to make them less attractive and less synergistic: for instance, "blind faith," "wishy-washy moderation,"[28] and "rigid stability." Family love can be "stifling"; knowledge can be "esoteric"; art can be "self-indulgent"; pleasures can be "libertine." But pejoratives can be added to any value, not just synergistic ones.

Synergy Co-opted? Cutting Through the Baloney

Yippie activist Jerry Rubin once asked how he could ever again tell a woman "I love you" when he lived in a culture that pummeled him with advertisements claiming "Your car loves Shell." Lovers, like transformationalists, cannot control what happens to words like "love" and "transformation." Likewise, in recent years "synergy" has been diluted, even corrupted, by overuse and misuse. A *New York Times* article reports that Monica Lewinsky's taped testimony to the Senate trying President Clinton "elicited some compassion but only fleeting interest Saturday in the 'cardio room' of the Synergy Fitness Club in midtown Manhattan."[29] This morning my daughter ate Lifestream Synergy Multigrain Cereal for breakfast. The self-described "socially conscious" makers of Synergy ask "Why Synergy?" on the back of the cereal box. The answer: "Because the whole is greater than the sum of its parts. Sensible and delicious breakfast from Lifestream . . . good for the bod!"

In *The Synergy Myth,* corporate titan Harold Geneen (1997: pp. xii–xiii) debunks the "carcinogenic slice of baloney called 'synergy,' the most screw-ball buzzword of the past decade." He maintains that synergy is "a fancy label that means whatever the speaker or writer wants it to mean," although generally it "is alleged to be some sort of alchemy whereby the whole be-comes greater than its parts." He leaves the door open to a meaningful syn-ergy: "True synergy is the rarest thing in the world. . . . It occurs when one entity that behaves in one way and another entity that behaves in another way merge into a third entity that starts behaving in an entirely new way."

Geneen is criticizing the corporate world's misappropriation of syn-ergy, all the way from rah-rah sessions aimed at making a company's em-ployees feel like one big happy family, to the merger of two large corpora-tions into a new one called Synergen ("If you toss a nickel, a quarter, and a dime into a box, you get forty cents. No magic there" [p. xiii]). He would presumably object to the November 23, 1998, cover of *Newsweek,* which pictures Ford's chairman-elect Bill Ford touting a sleek-looking car dubbed the "Synergy 2010" prototype.

On close analysis, however, Geneen's critique reveals not only how the business world misuses the term but also why, used properly, synergy can help explode the myths and implode the realities of corporate capitalism. A former chairman of ITT, Geneen is not much of a theorist and is regarded in the corporate world as something of a politically incorrect but entertain-ing loose cannon. Corporate apologists may not appreciate his labeling as "Baloney" the notions that "managers should nurture workers and strive to make the workplace a caring environment" and that "corporations should show 'social responsibility.'" Corporate chieftains should, rather, keep workers focused on "mak[ing] the company a profitable place" and "should never allow themselves to divert their attention away from their core cor-porate responsibilities" (pp. xviii–xix). Such is the scandalous rhetoric of the politically incorrect.

The Consequences of Synergy and Entropy

We shall return to the explosive and implosive implications of Geneen's musings, which bare the entropic underpinnings of corporate capitalism. For now, let us grant his point that "synergy" has been stretched thin by overuse. Rescuing it is essential to the argument begun in the previous chapter about a value reorientation that could transform the divide-and-conquer effects of affirmative action. The rescue requires clear definitions. As the previous examples illustrate, we might say that *quantitative* synergy refers to an interactive effect of two or more entities that is greater than the summed effect they would have in isolation: A x B is greater than A + B. In *qualitative* synergy, the synergistic effect is fundamentally different from the sum of its parts. The value synergies we will examine are typically both quantitative and qualitative.

At an inorganic level, the two gases hydrogen and oxygen synergistically interact to create the liquid water. At an organic level, the interacting cells in an animal's body somehow produce consciousness, which the cells individually cannot produce at all. At an interpersonal level, a pioneering family, whose members separately could not even survive, may together be able to thrive and multiply. Finally, if we consider the 100 members of a fishing village in complete separation, we will find them incapable of love, treachery, or commercial fishing; if, on the other hand, we consider them in interaction, then love, treachery, and commerce may flourish. Such synergies, both good and bad, are emergent properties of the interactions of the parts of a system.

One potent producer of synergistic effects is humans' pursuit of *synergistic values,* which are goods, or desired conditions, whose attainment by one person increases the likelihood of their attainment by others. This synergistic effect is the opposite of the zero-sum condition in which one person's gain is another person's loss. The collective effect of synergistic values is that citizens have a stake in one another's successes rather than their failures. If success means achieving the things we value, then pursuing synergistic values means that more of us will be successful than (a) if our value pursuits were unrelated, or, especially, (b) if they were related but mutually antagonistic. Social interaction becomes less win-lose and more win-win.

Let us take an example of each of these two conditions, (a) and (b), which negate synergy and reduce collective success. In these examples, we shall assume that you and I are friends, neighbors, colleagues, or acquaintances—that is, that we interact with each other:

(A) *Related versus unrelated value pursuits.* If we both value knowledge (learning, understanding, awareness, wisdom), then the more knowledgeable I become, the more likely you are to gain knowledge from your relationship with me, and vice versa. Conversely, if either of us were to suffer amnesia from a car accident, the other would be deprived of a potential source of new knowledge. Or if our value pursuits were unrelated, either because I moved to Asia and we lost contact, or because I came to value knowledge but not fun, and you came to value fun but not knowledge, then our value synergism would be lost. We would then have no stake in each other's success in gaining knowledge (or fun).

(B) *Related but antagonistic value pursuits.* Unlike the case of our both pursuing knowledge (a synergistic value), if we both pursue social status (an antisynergistic value), then an increase in my status will reduce your status relative to mine, and vice versa. Thus each of us has a stake in the other's failure, rather than the other's success, in attaining social status. Whereas under condition (a) our value pursuits are merely irrelevant to each other, under condition (b) they are actively hostile to each other. Whereas under (a), your gain does not affect me one way or the other, under (b) your gain is my loss.

Borrowing from the second law of thermodynamics, we might call such antisynergistic values, whose pursuit by two or more people is mutually antagonistic (or zero-sum), *entropic values.* Just as particles entropically colliding with one another entail a net loss of usable energy, value pursuits conflicting with one another entail a collective loss of achievable value. Unlike the case of knowledge, in which more for me potentially means more for my fellow citizens, the only way for my social status to increase is for someone else's to decrease. My high status must always be validated by someone else's low status. Culturally, let us define *entropy* as a society's loss of collective value (fulfillment, happiness, success) resulting from citizens' pursuit of antagonistic (competitive, zero-sum) values.

Synergistic value effects do not necessarily rely on individual saintliness, altruism, compassion, or any heroic qualities of human nature. I may be pursuing knowledge for selfish reasons, and I may exhibit it or share it with you for egoistic gratification, but I am still a greater potential resource for your own pursuit of knowledge than I would be if I had less of it myself. True, you might benefit even more from my knowledge if I cared about you and wanted you to benefit. But love and friendship—themselves examples of synergistic values—are not required in order for our mutual pursuit of knowledge to benefit us both.

Synergy, Entropy, and the Conventional Ideological Spectrum

Let us examine the way in which advocacy of synergy, and opposition to entropy, can be distinguished from the moralistic preachments of the politically correct left and right.

In the short run, Marxists and Christians hardheadedly appeal to the self-interest of their potential recruits, promising deliverance from capitalism and hell, respectively. But in the long run, both camps promise a heroic utopia by exhorting adherents to an altruistic standard allegedly more natural than self-interest—if only our natures could be freed from private property and/or Satan. I do not second-guess the millions of people who have sacrificed their own interests for others in distress or for the common good. But it is a different matter to expect the daily workings of society to depend on regular self-sacrifice by ordinary citizens. The body of historical, anthropological, biological, and psychological evidence casts doubt on ideologies that rely one-sidedly on either altruism or selfishness. Human nature has evolved capacities for both self-interested and self-sacrificing behavior, the combination of which confers selective advantages that have strengthened the species.[30] Each local mix of self-interest and altruism, including the concept of "enlightened self-interest," depends on a wide range of historical, sociocultural, and environmental factors.

Ideologies that shun this body of evidence do so at their own peril. Unrealistic claims about human nature expose proponents to charges of hypocrisy, irrelevance, or both. To the extent that believers act on their flawed assumptions, they hurt themselves in practical, political terms. For both Christian and Marxist ideologies, the golden millennium awaits a just-right combination of historical circumstances that will finally tame self-interest. A proper reading of sacred texts such as the *Book of Revelations* and *The Communist Manifesto* is supposed to reveal "mysterious" or "scientific" truths about natural altruism that are unavailable to infidels and sufferers of false consciousness. The view that psychologically complex, imperfectly ethical human beings may benefit from free markets or strong, secular authority is judged politically incorrect, even damnable.

Corresponding forces of PC on the right have encouraged an equally dogmatic commitment to elitist (among classical conservatives) and Invisible Hand (among classical liberals) assumptions equally at odds with the full body of evidence. This evidence casts doubt on the legitimacy of privileged elites, as well as on the beneficence of unfettered free markets (Lowi 1979). Conservative ideologues ignore the relatively egalitarian and communitarian models presented by indigenous societies, ancient Crete, Athenian and town-hall democracy, intentional communities, worker cooperatives, experiments in community self-determination, teledemocracy,[31] and state-level social democracies of the twentieth century.

Less dogmatic about human nature and less prone to political correctness than the traditional left and right are those feminists and environmentalists who advocate synergistic over entropic values. In *Maternal Thinking,* Sara Ruddick (1995) asserts, "The value of objects and accomplishments turns on their usefulness in satisfying needs and giving pleasures rather than on the money to be made by selling them or the prestige by owning them or the attention by displaying them" (p. 130). A synergistic ethic of caring links ecologism and feminism: "A defining task of [caretakers'] work is to maintain mutually helpful connections with another person—or animal—whose separateness they create and respect" (p. 131). Eco-feminists such as Carolyn Merchant (1989: p. 524) tend to agree with Aldo Leopold's warning that human values need to synergize with natural systems. In Merchant's view, the value entropy of profiteering accelerates environmental entropy. Value synergism is more clearly evident among pacifistic eco-feminists than among "eco-masculinist" militants such as Dave Foreman of Earth First![32]

Synergism as a Moral Position

Whether eco-feminist or not, synergism proceeds more modestly than Marxism, Christianity, liberalism, or conservatism, especially their politically correct versions. It begins, first, with the recognition that a wide variety of value preferences is consistent with human nature and with the requirements of a healthy and viable society.[33] For instance, whereas one society might thrive on the basis of tradition, security, family solidarity, and an ethic of friendship, another might emphasize individual freedom, artistic expression, social innovation, and self-actualization. Second, synergism assumes that society is better off if more of its members, rather than fewer, can achieve the culturally treasured values.[34] It follows, third, that it makes sense for societies—that is, for socializing authorities such as parents, teachers, and opinion leaders—to foster values whose attainment by one citizen has multiplier rather than divisive effects on its attainment by other citizens. Procedural liberals such as John Rawls and antiutopians such as George Kateb oppose collective resocialization as coercive. But as Robert Wheeler Lane points out, "It is a mistake to view the transmission of culture as a diminution of our freedom, for it is the very condition of becoming a person."[35]

Fourth, synergists fault, and seek to avoid, the widespread social pathologies that follow from citizens' pursuit of zero-sum, entropic values such as power, status, and wealth. Whether we like it or not, your high status must come at the expense of my low status; you may revel in power only as I grovel in powerlessness; and the eminence of the wealthy depends on the degradation of the poor. Here I refer to power, status, and wealth as ends, not as means to other ends. People may use whatever power, status, and wealth they happen to have for a wide range of purposes, including synergistic ones. An entropic culture entails a society divided between winners and losers, at war with itself. Although entropic ideologies, including that of corporate capitalism, assume that most losers will behave themselves, cross-cultural data show otherwise (Maslow 1964; Dye 1999). Instead of proclaiming "Darn my luck," many losers seek revenge, as reflected in Charles Derber's 1996 study of sociopathic "wilding" among both elites and masses.

An apt symbol of these losers is Luke Woodham of Pearl, Mississippi, who was "the chubby, poor kid at Pearl High School who always seemed to get picked on." He finally had enough. One day, he killed his mother with a butcher knife, then went to school and opened fire on his schoolmates, killing two, including his ex-girlfriend, and wounding seven others. Sixteen-year-old

Woodham wrote, "I am not insane. I am angry. I killed because people like me are mistreated every day. I did this to show society, 'Push us, and we will push back.' Murder is not weak and slow-witted; murder is gutsy and daring."[36] Woodham doubtless spoke for many others who stop short of killing. His words help us see how it can be that the wealthiest and most privileged country in the world also scores so high on indicators of social pathology such as crime, violence, child abuse, alcoholism, drug addiction, and broken homes.[37] Each violent youngster costs the United States $1.5 million, and the annual cost of crimes to the U.S. public had reached a staggering $450 billion by the mid-1990s.[38]

The situation of cultural entropy and social pathology has not improved in the decade since Marian Wright Edelman, president of the Children's Defense Fund, charged that "the standard of success for too many Americans has become personal greed rather than common good" and that one result is that "every 53 minutes in our rich land, an American child dies from poverty. It's disgraceful that children are the poorest Americans." The United States, she said, is an "ethically polluted nation, where instant sex without responsibility, instant gratification without effort, instant solutions without sacrifice, getting rather than giving, and hoarding rather than sharing are the too-frequent signals of our mass media, popular culture, and political life."[39] Interviewing hundreds of men and women over the last decade led reporter Susan Faludi to conclude that current consumer culture is "focused on money, on winning, and on dominating everything and everyone."[40]

Jean Bethke Elshtain (1998: p. 263) attributes some of this cultural entropy to the zero-sum mentality of identity politics, whose ethnic- and gender-based interest groups have the mentality that "one of us will win, and one of us will lose, and that's what it's all about: nothing but power of the most imposing sort." Elshtain is probably right, but a perusal of popular magazines such as *Black Enterprise* and *Working Woman* suggests that a more fundamental cause of cultural entropy is the entropic values of corporate capitalism.[41] In "What It Takes to Make It on Wall Street," Susan Caminiti advises *Working Woman* readers that above all else "women need the will to win" and that "whether you're a man or a woman, you have to be aggressive and not back down."[42] *Black Enterprise* addresses itself to audiences such as "New Power Generation" wannabes on subjects such as "How to Build a Winning Stock Portfolio." Recent covers of *Jump: For Girls Who Dare to Be Real* offer teen readers not only "The Best Back-to-Cool Clothes Ever," the secrets of "60 Days to a Ballerina Bod," and vital "Sexplanations," but also "Retail Details: Where to Get the Goods," "The Power of Puberty," and a quiz giving insight into how better to "Rule Your World."

The more entropically unforgiving—both "kick-ass" and "hard-ass"—a culture is, the more likely its losers are to resort to domestic abuse, crime, violence, corruption, manipulation, and deceit, and the more likely they are to fall victim to psychological disorders, family dysfunction, depression, alienation, anomie, suicide, substance abuse, and other forms of self-abuse (Goble 1970; Csikszentmihalyi 1991; Glendon and Blankenhorn 1995). The haunting videotapes made by killers Eric Harris and Dylan Klebold prior to the slaughter they carried out at Columbine High School in 1999 are pervaded by themes of cultural entropy. Because they had felt demeaned for so long, they lusted both for revenge that would punish others and for fame that would elevate them above others. Because Harris's family had moved so often, he was continually having to start all over "at the bottom of the ladder." He rails against Denverites, "with their rich snobby attitude thinkin' they are all high and mighty. . . . God, I can't wait 'til I can kill you people."[43] Klebold resented his popular and athletic brother, Byron, who, along with Byron's friends, continually "ripped" on Dylan.

In a *Time* special report, Evan Todd, one of the athletes wounded in the attack, confirms Harris and Klebold's view of the winner-loser jock culture. "Columbine is a clean, good place except for those rejects. . . . Sure, we teased them. But what do you expect with kids who come to school with weird hairdos and horns on their hats? It's not just jocks; the whole school's disgusted with them." Todd continues: "They're a bunch of homos. . . . If you want to get rid of someone, usually you tease 'em. So the whole school would call them homos." Ironically, the killers shared Todd's homophobic attitude: In one of the tapes, as Harris sights a gun's laser on Klebold, the latter says, "That is cool, dude. Every faggot's last sight."[44] In obscene language, Harris and Klebold proclaim their superiority over women, blacks, Jews, and homosexuals.

The winner-loser character of the society as viewed by Harris and Klebold has recently been implicated in the health problems of Americans. New medical evidence dramatically underscores the health costs of a class-stratified society of winners and losers. The results of 193 scientific papers published between 1994 and 1999 indicate that social class "is one of the most powerful predictors of health, more powerful than genetics, exposure to carcinogens, even smoking."[45] The best predictor of such killers as stroke, heart attack, and cancer turns out to be one's socioeconomic status. Because the key intervening variable seems to be stress related to one's low socioeconomic ranking, this finding indicts the zero-sum, entropic culture itself—a culture against which Eric Harris, in *Time*'s paraphrase, had wanted to "jumpstart a revolution of the dispossessed."[46]

Not only do countries with higher levels of inequality, such as the United States, have higher rates of illness and lower longevity than more egalitarian countries such as Sweden and Japan, but the same correlation between socioeconomic equality and health holds true within countries. "What do Biloxi, Miss., Las Cruces, N.M., and Steubenville, Ohio, have in common? High inequality, high mortality. Allentown, Pa., Pittsfield, Mass., and Milwaukee, Wis.? Low inequality, low mortality."[47] Status-ranking studies with animals show similar results, with, for instance, lower-ranking baboons and macaques having elevated levels of stress-related hormones and subsequent increases in pulse rates, fat buildup in arteries, and death from cancer, brain damage, and stroke. Among humans, the evidence indicates that "when a society creates steep discrepancies in income and wealth, it excites a preoccupation with material pleasures, money and status, and aggravates feelings of anxiety and inferiority that (it is all too accurate to say) eat away at people."[48]

These troubling findings should be of special concern to Americans, because "since the 1970s, virtually all our income gains have gone to the highest-earning 20 percent of our households, producing inequality greater than at any time since the 1930s, and greater than in any of the world's other rich nations (and many of its poor ones) today." It might shock Americans to learn that "Bill Gates alone is wealthier than half the American people put together." The critical issue, James Lardner finds, is "the ways in which we distribute money (and power and status) in the first place." That fact calls for "a basic change of thinking on the part of society."[49]

That the United States rates a gold medal in the Cultural Olympics of Hard-Ass is reflected in its rejection of national health insurance, its miniscule benefits for working parents of small children, its 25 percent actual poverty rate, its high incidence of physical violence and domestic abuse, its death penalty, and the shame attached to the social safety net guaranteeing citizens' most basic needs. Notwithstanding the connection between socioeconomic class and health, a recent study suggests that well-to-do members of an entropic culture suffer from intraclass status anxieties. According to a soon-to-be-published joint study by Columbia and Yale University researchers, "upper-middle-class adolescents have an even greater propensity for drug and alcohol use, depression and bouts of misbehavior than their inner-city counterparts."[50]

In 1998, the bipartisan National Commission on Civic Renewal warned about "a corrosive cynicism compounded with increasingly passive lifestyles and immoral conduct [that] has infected the United States at its roots."[51] While proclaiming that "the United States is still the greatest nation on Earth," the commission's report bemoaned a "cult of cynicism" and the fact that the United States "leads the industrialized world in violent crime, sexually transmitted disease, imprisonment, drug use and the production and consumption of pornography." Political psychologist Robert Lane reports "an alarming rise of clinical depression and other severe psychiatric disorders throughout the industrial world," citing as an example the fact that "Americans born after 1945 suffer depression at ten times the rate of those born fifty years before." He adds that "nearly half the current total population is likely to suffer some kind of mental illness during their lives."[52]

A report by Surgeon General David Satcher, released from the White House on December 13, 1999, summarized the results of hundreds of recent studies: "22 percent of the population has a diagnosable mental disorder . . .

mental illness, including suicide, is the second leading cause of disability." The report confirmed Lane's estimate that half of Americans will experience a mental or psychological disorder over their lifetimes.[53]

As child and family psychologists William and Martha Sears (1993) have argued for years, a need fulfilled is a need that goes away, while a frustrated need only mushrooms. But entropic values become needs that press ceaselessly upon us, like Hobbes's "endless striving for power after power, which ceaseth only in death." In essence, entropic needs enslave us to others by making our own happiness depend on their approval or disapproval and on their successes or failures relative to ours. David Levine, rejecting Hobbes's pessimistic assumption that human beings inevitably pursue entropic values,[54] advises, "When we eliminate concern for relative social position, we open up the possibility that the individual can achieve self-determination to a degree not otherwise possible."[55]

According to cultural historian Christopher Lasch (1979), a persistent critic of U.S. culture's marriage to entropy, Americans originally pursued competition out of concern for self-betterment and as a means toward some other end such as a job, a better standard of living, or political office. In the twentieth century, however, they have increasingly sought competitive success "as an end in its own right, the victory over your competitors that alone retained the capacity to instill a sense of self-approval" (p. 115). Consequently, "the American cult of friendliness conceals but does not eradicate a murderous competition for goods and position; indeed this competition has grown more savage in an age of diminishing expectations" (p. 124).

Both anecdotal and systematic evidence supports Lasch's lament. From schoolrooms to courtrooms, the evidence mounts that for many Americans, winning, even if fraudulently, has become paramount. "Cheating is pervasive among the nation's top high school students, according to a survey of juniors and seniors with at least a B average. Nearly 80 percent admitted some dishonesty, such as copying someone else's homework or cheating on an exam."[56] As schools are increasingly rewarded and punished according to students' test scores, teachers and principals are helping students cheat on the tests.[57] The O.J. Simpson murder trial featured lawyers "playing the race card," as reflected in the opposite outcomes of the criminal and civil trials, with the predominantly black, criminal jury finding Simpson not guilty and the mostly white, civil jury finding him responsible for the deaths of his ex-wife, Nicole, and her friend Ron Goldman. Criminologists worry about the growing appeal of legal tactics that purposely mislead. "An unethical courtroom 'trick' can be a very attractive idea to the prosecutor who feels he must win."[58]

William Ophuls (1997) bemoans the "moral entropy" entailed by liberal capitalism. In a review of Richard Lehan's 1998 *The City in Literature*, Sarah Marcus finds evidence of early-twentieth-century poets who foresaw much of what Ophuls and Lasch criticized later in the century: "Looking

backwards to an idealized past of cultural homogeneity, poets like Ezra
Pound and T.S. Eliot worried that a mechanized metropolis, driven by individualistic materialistic desires and the power of money would lead toward 'cultural entropy' and a desolate urban wasteland."[59] Of course, cultural homogeneity is not the only alternative to cultural entropy. Gene
Autry's idealized "Cowboy Code" incorporates both cultural diversity and
value synergism. According to Autry, the late cowboy, singer, actor, and
baseball-team owner, a true cowboy never takes unfair advantage of others,
always tells the truth and keeps his word, is gentle with children, the elderly, and animals, helps people in distress, is a good worker, rejects racially
or religiously intolerant ideas, and respects women, parents, and the law.
He is also a patriot who never shoots first or picks on the less powerful.

Unfortunately, as Freud (1961 [1927]: p. 13) recognized, in a culture
that pits its citizens against one another, patriotism takes on a shallow, negative, and illusionary character, displacing the aggressions of oppressed citizens away from their masters and onto foreigners. Like Hobbes, Freud
downplayed cultural variations and thus the social environment's role in
promoting friendly or unfriendly social relations. But like Marx, he clearly
understood the stake that entropic elites have in getting the masses to identify with them rather than resent them. In addition to the "illusion" of religion (Marx's "opiate of the masses"), Freud stressed the political importance of the "identification of the suppressed classes with the class who
rules and exploits them," by virtue of which "the suppressed classes can be
emotionally attached to their masters." Otherwise, "it would be impossible
to understand how a number of civilizations have survived so long in spite
of the justifiable hostility of large human masses" (p. 13).

The civilizations to which Freud is referring are precisely the most entropic ones, those pitting masters against slaves, lords against serfs, capitalists against workers, and commissars against citizens—not to mention
the politically divisive squabbles among underlings as they curry favor with
elites. Despite a socialization process shaped by elites and legitimizing
their rule, an entropic society remains one deeply divided against itself. Except in times of war, no measure of patriotic exhortation will make friendly
comrades and good citizens out of obdurate competitors. Indeed, authentic
patriotism, in the sense of caring about one's country, is now at a premium
in the United States and elsewhere.[60] Patriotism is supposed to be based on
public concern and national pride. But, in Lind's (1996: p. 233) depiction,
"America is not significantly freer or more democratic than other industrialized democracies today. It does, however, lead Europe and Japan in beg-
gars, murders, and prisons per capita."

In short, the synergistic perspective seeks to persuade not so much by
stipulating a specific set of politically correct values as by spelling out the
collective consequences of entropic versus synergistic categories of value
choice. Life offers us a large menu of synergistic choices, many of which

are avidly pursued even in notably entropic cultures like our own. With a big menu of nutritious value entrees, why should we set the table so that anyone starves?

Liberty, Equality, and Synergy

Maximizing choice while eliminating starvation was very much on the mind of political philosopher John Rawls (1971) when he set out to reconcile liberty and equality in his celebrated book *A Theory of Justice*. Full of good intentions but trapped in classical liberal tenets of possessive individualism, Rawls explicitly assumed that "the parties [to his social contract] took no interest in one another's interests" (p. 127). As noted by feminists such as Susan Moller Okin, Eva Kittay, and Mary Lyndon Shanley, this position basically ignores families, friendships, and other essential human relationships. Rawls thus cast the value pursuits of his citizens as haphazardly colliding billiard balls, and neglected the potential advantages of value synergism. Moreover, the "primary goods" he assumes all citizens seek lump means with ends, while betraying the capitalist underpinnings of his theory. He stipulates, for instance, that everyone seeks to maximize wealth and power.[61] Thus by assuming possessive individualists and by atomizing their value pursuits, he implicitly sacrifices the one ally he needs most: the synergistic values that alone can make compatriots of citizens and dramatically reduce the conflict between liberty and equality.

How do synergistic values minimize the conflicts between liberty and equality that have plagued political thinkers from Mill (1985 [1859]) to the present? As you and I freely pursue values whose achievement by either of us helps or elevates rather than harms or demotes the other, our libertarian successes carry with them a tendency to limit the growth of inequality between us. Unlike quests for power, wealth, and status, my pursuit of knowledge, friendship, craftsmanship, or mundane pleasures is likely to benefit you as well. Value synergism thus reduces the harms I might otherwise cause you—harms that Mill complained were used to justify social conformity and political repression. By contrast, Herbert Croly (1998 [1909]) favored an active government dedicated neither "to liberty [n]or to equality in their abstract expressions, but to liberty and equality insofar as they made for human brotherhood."[62] As Branko Horvat later argued, "Without human solidarity, inequality and unfreedom would immediately reappear."[63]

Like his mentor Mill, Rawls struggles mightily to reconcile liberties whose harmfulness to one another and to equality could be greatly reduced if citizens used their liberties to pursue synergistic rather than entropic values—a possibility that neither grasped. Like the seventeenth-century political philosophers examined by C.B. Macpherson,[64] Rawls simply assumes possessive individualists whose values are predominantly entropic. Rawls's

1971 attempted synthesis suffered both from dubious assumptions and from glaring contradictions, and it satisfied neither libertarians nor egalitarians, let alone conservatives or Marxists.[65] Most contradictory of all was his giving highest priority to liberty while requiring, magically, that the resulting inequalities be made maximally beneficial to society's worst-off members. A generation later, in *Political Liberalism* (1993: p. xvii), Rawls conceded that his general theory of "justice as fairness" had failed, but the missing link still eluded him: "The fact of a plurality of reasonable but incompatible comprehensive doctrines—the fact of reasonable pluralism—shows that as used in *Theory,* the idea of a well-ordered society of justice as fairness is unrealistic." He then simply takes citizens' incompatible values for granted. By virtue of this pessimistic conservatism, he retreats to a pluralist system of procedural justice that tries to make peace among the warring ideological factions of market society. Although "Rawls thinks liberal society can generate community,"[66] he never shows how. Indeed, his unconvincing attempt to humanize market society makes a good case, albeit unintentional, that liberal society actually undermines community.

In fairness to Rawls, we should recognize the challenge of persuading parents—black and white, men and women, Muslim, Christian, and agnostic, Democrat and Republican, libertarian and egalitarian—along with other socializing authorities, to shift their emphasis toward synergistic values. But surely this task is less daunting than Rawls's original hope of maximizing liberty while benefiting society's worst-off members. Those who doubt that the media might be used to foster value change should consider the impact that progressive soap operas in Mexico and Kenya appear to have had on viewers. Unlike Hollywood soaps, which invite escapism while modeling entropic values of wealth, status, and power, Mexico's popular *Accompañame* dramatized the advantages of birth control in an episode following which "registration at Mexico's family planning clinics jumped by 33 percent." The same message, portrayed in Kenya's influential *Ushikwapo Shikaman,* helped increase contraceptive use by 58 percent and to reduce the average desired family size of Kenyans from 6.3 children to 4.4.[67]

In the United States, it is difficult to estimate how much more entropic the culture might be without the influence of television shows such as *All in the Family,* which satirizes racism, sexism, and social intolerance; *Barney,* which emphasizes friendship, love, sharing, and compassion; or *Mr. Rogers' Neighborhood,* showcased earlier for its thirty-year advocacy of synergistic values.[68] The icons of U.S. soap operas may exhibit the entropic values of privilege and glitz, but they have serious cultural competition from Mr. Rogers: "For the generations who have grown up watching the slim fellow with the soft voice slip out of his jacket and into a sweater, change his shoes and feed his fish every day, few stars near his icon status."[69]

Americans believe that schools too can help address society's problems by teaching values. According to the Roper Poll's 1996 Survey of American

Political Culture, one of the three best ways—along with crime control and dads helping moms to build stronger families—that Americans think social problems can be corrected is by schools teaching good values. The national Character Education Project (CEP) began doing just that in 1993. Favoring "universal values," the CEP gets parents involved in discussions with educators about the most important values schools should teach. High on the list are respect, honesty, compassion, civility, nonviolence, and civic-mindedness. In 1998, ten schools in Denver won a four-year, million-dollar grant to foster these and related values. "What we are doing is a transformational process," says CEP spokeswoman Robin Johnston.[70]

Rawls (1971) began his influential treatise by begging the question of what kind of values a just society should be based on and in turn should foster. Indeed, his hypothetical framers were to choose political rules of justice from behind a veil of ignorance unbiased by any personal values. Horvat saw quickly what it took Rawls a generation to figure out: that conclusions about justice made by people subjected to a "special amnesia" about their personal histories and a "psychic amputation" of their values were bound to be unrealistic and unconvincing.[71]

The Liberal Fear of Prepolitical Values

We may ask why Rawls's unbiased framers would choose to maximize liberty and equality over, for instance, fraternity, security, tradition, health, family, love, friendship, religion, honor, wisdom, truth, beauty, self-actualization, creative expression, inner peace, community, or any of a number of alternative, widely esteemed values and goals that society might make paramount.[72] The answer seems to be (1) theoretically, Rawls's starting point is the sensibilities about justice of a particular people at a particular time, namely, citizens of late-twentieth-century capitalistic, pluralist democracies, and (2) empirically, liberty and equality as cornerstones of justice are what academic political theorists mainly write about. Granted, liberty and equality make it easier for more people to achieve other cherished values than do slavery and inequality—a classical liberal argument that makes Rawls's starting point seem less arbitrary. But it is equally true that loving families, community solidarity, friendship, and security make it easier for more people to achieve other cherished values than do dysfunctional families, anomie, enmity, and insecurity—and they may do so better than Rawls's favorites, freedom and equality.

To procedural liberals such as Rawls, for whom a political framework of liberty and equality is axiomatic, it seems arbitrary for philosophers to specify any prepolitical values, or substantive content of the so-called Good Life, as the proper purpose of society. Synergists, by contrast, do not begin with the naive assumption that political and social institutions can or should be "neutral" about what constitutes a good life. Unlike entropic values, synergistic values can help constitute a good life in which all members of society can share. They also make an optimal balance between freedom and equality easier to achieve. In turn, however, we shall see in Chapter 4 that conditions of social justice, including freedom and equality, do help to secure synergistic values from the threat of perverse transformation.

Notes

1. Adam Schefter, "Gibbs Takes Back His Life," *Denver Post,* January 4, 2001.
2. Episode of the PBS animated children's program *Arthur,* February 3, 1999.
3. Ronald Inglehart has suggested that modern citizens whose material needs have been met will pursue "postmaterialist" values, but these values could just as well be power and status as truth and beauty.
4. "Justice Tells Grads: Balance Family, Law," Associated Press, May 29, 2000.
5. Too much of the left's critique of capitalism is moralistic and platitudinous: capitalism and conservatism make us selfish; socialism or liberalism would make us altruistic, etc. This preaching mode—along with some useful insights—is exemplified in Mansbridge (1990), Etzioni (1996), Lerner (1996), Ophuls (1997), Nagle (1998), and Rorty (1998).
6. Csikszentmihalyi (1991: p. 165).
7. John Leo, "The Joy of Sexual Values," *U.S. News & World Report,* March 1, 1999, p. 13.
8. Work got a 7.2 rating; finances, 6.0; and sex, 5.5. Erica Goode, "Midlife Not Rife with Turmoil," *New York Times,* February 16, 1999.
9. Some partisans of parents, including Hewlett and West (1998), exaggerate parental altruism.
10. Reported in *Newsweek,* July 20, 1998.
11. "Exclusive Poll: 'We Hold These Truths . . .'," *USA Weekend,* July 4-6, 1997, p. 5.
12. Annie Murphy Paul, "Born to Be Good?" *USA Weekend,* July 23-25, 1999, p. 6. Recent research at the University of Kansas and the University of Arkansas has uncovered striking and unanticipated altruism in experimental subjects.
13. Adorno et al.'s (1950) classic study *The Authoritarian Personality* details some of the politically pathological consequences of lovelessness and other early childhood traumas.
14. Robert N. Bellah et al., *Habits of the Heart* (Berkeley: University of California Press, 1985).
15. Quoted in "Facing the Challenges of a Shared Future," *Princeton: With One Accord,* spring 1996, p. 3.
16. Robert Wright, "Where Anthropology Meets Psychology," *Time,* March 29, 1999, p. 117. Politically correct critics of the sociobiology pioneered by William Hamilton, George Williams, Robert Trivers, and Edward O. Wilson exaggerate its conservative implictions while ignoring its progressive ones.
17. Virginia Postrel, "The Hidden Power of Play," *Reader's Digest,* March 1999, p. 28.
18. Jeff Bradley, "Sour Note of the American Way," *Denver Post,* May 30, 1999.
19. Colin Turnbull, *The Forest People* (New York: Simon and Schuster, 1961).

20. "As in so many so-called 'primitive' cultures, every adult in this pygmy society is expected to be a bit of an actor, singer, artist, and historian as well as a skilled worker." Csikszentmihaly (1991: pp. 79–80).

21. In the documentary video *Rock & Roll: Punk, the Perfect Beat* (WGBH-Boston and the BBC, 1995, vol. 5), British punk rockers such as the Wailers and the Clash "recall how Jamaican reggae crossed international boundaries, deeply influencing punk and pop rock."

22. 1998 baseball fans may recall a similar reaction by opponents of Mark McGuire, after he hit his sixty-first and sixty-second home runs, first tying then beating Roger Maris's thirty-seven-year-old record.

23. Larry Evans's syndicated chess column, "'72 Match More Than a Game," December 27, 1998.

24. Elisabeth Lasch-Quinn, who edited her father's last, posthumous work (Lasch 1997), chose this Emerson quote as the dedication to the book, which her father had "lost himself" in crafting.

25. The pure pleasures I list here overlap Csikszentmihalyi's (1991: p. 46) categories of "pleasure," which he sees as homeostatic, simple, and uncreative, and "enjoyment," which is dynamic, complex, and creative. Reminiscent of J. S. Mill's distinction between higher and lower pleasures, this distinction reflects intellectuals' sublimative preferences for art and science over eating and sex.

26. Jeffry Scott, "Trying to Slip in Some Fun," Cox News Service, February 23, 1999.

27. In Chapter 4, I examine how synergistic values can become perversely transformed into their opposites.

28. "Extremism in the defense of liberty is no vice; moderation in the pursuit of justice is no virtue," said 1964 presidential candidate Barry Goldwater, in a famous line penned by community activist and speechwriter Karl Hess.

29. Susan Sachs, "Viewers Appraise Lewinsky," *New York Times,* February 7, 1999.

30. See, for instance, Cathy Madison, "Don't Buy These Myths," *Utne Reader,* no. 90, November-December 1998, p. 55, and Natalie Angier, "Society's Glue: Science Examines Empathy's Role for Man, Beast," *New York Times,* September 28, 1995. See also Robert A. Hinde, *Biological Bases of Human Social Behavior* (New York: McGraw-Hill, 1974); Jane J. Mansbridge (1990); Margaret Mead, ed., *Cooperation and Competition Among Primitive Peoples* (Boston: Beacon Press, 1961); Abram Kardiner, *The Psychological Frontiers of Society* (New York: Columbia Press, 1945); and Alan Page Fiske, *Structures of Social Life: The Four Elementary Forms of Human Relations* (New York: Free Press, 1991). Fiske's four basic social relations—communal sharing, authority ranking, equality matching, and market pricing—are well-documented and, together, make a strong prima facie case against the politically correct narrowings of both left and right. While the left prizes communal sharing and equality matching, the right favors authority ranking and market pricing.

31. See Ted Becker and Christa Daryl Slaton, *The Future of Teledemocracy* (Westport, CT: Praeger, 2000).

32. Zero-sum tendencies are apparent in Foreman's approach to population control: he recommends that "no welfare payments or food stamps be provided to parents with more than two children, that capital punishment be the penalty for murder, rape, kidnapping, and other violent crimes, and that further immigration to the United States be prohibited" (Lee 1995: p. 62). By contrast, many aspects of the mythopoetic men's movement, despite its embrace of the warrior myth, overlap synergistic ecofeminism. See Bly (1992). More recently, Foreman has moderated his views.

33. Galston recognizes that the quantitative diversity of values in a society may affect social solidarity, but, like most liberals, he misses the qualitative effects on solidarity of synergistic versus entropic values. William Galston "Value Pluralism and Liberal Political Theory," *American Political Science Review* 93, no. 4, December 1999, p. 776.

34. "Each society can then be evaluated in terms of how much psychic entropy it causes, measuring that disorder not with reference to the ideal order of one or another belief system, but with reference to the goals of members of that society. A starting point would be to say that one society is 'better' than another if a greater number of its people have access to experiences that are in line with their goals." Csikszentmihalyi (1991: p. 78).

35. Robert Wheeler Lane, *Beyond the Schoolhouse Gate: Free Speech and the Inculcation of Values* (Philadelphia: Temple University Press, 1995), p. 172. Indeed, there is no neutral choice whereby we can somehow avoid political socialization: "Since the socialization of children is inevitable, the pressing questions are who will do the socializing and what information and values will be inculcated" (p. 173). The best antidote to conformity is to include the independence fostered by critical and creative thinking among the values taught. An example is the media-literacy movement spreading from Europe, Australia, England, and Canada to U.S. cities such as Seattle, where the Creating Critical Viewers program in public schools equips children to view television—and, by extension, other socializing influences—with an independent, critical eye. Kay McFadden, "Seattle School Teaches Kids to Watch TV Critically," Knight-Ridder News Service, July 9, 1998.

36. Gina Holland, "Teen Left Note Before Rampage at School, Saying, 'I Am Angry.'" Associated Press, October 3, 1997.

37. Csikszentmihlyi (1991); Derek Bok, *The State of the Nation* (Cambridge: Harvard University Press, 1996); Dye (1999).

38. Fox Butterfield, "Survey Finds That Crimes Cost $450 Billion a Year," *New York Times,* April 22, 1996.

39. "Veterans of Change, Ready for More," *Stanford Observer,* June 1990, 13.

40. Susan Faludi interview with Sue Halpern, *Mother Jones,* September-October 1999, p. 38. Celebrated among feminists for her 1991 book *Backlash,* Faludi (1999) has more recently focused on the sufferings of men embroiled in the cultural war of all against all. "Men," she says, "don't want to live in a world run on retail values any more than women do. Like women, they want to be needed and useful participants in society."

41. Max Weber observed: "The more the world of the modern capitalist economy follows its own, immanent laws, the less accessible it is to any imaginable religion with a religious ethic of brotherliness." In Michael Harrington (1992: p. 299).

42. Susan Caminiti, "What It Takes to Make It On Wall Street," *Working Woman,* March 1999, pp. 57, 60.

43. *Time* magazine special report, downloaded from <www.Time.com> on December 13, 1999.

44. Ibid.

45. Erica Goode, "Lack of Status Weighs Heavily on Health," *New York Times,* June 1, 1999. "What matters is not simply whether a person is rich or poor, college educated or not. Rather, risk for a wide variety of illnesses, including cardiovascular disease, diabetes, arthritis, infant mortality, many infectious diseases and some types of cancer, varies with relative wealth or poverty: the higher the rung on the socioeconomic ladder, the lower the risk. And this relationship holds even at the upper reaches of society, where it might seem that an abundance of resources would even things out." Milyo and Mellor offer alternative possible interpretations of the

correlation between social ranking and health. See Jeffrey D. Milyo and Jefficer M. Mellor, "Is Inequality Bad for Our Health?" *Critical Review,* 13: 3–4, 2001, pp. 359–372.

46. *Time* magazine special report, downloaded from <www.Time.com> on December 13, 1999.

47. James Lardner, "Widening Income Gap May Narrow Our Lifespans," *U.S. News & World Report,* August 23, 1998.

48. Ibid.

49. Ibid.

50. "Suburb Kids Have Plenty of Problems," *USA Today,* August 16, 1999.

51. Thomas Hargrove, "Americans Are Own Worst Enemy, Civil Study Claims," Scripps Howard News, June 25, 1998.

52. Robert E. Lane, "The Happy Mask of War and Violence: Lessons for Market Democracies," cited in Lance Bennett, "The Uncivic Culture: Communication, Identity, and the Rise of Lifestyle Politics," *PS: Political Science and Politics* 31, no. 4, December 1998, p. 757.

53. Robert Pear, "Health Czar Puts Focus on Mental Illnesses," *New York Times,* December 13, 1999.

54. "But man, whose job consisteth in comparing himself with other men, can relish nothing but what is eminent." Thomas Hobbes, *Leviathan* (New York: Macmillan, 1962 [1651]), p. 131.

55. David Levine, *Needs, Rights, and the Market* (Boulder, CO: Lynne Rienner, 1988), p. 139.

56. Carole Feldman, "80% of Top High-Schoolers Admit Not All Grades Earned," Associated Press, October 20, 1993. A 2000 survey by the Josephson Institute of Ethics found that 70 percent of high-school students report cheating within the last year. Gisele Durham, "Teens Lie, Cheat a Lot, Study Finds," Associated Press, October 17, 2000.

57. "Teachers, Principals the Culprits in Recent Cheating Scandals," Associated Press, June 8, 2000.

58. Bennett Gershman, in Sullivan and Victor (1996: p. 113).

59. October 1998 posting of H-NET BOOK REVIEW, at <http://www2.h-net.msu.edu/reviews/showrev.cgi?path=17044907946051>, of Richard Lehan, *The City in Literature: An Intellectual and Cultural History* (Berkeley: University of California Press, 1998).

60. Nothing is less patriotic than global corporations, as reflected in the comment of a vice-president of Colgate-Palmolive: "The United States does not have an automatic call on our resources. There is no mindset that puts this country first." Quoted in William Greider, "The Global Marketplace: Closet Dictator," in *The Case Against Free Trade* (Berkeley: North Atlantic Books, 1993), p. 209. At the same time, the U.S. military faces unprecedented problems recruiting personnel, partly because of widespread public cynicism. John Omicinski, "Military Scrambles for Recruits in Cynical Nation," Gannett News Service, May 20, 1999.

61. His justification for this assumption, however, regards wealth and power primarily as means to other ends and thus really as secondary, not primary, goods.

62. It is clear that social synergy took priority over liberty, equality, and democracy for both Croly and his mentor Faguet. Crediting Faguet for emphasizing fraternity, Croly wrote, "The salutary and formative democratic purpose consists in using the democratic organization for the joint benefit of individual distinction and social improvement." Herbert Croly, *The Promise of American Life* (New York: Macmillan, 1909), excerpted in Dolbeare (1998), p. 422.

63. Branko Horvat, "Ethical Foundations of Self-Government," *Economic and*

Industrial Democracy, no. 1, 1980, p. 11.

64. C. B. Macpherson, *The Political Theory of Possessive Individualism* (London: Oxford University Press, 1962).

65. See, for instance, Allen Buchanan, "A Critical Introduction to Rawls' Theory of Justice"; Alan H. Goldman, "Responses to Rawls from the Political Right"; and Leslie Pickering Francis, "Responses to Rawls from the Political Left," all in Blocker and Smith (1980).

66. Leslie Pickering Francis, in Blocker and Smith (1980: p. 490).

67. Andy Steiner, "As the World Turns: Beyond Hollywood, Soap Operas Spread Social Change," *Utne Reader* 91, January-February 1999, p. 24.

68. It is fashionable among middle-class progressives to debunk *Barney* as simple-minded and sappy, a cynicism Hollywood has tried to tap in such camp movies as *Babe: Pig in the City,* which attracted hip adults but bombed at the box office because of its minimal appeal to children.

69. Nancy Hewitt, "Mister Rogers Firmly Planted in TV Neighborhood," *Los Angeles Times,* February 21, 1998.

70. Carlos Illescas, "10 Denver Grade Schools Will Teach 'Universal Values,'" *Denver Post,* October 22, 1998.

71. Branko Horvat, "Ethical Foundations of Self-Government," *Economic and Industrial Democracy,* no. 1, 1980, p. 5.

72. For communitarian Amitai Etzioni (1996) the "self-evident" choice, in lieu of liberty and equality, is personal autonomy and moral order, with equality, ecology, and other values relegated to a subordinate position.

4

Beyond Liberalism and Communitarianism: The Invisible Hand of Synergy

"You know, the unhappy truth about our time, I think, from the fifties until now, is that you're either a winner or a loser, and that makes most of us suffer a lot."

—Yale alumnus and filmmaker Bob Mason[1]

"Don't waste your time on jealousy. Sometimes you're ahead, sometimes you're behind. The race is long and, in the end, it's only with yourself."

—Kurt Vonnegut, to MIT graduating seniors[2]

"We know that individual liberty and individual happiness mean nothing unless both are ordered in the sense that one man's meat is not another's poison."

—Franklin Delano Roosevelt[3]

Value Synergy as the Other Invisible Hand

In a column entitled "'Values' Just a Sign of the Times," E. J. Dionne attests to "a quiet revolt against materialism" that "reflects a concern that the marketplace, for all its splendors, may produce value but not values."[4] Equally concerned about value and values was Adam Smith, the moral philosopher who founded modern political economy. As we shall see in Chapter 8, the left has not given the politically incorrect Smith (1759, 1776) his due, and that blind spot has come back to haunt not only radical critics of capitalism but every state-socialist regime.[5] Unlike much of the left today, Smith took the issue of values to be an important one: "For to what purpose is all the toil and bustle of this world? What is the end of avarice and ambition, of the pursuit of wealth, of power, and pre-eminence?"[6] In this chapter we must ask how the economic synergies that Smith discovered in the free market relate to the value synergies that are possible in a free culture. Are the two kinds of synergy identical or distinct? If distinct, are they mutually advantageous, mutually antagonistic, or unrelated? What, if any, is the overlap between market values and either synergistic or entropic values?

Anything with a market value must be in limited supply, or it would not trade on the market, because its exchange value would be zero. A desirable good, service, or condition that was limitless, like air or dirt, would command no price on the free market.[7] Is a synergistic value free or costly? It may be either or both. Knowledge, like artistry or friendship, may cost only time and energy to acquire, but certain kinds of knowledge, artistry, or friendship may require costly education or travel. Both the money and the opportunities foregone in, say, learning mathematics, Chinese, or music theory, cost me other possibilities, some of which may have market value. But I can attain such learning without taking it away from anyone else. Any scarcity of a synergistic value stems from the difficulty and costs of attaining it, not from the fact that attaining it requires taking it away from somebody else.

Many synergistic values require us to enter the market in order to achieve them to the level we desire. For instance, doing my kind of art may require that I buy costly materials or pay to study with a master. It may also require me to sell my art in order to make a living. Pure pleasures like fly-fishing may take me to remote locations that are expensive to reach. Being the best homebuilder I can be means that I need to buy costlier materials and hire more expensive subcontractors than if my only concern were minimizing costs in order to maximize profits. In short, a positive-sum value is not necessarily free of cost or of market constraints. Markets can serve or impede synergistic goals. On the one hand, free markets may give me a better chance of procuring what I need to pursue my synergistic goals than, for instance, a state-run economy whose managers prohibit me from selling my art on the grounds that it is decadent.[8] On the other hand, if free-market advertising seduces my potential clients into buying expensive clothes, cosmetics, and face-lifts, they may be unable to afford my paintings.

Useful goods and services in limited supply will always need to be exchanged by producers and consumers at some agreed-upon price.[9] In *The Wealth of Nations,* Smith (1776) showed how free-market consumers and producers unintentionally promote the common good by pursuing their own economic interests. Economic freedom allows suppliers to produce what they want to, while competition for profits with other producers gives them an incentive to satisfy consumers' demands with an optimum balance of high quality and low cost. Economic freedom also permits consumers to buy what they want, to pick and choose among alternative goods and services, and thus to let producers know how well they are satisfying consumers' wants. The pricing mechanism balances producers' supply of goods and services with consumers' demand for them, and it facilitates exchanges of money for goods and services. Free markets also encourage a division of labor, which, along with new technology, increases productivity, thus providing a wider range of goods and services to consumers while reducing costs and temporarily increasing profits for producers. Increased consumption and production fuel economic growth, and the resulting larger economic pie may benefit society as a whole.

Consumers' so-called sovereignty in defining market values by their purchases masks the fact that consumer choices have been influenced by earlier socialization processes that shaped the consumers' values prior to their entering the market. Perhaps, for instance, I don't care about being better dressed than my neighbor, because for me fashion either is unimportant or is a means of purely personal expression. Consequently, my demand for trendy or high-fashion clothes will be minimal. Similarly, competition for jobs that confer high status will not for that reason attract people whose values deemphasize status. Nor will maximizing profits interest those who care little about wealth but much about the quality of their work. The free market involves competition for contested items—among consumers for goods, workers for jobs, and producers for profits—but only among those who actually value the items. The magic of the market, Smith's Invisible Hand, is that the participants' market competitions, while temporarily hurtful to the losers, provide net benefits to the economy as a whole. The magic of synergistic value pursuits—a second Invisible Hand—is that they counteract market scarcities by increasing net value achieved. Knowledge acquired multiplies; craftsmanship inspires apprenticeship; friendship encourages friendliness; a single loving family can inspire its peers and generate loving successors; connoisseurs of pleasure spread their genius simply by being themselves. Even if I cannot afford to outbid other purchasers for a car, yacht, or home, I can "afford" to gain knowledge, craftsmanship, friendship, and cost-free pleasures of everyday life. The latter will seem empty, however, if I am addicted to entropic one-upmanship.

The more synergistic the values pursued in a free-market society are, the fewer are the participants who must be losers, and the less true is Bob Mason's lament that "the unhappy truth about our time, I think, from the fifties until now, is that you're either a winner or a loser, and that makes most of us suffer a lot." By contrast, the pursuit of entropic values such as power, status, and wealth (alluded to by Adam Smith) exacerbates the inherent scarcity of market values. It thereby encourages a cultural war of all against all, which Hobbes attributed to human nature but which also feeds culturally on entropic value choices by institutional authorities and ordinary citizens.

In short, market values, though inherently limited, can breed economic synergy, especially through an expanding economy.[10] They can also facilitate either synergistic or entropic values pursued by market participants. The losses entailed by market competition can be at least partially offset by value synergism. For instance, I may benefit from reading scholarly works published in lieu of my own rejected manuscripts. I certainly benefit from preferring poetry to Porsches that I can't afford anyway.[11] If I enjoy gambling but value the well-being of Indian reservations and Colorado's environment, I can place my bets in Indian casinos or with the Colorado lottery, which helps fund environmental protection. In either case, even if I lose in one respect, I win in another. On the other hand, value entropy exacerbates market losses, as in the case of my not only failing to get the job or score the deal that would have afforded me a Porsche but also suffering a loss of social status and power by my failure.

Like Smith's Invisible Hand of market economics, the Invisible Hand of value synergism does not depend on altruism or on conscious efforts to promote the common good, although, like Smith's, it can benefit from altruism and purposive policy. Keynesian and neo-Keynesian policymakers have supplemented Smith's Invisible Hand with visible economic planning to stabilize the market system and save capitalism from economic depression, social collapse, and political revolution. Similarly, a conscious effort by cultural authorities, including parents, to nurture synergistic values would later culminate in the unintended synergism of value synergists who are simply going about their business. In time, synergistic resocialization can increase the number of professional and amateur artists doing their art, of professional and lay scientists accumulating knowledge, of restaurateurs and domestic chefs creating culinary delights, of parents nurturing their children. Authorities and citizens who foster synergistic values increase the percentage of value pursuits that are positive-sum rather than zero-sum.

Both invisible hands benefit from the fact that they can do their magic without the help of model Christians or model Marxists heroically dedicated to the public good. Historian Patricia Limerick has recommended that we treasure the heroic moments people are capable of, and appreciate their extraordinary contributions to social value, but not count on saintliness in either leaders or citizens.[12] There is nothing heroic about ordinary people seeking ways of making their daily lives fuller, more challenging, or more enjoyable without besting their neighbors, but such synergism does keep them out of trouble by giving them something better to do than going for one another's throats. Under sufficiently oppressive conditions, of course, even ordinary pursuits may take on a heroic character. Indeed, prosynergy parents today must fight social forces that promote entropy, partly because their children need to learn how to survive other people's frenzy for power, status, and wealth (Hewlett and West 1998).

Using Justice to Avoid Perverse
Transformations of Synergistic Values

I have yet to give a talk on synergism without someone in the audience raising an obvious objection: "Can't your synergistic values be transformed into their exact opposites?" Yes, they can, I am sorry to say. Certain conditions can turn my pleasures into your pains, tempt me to use my knowledge to preserve your ignorance, turn creative impulses destructive, and even transform the energy of love and friendship into hatred. For instance, an ethic of "keeping up with the Joneses" converts the family from a locus of love into a command center of competition. Synergistic values are not inherently scarce or competitive, but they can become so. What are the conditions in which such perverse transformations are most likely to occur? They are precisely the conditions targeted as unjust by liberal democratic theorists such as Rawls: namely, arbitrary deprivations of freedom and equality.

An instructive example is this sadly beautiful passage from W.E.B. Du Bois's *The Souls of Black Folk:*

> I remember well when the shadow swept across me. I was a little thing, away up in the hills of New England, where the dark Housatonic winds between Hoosac and Taghkanic to the sea. In a wee wooden schoolhouse, something put it into the boys' and girls' heads to buy gorgeous visiting-cards—ten cents a package—and exchange. The exchange was merry, till one girl, a tall newcomer, refused my card,—refused it peremptorily, with a glance. Then it dawned upon me with a certain suddenness that I was different from the others; or like, mayhap, in heart and life and longing, but shut out from their world by a vast veil.

While others might have crumbled in despair or pleaded for acceptance, young Du Bois showed his proud resilience: "I had thereafter no desire to tear down that veil, to creep through; I held all beyond it in common contempt, and lived above it in a region of blue sky and great wandering shadows. That sky was bluest when I could beat my mates at examination-time, or beat them at a foot-race, or even beat their stringy heads."[13] The injustice of racism had turned beauty and kindness into ugly rejection—had turned synergy into entropy—and had converted Du Bois himself to the ethic of conquest from which his own people had suffered for centuries. He would dedicate himself to punishing his tormentors by conquering them in every way possible. For him and his fellows, the world had become a zero sum of winning and losing. Later he would reconsider this entropic choice and contribute the fruits of his stunning literary genius to the world.

Although the devil is always in the details, let us generally agree with liberal democratic theorists in labeling unjust any institutions, laws, or policies that unfairly elevate some people over others or that arbitrarily deprive people of liberty. Such conditions cause festering resentments between the unfairly advantaged and the unfairly disadvantaged—and even, as Marx and Bellamy pointed out, among the disadvantaged struggling to ascend and among the advantaged fearful of falling. These perpetual fears and resentments transform value pursuits that mutually benefit citizens into sources of further division.

Pleasure Perversely Transformed

Injustice typically wins one group's pleasures at the expense of another group's pain. Roman citizens enjoyed watching Christians being thrown to the lions. The pleasures of the Southern aristocracy depended on the labor of black slaves. Nineteenth-century fun on the frontier was paid for by pioneers' expropriating of Native peoples. The luxuries of America's billionaires were made possible by rank-and-file laborers paid but a pittance of the market value they had created. The perks and powers of the Soviet coordinator class were purchased by the disfranchisement of the nominally sovereign socialist proletariat (Albert and Hahnel 1981).

Knowledge Perversely Transformed

Injustice allows knowledge to be used as a weapon by one group to control another, as an instrument for keeping opponents in the dark. Black slaves in the South were legally forbidden to learn to read. Today, corporate insiders use privileged knowledge to get unfair and illegal advantages in stock transactions. Tobacco companies hide medical facts about their product to avoid liability and protect profits. Ford Motor Company lawyers persuaded the court to suppress written evidence that Ford executives knew ahead of time about the often fatal gas-tank flaw in the Ford Pinto but decided to go ahead with production anyway.[14] Like the FBI and the CIA, the Soviet secret police selectively exposed facts harmful to their opponents while censoring information damning to themselves. In conditions such as these, one person's knowledge becomes a source not of another person's enlightenment, but of other people's fear, confusion, and oppression.

Art Perversely Transformed

Injustice often means that creativity is used for destructive purposes. Inventors who might have been making better medicines, farm tools, or irrigation systems have instead devised torture chambers, land mines, and nuclear bombs. A great deal of imagination and artistry has gone into tobacco advertisements targeted specifically at vulnerable youth, women, and ethnic minorities, because the wealthy companies value their profit margins over alternative values such as truth, health, and compassion. Television critics have noted the technical and imaginative superiority of commercials over programs, a consequence of the fact that it is the ad that sells the product. Unfortunately, these commercials are used to convince women that they need antidotes to their unattractiveness, to persuade men to buy gas-guzzling cars that will add to their sex appeal, and to induce young people to buy the really cool clothes that will make them popular with their friends. Hollywood uses the creativity of writers, actors, and directors to make C-grade films that push violence, exploitative sex, and the glitter of power, wealth, and status.

Family Values Perversely Transformed

Injustice penetrates the household, not only via patriarchy and ageism, but also when frustrated employees take out their aggressions on their children and spouses. Relationships that start out loving can turn hateful if family members are pushed to the breaking point by demeaning attitudes of bosses, by ethnic discrimination, or by the sex wars that have arisen as women have struggled for equal dignity and fuller opportunities.[15] The love, trust, and respect that enrich family life are undermined by adultist practices that demean children and arbitrarily restrict their options. The "generation gap" that divides families reduces children's identification with parents and makes them more susceptible to peer pressures and consumerism. Not only do entropic forces of consumer society help turn love energy into envy, jealousy, and hatred, but, as we shall see in Chapter 7, they undermine the potential of families as empowered political actors seeking family-friend-lier policies from business and government.

Friendship and Love Perversely Transformed

Injustice often makes enemies of former or potential friends. In a society that stresses interpersonal comparisons along a winner-loser dimension, friend-ships can be threatened when Friend A fears that Friend B's new acquain-tance C might tip the balance of power against A. If social status or power is seen as a function of how many friends one has, or how wealthy one is, then a new friend or promotion may "demote" one's original friend. In *The Devil's Dictionary* (1993 [1911]: p. 6) Ambrose Bierce defined antipathy as "the sen-timent inspired by one's friend's friend." The very intensity of a close friend-ship can make its perverse transformation into enmity unusually painful, es-pecially when the friendship was also a lovership. Shulamith Firestone writes, "Love demands a mutual vulnerability or it turns destructive: the de-structive effects of love occur only in the context of inequality."[16]

Craftsmanship Perversely Transformed

Highly competitive societies stack the cultural deck in favor of those blessed with the particular competitive skills favored by their society's rules. In a culture of winners and losers, the synergistic pursuit of a craft can easily get sidetracked into an entropic pursuit of fame. Achieving fame imposes costs not only on those put in one's shadow, but on oneself. According to singer and pop idol Madonna, the increasing quest for fame promised to fill her up but instead emptied her out. "Fame consumes you, exhausts you and finally depletes you," she told the *New York Post*. "I do blame fame for prematurely ending a lot of the relationships in my life. . . . The only relationship you have [is] that relationship with your fame. Everything else comes second, or third, or fourth, [but] at the end of the day, fame is not love."[17] When profit is paramount, craftsmanship is often sacrificed for the bottom line. When the pursuit of power prevails, those whose craft is properly to serve the public good are often silenced, corrupted, or eliminated.

Ties That Bind, Sins That Shred

We need look no further than Mahatma Gandhi's "Seven Deadly Sins" to grasp the institutional and personal tendencies that can transform synergistic values into their entropic opposites: (1) wealth without work, (2) pleasure without conscience, (3) knowledge without character, (4) commerce without morality, (5) science without humanity, (6) worship without sacrifice, and (7) politics without principle. A prominent tendency of corporate capitalism is to reward those who are already privileged and powerful while exploiting or ignoring those who are not. In *Chaos or Community?*, Holly Sklar (1995: p. 13) highlights the unfavorable economic conditions facing the poorest quarter of U.S. families, including the working poor. A family of four needs an income "of about 155 percent of the official poverty line to buy minimally sufficient food, housing, health care, transportation, clothing and other personal and household items, and pay taxes." By this more accurate standard, official poverty rates of 15 percent jump to 25 percent. When asked collectively to develop a minimally sufficient budget for a family of three, the students at my working-class, commuter campus consistently exceed the official poverty line by about 100 percent.

   In addition to the health consequences of inequality discussed in Chapter 3, Robert Reich warns of another pathological consequence of U.S. society's becoming divided into a relatively few winners and millions of losers: "We are on the way to becoming a two-tiered middle class composed of a few winners and a larger group left behind, whose anger and disillusionment is easily manipulated. Today the targets of rage are immigrants, welfare mothers, government officials, gays and an ill-defined 'counterculture.' As the middle class continues to erode, who will be the targets of tomorrow?"[18] Feminist Betty Friedan (1997: p. 12) worries that if women's economic gains come at the expense of men, gender wars will hurt men and women alike: "Now I see the impossible paradox for women: *women are achieving what begins to look like equality because men are doing worse. Is their loss really our gain?*" (emphasis in original).

   Justice defined as "to each according to work" has come closer to realization under socialism than capitalism (Przeworski 1991). Under capitalism, the more accurate formulation is "to each according to ownership and work," in that order. *Ceteris paribus,* those who work hard get ahead more than those who do not, but those who own more get ahead more than those who work hard. When Bill Gates doubled his wealth in 1998 from $25 billion to $50 billion, he worked no harder than millions of Americans who gained no wealth at all. In the United States, justice so defined has, ever since the New Deal, been publicly supplemented by Judeo-Christian mercy, defined as "to each according to need," which also entails a version of Jesus's and Marx's "from each according to ability," since it is the able who must care for the needy. If this standard were applied across the United States, not only the American people but their synergistic values would be better protected from perverse transformation.

Given the mixed U.S. tradition of capitalist justice and Judeo-Christian mercy, it is not surprising that Americans support the safety-net concept in varying percentages, depending on which part of the net they are asked about. A majority of *Newsweek* readers in 1998 viewed as rights a good public-school education (86 percent), adequate medical care (74 percent), adequate housing (58 percent), and a good job for anyone willing to work (50 percent), whereas only a minority accord everyone a right to an adequate standard of living (41 percent), a reasonable amount of leisure time (29 percent), enough money to live on in retirement (28 percent), a college education (22 percent), and a raise in wages and salary every year (10 percent).[19] In any case, when a large percentage of a populace lacks the basics of a dignified life, envy and resentment are likely to short-circuit the positive-sum effects of synergistic values.

Perverse transformations of synergistic value are disappointing, like losses in the competitions of the marketplace. Avidly pursuing but losing something, whether a friendship or a job, is painful, but that fact does not mean that the pursuit was ill-advised or that markets and friendships are zero-sum games after all. In the long run, working hard to achieve our ends is a strategy that pays off. This lesson may be hard to accept when the long-term gain is presently invisible and the short-term loss all too palpable. Synergistic, positive-sum possibilities do not insure any of us against loss, but entropic, zero-sum goals ensure many of us of loss. Conditions favoring mutual rather than competitive success are especially beneficial for children as they develop. Becoming a "loser" in childhood can be a devastating blow. Despite the danger that even a synergistic value such as friendship, knowledge, or parental love can be lost, perversely transformed, or otherwise traumatizing, e.g., via marital discord or divorce, there is no "safe" strategy whereby children can protect themselves from disappointment by avoiding friendship, love, and learning. Any such strategy is a loser from the start.

Might an all-consuming synergistic pursuit, though not perversely transformed into its opposite, eventually sacrifice its synergism and even become entropic because of its manic nature?[20] Consider a compulsive friendship that allows the friends neither other friends nor the time and energy to pursue other values. Or ponder the situation of artists or scholars so wrapped up in their work that they endanger their health, lose their friends, or hurt their families. The unattractive quality of such lives may well create a backlash that turns others off from the very pursuit of close friendship, dedicated scholarship, or serious art. But synergistic values have no monopoly on monomania, as seen in lives dedicated to a desperate pursuit of power, wealth, and status. Despite its costs, monomaniacal dedication to friendship, knowledge, or art is less likely to devastate innocent bystanders than is monomaniacal dedication to wealth and power. Painter Vincent Van Gogh and poet Sylvia Plath killed only themselves; industrialist John D. Rockefeller's police killed almost a hundred mining men, women, and children at Ludlow, Colorado, and tyrant Adolph Hitler sent millions of Jews, Gypsies, and others to death camps.

Freedom and Equality as a Defense Against Injustice

The cry for freedom, justice, and equality is best understood as a political defense against oppression. In this vital role, it is a staunch ally of synergy. Arbitrary subjection to slavery, injustice, or inequality is intensely painful. The converse is less true: Being free, equal, and justly treated—especially if we are used to it—may give us peace of mind when we compare ourselves with the oppressed, but it is not ecstatically pleasurable. In fact, the absence of oppression has no substantive content at all but, rather, sets the stage for what we want to do with our lives when nothing unfairly holds us back. If we collapse the three conditions into one by viewing justice as the optimal synthesis of freedom (or liberty) and equality, then justice may be seen as the political umbrella under which we all have the least-encumbered chance of fulfilling our human potential.

This umbrella of justice, under which publicly fostered restraints and inequalities are limited to ones that prevent serious harm to others, is analogous to Marx's vision of communism as the end of human prehistory—that is, as the beginning of our opportunity to realize our fullest potential as self-aware, social, and creative beings. But unlike the communist umbrella, this one does not suffer from structural defects through which the rain of reality would surely pour: namely, the abolition of markets and government, premised on the replacement of self-interest by social responsibility. Rather, the synergistic umbrella of justice allows value synergies to flourish by outlawing arbitrary inequalities and gratuitous restrictions on freedom. This prohibition would minimize the perverse transformation of synergistic values into their entropic opposites.

Have we simply sneaked liberal justice in the back door under the cloak of synergy? We have not, although we grant liberal democracy its due by recognizing the great, entropic harms done by arbitrary unfreedoms and inequalities. Unlike straight liberal justice, the liberal-synergistic umbrella starts with synergistic values as the proper foundation of society and then insists on the kind of libertarian-egalitarian social justice that protects citizens from threats to their synergistic value pursuits. These pursuits cannot trump justice, because any condition that systematically and unfairly subjects one person to another is entropic, not synergistic. Arbitrary inequality allows the unfairly advantaged to extract value—economic, political, social—from the unfairly disadvantaged. Arbitrary coercion allows the unfairly empowered to extract liberty, and the myriad values it affords, from the unfairly constrained.

Cross-culturally, this umbrella of prohibition would permit a range of formulas, depending on the relative importance accorded various forms of liberty and equality. For instance, a society somewhat more dedicated to liberty than equality might permit stridently aristocratic forms of literary and artistic expression that bluntly satirized "inferior" modes of living. Another society, leaning more heavily toward equality, might legislate against a wider range of "words that wound" as well as other forms of expression judged demeaning to others.[21] To keep itself honest and vibrant, a synergistic society would do well to permit the full range of free political activity prized by liberals, even including freedom for a hypothetical Entropy Party whose purpose was to replace synergism with entropism.

Robert Nozick suggests that utopian visions are more attractive and defensible as they are more numerous and varied—that is, when they give prospective citizens real choices.[22] I agree. However, under the synergist umbrella, some prohibitions must be universal: no slave-owners and slaves, no lords and serfs, no billionaires employing impoverished workers, no unaccountable vanguards or commissars, no public discrimination on the basis of race, gender, age, or any other irrelevant criteria, and no nest-fouling ecocide. Anything less is dangerously entropic and unjust.[23] Synergism's ability to accommodate a rich cross-cultural diversity of value options differs from Michael Walzer's cultural pseudo-relativism, whereby anything goes—anything is "just"—so long as people in a society "live in a way faithful to the shared understandings of the members," in other words, so long as a people live up to Walzer's own criteria for The Good, including consistency, faithfulness, sharing, understanding, and majority rule (in the event "the members" are not unanimous).[24] Confronted, for instance, with the traditional Ghanaian system of Trokosi, or ritual sexual slavery of young girls atoning for their adult relatives' sins, Walzer would ask how faithfully its practitioners were following understandings shared with other Ghanaians.[25] A synergist would judge such practices entropic, unjust, and wrong.[26]

Structuralist-progressive readers may long since have grown impatient with my emphasis on values rather than institutions. But structuralists deserve a corrective dose of values, because structuralism has grievously discounted the importance of values, in effect defaulting to conservatives, especially on the vital issue of personal and family values. However, changed values alone, if unaccompanied by institutional transformation, will inevitably abort. Only a minority of people will persist in pursuing knowledge, friendship, art, family, craftsmanship, or mundane pleasures as primary values if the institutional rules and practices favor entropic predators that mercilessly hound everyone else to defend themselves. Institutional and cultural change must go hand in hand.

Although a range of laws, policies, and institutions can accommodate cultural synergy, the following chapters will—as food for thought—recommend specific directions of institutional change that progressives typically ignore, partly for reasons of political correctness. In general, these directions involve (1) political structures whose strong leaders are held effectively accountable by the vigorous engagement of ordinary citizens in the political process; (2) economic structures whose (mostly public) necessities and public-amenities sector is democratically planned and regulated by the people and their accountable delegates, and whose (mostly private) luxury sector outlaws absentee ownership while encouraging sole proprietors, partnerships, and economic cooperatives to avail themselves of the freedoms and incentives of the market; (3) constitutional protections for all citizens, including youth, against arbitrary discrimination in public matters; and (4) constitutional protection of the natural environment and its inhabitants against ecocidal production and consumption.

Good Competition Versus the Tragedy of Triumph

If synergy is better than entropy—because, *ceteris paribus,* more people benefit—does it follow that all competition is bad? I think not. Although any competition whose participants care about the outcome involves an element of disappointment and value entropy—a zero sum of winning and losing—the key issue is whether other, synergistic benefits outweigh the entropic costs. Classic synergisms of competition are (1) fun, (2) enhanced craftsmanship, and (3) Smith's Invisible Hand benefits of economic exchange, specialization, and growth. Among good friends or worthy opponents, playing chess, tennis, or Monopoly (unlike playing its politically correct alternatives Class Struggle and Anti-Monopoly) is just plain fun, despite any disappointment associated with losing the game.[27] Such competitions can also build our skills and provide entertainment, even artistry, for spectators. Games, especially sports, can provide employment, increase demand for equipment, improve health, and have multiplier effects in related industries.[28]

The key to the ratio of synergy and entropy in competitions is how important winning is to the participants, compared with other values. "The mania for winning," says Lasch (1979: p. 186), "has encouraged an exaggerated emphasis on the competitive side of sport, to the exclusion of the more modest but more satisfying experiences of cooperation and competence." The issue of balance is reflected in the competing aphorisms "It's not whether you win or lose; it's how you play the game" versus "Winning isn't everything; it's the only thing." The latter expresses a particularly virulent form of value entropy, since in most competitions it implies a single winner and many losers. I once had a student who was perennially depressed about himself as an athlete, because in high school he had been the second-best wrestler in his weight class in a large metropolitan area, whereas, a generation earlier, his father had been first and still reminded him of the difference. Many of today's sports psychologists try to teach athletes that they are more likely to win if, ironically, they forget about winning and losing and focus on doing their best, on the craftsmanship of their sport, and on having fun.

Defenders of winning as the singular purpose of competition often say that it is the hunger for victory that brings out the best in the competitors and helps them improve. The truth is often just the opposite. The argument may be valid when competitors are evenly matched, but, as reflected in Las Vegas betting lines, equality is the exception rather than the rule. In a typical competition, the participants know ahead of time who is likely to win. If the main goal of the competitors is to win, and the outcome is virtually predetermined, then neither favorite nor underdog has much incentive to excel. No matter how hard the inferior competitor tries, he or she will probably lose, while the superior player can usually win without great effort. Thus most competitions bring out the best in opponents only when goals other than winning—enjoyment, self-improvement, self-respect, craftsmanship—are paramount. The legal gymnastics performed in November 2000 by Al Gore and George W. Bush in their all-out attempts to win the presidency probably served to delegitimize both the election and the office itself.

In effect, then, a primary focus on winning may be a formula for mediocrity rather than excellence. This fact may explain why American students and athletes, whose mentors stress winning more zealously than in many other countries, have in many cases lost ground to their international peers. It certainly explains why U.S. distance-running competitions have doctored their entrance requirements to reduce the number of entrants from nations such as Kenya, whose athletes dominate their U.S. counterparts. U.S. race organizers find the superiority of African, Latin, and Asian runners embarrassing, and prefer to "dumb down" their races to allow for more American "winners." On TV's *Politically Incorrect,* host Bill Maher has called this ploy "affirmative action for slow white guys."

The ethic of victory at all costs may also explain the new bureaucratic hoops erected to disqualify Jamaica's child spellers just as they were beginning to best their U.S. counterparts. Both Kenyan athletes and Jamaican spelling coaches have wondered aloud why Americans do not focus their efforts on more diligent training rather than on disqualifying superior competitors.[29] Americans' resentment of superior competitors also helps to explain the periodic acts of vandalism and violence in Montana, South Dakota, and elsewhere against the communal farms of pacifist Hutterite colonies, disliked by competing capitalist farmers because the Hutterite farms are more efficient, diverse, and profitable than their own.[30]

The race to win the Cold War took a serious toll on Olympic athletes from both the United States and Soviet Bloc countries such as East Germany, many of whose athletes took steroids and other drugs to enhance their performance. Like many other professional athletes, NFL defensive lineman Lyle Alzado bulked up with steroids for many years—and paid for it with his life. Whether we pay for an addiction to winning-as-the-only-thing with mediocrity, discrimination against opponents, or health problems and early death, we are engaged in an apparent paradox of the tragedy of triumph. In order to win at all costs, we forfeit other values that are more meaningful, more lasting, and more widely achievable. In addition, a mania for winning often carries other unattractive qualities in its wake. "Try to hate your opponent," advises billiards competitor Danny McGoorty. "Even if you are playing your grandmother, try to beat her fifty to nothing." World boxing champion Sugar Ray Robinson once commented, "Hurting people is my business."[31]

We fail to appreciate the many factors beyond our control that affect the outcome of a competition, especially who our opponent happens to be. If I sit down across the chess table from Bobby Fischer, I lose. If I play my father, on the other hand, I win. If Fischer and I compete with my father on the violin, he beats us both. "Upsets" usually signify that the superior competitor had a bad day. What do these victories and defeats really mean? In an age of mass media awash in a culture of spectacle, the importance of victory and defeat is grossly exaggerated, often accompanied by much sound and fury, thrill and agony, idolization and demonization. The largely coincidental nature of who wins makes it doubtful that it signifies anything inherently important. Of course, cultural norms can give it importance, as when an Olympic gold medalist wins many lucrative advertising contracts while the silver medalist receives none, even if the margin of victory was a tenth of a point or a hundredth of a second. The pathological outcomes of winning at all costs can become important indeed.

One of these pathologies should especially concern progressives: value entropy on the left. In recent years, liberals and radicals may have gotten better at the self-criticism they long parroted from communal founder John Humphrey Noyes (1876) and Chinese leader Mao Zedong (1956). But their nominal embrace of synergistic values such as love, community, and compassion remains uncomfortably married to concerns for their own power, status, and influence within activist organizations. Activist egos often seem a match for those of corporate executives or Democrats and Republicans trying to claw their way to the top of establishment hierarchies. Bitter interpersonal and interclique feuding has weakened liberal Democrats, unions, the affirmative-action lobby, black radicals, Marxist groups, the feminist movement, the American Indian Movement, environmental organizations from the Sierra Club to Earth First!, and third parties such as the Greens. Nasty infighting is probably no more common among liberals and radicals than it is among conservatives and reactionaries. But it stands out more markedly in contrast with espoused progressive ideals than it does, for instance, among conservatives who preach a gospel of profit, self-interest, and possessive individualism.

An example of both the problem and an attempt to solve it was the 1998 founding of the Black Radical Congress (BRC), which hopes to overcome traditional divisions among black activists by taking a more inclusive approach to black militancy. At the BRC's founding meeting in Chicago, "the high profile of black feminists and gays and lesbians forced the congress to address the blind spots of traditional black radicalism: sexism and homophobia." Progress was reflected in the fact that "when lesbian activist Barbara Smith remarked that it was the first time she'd been invited to a meeting of black leftists, she received a rousing ovation." As black feminist Barbara Ransby commented, "We cannot replicate the same competitiveness, elitism, and chauvinism so prevalent in larger society. We have to forge a different path." [32] But the outcome was uncertain, as other participants disagreed that "homophobia should be as central as race and class" or took issue with the black capitalism of Louis Farrakhan and the Nation of Islam.[33]

Of course, serious discussion and debate of important issues are a healthy antidote to political correctness. The ideal outcome is a synthesis more beneficial to all participants than any of the original, conflicting positions. But the painful turmoil of ego-driven and special-interest disputes often leaves a wake of bitterness and division that undermine the very purpose of progressive organizations. The challenges of transforming a powerful system of capitalist political economy will impose losses enough. In addition, the damage of internal strife, irrespective of who "wins," suggests that in the entropic war of all against all, progressive transformation can suffer not only from the misfortune of defeat but also from the tragedy of triumph.

Pioneers of Synergism

The origins of synergistic theory can shed light on what I have called the Invisible Hand of Synergy. In the 1930s, cultural anthropologist Ruth Benedict became troubled by the cultural relativism with which she had become associated. She began to seek some third alternative to relativism and its opposite, value absolutism, more often associated with religion than anthropology. "She took four pairs of cultures, which she had selected because they were different, and, on huge sheets of newsprint, wrote all that she knew about these cultures." On the one hand, the Zuni, the Arapesh, the Dakota, and the Inuit "produced nice people," were characterized by affection, and were "good cultures—those she liked." On the other hand, the ones "that she disliked," the Chuckchee, the Ojibwa, the Dobwo, and the Kwakiutl, were "surly and nasty," exhibiting hatred and aggression (Goble 1970: pp. 111–112).

Benedict tried to account for this pattern of difference with the variables of race, geography, climate, size, wealth, and complexity, but none of these explanations worked. Trying but rejecting the distinctions "high morale" versus "low morale" and "secure" versus "insecure," she borrowed a term from biology and finally settled on "high synergy" versus "low synergy."[34] As Goble puts it, "The high synergy societies were those where people cooperated together for mutual advantage, not necessarily because they were unselfish but because the customs of society made cooperation worthwhile" (p. 112). In her original, unpublished 1941 lecture notes, Benedict wrote, "Societies where non-aggression is conspicuous have social orders in which the individual, by the same act and at the same time, serves his own advantage and that of the group." Such synergistic behavior occurs "not because people are unselfish and put social obligations above personal desires, but when social arrangements make these two identical. . . . Their institutions insure mutual advantage from their undertakings."[35]

It was humanistic psychologist Abraham Maslow who discovered Benedict's distinction between high and low synergy in the lecture notes she had given him.[36] Her distinction fit nicely with his own theory of a universal hierarchy of human needs, since a high-synergy society was much more likely than a low-synergy one to fulfill the five universal needs Maslow (1943, 1954) had identified: survival, security, affection, respect, and self-actualization. Maslow picked up on Benedict's characterization of low-synergy societies as bad ones in which "the advantage of one individual becomes a victory over another, and the majority who are not victorious must shift as they can" (Goble 1970: pp. 112–113). The two were taken by the fact that in high-synergy societies, "wealth seemed to have been spread around more. In the bad society wealth made more wealth and poverty more poverty" (p. 113). In low-synergy societies such as the Kwakiutl, the rich used a range of economic devices to exploit the poor, including slavery, high interest rates, and unfair taxation.

Maslow found that in high-synergy societies, gods are portrayed as using their powers to benefit the whole, whereas in low-synergy societies gods tend to be viewed as malevolent and religious authorities as using their powers for personal profit. In cross-cultural studies, Benedict found and Maslow confirmed a broad impact of synergistic versus nonsynergistic approaches "in the style of prayer, the style of leadership, the style of family relationships, the style of relationships between men and women, the vocabulary of sexuality, the types of friendship," etc. (p. 113). Maslow described U.S. society as mixed, with important sources of high and low synergy. Some cultural elements support generosity and security, while others, such as competitive grading in schools, "make one man's gain another man's loss." Low-synergy intimacy, especially in the lower classes, involves an inability to see relationships as mutually advantageous, "with the conclusion that whoever loves more is a sucker or must get hurt" (p. 114).

Maslow explicitly connected low synergy with social pathology, and high synergy with societal health. He envisioned "a society with psychologically healthy people where there will be less crime, less mental illness, less need for restrictive legislation." He believed that, unlike the antisynergistic society seen as natural by Hobbes and Freud, a high-synergy society could accommodate rather than repress human instincts and "would encourage people to develop their potential for love, cooperation, achievement, and growth" (p. 115). Clearly, many of the arguments I have made regarding synergy and entropy can be traced to a line of thought begun by Benedict and developed by Maslow. Cultural values and individual psychology must count heavily in any adequate account of social, economic, and political phenomena. It is no coincidence that the societal importance of cultural synergy was first made explicit by a cultural anthropologist and a personality psychologist.

In this chapter, I have developed the Benedict-Maslow train of thought even further, with an eye to social transformation. I have focused on the values aspect of synergy, as distinct from the structural and institutional aspects emphasized by Benedict and Maslow, by Adam Smith, and by most progressive activists. I have chosen this focus not because values are more important than social structure and institutions—with which they vitally interact—but because they have been largely ignored by the political left, in part because it has been politically correct to do so. Borrowing from physics, I have reconceived "low synergy" as having a substantive content, *competitive entropy,* in order to emphasize people's active pursuit of values that serve to divide and, in some respects, conquer them. I have suggested that synergistic values comprise an additional Invisible Hand that can correct for the entropic deficiencies of market society that were ignored by Smith's original Invisible Hand and that are sugar-coated by market enthusiasts such as Hayek, Friedman, Nozick, and Charles Erasmus.

Benedict and Maslow see synergistic effects as involving conscious cooperation and as simultaneously benefiting the cooperators. Such synergisms are common, but the Invisible Hand of value synergism captures a broader range of effects that are *unconscious* and *delayed.* Two citizens who are seeking friendship, knowledge, beauty, or craftsmanship may be unaware of each other's strivings, yet in time may come to benefit from

them. The more visible hand of active cooperators imposes higher requirements of communication, kindness, or enlightened self-interest than are required by synergists who in the short run are simply "doing their thing"
while unintentionally serving to create conditions that eventually help their
fellow citizens. Maslow emphasizes that "the society with high synergy is
one in which virtue pays" (Goble 1970: p. 112), a society, in other words,
in which being nice to others redounds to one's own benefit. A synergistic
value, on the other hand, is one that can be pursued self-interestedly and
still have "nice" effects on others.

Capitalism, Communitarianism, and Synergism

How does synergism relate to the communitarian critique of liberalism and
to liberalism's economic sibling, corporate capitalism?

The Neocommunitarian Movement

In the 1990s, a group of mostly U.S. intellectuals appropriated the term
"communitarian" from a movement of practical communitarians dating
back more than three centuries in the United States and including such famous intentional communities as the Shakers, Oneida, the Amana colonies,
and the Hutterites.[37] Today's neocommunitarian movement, as it should
properly be called, was founded in response to Americans' growing exag-
geration of the importance of individual and group rights as opposed to social responsibilities. The original, intentional communitarians have all
along found the balance in this country to be excessively tilted against social responsibility—even from the founding of the republic, if not before.

In an early review of the (neo)communitarian movement, officially
launched in 1991 by sociologist Amitai Etzioni, political scientist William
Galston, law professor Mary Ann Glendon, and other academics, Walter
Shapiro asked whether the emphasis of communitarianism would be on "A
Whole Greater Than Its Parts?"[38] Have these communitarians become the
new synergists? The initial issue of their journal, *The Responsive Community,* stressed that "the rights of individuals must be balanced with responsibilities to the community"—a cliché that admittedly needs repeating. But
an urge to balance rights with duties, autonomy with a moral order, has no
necessary connection with creating a whole greater than the sum of its
parts, or with the social benefits of cultural synergy. In fact, Etzioni's periodic fulminations against the American Civil Liberties Union (ACLU) sound
strictly zero-sum: by according too many rights to criminals, he charges, the
ACLU is taking away the rights of victims and innocent members of society.

In fairness to communitarians, a greater sense of social responsibility
would no doubt moderate the entropic excesses of liberal individualism.

But even John Locke, Adam Smith, and John Stuart Mill recognized the importance of individual responsibility to the community. As Harold Geneen might say, "No synergistic magic there." Brian Stiltner argues that the (neo)communitarian and liberal camps are best combined under the rubric "communal liberalism."[39] Lacking any clear agreement on alternative values and institutions, most communitarians have fallen back on the carrot of moral preachment and the stick of state coercion: "Be more responsible, or else!"

But synergistic values, which some communitarians espouse some of the time, can provide a third alternative. As more citizens pursue synergistic values, fewer of them need to be preached at or jailed, because fewer of them are using their rights and liberties to hurt others. Despite their lack of a transformational alternative, communitarians have had a salutary effect in attacking a number of politically correct shibboleths. For instance, communitarians are willing to call a criminal a criminal, whether white or black, and to argue that U.S. society should consider more dramatic measures to protect the innocent. They also recognize the importance of strong families, even when parental responsibilities conflict with careerism, and they target the left's weakness in addressing the forces that are swamping families and undermining parental authority.

But it is not enough to say that the community is important. Progressives need to address what values the community is based on, is going to stand for, and is going to foster in its members. Indeed, as Etzioni (1996: p. 89) stresses, "The question of what the society considers good and how it is to be judged cannot be avoided." But for the most part, he and other communitarians do avoid any systematic answer to just that question. Etzioni's "new golden rule" amounts to little more than the truism that individual autonomy must be balanced by social responsibility. To state that having a moral order is a core communitarian value is to beg the question of what values will comprise this core. At the end of his book, he tags on some "corollary and secondary values" that he deems consistent with autonomy and order: "a measure of social justice," an unspecified degree of equality, "promoting peace," "some feminist values," and "stewardship toward the earth" (pp. 251–252). But he gives little rationale for these particular attachments to his truistic communitarian core.

Most noticeable by its absence is any critique of the entropic values whose pursuit is systematically compromising all of the nice-sounding values he does endorse. For the most part, communitarians seem unaware or unconcerned that they have by default reaffirmed the cultural values of liberal individualism.[40] Civil libertarians, feminists, and others have attacked communitarians as "conservative" for espousing stricter crime control and "family values." The more troubling conservatism of communitarians is their slighting of Americans' unabated struggle for power, wealth, and status—the very ethos that has severely frayed the communities they hope to salvage. Their critique of affirmative action focuses on the individualism of its "rights talk" (Glendon 1991), not the entropic values that rights are used to achieve. It is not only excessive individualism itself, but what individuals are pursuing, that threaten to dissolve our families, neighborhoods, cities, and nation.

In "Compassion and Political Correctness," Geoph Kozeny (1998: p. 80), a voice of the long-time communitarians, could just as well be speaking for Etzioni's neocommunitarians. "What," he asks, "will it take to build a society that empowers and inspires each individual to manifest his or her full potential while also advancing the common good in a way that is sustainable?" While opposing oppression and injustice, Kozeny warns against the blinders of an "us versus them" mentality that could prevent progressives from learning from their opponents. Anticipating my concerns in Chapters 5 and 6, he cautions adults against a "misguided sense of infallibility" that inclines them to disregard the voices of young people. Whether in our families, schools, communities, or "large-scale political struggles, both sides carry the misguided illusion of infallibility" (p. 79).

Popular Commentary on Synergy and Entropy

As implied by the complaints of protocapitalist Harold Geneen, strands of synergism have pervaded contemporary popular culture. Influential fix-it maven and former business professor Stephen Covey (1994, 1997) pushes synergy when he advises millions of his followers on their priorities, and on the habits of effective people and effective families. Effective families, for instance, should think in "win-win" terms of mutual respect and support, and should synergize by using "creative cooperation" to achieve a family whole that is greater than the sum of its parts. Covey (1994: p. 219) believes that "the passion created by shared vision creates synergistic empowerment. It unleashes and combines the energy, talent and capacities of all involved." Covey (1997: p. 174) charges that U.S. society "is literally saturated with win-lose: forced ranking systems, normal distribution schools, competitive athletics, job openings, political contests, beauty contests, television, and lawsuits." But he offers no critique of the political economy that requires this entropic system. The bread of his Franklin Covey Company is thickly buttered by corporate and governmental America, and nowhere does he suggest transformational alternatives to the current system. In a tacit loss-loss addendum to his win-win philosophy, Franklin Covey executives announced plans in 1999 to fire six hundred workers in an effort to reverse recent losses. By accepting the institutional status quo, Covey begs the question of how families (or companies) whose members are pursuing entropic values such as power, wealth, and status can consistently "synergize" their efforts, even internally, let alone with their neighbors.

Another best-selling author, psychologist Mihaly Csikszentmihalyi (1991), makes brief reference to Benedict and Maslow's concept of synergy, referring to their "interesting treatments of the positive integrative effects of culture" (p. 244). He defines a good society as one that minimizes psychic entropy by enabling as many citizens as possible to fulfill their goals. But rather than identify values that might minimize entropy by benefiting both the pursuers and their fellow citizens, he reduces all value pursuits to one, which is allegedly "the foremost goal of every human being," namely "optimal experience," or "flow" (p. 78). Flow is defined as "the state in which people are so involved in an activity that nothing else seems to matter; the experience itself is so enjoyable that people will do it even at great cost, for the sheer sake of doing it" (p. 4). So defined, flow turns out to be as dangerous as it can be wonderful. Far from being as synergistic as the word itself sounds, flow may be highly entropic. "The Athenian *polis,* Roman law, the divinely grounded bureaucracy of China, and the all-encompassing spiritual order of India were successful and lasting examples of how culture can enhance flow—at least for those who were lucky enough to be among the principal players" (p. 81). The "lucky enough" qualifier is quite a zinger, since it excludes the great majority of residents in all four of the exemplary societies he cites. Especially unlucky in these flowing societies were the Greek and Roman slaves, Christians fed to the lions, the lower castes in India, Chinese peasants, and women in all four societies, including the Chinese women whose feet were bound to prevent them from escaping their oppression. Indeed, "Adolf Eichmann, the Nazi who calmly shipped tens of thousands to the gas chambers, was a man for whom the rules of bureaucracy were sacred. He probably experienced flow as he shuffled the intricate schedules of trains, making certain that the scarce rolling stock was available where needed, and that the bodies were transported at the least expense" (p. 231).

Aside from best-selling authors, academia has taken an interest in synergy. What universities need now, according to the Boyer Commission's *Reinventing Undergraduate Education* (1996), is "a synergistic system in which faculty and students are learners and researchers, whose interactions make for a healthy and flourishing intellectual atmosphere" (p. 11). Part of this system involves the "reward structures in the modern research university[, which] need to reflect the synergy of teaching and research" (p. 32). But these synergies are structural, not values-based, as the commission declined to tackle PC-laden issues such as the content of education, the value of the Western canon, and values generally, although multicultural diversity "is a critical element in building community values" (p. 35).

Left-wing curmudgeon Jim Hightower brings us back to the topic of "synergy misappropriated," raised earlier by Geneen (1997), but with the opposite twist: "In practice, what synergy means is that one division of the conglomerate scratches the back of another division, and vice versa. . . . A Disney ad sponsored a show about a Disney theme park, all of it airing on a Disney network. Disney, Disney, Disney. Synergy."[41] We go from a right-wing critique of synergy as mush to a left-wing critique of synergy as conspiracy. But these are both straw synergies, corrupted by energy-sapping entropy. The "synergy" Geneen dislikes saps the energy that corporations need in order to be tough-minded enough to beat out their competitors. The "synergy" Hightower dislikes is corporations' conspiratorial way of avoiding free competition (which might keep them honest) and thereby beating out their competitors.

An authentic strand of synergy is alive in the thought and practice of the original, pre-1991 communitarians: namely, people who live in intentional communities numbering in the thousands across North America and around the world. From the Hutterites of Canada, Montana, and South Dakota, to Twin Oaks in Virginia and The Farm in Tennessee, to the kibbutzim of Israel and eco-villages across the globe, communal residents have long used cooperative economics and consensus decisionmaking to create conditions in which the benefit of each is intended to be the benefit of all. These intentional communities assume that all citizens are imbedded in a community fabric whose strength relies on an ethic of responsibility for the well-being of others. By contrast, Etzioni's postliberal neocommunitarians seem to have discovered community responsibility as an afterthought, as a reaction to the recent excesses of liberal individualism.

Leading members of the Fellowship for Intentional Community, including communal founder Laird Schaub, have recently been attracted to Hunter, Bailey, and Taylor's (1998) system of "co-operacy" as an alternative to autocracy and democracy. Whether in one's community, neighborhood, or workplace, co-operacy seeks consensus through the active involvement of all members or residents, rather than rule by leaders or majorities. It emphasizes the ideals of connectedness and well-being of all the participants, their empowerment through communal interaction, the synergism of institutionally "making music together," the pursuit of universal rather than parochial values, and relations that release rather than waste collective energy. In all of these respects, co-operacy is synergistic.

But the authors of *Co-operacy* explicitly define synergy as "what a team can achieve" (p. 84) if it makes proper distinctions and connections between, for instance, individual energies and group goals. As in the case of Covey's "creative cooperation" and neocommunitarians' ethic of social responsibility, co-operacy's application of synergy is visible and purposive for the synergizers. The Invisible Hand of Synergy goes further, including not only the conscious, cooperative synergism that is in effect the visible tip of an iceberg, but the deeper waters of synergistic pursuits whose reciprocal benefits are not consciously planned but arranged "as if by an invisible hand." The role of planning in this larger ocean of synergism rests in the decisions of socializing authorities about what values to foster in families, schools, workplaces, media, government, and places of worship. Similarly, the role of systemic planning for Smith's economic Invisible Hand lies not in the hands of producers and consumers but in the minds of public officials who define the legal parameters of ownership and market exchange.

A key asset of the Invisible Hands of free markets and synergistic val ues is that they do not rely excessively on social virtues such as rationality, compassion, public spiritedness, and altruism. In the blissful visions of Christians and communists, these virtues abound. In the real world of the present and foreseeable future, synergistic systems would do well to welcome these virtues when proffered but to anticipate them with clear-eyed hope rather than starry-eyed optimism. In works such as Holly Sklar's (1995) *Chaos or Community?* and South End Press Collective's (1998) *Talking About a Revolution,* progressives seem to be moving in a synergistic but also realistic direction. Sklar sees "successful communities and nations [as] greater than the sum of their parts—and not torn apart." She declares, "It is time to envision our nation as a mutually-beneficial community, not a zero-sum game of winners and losers" (p. 176). Her proposals—from all-age social security and workers' rights, to universal health care and environmentally sustainable development—indicate that it will take clear heads and hard work, not politically correct wishful thinking, to realize this vision.

Synergy, Entropy, and Capitalism

Is capitalism the positive-sum, synergistic game imagined by Adam Smith and Harold Geneen? Smith did not use the term and Geneen does not like it, but neither has doubted that the hard-nosed, competitive pursuit of economic self-interest will benefit society much better than will the detailed planning of systemic do-gooders. Depending upon our ideological interests, we could spin out alternative algorithms whereby the material synergies of market efficiency either outscore or underscore the psychological entropies of status lost, of impoverishment, and of powerlessness. But by placing a reasonable value on key costs and benefits seldom included in the calculus of capitalists, progressives can correct for the roseate myopia of capitalist cheerleading while avoiding politically correct distortions of their own.

First, for a culture sown from Judeo-Christian morality and built on the principle of law, it seems reasonable to assign a high cost to the profiteering theft of indigenous lands and destruction of indigenous cultures, acts that have been officially regretted by U.S. courts, which nonetheless refuse to enforce U.S. treaty obligations to the indigenous peoples of North America.[42] Second, for a society in which a large majority favors environmental protection, it seems reasonable to assign a high cost to the relentless environmental destruction, depletion of nonrenewable resources, and health problems wrought by unchecked industrialism at home and abroad (Kay 1998; Brown, Flavin, and French 2000). Third, for a democratic political system justified by the principle of equal voice, it seems reasonable to assign a high cost to wealthy interests' buying of votes through campaign financing, mass advertising, and lobbying, and to the resulting cynicism of Americans toward their political institutions (Nader 1997; Kay 1998).

It is not reasonable to blame capitalism for slavery, racism, sexism, and ageism, all of which preceded it. But it is reasonable, fourth, to charge capitalists with having taken advantage of these historical inequities until it was no longer profitable to do so. One of the reasons why historically legal oppression continues to disadvantage its victims' offspring long after the oppressive laws were overturned is that the rules of capitalist accumulation enable the initially advantaged to multiply their advantages exponentially. The secret to class dominance under capitalism resides less in the market freedoms praised by Adam Smith than in the special laws of ownership that permit some people to profit off the labor of others—and to pass on the resulting wealth to their economic and biological progeny—while claiming with a straight face that success in life is a result of one's own efforts.

Marx was wrong on some important issues, but he was right about the fact that capitalism tends to reduce social relationships to their cash value. When family obligations get in the way of parents striving to "make it" in the marketplace, the needs of children are often neglected. Historically, as marriage itself came to encumber the worker mobility that employers increasingly required, divorce rates skyrocketed. As traditional, precapitalist religious norms of treating others kindly came to threaten profits, the Golden Rule gave way to the Rule of Gold. When the global economy presented large corporations with the choice of patriotic duty versus global profits, most chose profits. U.S.-based multinationals such as Ford, Chrysler, General Motors, Standard Oil, and ITT allowed their German subsidiaries to continue supplying Hitler's armies during World War II, then sought and received reparations from the U.S. government for damage done to the companies' German plants by Allied bombers.[43] Since World War II, U.S.-based oil companies have readily sacrificed U.S. oil independence for increased U.S. reliance on foreign oil because it has been more profitable to the companies than domestic oil.

More subtly, the out-of-sight, out-of-mind treatment of our elderly reflects their loss of market value; as retirees, they become useless as workers and marginal as consumers. The very young, who are costly rather than profitable, are treated even worse than seniors, although the superficially advantageous "youth culture" targets children and their parents for endless consumer purchasing. Developers, who are inconvenienced by solidary communities that resist locally harmful developments, pursue a wide range of tactics to weaken local communities and neighborhoods (Domhoff 1998). In these struggles, they use their political clout, bought with campaign contributions and secured by lobbying, to recruit government to their side in growth-versus-preservation conflicts.

These serious costs of capitalism have misled leftists to fault the market itself, when in fact it is outside ownership of capital, monopolistic restrictions on free markets, governmental subsidies of business, minimal prosecution of corporate criminality, lax environmental laws (Chivian et al. 1993), and a culture of entropy that account for most of the entropic consequences of market society. There are ways in which economic democracy in public and private sectors can minimize the entropic costs while maximizing the synergistic benefits of a market economy. When corporate decisions are made by large shareholders and their managers, these corporations cannot be held accountable either by their workers or by the communities in which operate.

Not many top corporate executives are willing to be as politically incorrect in public as Harold Geneen. Geneen (1997) not only accords business the right but charges it with the duty to toe the bottom line against all competing considerations, no matter how socially valuable or morally praiseworthy they may be. Forgetting that the historical rationale and legal condition for granting corporations limited liability was that the incorporated firms must serve the public interest, he declares, "The business of business is business. But a lot of people don't understand that simple concept. Business, they say, must be 'socially responsible.' What blather. Management's first duty is to satisfy shareholders" (p. 161). In peeling off layers of corporate rationalization, Geneen lays bare the dangers of outside ownership of capital. In debunking do-gooder executives who kowtow to the pressures of political correctness, he advises that management "shouldn't take a position on the controversial social and moral issues of the day without the consent of its owners" (p. 162).

In other words, any corporate policies that might promote clean air, the stewardship of the earth, food for the hungry, fairness to workers and their families, elimination of racism and sexism, good government, reduced corporate corruption, and the prevention of war should be subject to veto by stockholders whose overriding interest is profit. With Dickensian overtones, Geneen skewers the hypocrisy of corporate "charity": "The big to-do that many companies make, often around Christmastime, about giving a portion of their sales or profits to charity is so much humbug. They're doing no such thing. What they're doing is a cute kind of advertising" (p. 162). Indeed, he portrays as a sham some corporations' endorsement of synergistic values such as love, community, kindness, and charity. In December 1995, American Express showcased its holiday philanthropy around the theme "Take the time out to love someone," while Chemical Bank sponsored a Radio City benefit for poor children. Geneen's response: "It was all very touching. And very phony. You can hardly walk into a shop these days without getting hit over the head with corporate America's civic-mindedness" (pp. 162–163).

Even if Geneen is being a little hard on his capitalist brethren, both logic and evidence indicate that when push comes to shove, investor-owned companies seldom sacrifice much profit or market control for communitarian, humanitarian, or ecological purposes. Regarding corporate contributions to the Rain Forest Fund, Geneen says that "you can bet that if their contributions were significant enough to put them at a cost disadvantage [relative] to their competitors . . . they'd cut the program in a second" (p. 163). He has good reason to dismiss pseudo-synergistic corporate posturing. But he cannot simply decree into being a market economy whose participants exclusively value wealth, power, and status. While he may know his corporate comrades well, he shows little understanding of the rich variety of values that can motivate ordinary workers, consumers, families, and citizens.

Conclusion: Values as a Blind Spot of the Left

Values should be the Achilles' heel of the right. Instead, they have become a blind spot of the left. Progressives have hesitated to argue for the importance of values in social transformation, especially values with traditional or conservative overtones, such as public order, personal discipline, social responsibility, and commitment to family. Implicitly, leftists have continued to harbor utopian hopes for an enlightened and altruistic citizenry capable of noble self-sacrifice, public-spiritedness, social cooperation, and rational planning. They seem less aware that more mundane, less heroic pursuits of a synergistic nature might promote progressive ends more reliably than the politically correct vision and fervor they have long promoted.

Commentators on "the pure, venomous voices of America's culture wars," intensified by the Clinton impeachment proceedings, may be missing the point, or at best scratching the surface. "Echoing views held by many observers, [Theodore] Roszak says the right fundamentally won the political war, given the dominance of conservative policies today. But the left won the key cultural battles over issues such as sexual freedom and tolerance for individual lifestyles."[44] But in a society whose members feel pressed each morning to gird up their loins for another day of getting ahead, these "key cultural battles" comprise at most a sideshow. When Americans use their freedoms to prey on others while "tolerating" lifestyles of conquest and defeat, any cultural victory of the left over social conservatism rings hollow.

I have criticized certain utopian tendencies of the traditional left and its often unspoken spiritual allies. Nevertheless, I confess to hoping and sometimes believing that "healthy, well-functioning human beings have a basic and pervasive need to transcend themselves; that is, to identify themselves as a part of larger, ongoing, and enduring processes, projects, institutions, and ideologies."[45] And I confess to sympathy with the notion that "the communion with the whole human family and of all beings is as rational as it is indispensable. A mystical bond with all other beings is one which alone secures the sense of belonging, without which we remain aimless and lost."[46] But the beauty of the Invisible Hand of Synergy is that it benefits from such sublime intimations to the degree they are correct, but does not throw itself up in despair if they prove less forceful than their partisans anticipated.

Notes

1. Quoted in Calvin Trillin, *Remembering Denny* (New York: Warner Books, 1993), p. 50.

2. Commencement address, Cambridge, Massachusetts, May 1997.

3. Franklin Delano Roosevelt, 1932 Commonwealth Club Address, in Dolbeare (1998: p. 463).

4. *Washington Post,* August 3, 1999.

5. Smith was as politically incorrect among traditionalists in his own day as he is among U.S. progressives today. Nevertheless, notes Robert Heilbroner, "Smith is not, as is commonly supposed, an apologist for the up-and-coming bourgeois." Rather, "he is an admirer of their work but suspicious of their motives, and mindful of the needs of the great laboring mass." *The Worldly Philosophers,* 3rd ed. (New York: Clarion, 1967), p. 48.

6. From the *Theory of Moral Sentiments,* quoted in Heilbroner, ibid., p. 66.

7. Of course, entropic industrialism has made even clean air and usable topsoil scarce and costly.

8. Mao condemned Beethoven's music for its "bourgeois decadence." Stalin outlawed the music of Shostakovich, Prokofiev, and Khachaturian for their "formalistic perversions."

9. State socialism does not avoid this exchange. The socialist state in effect tells producers and consumers what price they must "agree" on, as well as what quantities are to be supplied at that price. If the official price is too high, rogue producers or corrupt middlemen will offer the good at a lower price on the black market. If the official price is too low, artificial scarcities will develop, often because producers are being underpaid and respond by slacking off. In either case, the state enterprise is likely to operate at a loss, which must be paid for by, in effect, taxing more productive enterprises.

10. The entropic effects of ecologically unsustainable growth is a topic of Chapter 8.

11. Of course, sour grapes don't count as synergy.

12. Patricia Nelson Limerick, "A Hard Look at Heroes: Measure by Heroic Moments," *Denver Post,* June 7, 1998.

13. W.E.B. Dubois, *The Souls of Black Folk* (Chicago: A.C. McClurg, 1903), excerpted in Dolbeare (1998: p. 382).

14. Mark Dowie, "Pinto Madness," *Mother Jones,* September-October 1977, pp. 18–32.

15. "Capitalism turns everything into commodities, and the power inequalities change wives and children into property, thus perverting loving relationships." Lois Rita Helmbold and Amber Hollibaugh, "The Family: What Holds Us, What Hurts Us" (1983: p. 191).

16. Quoted by Helmbold and Hollibaugh (1983: p. 196).

17. August 28, 1998.

18. Robert Reich, quoted in Freidan (1997: p. 27).

19. 1998 Roper Starch Worldwide survey of 1,000 *Newsweek* readers. U.S. Census Bureau reports show no significant improvement in the conditions of the nation's poorest quintile in the 1990s.

20. The costliness of an all-consuming value, even a synergistic one, is analogous to Etzioni's (1996: pp. 35–45) "inverting symbiosis," whereby excessive liberty, like excessive morality, undermines itself.

21. Mari Matsuda et al., *Words That Wound* (Boulder, CO: Westview, 1993).

22. Robert Nozick, *Anarchy, State, and Utopia* (London: Basil Blackwell, 1974).

23. Ecocide is unjust because it unfairly subordinates the well-being of all other species to that of humans, and because it arbitrarily restricts the liberties of other species.

24. Michael Walzer, *Spheres of Justice* (New York: Basic Books, 1983), p. 313.

25. Ann M. Simmons, "Ghanaian Practice Under Fire: System Enslaves Women," *Los Angeles Times,* July 22, 1999.

26. Synergists thus defy George Will's notion that "talk of values," being relativistic, "should be abandoned" and replaced by "talk of virtues," which are absolute. George Will, Commencement Address, Lafayette College, May 28, 2000.

27. In class simulations, my students' verdict on politically correct antidotes to Monopoly like Anti-Monopoly and Bertell Ollmann's Class Struggle is: B-O-R-I-N-G. Once again, paradise lost proves more interesting than paradise regained.

28. Commercialized sports may also, of course, entail a great deal of waste.

29. Deb Riechmann, "Island Spellers Stung by Change in Rules," Associated Press, January 13, 1999.

30. Jim Robbins, "Arsonists Try to Drive Out Hutterite Families: Peaceful Sect Starting New Montana Colony," *New York Times,* April 16, 1998.

31. Robert Byrne, *1,911 Best Things Anybody Ever Said* (New York: Fawcett Columbine, 1988), pp. 338–339.

32. Marcia Davis, "The Red and the Black: An Emerging Black Political Movement Looks to the Left," *Utne Reader* 91, January-February 1999, p. 16 (excerpts from earlier articles in *The Nation, In These Times,* and *The Black Scholar*).

33. "Despite his elaborate masquerade of pro-black militancy," charged Manning Marable, "Farrakhan can be best understood as an advocate of Reaganomics and [a] conservative social policy orientation." Quoted in Davis, ibid.

34. Various forms of the word *synergy* have been in scientific use for centuries. In physiology, for instance, "synergic" is defined as "working together, co-operating, as a group of muscles for the production of some movement." *The Oxford English Dictionary* (New York: Oxford University Press, 1971), p. 381.

35. Quoted in Goble (1970: p. 112).

36. "Synergy: Some Notes of Ruth Benedict," *American Anthropologist* 72, April 1970, pp. 320–333, and "Synergy in the Society and the Individual," *Journal of Individual Psychology* 20, 1964, pp. 153–164.

37. See the journal *Communal Societies,* published by the Communal Studies Association, as well as *Communities: Journal of Cooperative Living* and *Communities Directory,* both published by the Fellowship for Intentional Community.

38. Walter Shapiro, "A Whole Greater Than Its Parts?: American Individualism Draws Fire from a New Intellectual Movement That Re-Emphasizes Social Obligation," *Time,* February 25, 1991, p. 71.

39. Brian Stiltner, *Religion and the Common Good: Catholic Contributions to Building Community in a Liberal Society* (Washington, DC: Georgetown University Press, 1999).

40. See, for instance, William Galston, "Value Pluralism and Liberal Political Theory," *American Political Science Review* 93, no. 4, December 1999, pp. 769–778.

41. Jim Hightower, *There's Nothing in the Middle of the Road but Yellow Stripes and Dead Armadillos* (New York: HarperCollins, 1997), p. 140.

42. For documentation of this sordid chapter in U.S. history, contact Glenn Morris, Director, Fourth World Center for the Study of Indigenous Law and Politics, University of Colorado, Denver.

43. Morton Mintz and Jerry S. Cohen, *Power, Inc.* (New York: Bantam, 1976), pp. 293 ff. and 497 ff.

44. Josh Getlin, "Scandal Reveals Cultural Shifts," *Los Angeles Times,* February 8, 1999.

45. Ernest Partridge, "Why Care About the Future?" *Alternative Futures* 3, no. 4, fall 1980, p. 90.

46. Henryk Skolimowski, "Evolutionary Illuminations," *Alternative Futures* 3, no. 4, fall 1980, p. 13.

5

The Missing Child in Transformational Politics

"What power do children themselves have? Right-wing politics resists thinking about rights for children."

—Mary John[1]

"Many fathers in the late 1950s gave up their traditional setting of limits. . . . The children soon saw they had been put into power."

—Robert Bly[2]

"All over the world, children are asking to be heard."

—Craig Kielburger (1999: p. 288)

"Not since Anne Frank has a child so effectively borne witness to the madness of adult reality."

—Kirkus Reviews on Craig Kielburger's *Free the Children*

In the zero-sum culture of entropy, it is first and foremost children who become the losers. Mary John's accurate statement overlooks the fact that left-wing politics also resists thinking about children's rights. Robert Bly's poetic license, so often put to wise use, here mistakes children's abandonment (Bly 1997: p. 132) for their empowerment (pp. 6, 161). In *Free the Children,* sixteen-year-old author and children's-rights activist Craig Kielburger (1999) gives witness to what young people can do when they are forsaken by adults. With the recent surge in school violence, concerned adults have done a great deal of hand-wringing about "the child problem," about "what is so tragically wrong with young people these days." While blaming school cliques, mass media, administrators, permissive parents, godlessness, guns or gunlessness (take your pick), and other bugaboos, the politicians, preachers, pundits, and panderers have all but ignored the issues in our divisive culture of winning and losing, of Americans' collective pursuit of entropic values and its pathological consequences. For reasons not so mysterious, they have also avoided another central issue: the political silencing of young people and its consequences.

Missing Children: An Introduction to Adultism

As revelers rang in the new year of 1998, Judge Michael Mason of Maryland was busy deciding the fate of a youngster named Cornelius.

> The clock is ticking for Cornelius. In a few weeks, this happy 2-year-old will be ripped away from the only mother he's ever known and returned to the care of his birth mother, a 23-year-old twice-convicted felon who killed another of her four children. [Judge Mason] ordered Cornelius removed from the custody of Laura Blankman, the foster mother who is trying to adopt him, and turned him over to Latrena Pixley, the troubled young woman who gave birth to Cornelius while on probation for the murder of her 6-week-old daughter.[3]

The mother, Latrena Pixley, had killed Cornelius's sister Nakya because she was crying from hunger. "A police officer in training, Laura Blankman, whom Pixley had met a few years earlier, felt sorry for Pixley and offered to keep her baby on weekends. Blankman's baby-sitting job quickly evolved into a full-time guardianship" as Pixley continued to get into trouble with the law. "Eventually, Blankman, whom Cornilous [sic] had begun calling 'Mommy,' sought to adopt the boy, and Pixley protested."[4] By court order, Cornelius was to be sent "to a halfway house in dangerous northeast Washington, D.C., a crime-ridden, drug-infested area where his mother temporarily lives because she has no job or other means of support." Columnist Linda Chavez noted: "The case stands as a monument to the cruelty of a system that cares more for preserving the parental rights of dangerous and irresponsible adults than protecting children."[5] The legal battle to determine Cornelius's fate was joined by the child advocacy group Hear My Voice, and in January 2000, Judge Mason's decision was overturned by the Maryland Supreme Court, which awarded Blankman custody of Cornelius.

Other children have not been so lucky. In "Shackled in the Land of Liberty: No Rights for Children," Mohr, Gelles, and Schwartz (1999) show how and why cases like Cornelius's are widespread.[6] "The core ideological value [of the child welfare system] is that children do best when raised by their biological parents. One version of this ideology is the notion that even the best foster or adoptive family is not better for a child than a marginal biological family" (pp. 45–46). Parental rights carry far more clout in the courts than children's rights. Not only has "the child welfare system . . . been in crisis for nearly three decades," but abuses of children by the system have been so numerous and severe that "at least 27 states and many more localities are under court order to improve child welfare services" (p. 47). Despite the Adoption and Safe Families Act of 1997, intended to protect just such children as Cornelius, "children and their 'best interests' are given minimal consideration in child welfare proceedings" (p. 47).

Political correctness is also implicated in the initially perverse ruling on Cornelius: The birth mother and murderess is black; the foster mother and policewoman is white. Some progressives argue, and the government often agrees, that prospective parents should not adopt children of a different race.[7] These progressives take special umbrage at the notion that particular white parents might do a better job of rearing a nonwhite child than the child's nonwhite biological parents.[8] This argument, based on no scientific evidence, dresses up old-time prejudice in the garb of right-on progressivism. In the case of Cornelius, the court initially gave priority to the rights of biological parents and to same-race adoption over the child's well-being.

Similarly, when Texas tried to prevent a white and Native American couple from adopting their two black foster children, on grounds that "it would be in the kids' best interest to place them in an African-American home," it was a *conservative* advocacy group, the Institute of Justice, that helped the multiracial foster parents win a lawsuit after "more than two heart-wrenching years." Contrary to the race-matching guardians of PC, "the few available academic studies have shown that the adopted children grow up well-adjusted and comfortable with their ethnic identity."[9] Some adoptive parents are striking back with lawsuits charging government with racial discrimination against them and their would-be adoptive children.[10]

In fact, political correctness contributes more broadly to the left's general silence on the inequality of rights between adults and children. Lower-class parents tend to deal more harshly with their children than do middle- and upper-class parents.[11] Pleas for the rights of children may therefore offend partisans of the proletariat. Nonwhite parents are more likely than whites to use authoritarian measures, including physical discipline, on their children; to substitute infant formula for breastfeeding; and to subject their children to second-hand cigarette smoke.[12] Health-based arguments against these practices may raise the specter of "racism." The view that very young children do better when at least one parent is at home antagonizes some feminists, who see such thinking as tantamount to imprisoning mothers at home who would rather be in the (paid) workplace.[13] Like childless employees who feel put upon by parental leave, gay activists who address family issues usually focus on the rights of adult gay partners.[14] In short, the well-being of children takes a backseat to more salient concerns of many otherwise progressive groups.

It seems natural to most adults—left, center, and right—that along with their greater responsibilities, they should also have more rights than children. There is no denying that children, on average, have less knowledge and experience than their elders, or that infants come into the world totally dependent on their elders. In addition, most adults believe that age confers wisdom, that adults know what is best for children, and that adults generally take good care of children. To adults, age-based restrictions seem well-intended and sensible. What, after all, is arbitrary about allowing sixteen-year-olds, but not three-year-olds, to drive a car? What is capricious about laws that would prohibit an eight-year-old from deciding how the family budget should be spent? Aren't grade-schoolers protected by laws that prohibit them from drinking hard liquor or having consensual sex with their parents' adult friends? Shouldn't young people be protected from a forty-hour work week at wage labor? Don't youth curfews help keep teenagers out of harm's way? And wouldn't enfranchised ten-year-olds either vote the way their parents told them to, or, alternatively, vote for unlimited cartoons, candy, and recess? Isn't it true, after all, that elders know best?

Because most adults, even progressive adults, when they ask these questions, do so rhetorically rather than seriously, the assumptions underlying them are seldom questioned. Liberal, socialist, and, more recently, transformational perspectives on social policies and social change typically subsume children under the demographics of their parents—as poor children, children of color, children parented by a single mother, or children from certain kinds of families or geographical areas. When children are singled out for political attention by progressives, it is because they are viewed as needing help from sympathetic adults who can and should reshape public policy to treat them better. What is missing in transformational theory and practice is young people as political actors with voices of their own. Indeed, pioneering cases of actual or potential youth empowerment, such as Free the Children and Kids Voting USA, have come under the shadow of criticism by observers such as Neil Postman (1994), whose book *The Disappearance of Childhood* argues that today's society is making children grow up too quickly.

This chapter looks more closely at the assumptions underlying age-based differences in rights and responsibilities, and offers evidence that calls these assumptions into question. A key issue concerns what the average differences among people of different ages imply, legally and politically. If close scrutiny reveals many age criteria to be not only arbitrary but detrimental to young people, we may speak of the problem of *adultism*—a form of ageism that afflicts and demeans young people.

In *The Missing Child in Liberal Theory,* John O'Neill (1994) refers to "the political issue of *child mutism*," noting that "the child's experience of justice and care is determined by its unequal relations with adults and elder children" (p. 46). O'Neill shows why liberal theory, with its assumption of atomized, marketable individualists, does not and cannot deal coherently with families or their dependent children. He credits Pateman (1988) with showing that "contract theorists from Hobbes to Rawls have assumed that the child is entirely in the power of its male parent" (p. 40). In Elshtain's (1982: p. 289) characterization: "Children have been the companions of women in the closet of political science. . . . Children remain both silent and invisible"—and much more so than women, I would add.

It may not be surprising that adult liberals, contract theorists, and political scientists would overlook the issue of children's rights and the very notion of children's oppression as a class. But it is disappointing that so few transformationalists do any better, especially when we consider (in Chapter 6) evidence that young people constitute the largest severely oppressed class in the world. If social transformation were to mean fewer wars, reduced crime, less starvation and malnutrition, better care for the planet, less family violence, fewer broken homes, more sustainable economies, and better health care, no group would benefit more than children. If nobody needs social transformation more than young people, it would behoove progressives to start paying more attention to the plight of young people, especially if allowing their active involvement might strengthen the forces of transformation.

Of the interest groups that do pay attention to children's problems, how well do they represent the interests of the children they purport to help? One of the best recent critiques of adult interest groups as biased representatives of the interests of children is Cathy M. Johnson's "Who Speaks for Children? Representation in the Policy Process" (1994). She examines the arguments made by an array of groups during congressional hearings on the Family and Medical Leave Act in 1993, the adoption of child-care grants and tax credits in 1990, and discussions about work versus welfare surrounding the Family Support Act in 1988. All of the interest groups claimed to be prochild and profamily. But Johnson documents the consistent subsuming of children's interests under those of the testifying adult groups.

> While numerous groups testified and many of them profess to represent children, most of them organized around the interests of another constituency, for example, labor, women's rights, civil rights, religious organizations, health professions, charitable institutions. Even organizations oriented around children tend to have some other interest important to their existence. For most groups this is an occupation—nurses, educators, pediatrics, child care—that is likely to influence . . . the positions they take. (p. 3)

Although liberals opposed welfare reform's mandatory work requirements for mothers with small children, their effectiveness suffered from a lack of any "policy theory about children on which to hang their opposition to mandatory participation" (p. 25). Johnson found the adult interest groups' arguments in the policy debates about children to be predictable on the basis of the adult interest at stake. "Groups see children's interests through the prism of their own needs" (p. 25). She calls for "new and creative ideas" to overcome this unsatisfactory representation of children's interests by adults. But she explicitly rejects giving young people a political voice of their own: "Because we do not expect or trust children to voice their own needs and wants, we need to come up with some other way to identify what is in children's interests" (p. 26). In short, the new and creative ideas will continue to be paternalistic—or maternalistic.

The Political Construction
of Childhood Versus Adulthood

Philippe Ariès's classic work *Centuries of Childhood* (1962) showed that the very concept of childhood as a radically distinct status from adulthood is a cultural construction developed only recently in Western history. Even today, cultures vary dramatically regarding the typical rupture, if any, between childhood and adulthood.[15] Stephanie Coontz (1997) speaks of three stages in the Western evolution of "childhood." For a long period of time, young people were socially included along with adults in both knowledge and participation. Then they were excluded in both areas—the situation we are most familiar with. But "now, we try to exclude them from participation, but we're unable to exclude them from knowledge. It's the most pathological situation you can get." Along with Postman (1994), Coontz and others worry about the harmful effects of children growing up too fast. "We have been blurring the boundaries between childhood and adulthood for some time in all the different realms of life," says Kiku Adatto, head of Harvard's Children's Studies Program, ignoring the crystal clarity of adults' official political monopoly.[16] Chapter 6 in this book asks whether any benefits from enfranchising minors would be more than offset by the ill effects of pressuring children into shouldering responsibilities prematurely.

In addition to a broad cultural construction of the distinction adult-versus-child, there is a more specifically political construction. In asking how in modern times one person gets designated an "adult" and another a "child," we might recall psychiatrist R. D. Laing's similar question about the distinction "sane" versus "insane." An "insane" or "abnormal" person is someone markedly different from those with the legal power to assign psychiatric labels, who naturally consider themselves sane and normal. For instance, homosexuality was long defined, by heterosexual psychiatrists with the power to do so, as a psychological disorder. A similar situation exists with respect to race. Why were Americans with a single African grandparent, or even great-grandparent, legally defined as black? ("Those black genes must be mighty powerful," quips comedian Dick Gregory.) The historical answer is that those with the legal power to label, namely whites, decided so. Similarly, a "gentile" to an orthodox Jew or Mormon is someone different enough from them to be defined by them as "other," or "outsider."

Similarly, a "child" is someone sufficiently younger than those doing the legal defining, namely self-defined "adults," as to be considered less than adult and thus undeserving of the rights and privileges of adults. Adults view this distinction as natural and benign, intended to ensure the proper care of dependents. Like most privileged groups, adults consider their privilege justifiable because it is ostensibly beneficial to those they have subordinated. Men are to look out for their women; masters, for their slaves; believers, for infidels (by converting them); adults, for children.

Progressives advance many arguments about how their new policies and institutions will benefit all classes and groups, including children. But, as exemplified by Cathy Johnson (1994), they say little about the transformational possibilities of young people speaking, acting, and deciding for themselves. Progressives may well be less authoritarian than conservatives in their child-rearing practices, just as they are more environmentally friendly than conservatives. In these arenas, they are satirized by the right as politically correct permissivists and tree-huggers. Because they feel more enlightened than conservatives on these issues, they seem willing to rest on their laurels and ignore the possibility that far from being "too radical" regarding children and ecology (as the conservatives charge), in fact they are not radical enough.[17] That is, if they wish to be transformational rather than merely reformist.

Age as an Apparently Benign Criterion of Rights and Responsibilities

Adults' belief in their own wisdom, guidance, and beneficence runs consistently across the ideological spectrum. Notwithstanding the disproportionate suffering of children under the stewardship of adults (Chapter 6), to most adults these beliefs are not only plausible—they are an article of unquestioned faith. A good example is the *San Francisco Chronicle*'s editorial complaint of November 14, 1991, against an unusual crack in the wall of political adultism:

> It may well be, as some have contended, that Paul Kim, a 16-year-old senior at Grace M. Davis High School in Modesto, is the brightest member of the state Board of Education. But it is not reasonable that someone his age should have the authority to vote to spend $170,000 in public funds. As it happened, Kim turned out to be the decisive vote to authorize the board to hire a private lawyer to sue state Superintendent of Public Instruction Bill Honig in an effort to wrest greater control over the state's educational policy [an effort the *Chronicle* opposed].

Why, we might ask, was Kim's right to vote unreasonable? The editors, confident that their "reasoning" was self-evident, never bothered to explain it. A *Denver Post* editorial of February 25, 1992, admits: "Teenagers are right. It's hypocritical for the state to permit them to buy a car at 16, and to cast a ballot at 18, while telling them they won't be trusted with a beer until they're 21. But unfair as this may be, it's the law." Adults prevail; end of debate.

Perhaps the rudiments of critical argumentation atrophy with ageism, though not necessarily with age. The *Chronicle* and *Post* unintentionally remind us of Freud's (1927: pp. 77–78) lament regarding "the depressing contrast between the radiant intelligence of a healthy child and the feeble intellectual powers of the average adult." Goethe went even further: "If children grew up according to early indications, we should have nothing but geniuses." It seems likely that the way adults treat children may stunt children's radiance and genius. Before automatically embracing adultist assumptions, let us look at some cases of unusual young people in action.

"Precocious" Children

When fifteen-year-old Chelsea Clinton accompanied her mother on a tour of India and Pakistan in 1995, she declined invitations to "kiddie" events, preferring instead to participate in the same activities as the First Lady. Molly Moore of the *Washington Post* noted the importance of the First Child's "symbolic role: A young woman with a bright future standing before young South Asian women who may not be allowed to finish school because they are needed at home, who will be married off at a young age to boys they have never met and who face lives of drudgery and misery." Moore reports that Chelsea "appeared at ease sitting amid a crowd of about 250 impoverished women—ragpickers, vegetable vendors and garment makers—during a visit to a branch of the Self-Employed Women's Association, a union of poor working women."[18]

On this trip, administration officials were taken aback by Chelsea's insistence on doing "adult" things—but insist she did. (In her youthful activism, Chelsea may have been following in the footsteps of her father. "The president said he was only 9 when [civil-rights pioneer Rosa] Parks refused to stand up. He and his friends 'couldn't figure out anything we could do since we couldn't even vote. So we began to sit in the back of the bus when we got on.'"[19]) It is hard to say what impact Chelsea may have had on future choices made by young women who saw her, but "throughout Pakistan and India, young women have related enthusiastically to Chelsea as they accompany her through their schools, villages and homes."[20] Feminist scholars of South Asia have recently reported on the dramatic effect discrepant role models are having in opening Asian women's eyes to choices they never thought they had, and in inspiring them to rebel against arbitrary limitations on their choices.[21]

"So what?" an adultist critic might retort. "Chelsea Clinton was hardly a typical fifteen-year-old." One could say the same thing with even more force about young Mozart, who began composing music at the age of five; about John Stuart Mill, who edited his famous father's political-economy manuscripts at age eight; about mathematician John von Neumann, who "could divide eight-digit numbers in his head by age six"[22]; or about Jean Piaget, who published his first scientific article at age ten. Famous people are never "typical," but there is no dearth of less celebrated examples, including young composers such as Ashley Meagher (ten),[23] authors Mike Joyer (ten) and Zach Robert (eleven),[24] painter Alexandra Nechita (ten),[25] high-energy-physicist Natalia Toro (fourteen),[26] and mathematician Sarah Flannery (sixteen). [27] Nechita's paintings sell for $50,000 each to celebrities such as comedian Ellen DeGeneres and businessman Lee Iacocca, and Flannery's new e-mail code increased e-mail speeds by a factor of ten. Katie Shaughnessy, sixteen, is one of many teens hired by Nintendo as telephone troubleshooters to help befuddled adults beat problems they're having with their new Nintendo games. Here is a typical interaction with a customer:

> Customer: "I've pressed every button on my TV set and my cable converter trying to get this thing to work. I set it to Channel 3, then I set it to Channel 4—nothing." [Two children are wailing in the background that they want to play the game—now.]
> Katie: "M'am, I'd like you to try setting it to Channel 2." [She speaks with the calm, impassive voice of an air traffic controller.] "Now do you see where it says 'input' on your remote control? Press that. Anything? No? OK, press it again."
> Customer: [After a pause] "Wait! Hey, there it is! Wow, it's on. Hey, kids, it's working! Hey, thanks!"

"It's fun when you can help people," says Katie. "It's, like, 'Cool! I can fix somebody's problem.'" Her teen colleague Daniel Wells is asked why, unlike adult new owners of Nintendo, he and his friends never have any problems with it. His disarming reply: "Maybe we're just more, you know, advanced." What Aaron Barton likes best about the job is that adults are turning to him for advice: "Here I feel like I'm really getting treated like an adult."[28]

An Iceberg's Tip of Other Exceptional Children

Let us momentarily set aside the issue of *political* maturity and focus simply on the issue of maturity—and its purported link to age. We might create an acronym to dub the conventional view the KRRESI (pronounced "cr-razy") theory, which assumes that adults are automatically superior in the KRRESI virtues of Knowledge, Rationality, Responsibility, Experience, Selflessness, and Intelligence. The theory holds that because young people have small brains, a dearth of experience, and negligible consciences, they should forfeit a variety of rights that adults enjoy. Even if we ignore the likelihood that billions of adults may also lack these virtues and thus be exceptions to the rule of adult superiority, many children are clear exceptions to it.

Kids Flying

It is common knowledge that millions of young Americans easily defeat their elders at video games, mostly because of their greater "time on task" than Mom and Dad.[29] Less common is our knowledge of the large number of young people who are skilled pilots of real airplanes, including interstate pilots Thad Mitchell (fifteen), John Kevin Hill (eleven), Tony Alienga (eleven), Victoria Van Meter (eleven), Christopher Lee Marshall (ten), Erik Fiederer (ten), Elliot Shoup (nine), Rachel Carter (nine), Killian Moss (eight), Bill Morency (eight), and Daniel Shanklin (seven). In the aftermath of the 1996 fatal crash on takeoff of a plane piloted by seven-year-old Jessica Dubroff, a hue and cry arose to ban child pilots. For instance, Congressman John Duncan Jr. (R-Tennessee), chairman of the U.S. House Aviation Subcommittee, proposed legislation to prevent anyone so young from piloting an airplane, saying, "I think it is a crime that a 7-year-old was allowed to fly this plane."[30]

This adultist legislation failed, largely because young pilots, their instructors, and their parents revealed the illogic underlying proponents' arguments. Most important was the lack of evidence that Jessica's young age had contributed to the crash. The immediate cause of the tragedy was a sudden wind shear whose fatal effects could probably not have been prevented by even the most skilled of adult pilots. Of course, the crash could have been prevented had the relevant adults, Jessica's parents and her flight instructor, wisely chosen to delay the takeoff because weather conditions were ominous.[31] No one suggested that the three adults' poor decision showed that adults should be banned from making such decisions. Advocates for an age restriction on flying failed to cite any studies showing higher-than-average crash statistics for young pilots. It is interesting to recall eleven-year-old Tony Alienga's flight around the world in 1989, during which there was also a crash (with minor injuries only), which occurred when the boy's father was at the controls to give his son a rest. No one used this crash to suggest that thirty-something fathers should be banned from flying.

Kids Dying

On my son's first birthday, August 21, 1994, I read about the death of fifteen-year-old Bennie Agrela, who had undergone two liver transplants and decided he could no longer stand the horrendous side effects of his antirejection medication. When Agrela had first stopped taking the drugs, he was removed from his home by the Florida Department of Health and Rehabilitative Services and forced to take the medication. He went to court to seek the right to return home on his own terms, and his testimony proved so powerful that Circuit Judge Arthur Birken overruled the state, permitting Agrela to go home to die. "He went in a very good way. We're very happy," Agrela's sister told the *Fort Lauderdale Sun-Sentinel*. He didn't complain of any pain." Early that morning, "Agrela opened his eyes and called out to his mother, who had kept a bedside vigil. He raised his arms and said, 'Mami, hug.' The two embraced. Agrela smiled and took in his last breath." Prior to Judge Birken's intervention, the authorities had determined that Bennie's age disqualified him from knowing or deciding what was best for himself.[32]

Kids Saving Others from Dying

"Girl Hikes Desert to Save Family" is a story that can be multiplied thousands of times about children who act decisively and courageously in times of great peril to themselves and their loved ones. This thirteen-year-old "hiked nearly twenty miles through the Mohave Desert to find help for her stranded family." She was able to direct Edwards Air Force Base personnel to her mother and twenty-two-month-old brother. The family's ordeal had begun when the car ran out of gas.[33] In Darwin, Australia, five-year-old Paul Harrington saved his eight-year-old sister's life by grabbing the tail of a crocodile that was dragging her into the water. The distracted reptile dropped the girl, whose father killed it with an ax.[34]

In preparation for becoming a baby-sitter, twelve-year-old Aviva Landie took a first aid course—and learned enough to later save the life of four-year-old Gabe Levin, who was choking on a jelly-and cheese-covered Passover cracker.[35] When an eleven-year-old boy from Colorado City, Colorado, saw his three-year-old sister choking on a pea pod, he saved her life with the Heimlich manuever he had learned from a television show. Similarly, ten-year-old Michael Short used the Heimlich maneuver he had learned in Cub Scouts to save the life of his eight-year-old sister, who was choking on ice. Five-year-old Brandon Newberg learned the Heimlich manuever while watching *Rescue 911* and used it to save the life of his three-year-old brother, who was choking on a quarter.[36]

Touchingly, if less dramatically, professional football star Chris Zorich reports on one of the myriad ways in which young people respond to his various programs to help the needy and dying: "I was walking down the street and this 7- or 8-year-old kid comes up and has a dollar bill in his hand and gives it to me [and says,] 'I don't want your autograph, I want you to give this to the kids you help.'"[37] In recent years, postal workers at Christmas sadly report an increasing incidence of children's letters to Santa Claus asking not for toys but for food and clothing, often for other family members. A Chicago youngster, for instance, asked for "boots and gloves for my brothers so they can go to school warm."[38]

Although young people's repertoire of compassionate behavior typically expands as they develop, incidents such as the following suggest that it is fruitless to draw any age line for the earliest possible appearance of feelings of responsibility for the well-being of others. This headline made me think of my own children, who were a few months younger than these children: "2-Year-Old Cares for Baby Sister for 2 Days After Mom Dies."

> For two days after his mother died in their apartment, 2-year-old Thomas Hubbard fed his baby sister cereal and took care of her, not letting in the new babysitter because she was a stranger. Through the door, he told her his mommy was sleeping. . . . While his mother lay dead, Thomas, nick-named 'Tray,' watched over his 1-and-a-half-year-old sister, Kiana. He couldn't get milk for her because [his mother] had put child locks on the refrigerator door, so he fed her cold cereal and crackers, family members said. . . . Thomas, who turns three in April, also knew Kiana was wet, but could only stuff toilet paper in her diaper.[39]

Toddler Tray's resourcefulness and concern for his sister helped both of them survive. In April 2000, this feat was exceeded by two-year-old Linda Hoell, who cared for her fourteen-month-old sister, Arianna, for three days after their father died in Norfolk, Virginia.

Kids Just Dying to Help Out

Fifteen-year-old Justin Thran's long-time philanthropic activities began ten years earlier, when his father drove him by a cemetery during a burial for a man who had died of a heart attack, leaving four children. "What are they going to do for Christmas?" the five-year-old had asked. Learning that a local church was taking donations, Justin decided to contribute an armful of his favorite toys. At ten, he wrote a school essay making a wish to Santa. "I made a wish that no one would go hungry," he said. Since that time, he has built birdhouses with the help of his carpenter father, selling them and donating the thousands of dollars of proceeds to a food bank and other charities.

Children sometimes make sacrifices for their pets and other animals. Seven-year-old Juliette Harris was bitten by a bear cub she had found in the woods. State health officials said the cub would have to be killed to determine whether it had rabies, which would require Juliette to get rabies shots. But Juliette offered to take the seven shots without knowing the diagnosis—each with a five-inch needle—in order to save the cub's life. "I just didn't want that cute baby bear to die," she said.[40] Seven- and eleven-year-olds Cutter and Tanner Holt gave their life savings of almost $150 to a shelter for homeless dogs and cats. "We had all this money and we have enough stuff in our room," said Tanner. "We didn't want to waste it on other electronics."[41] In recent years, the federal government has been recognizing dozens of heroic children as "safety stars" by inviting them to make an appearance on Capitol Hill.

Kids with Brains to Die For

Some children are embarrassingly more intelligent and knowledgeable than many adults. Avi Ben-Abraham, the real-life model for television's *Doogie Howser, M.D.*, could read and write at age two and earned a medical degree at age eighteen—a world record.[42] This feat inspired Balamurati Krishna Ambati, who had mastered calculus at age four, to enter New York University on a full scholarship as a premedical student at age eleven in an effort to get his M.D. by age seventeen. NYU's director of scholarships was criticized for favoring the young prodigy, and replied, "What if we had told Mozart that he was too precocious?" To adults who had accused Ambati of caring only about breaking Ben-Abraham's record, the eleven-year-old countered that his experience of being burned by scalding water at age three had piqued his interest in pursuing a medical degree: "After that," he said, "I started to think about assuaging human suffering." [43]

Both of these records may well fall to Masoud Karkehabadi, who began college at age nine, transferring to the University of California, Irvine, at ten. "I want to be a brain surgeon," said the ten-year-old, "because the brain is the least-understood organ, and I want to be able to find the cure for Alzheimer's because I want to use my gift to help society." He had read newspapers at age four, easily reciting everything he read. "Two years later, when his aunt was having trouble with an obstetrics class required for a nursing degree, Masoud picked up her textbook, read it, explained it to her and helped her pass the class." As a nine-year-old college student, Masoud won over some initially hostile, much older classmates by tutoring them in algebra and anatomy. His father, Mike, describes himself as having been selfish at age nine and ten, "but Masoud is so in love with people. He has such a big heart, he wants to help everyone."[44]

Multiple world record holder Michael Kearney has nothing to fear from such competition. "Just like other kids" in his own eyes but "severely gifted" according to experts, Kearney graduated from high school at age six, got his B.A. at ten, and received his M.A. in biochemistry at fourteen. He had been speaking in complete sentences from age six months and could read soup can labels at fourteen months. "From the start," says his father, "it appeared to [his mother] Cassidy and me that when Michael was not allowed to learn new things he was actually in pain." So his parents taught him at home through high school. In no hurry to finish his Ph.D. in record time, he decided to take a break before starting doctoral studies at Berkeley or Purdue.[45]

Political Children at the Grass Roots

The preceding cases are but a small sampling of the millions of unusually talented and conscientious young people. But what do children's sheer IQ, artistic or literary talent, and early compassion have to do with their under-standing of public issues? What do precocious brains have to do with po-litical participation? Logically, they have a great deal to do with it, because they refute the notion that the politically important KRRESI virtues, in-cluding knowledge, responsibility, and experience, are rare or nonexistent in children. And in fact, children exhibit their political energy and insight on a daily basis, despite formal disfranchisement by adultist legal systems. As social problems intensify but adults become less involved in politics, in-creased participation by young people is taking up some of the slack. Let us look at some examples of politicized young people.

Age-Based Differences in Political Attitudes

Before we examine cases of young political activists, what can we say in general about children's political attitudes? Despite the strong influence parents have on their children's political thinking—an influence that con-tinues into adulthood—children worldwide differ from their elders on some vital political issues. A wide variety of opinion polls and cross-national re-search, as well as numerous parallel voting systems (as in Costa Rica, as well as dozens of states in the United States, where Kids Voting USA al-lows children to cast nonbinding votes along with adults), suggest that on many issues children as a class are more progressive than adults.[46] Chil-dren, more than adults, favor environmental protection, diplomacy over militarism, gun control, alternatives to corporal punishment, compassionate social programs, public aid to education, funding of academics over athlet-ics, drug-rehabilitation programs, protection of free speech and artistic expression, equal rights for gays and lesbians, sex-education and condom-distribution programs, national health insurance, and governmental invest-ment in public amenities such as parks, libraries, and museums.

Skeptics might argue that these children's preferences are based on naively idealistic assumptions—a charge made by adult conservatives against adult progressives with these same preferences. Regarding environ-mental protection, EPA head Carol Browner suggested a different interpre-tation: "Kids fundamentally get it," she says. "Why would you hurt your environment? Why would you hurt the place that you live in?"[47] Children have not yet learned from adults that more is better, that growth is more im-portant than stewardship, that economic growth should trump ecological re-sponsibility. Similarly, is it naivety or realism that makes kids more antiwar than adults? When schoolchildren were asked in 1991 why the United States was bombing Iraq, some of them said that the United States was try-ing to liberate Kuwait, but "overwhelmingly they said we are fighting for oil." Many of the children found the U.S. attack on Iraq to contradict adults' teaching that fighting is the wrong way to solve conflicts.[48] Perhaps the greatest political resource offered by young people is that they are less jaded and less prone to self-fulfilling prophesies of political pessimism than adults (Kozeny 1998: p. 79).

In the area of religious, ethnic, and racial prejudice, not only are children less biased than adults, but this average difference is greater, the younger the child. Young children seem to have no concept of racial difference until they are taught one. Indeed, until my own children were introduced in school to the concept of race on Martin Luther King's birthday, neither my wife nor I had ever heard them use skin color to describe their racially varied playmates. As Lieutenant Cable sings in *South Pacific*, "You've got to be carefully taught to hate and fear."[49] Although children are capable of pettiness and cruelty, they have not yet imbibed the full potion of adult lore on the inferiority of other races and cultures or the superiority of one's own true religion as compared to other, false ones. Children "naively" accept one another despite racial or ethnic differences—until adults teach them otherwise.

> In 1990, Arizonans approved a holiday to honor Martin Luther King, by a 3-1 margin. This is not a misprint. The catch: the ballots didn't count. The people casting them, all participants in the Kids Voting program, were under eighteen. While the state's "real" electorate defeated the King referendum and a school-funding issue, children approved both, though they knew that King Day would simply replace another school holiday.[50]

A survey reported on ABC's *Nightline* found another strong indication of differences in the racial attitudes of children and adults. Except for *Monday Night Football,* which made the top ten shows for both black and white viewers, no top-ten favorite of whites made the top-ten list of blacks (and vice versa). In stark contrast, a much higher percentage of young people are crossover viewers. For instance, few adult whites watch *Moesha,* and few adult blacks watch *Seinfeld,* but the same cannot be said of young viewers, many of whom "cross over" to watch shows whose main characters are racially different from themselves.[51] According to the University of California's annual national survey of incoming college freshmen, "sixty-three percent of college freshmen say they socialize frequently with someone from a different racial or ethnic group"—about twice the rate for adults. In short, "youth equals diversity."[52]

As we might expect, the case with gender prejudice is less clear, partly because males and females do differ in biologically important ways, and partly because adults start gender-tracking and stereotyping girls and boys at such an early age. Parents dress their little girls and boys in different colors, buy them different toys, encourage them to pursue different activities, and thus exaggerate whatever natural differences exist between the sexes. The media, having already shaped these parental attitudes about gender, then perpetuate and exaggerate the gender differences instilled in children's minds by parents. Nature and nurture are harder to sort out with gender than with race. Left to their own devices, young children are much more likely to notice, and to regard as important, the difference between boys' and girls' genitalia than the different skin colors of their playmates.

Nonetheless, many young people are less sexist than many adults, especially than adults influenced by patriarchal religions or convinced that sexism sells. In a nationally published article on sexist advertising, eleven-year-old Emily Hume of Chicago blasted adult-created commercials for their sexist impact on youngsters: "I think these little things in commercials really can make a person think: 'Well, if people are sexist in commercials, then I guess it's OK.' Well, it's not! As a girl, I hear boys say sexist things all the time." Hume argued that turning the tables on boys by subjecting them to stereotyping might help them correct their own behavior. "I hope that in the future," she wrote, "ad companies will wise up and see that girls and women have been neglected long enough. And we're not going to put up with it anymore!"[53]

On the related issue of sexual orientation, young people have grown up in an era far more tolerant of homosexuality than the preceding two generations. Not surprisingly, young people express less homophobia than adults.[54] Unlike Republican Senate Majority Leader Trent Lott and adult Utah politicians, most young people do not believe that homosexuality is a sin.[55] In 1998, when high-school psychology teacher and state-champion volleyball coach Wendy Weaver of Salem, Utah, was fired as coach for being a lesbian, most parents supported the authorities while most students and players supported Weaver. Encouraged by the young people's support, Weaver sued the school district. Federal judge Bruce Jenkins ruled that the district had violated Weaver's constitutional rights of free speech, equal protection, and due process.[56]

Beginning in early 1998, gay student clubs in high schools across the country started claiming a constitutional right to be treated like any other student group. In Utah, conservative adults scored a Pyrrhic victory over the Gay-Straight Alliance of students at Salt Lake City's East High School when the school board banned all extracurricular clubs throughout the district rather than allow a "deviant" club that was upsetting state legislators in Mormon-dominated Utah.[57] Federal law prohibits discrimination against school clubs on the basis of unpopular ideas. Opposing the discriminatory adult majority in Utah government "were civil libertarians and hundreds of high school students—only a few of them gay—who rallied and marched on the statehouse to save their extracurricular clubs. But their efforts proved fruitless." Sacrificed to the politicians' homophobia were such clubs as Young Republicans, Young Democrats, Students Against Drunk Driving, Polynesian Pride, and the Aztec Club for Latinos. Students and teachers at East High say that "school spirit has evaporated, students don't socialize as much, and class and racial rifts are deeper than ever." Ironically, the Gay-Straight Alliance benefited from the publicity, becoming a thriving community group that rents space at the high school.[58]

It is not only in Utah that adults are intolerant of young people's political choices, and sexual preference is but one of many areas in which adults try to limit or silence youth politically. For instance, many school boards across the country have sought to censor or ban student newspapers. A typical case occurred in 1998: "When a Phoenix high school student tried to distribute an independent newspaper at his school this fall, school officials confiscated the copies and the school's lawyer sent a letter to the 17-year-old student threatening legal action."[59] It is easy to see why conservatives might shy away from efforts to empower young people—except for specific youth constituencies that might favor conservative viewpoints, for instance crackdowns on drug dealers. More important for our purposes is the fact that transformational practitioners show little interest in empowering the young, despite children's typically more progressive political attitudes. It is debatable how much of this indifference reflects the calculated self-interest of adults, even progressive adults, and how much reflects traditional, unreflective adultism.

A 2000 poll of 650 fifteen- to eighteen-year-olds suggests that young people are more likely than adults to pursue synergistic (win-win) as opposed to entropic (win-lose) values. "Teens say that being happy, having the respect of family and friends, and having a happy family life are the surest signs of success." They perceive large corporations as hostile to these values. Compared with adults, the teens are "less likely to say being aggressive, competitive, and focused on winning are important components of leadership." [60] Why *are* children more politically progressive than adults on issues such as ecology versus growth, peace versus war, and racial differences? The answer is complex and is tangential to the main focus of this chapter, which is the arbitrariness and illogic of adultism. More important than why, or even whether, young people are more liberal or radical than adults is their right to a voice and their right to be judged according to qualities other than age. Yet three reasons for young people's progressive attitudes do seem worth mentioning.

First, as we shall see in Chapter 6, no class of human beings so numerous is as mistreated, neglected, and oppressed as young people, who therefore have a vested interest in challenging the status quo. Second, the critical and creative acumen of children is less atrophied by religious and political dogma than is that of their elders. Third, today's primary and secondary schools encourage students to think more critically about public issues than schools did for earlier generations of students, who are now adults. Learning the three R's did not alert mom, dad, grandma, and grandpa to problems of poverty, racism, sexism, militarism, or global warming.

Children as Political Actors

In the general exuberance over South Africa's new democracy in 1994, many people may have forgotten the Soweto Riots of 1976, "a children's crusade against apartheid that historians regard as the beginning of the end of white-minority rule"[61] Reflecting on the hundreds of children from South Africa and elsewhere whom he had interviewed, psychologist Robert Coles (1986) reported: "What I have heard may be called the expression of a political morality" (p. 302), which in children's warnings about nuclear war "is never too distant. These children realize that what their countries or other countries do may well affect how, or indeed whether, they will live" (p. 303). Similarly, many disfranchised children, including future president Bill Clinton, took it upon themselves to participate in the U.S. civil rights movement as well as the movement against U.S. involvement in the Vietnam War. In addition, many children participated in these movements along with their parents. After years of interviewing American Indian children, Coles was surprised to discover that "a rather subtle and canny knowledge of political affairs is not necessarily beyond the ken of ordinary boys and girls" (p. 11).

More recently, Yugoslav antiwar activist Zlata Filipovic, age thirteen, wowed the U.S. Congress with her testimony on the injustices of the war she and other children were suffering in Bosnia. She said that unlike many Yugoslav adults, Bosnian children did not think of themselves as Serbs, Croats, or Muslims, but as interchangeable victims of war. Her book, *Zlata's Diary: A Child's Life in Sarajevo* (1994), was already a best-seller in France before it was published in the United States. Filipovic resisted attempts by some of the admiring U.S. lawmakers to put their own spin on her experiences. When New Jersey Republican Chris Smith suggested that it was prayer and faith in God that had given her the strength to survive her ordeal, she gently demurred, saying that it was the love among her family that had been the key. Resisting accolades for her testimony, she said, "Any child in Bosnia could sit here."[62]

Even younger children have addressed even more august bodies. "Eleven-year-old Tajasvi Srimushnam, from Arizona, recently addressed the United Nations General Assembly concerning environmental projects he helped create at his school and on his own. At the top of that list is the purchase of 24 acres of South American rain forest, bought with funds from the school's own recycling program." Speaking as a member of the UN Global Youth Forum, he declared, "No matter how much of the rain forest is destroyed, these 24 acres are safe."[63] Many other children's groups have raised money to save whales and other endangered species, to provide medicine to Iraqi children hurt by the U.S. economic boycott, and to buy Sudanese children out of slavery.[64]

In schools around the world, more and more children are challenging their parents and school authorities to live up to the environmental principles being taught in the schools. Ecological researcher Lannis Temple talked to 2,400 children in fifty-five schools in thirty-six countries on six continents. He found that school children worldwide have a very positive orientation toward ecology. "What most concerns children are adults. Children 'see plants, animals and water as one family,' he says. 'They are concerned about adults and their behavior. They wonder why adults disregard nature.'" Nine-year-old Franzisca Ebert of Berlin asked: "Why do we build cars with catalytic converters when they pollute the environment?" From refusing Styrofoam, to demanding recycling, to boycotting net-caught tuna,[65] to opposing toxic development projects, "kids are saying to adults: Be more like us."[66]

It is not unusual for students to walk out of classes to protest some antiecological practice of their schools, as in the case of two hundred students from Southern Hills Junior High in Boulder, Colorado, who objected to "the school's use of colored paper that is not recycled."[67] It is not only parents and schools that are taking notice. "So many young people embrace environmentalism—the favorite cause of 75 percent of 10,000 students surveyed by the consulting firm Bedford Kent Group—that corporations have begun to respond." For instance: "Spokesmen for Star-Kist, the canned-tuna giant, said its decision to stop using net-caught tuna was in part due to the anti-net campaign of 17-year-old Joel Rubin."[68] After Kids for the Preservation of Clear Creek Canyon gave moving testimony that helped defeat a proposed 320-acre mining quarry in a picturesque canyon, Chicago developer O. R. Goltra complimented his youthful adversaries for the quality and diligence of their efforts.[69]

Members of the youth advisory board of the nonprofit group Earth Force promote bicycling for both health and environmental reasons. "Biking is fun, biking is healthy and biking is good for the environment," says Anrit Chaudhuri, thirteen, of Cambridge, Massachusetts. "If you bike four miles instead of driving in a car you can reduce air pollution by 15 pounds." Helping Chaudhuri lobby in Washington in September 1998, Anissa Medina, also thirteen, explained Earth Force's strategy as seeking "to make America more bicycle friendly, community by community." The group promotes more bike racks and routes at schools, more bike-safety measures, and youth involvement in other environmental-protection programs.[70] At age twelve, activist and author Danny Seo (1997) founded Earth 2000, a movement of over 20,000 teenagers to protect animals and the environment. In his early teens, Ben Smitowitz helped found the International Student Activism Alliance in order to give a voice to disenfranchised teens (Vittorini 2000: p. 35).

In Los Alamos, New Mexico, where the atomic bomb had been developed a half century ago, "children proposed [in 1995] to place a peace memorial near the new Los Alamos library on the 50th anniversary of Hiroshima. Children from 50 states and 53 countries competed to design a statue." But the peace initiative irked Los Alamos adults, whose identities were tied to the town's atomic history. Officials such as councilor Jim Greenwood worried aloud about "the so-called peace activists" who might use the memorial as "a rallying point to indict the town for its role in creating nuclear weapons." The county commissioners turned down the memorial, leaving the children in tears. Fourteen-year-old David Rosoff, who had helped get 41,000 signatures and raise $20,000, said, "I am very, very frustrated because they can't seem to get past the past."[71]

In Oakland, California, on the other hand, children "were a major force in getting [Healthy Cities] legislation passed," creating a program that addresses education, housing, economic development, security, and law enforcement. Children have actively promoted similar campaigns in Quebec, Milan, and Seattle. Since 1983, Seattle children have helped preserve the physical and social environment through the program Kid's Place, which has spread to many other cities in Europe, Japan, and North America. "The results have included new parks and play areas, pedestrian bridges, neighborhood centres and clinics for adolescents. Young people have won approval for midnight basketball games and have persuaded principals to keep schools open late so they can be used for recreation."[72] In the wake of a rash of school shootings in the late 1990s, a group of fifty teenagers from nineteen states went to Washington, D.C., in the summer of 1999 urging Congress "to listen to them when making decisions that will affect their lives." Said high-school senior Travis Brennan, "There's no way that someone who's 35 can have the same perspective as us. If you're talking about funding programs, it's only logical that you would talk to the people those programs are going to affect."[73]

Students in the United States have yet to achieve the dramatic, nationwide political effects occasionally achieved by their peers in other countries. In Venezuela, for instance, junior-high and high-school students in November 1991 shut down schools throughout the country in protest over poverty, inflation, and public transportation. In urban Brazil, "emancipated street children organized into a national movement, [and] have grabbed center stage from time to time as self-conscious political actors demanding their citizenship and civil rights" (Scheper-Hughes and Sargent 1998: p. 15). It was two teen employees in Squamish, British Columbia, who initiated the first unionized McDonald's in North America.[74] The Canada-based, child-run organization Free the Children has done just that in changing several nations' policies on forced child labor.

Even first-graders regularly surprise their elders with their understanding and passion for public issues. In "If I Were President" role-playing exercises, primary schoolers' favorite targets are saving whales and other endangered species, cleaning up pollution, getting rid of war, guns, and harmful drugs, helping poor people out of poverty, improving schools, lessening violence on television, and preventing adults from being mean to children. Teacher Saverio Greto, who uses such role playing in class, finds not only the idealism but the sophistication and hard-headed realism of such young students especially remarkable. "I don't feel like I was that aware of social issues back when I was in elementary school," Greto said. "I would have written something about Dick and Jane."[75]

In Phoenix, twelve-year-old Abby Weinzer started Operation Sleep Sac to provide new sleeping bags, toiletries, and stuffed animals for the homeless, eventually winning material support from businesses, schools, and government. "Abby had a very professional-looking prospectus," said Phoenix city councilman Tom Milton, "but people were not taking her seriously because of her age."[76] Even younger but hard not to take seriously is ten-year-old breast-feeding advocate Simon Wyatt, whose Baby Bottle Blaster web page (<http://www.lightlink.com/hilinda/simon/bbb.html>) declares: "Down with baby bottles! (Ick! What useless garbage)/ Babies don't need bottles!" He and younger brother Timmy make it clear that the scientific data support them, not the formula favorers.[77] Eleven-year-old Michael Munds has raised money for the needy since he was three. "He just finds a cause and says, 'I'm going to do it,'" said his mother, Gayle Mundis. "I just follow him and drive him wherever he needs to go. This is a gift from God, something that is natural to him. His outlook is different. He tries to imagine what it's like to be in those situations."[78] He has raised nearly $90,000, choosing "causes that don't get a lot of attention."

In spring 2000, a four-year campaign begun by eleven-year-old researcher and activist Hunter Scott finally paid off when Congress officially redeemed the name of World War II Navy captain Charles Butler McVay III, who had been unjustly court-martialed for actions allegedly leading to the sinking of his cruiser Indianapolis by the Japanese in July 1945. In *Everyday Heroes,* Vittorini (2000) chronicles dozens of additional examples of children who exhibit courage, compassion, and an activist concern for the public good.

Children Against Adultism

In addition to supporting poor people, peace, and Mother Earth, children are increasingly fighting adultism itself. Junior-high student Johanna Jensen's winning design for a bookmark given out by The Tattered Cover, one of the world's largest bookstores, reads: "Books do not discriminate on the basis of age, color, sex, or creed. Reading is a gift available to everyone." Children are sensitive to age stereotyping and to unfair rules, and more and more of them are concluding that automatic age restrictions are unfair. On January 8, 1998, Ann Landers published a letter read by millions of readers in newspapers throughout the country:

> I am a 16-year-old girl who is tired of dealing with teenage discrimination. Whenever I go into a store—it doesn't matter if it is a convenience store, a clothing store or even a video store—someone follows me around to be sure

I don't steal anything. This is insulting. Another recurring problem happens when I go to a restaurant with friends. Teenagers always get horrible service because the waiter or waitress assumes we will leave a poor tip. I have never failed to leave at least 15 percent, and my friends do the same—even if the service isn't great. Please let your readers know that if adults don't give teenagers a chance, we cannot prove that we are honest and decent.

At its best, political correctness has helped curtail derogatory stereotypes and comments against women, ethnic minorities, the disabled, gays, and seniors. It has yet to curb much of the insulting anti-youth behavior protested in this letter. There is little PC pressure to curtail demeaning comments about young people as "rug rats," "spoiled brats," or "Generation Xers."

For more than a decade, young people across the country have also been protesting arbitrary restrictions on their legal rights. At Pojoaque schools in New Mexico, the youth-authored *Youth Voice* argues that mere age should not lessen the constitutional protections afforded Americans:

Does the Bill of Rights apply only to adults? Some teens feel as if it does. Why do teen civil rights threaten adults when teens exercise them? Many times the constitutional rights of juveniles are violated. We feel this is wrong. . . . Student newspapers are often censored, yet adult newspapers are not. This is a violation of the First Amendment, which grants us freedom of the press.

In this column, published in Santa Fe's daily newspaper *The New Mexican,* the teen writers criticized the Supreme Court's decision in *Hazelwood School District v. Kuhlmeier* (1988) for permitting censorship of student newspapers: "We see this as saying that it is legal for adults to break the law by violating student rights. How can you explain different interpretations of the United States Constitution simply because of age?"[79]

Students across the country have also been protesting youth curfews, enlisting adult allies such as the American Civil Liberties Union to defend their rights. When high-school cheerleader and top-ranking student Kristine Kvalvik was arrested for violating a Phoenix curfew of which she was unaware, the ACLU went to bat for her. Kvalvik objected not only to the arbitrariness of the 10 P.M. curfew but the rudeness of the arresting officers and their refusal to read her her rights. "I asked, but they didn't notify me of any rights that I have," she said of the police, adding ironically: "I guess I've watched too much TV."[80] Despite her superlative high-school record and the strong support of her parents, fifteen-year-old Kvalvik's crime of sitting and chatting in a park with friends after 10 P.M. led a juvenile court judge to declare her an "incorrigible child" and to fine her $56 or fifteen hours of community service.

Another favorite target of youth protest against adultism is dress codes. Students at Northglenn High School in Colorado pointed out contradictions in the school's dress code. As a student organizer noted, "Baseball caps are banned. Punk haircuts aren't. Cowboy hats are banned. White shoelaces aren't, though some Skinhead groups . . . use them in certain ways as a signal of White Power." Stacy Ehrlick, fifteen, asked, "Will you ban the American flag because it's related to skinheads?" She predicted that "gangs will continue to come up with such a variety of hairstyles, clothing styles, hand signals and symbols that school officials will never be able to keep up with them." The students criticized authorities for taking a superficial approach to dealing with gangs. Banning clothing styles fails to get to "the heart of the problem," according to teen Greg Magee. "You've got to consider why kids get into gangs. Maybe they have no pride, no money, feel there's no out for themselves. They have to see a way to feel proud." [81]

Young people are opposing corporal punishment, which is considered assault and battery if carried out against adults. In the state of Washington in the fall of 1992, a group of Shoreline school district fourth-, fifth-, and sixth-graders discussed pending legislation in the state legislature to ban corporal punishment in schools. They read and debated arguments pro and con, decided to support the ban, and designated four children to testify before two legislative committees. In their spring 1993 testimony, the youngsters cited studies showing the harmful effects of corporal punishment (see Chapter 7), and statistics indicating decreased school vandalism and dropout rates in the twenty-two states that had banned corporal punishment. Their testimony was well received by the legislature, which had defeated the bill eight years in a row. "Educators and psychologists applauded [the students'] clear and conclusive commentaries. Paid lobbyists deferred their testimony to the Shoreline students. One by one, each lobbyist stood up and asked to go on record in support of the children's statements." The bill passed and was signed into law by Governor Mike Lowry.[82] Students in Minnesota help prevent corporal assault in another way. Prairie Creek School in St. Olaf, an alternative K–5 school, is one of the state's many in which students run their own conflict-resolution programs. "When a conflict breaks out, the children who were trained take aside the children who are having the conflict and mediate the session, allowing those involved in the dispute to find their own solutions."[83]

Unlike adults, children in many parts of the world can be sold into bondage. One of the most revealing cases of child activism is that of Pakistani carpet-factory worker Iqbal Masih, who was assassinated in April 1995 at the age of twelve.[84] Masih was killed for organizing his fellow child laborers—3.4 million under age fourteen in Pakistan alone—and for publicizing their plight at the United Nations and elsewhere.[85] Masih's parents had sold him into bondage at the age of four, and for many years he had toiled in a carpet sweatshop before escaping to embark on his organizing campaign. The world of adults implicated in this murder included not only the wealthy owners in the carpet industry but the Pakistani government, which permitted—and continues to permit—the sweatshops in which young children are virtually enslaved to the dictates of profiteers.[86] Masih's murderers killed the child organizer, but they did not kill his idea, which inspired an illustrious protégé.

After reading of Masih's death in the newspaper, twelve-year-old Craig Kielburger, of Toronto, persuaded some of his friends to help him start Free the Children,[87] which in four years has attracted five thousand members in twenty-five countries, from Pakistan to Central America and the Philippines, and from Canada to South Africa. The only international human-rights organization run by children, Free the Children has raised more than a million dollars to fund schools, health kits, and alternative sources of income for poor children's families through donations of land, sewing machines, and dairy animals. It also provides donated materials, volunteer labor, and mentors for freed children. The group helped persuade Nike to change policy in its shoe factories, which are now officially forbidden to employ anyone under the age of eighteen. It also helped get the Canadian government to institute its Rugmark customs screen, which targets imports into Canada from any employer of child labor or of underpaid or mistreated adult labor.

The teenaged Kielburger, who travels widely both organizing and lecturing, was recently awarded the Franklin and Eleanor Roosevelt Medal of Freedom, joining previous recipients Harry Truman, John F. Kennedy, Elie Wiesel, and Desmond Tutu. A motto of Kielburger's organization is "Kids Can Free the Children."[88] Free the Children has helped inspire many other groups of children to join the campaign against forced child labor.[89] The full title of his recent book (1999) is *Free the Children: A Young Man Fights Against Child Labor and Proves That Children Can Change the World*. Howard Cohen (1980: p. 106), a friend of children's rights, once reassured adults who might fear his proposal to allow children to participate politically: "As a matter of fact, it is highly unlikely that children as a group would have the time, energy, interest, or sophistication to organize themselves into concerted action." Free the Children, like other children's movements, has proved him wrong.

Children against adultism have picked up a variety of adult allies, including state legislatures that have restored some of students' First Amendment rights and governing bodies that have included youth members. On neighborhood-improvement policy, Denver City Council member Susan Barnes-Gelt found that youth consultants "seem to recognize better than adults the large number of empty park spaces there that could be better used." Mayor Wellington Webb called "having kids offer ideas for their own neighborhoods . . . an imaginative step forward."[90]

The members of Ortega Middle School's Accountability Plus Committee, consisting of parents, teachers, administrators, and students, elected eighth-grader Kanji Kawanabe as chair. "Kids are not generally given enough responsibility," said Kawanabe, a straight-A student whom other members of the committee praised for his strong and effective leadership. "Adults are often blown away by how thoughtful and insightful kids are," said the Colorado state commissioner of education. "The contribution they make is astounding. What happens to kids is at the heart of the day-to-day operation of a school."[91] Impressed by Free the Children, Canadian minister of external affairs Lloyd Axworthy says the youngsters have "debunked the notion that children have nothing to contribute to government policy debates" (Kielburger 1999: p. 287).

Some courts and lawyers' groups such as the American Bar Association have begun to support children's legal rights, including the right to legal standing and representation. They have been joined by such advocates as former attorney general Janet Reno and former first lady and New York senator Hillary Clinton. A number of legal scholars have taken up the case for children's rights: "The neglect of children's rights, their invisibility, and their lack of representation in present systems lead to the inevitable abuses of the same children who should receive protection within those systems under the Fourteenth Amendment to the Constitution."[92]

In the extreme case of children killing abusive parents—an extreme becoming less rare in the United States—some lawyers, juries, and judges are coming to view these killings as justifiable self-defense. A highly publicized case is that of fifth-grader Druie Dutton and his eighth-grade brother, Herman, who in 1993 killed their sleeping father, Lonnie Dutton, with a hunting rifle. The boys told authorities they had killed their father "because they were tired of his beatings and of watching him sexually molest their 10-year-old sister." In the Duttons' farming town of Rush Springs, Oklahoma, the 1,400 residents rallied in support of the boys. A bully since childhood, Lonnie Dutton had not only repeatedly abused all four of his children but threatened townsfolk as well. The prosecutor, defense attorneys, and judge agreed on a plea bargain that released the boys to therapeutic foster homes, touching off a celebration in their hometown.[93] A study by the Hazelton Foundation found that 63 percent of eleven-to-twenty-year-old males who commit murder "killed the person battering their mother."[94]

PC's Silence on Adultism

Children should not have to become vigilantes in order to protect themselves or defend their rights. We should be thankful to the adults who rose, if belatedly, to defend the Dutton children. The problem with most adult defenses of children, however, is that at best they redress the *excesses* of adultism, not adultism itself. Adultism is itself implicated in children's violence against their parents. Most people judge violence as defensible only as a last resort. Prior to taking up arms, we are expected to try persuasion, letter writing, organizing, lobbying, campaigning, voting, running for office, politicking, horse trading, boycotting, marching, striking, and civilly disobeying. But practically and legally, these prior resorts are rarely available to children. When children's families, or their physical, social, economic, and legal situations, betray them, their political disempowerment restricts their choices to flight, self-defense, or silent suffering. All three of these options are fraught with danger, as demonstrated by the case of assassinated child activist Iqbal Masih, cited earlier.

Young people's oppression is revealed in our daily talk. Politically incorrect language is criticized for demeaning people by implying their inferiority. The inequality suggested by racial or sexual slurs, or by such usages as "retarded," "handicapped," "old people," "old farts," and "geezers," has become unacceptable among those who value equal dignity for all. But what about those whose disadvantage is based not on advanced age but on lesser age? Little heat is felt by bigots who demean children with expressions like "rug rat," "curtain climber," "whiny kid," "wet behind the ears," "adolescent," "juvenile delinquent," "spoiled brat," "young punk," "me generation," or "typical Generation Xer." There is no PC police for the young.

This inconsistency of PC language norms is not a coincidence. The world in which PC has developed is a world politically monopolized by adults. These adults, whether politically correct or incorrect, do not view adultism as a problem, either because the problem indicts them or because they are unaware of it. When made aware of it—as I have done on talk radio, in town meetings, and at scholarly conferences in the United States and abroad—adults react with disbelief and outrage. One caller on a radio talk show, a retired airline pilot, was so incensed by my proposal for allowing children to vote (Chapter 6), that he called the chancellor of my campus and demanded that I be fired for incompetence.

Almost nothing is more certain to most adults—black and white, male and female, rich and poor, left and right—than the legitimacy of the privileges of adulthood. We might expect adult leftists to examine the logic of adultism more readily than the adult right. Indeed, progressives already feel, often justifiably, that they do better by young people than do authoritarian, tradition-bound conservatives. But examining their own dogmas requires a critical acumen discouraged by PC. Moreover, the historical record is unclear on whether the left, once privileged, is any more likely than the privileged right to give up its advantages merely because they are arbitrary and unfair. In any case, most adults remain wedded to their hegemony over young people yet befuddled by youthful disrespect toward them.

Of course, if adults are using their monopoly of power to take especially good care of the young—better than could a polity that included young people—then despite any illogic of the adult monopoly, defenders of adultism could at least make a utilitarian case for the continued disfranchisement of the young. We begin Chapter 6 by examining this possibility.

Notes

1. Mary John, "Children's Rights in a Free-Market Culture," in Stephens (1995: p. 126).

2. Robert Bly (1997: pp. 5-6).

3. Linda Chavez, "Killer Mom Awarded Custody," *Denver Post*, January 7, 1998.

4. Kathleen Parker, "Where's Common Sense in Child Custody Case?" *Orlando Sentinel,* July 16, 1998. In news accounts, the child's name is variously spelled. The pronunciation is apparently "Cornelius," but the court record spells his name "Cornilous."

5. Chavez, "Killer Mom Awarded Custody."

6. Readers may review similar contested adoption cases at the Hear My Voice website: <http://www.hearmyvoice.org>.

7. In Minnesota, for example, the Minority Heritage Protection Act mandates same-race adoption, and defines a child who is 10 percent black and 90 percent white as legally black. Lind (1996: p. 122).

8. "Black activists have replaced white supremacists as the advocates of same-race adoption." Lind (1996: p. 122).

9. Brenda C. Coleman, "Interracial Adoptions a Flash Point," Associated Press, January 3, 1997. Related studies show that "contrary to popular belief, just being biracial does not pose additional psychological risks. Research shows that most biracial children who grow up in supportive environments, families and neighborhoods and so forth have a self-esteem just as normal as anybody else's." Psychologist Marguerite Wright, as quoted in Sara Steffens, "What Shatters Children's Racial Innocence?" Knight Ridder News Service, September 6, 2000.

10. *USA Today,* April 21, 1999.

11. Coontz (1997: pp. 149–150); Hewlett and West (1998: p. 117).

12. A study published in *Pediatrics* in January 1995 found that "inner-city mothers were more likely to spank than well-to-do suburban mothers" and that "mothers who had been spanked as a child both spanked more frequently and believed more strongly in spanking." Brenda C. Coleman, "Mothers Still Turn to Spankings, Survey Finds," *Cincinnati Enquirer,* January 11, 1995. A February 1997 Gallup Poll found that blacks most strongly favored spanking, followed by southerners and Protestants, whereas easterners and liberals were least likely to favor spanking. Brigid Schulte, "Spanking Backfires, Study Finds," Knight-Ridder News Service, August 15, 1997. "In one study, non-white women were five times more likely than whites to wean their babies before twenty-six weeks" (Baumslag and Michels 1995: p. 205). In a study of poor, inner-city mothers, "there were proportionately more African-Americans feeding formula (53 percent compared with 24 percent feeding human milk)," and health outcomes were worse for the formula-fed babies. S. M. Bass and M. W. Groer, "Relationship of Breastfeeding and Formula-Feeding Practices with Infant Health Outcomes in an Urban Poor Population," *Journal of Perinatal and Neonatal Nursing,* no. 11, 1997, pp. 1–9. In 2000, the surgeon general reported that only 19 percent of black mothers were nursing their infants for the first six months, compared to over 30 percent of nonblack mothers. Lauran Neergard, "Black Moms Not Feeding Enough, Study Says," Associated Press, November 7, 2000. Tobacco companies have targeted lower-class and nonwhite audiences as particularly susceptible to culturally tailored cigarette ads. Children are harmed by secondhand smoke, and some young people have organized antismoking campaigns. John Schwartz, "Carcinogen Passed to Fetuses; Study: Smoking Moms Transmit Agent," *Washington Post,* August 24, 1998; Sheba R. Wheeler,

"Students' Anti-Tobacco Crusade Reaches the Halls of Congress," *Denver Post,* February 1997.

13. In *Beyond Gender,* Betty Friedan (1997) takes issue with this tendency among feminists.

14. An interesting study of gay employees' attitudes toward employee benefits for families with children is Maureen Scully and W. E. Douglas Creed, "Restructured Families: Issues of Equality and Need," in Pitt-Catsouphes and Googins (1999: pp. 47–65).

15. For instance, during a visit to Bali in 1978, I was surprised to find no evidence of self-conscious, stereotypically "adolescent" behavior or "identity crisis" among Balinese teens I spent time with. When I mentioned this experience to psychologist Erik Erikson as an exception to his stages of psychological development, he replied with a twinkle in his eye that I had probably misread the teens' behavior. I cite additional evidence later.

16. Quoted in Peter Applebome, "Age of Childhood Innocence May Be Ending," *New York Times,* May 21, 1998.

17. I make this argument regarding ecology in Chapter 8.

18. Molly Moore, "Chelsea Taking Spotlight on Tour," *Washington Post,* March 31, 1995.

19. Catherine Strong, "Congress Lauds Civil Rights Heroine," Associated Press, June 16, 1999.

20. Moore, "Chelsea Taking Spotlight on Tour."

21. Seminar with Brooke Ackerly and Jana Everett, Denver, Colorado, March 2, 1998.

22. Nathan Myhrvold, "John Von Neumann: Computing's Cold Warrior," *Time,* March 29, 1999, p. 90.

23. Jeff Bradley, "Fifth-Grader Going Places as Composer," *Denver Post,* February 12, 1992.

24. Carol Kreck, "It's Just a Book—No Excuses," *Denver Post,* January 4, 1990.

25. Peter Plagens, "Even a Kid Could Do It," *Newsweek,* June 3, 1996.

26. Sean Kelly, "Boulder Teen Wins 'Junior Nobel,'" *Denver Post,* March 9, 1999.

27. "Irish Teen Boosts Pace of E-Mail," Associated Press, January 14, 1999.

28. Sam Howe Verhovek, "Teenagers Are Game for Work: Play Counselors Solve Nintendo Problems," *New York Times,* December 31, 1998.

29. Personal conversations with computer scientist Clayton Lewis.

30. Christopher Lopez, "Young Pilots Defend Flights," *Denver Post,* April 12, 1996.

31. Jessica's father and her flight instructor were also killed in the crash.

32. "Liver Patient Dies 'in a Very Good Way': Teen Fought to Stop Taking Medication," *Ft. Lauderdale Sun-Sentinel,* August 21, 1994.

33. Associated Press, December 19, 1997.

34. "Boy Saves Sister from Crocodile," *Rocky Mountain News,* February 8, 2000.

35. "Sitter Saves Boy Choking on Cracker," *Denver Post,* April 18, 1998.

36. "Thousands of Lives Saved by Heimlich Maneuver," *Denver Post,* November 26, 1997.

37. "Zorich: A Man for All Seasons," Associated Press, December 25, 1997.

38. "Dear Santa: My Uncle Craig Sold the Nintendo Because He Is on Drugs," *Wall Street Journal,* December 21, 1993.

39. Associated Press, February 19, 1996.

40. "Child Takes Rabies Shots to Save Cub," Associated Press, May 15, 1996.

41. "Boys' Savings Go to Dogs, and Cats," Associated Press, February 12, 2000.

42. "Human Icicles Waiting for Way to Beat Death," *Salt Lake Tribune,* January 5, 1992.

43. Alessandra Stanley, *New York Times,* May 7, 1990.

44. Jeff D. Opdyke, "'But . . . I'm Just a Kid': College as Easy as Climbing Trees for Genius, 10," *Orange County Register,* February 29, 1992.

45. Tim Tesconi, "Tennessee Boy Graduates with Master's Degree at 14," *New York Times,* August 11, 1998.

46. See, for instance, "If Teens Ran the Schools: 72,000 Teens Speak Out in Exclusive Survey," *USA Weekend,* August 23-25, 1991; Bedford Kent Group Survey, 1992; Lannis Temple, *Dear World: How Children Around the World Feel About Our Environment* (New York: Random House, 1993); Nickelodeon's six-hour documentary "Nickellennium" on children's views worldwide, December 31, 1999; and the children's Harris poll established in 1999 (<http://www.i-matter.com>).

47. "Browner Mixes Job, Parenting," Associated Press, September 12, 1993.

48. Carol Kreck, "War Fills Kids with Worries, Questions," *Denver Post,* January 18, 1991.

49. Psychologist Marguerite Wright notes: "Kids are not born with this [racism]. We give it to them . . . Children, when they're young, they think it's absurd. A lot of them laugh when they learn that people judge other people because of their skin color." Sara Steffens, "What Shatters Children's Racial Innocence?" Knight Ridder News Service, September 6, 2000.

50. "The Election Connection: Want to Get Adults to Vote? Send in the Kids," *Newsweek,* October 26, 1992, p. 74.

51. *Nightline,* May 6, 1998.

52. Brad Edmonson, "The Multicultural Myth: Diversity Depends on Where You Live," *Utne Reader,* no. 91, January-February 1999, p. 18.

53. Emily Hume, "Do Commercials for Toys Favor Boys?" *USA Weekend,* June 25-27, 1993.

54. For instance, an ICR (Media, Pennsylvania) poll conducted for Associated Press in 2000 found young people to be more supportive of gay marriage than were their elders.

55. Associated Press release, June 16, 1998.

56. "Lesbian Teacher Wins School Suit," Associated Press, November 27, 1998.

57. This intolerance is ironic in light of historical discrimination against Mormons for their practice of polygamy.

58. Kristen Moulton, "School Club Ban Backfires: Salt Lake City Students Hurting; Gay Group Thrives," Associated Press, December 19, 1998.

59. Tracy Breton, "Student Publications Face Increased Curbs on Speech," *Providence Journal,* January 14, 1999.

60. Jacqueline Fitzgerald, "Teens Lukewarm on Corporate Roles," *Chicago Tribune,* November 21, 2000.

61. John Daniszewski, "Blacks Flock Back to Schools," Associated Press, June 16, 1994.

62. "We Just Knew That at Any Moment We Can Be Killed: Bosnian Awes U.S. Lawmakers with War Tales," Associated Press, March 11, 1994.

63. "Eleven-Year Old Addresses U.N.," *Integrity* 3, 1991, p. 8.

64. Adult human-rights groups disagree among themselves about the net costs and benefits of buying Sudanese out of slavery, since doing so provides an economic incentive to prospective slavers.

65. The nets incidentally catch and kill dolphins as well.

66. Ann Hicks, "Kids Feel Positive About Ecology: Adults' Actions Are Top Concern, Author Finds," *Cincinnati Enquirer,* April 22, 1993.

67. "Paper Not Recycled, So Students Walk Out," *Denver Post*, March 26, 1992.

68. "YES Group Points out Protection Not a Fad," *Denver Post,* April 22, 1992.

69. Hector Guttierez, "Kids Join to Oppose Quarry: Youths Want to Preserve Clear Creek for the Future," *Rocky Mountain News,* February 16, 1990.

70. Lawrence L. Knutson, "Young Cyclists Push Bike-Friendly Nation," Associated Press, September 18, 1998.

71. Jim Carrier, "Worlds Apart: Atomic Legacy Culture," *Denver Post,* June 11, 1995.

72. UNICEF, *The Progress of Nations 1997* (New York: UNICEF Division of Communication, 1997, pp. 60–61).

73. Sara Kugler, "Teens Plea for Voice in Halting Violence," States News Service, June 30, 1999.

74. *Utne Reader* 91, January-February 1999, p. 18.

75. Bill Briggs, "First-Graders Show a Lot of Promise(s) as President," *Denver Post,* March 27, 1995.

76. Lori Baker, "Helping Homeless Is Teen's Mission," *Arizona Republic,* January 17, 1999.

77. In Chapter 7, I review the scientific findings on the superiority of breast-feeding compared to formula feeding.

78. Angie DeVine, "Boy, 11, Raises Funds for Disaster Victims," *Denver Post,* November 6, 1999.

79. Allena Walsh, Crystal Coleman, Heather Shelburn, and Adam Muller, "Youth Voice: Teens Feel They Merit More Representation," *The New Mexican,* July 2, 1989.

80. Eric Miller, "Teen Challenges Curfew Law: ACLU Aiding Cheerleader in Case Against Phoenix Ordinance," *Arizona Republic,* October 17, 1993.

81. Janet Bingham, "Students Protest Dress Code," *Denver Post,* October 23, 1991.

82. Colleen Foye Bollen, "When Children Take Action," *Mothering,* spring 1994, pp. 89–91.

83. Mary Lou Salazar, personal communication. See her "Peace Education in the Denver Public Schools," *Peace Education Miniprints,* no. 78, March 1995.

84. See Kielburger's (1999: pp. 200–224) discussion of the controversy over Masih's exact age.

85. Amir Zia, "Pakistan's Poverty Forces Kids to Work," Associated Press, June 3, 1999.

86. Kathy Gannon, "Little Hero: Young Boy Who Crusaded Against Child Labor Killed," Associated Press, April 18, 1995. See also Kielburger (1998).

87. Website <http://www.freethechildren.org>

88. CBS, *60 Minutes,* "One Child's Labor," October 3, 1999.

89. Steven Greenhouse, "Child-Labor Issue Ignites a Multifaceted Youthful Crusade," *New York Times,* December 25, 1996.

90. J. Sebastian Sinisi, "Forum Culls Ideas from 35 Children," *Denver Post,* April 6, 1997.

91. Janet Bingham, "Students Help Pick Their Boss: Youngsters' 'Two Cents' Proves Surprise to Elders," *Denver Post,* June 3, 1991.

92. Mohr, Gelles, and Schwartz (1999: p. 38).

93. Sam Howe Verhovek, "Town Rallies Around Sons Who Killed Dad: Citizens Say Boys 'Scared Silent' on Abuse," *New York Times,* July 26, 1993.

94. "More Legal Protection for Kids Urged: Conference Aims at Reversing Deteriorating Status of 'Pediatric Law,'" Associated Press, April 8, 1990.

6

Beyond Adultism: Political Empowerment for Young People

"There is a growing movement around the world of children and youth seeking a voice and the right to participate in issues that affect them. . . . We see no reason why today's youth should not also be today's leaders."
— Craig Kielburger (1999: pp. 287, 314)

". . . nor shall any State . . . deny to any person . . . the equal protection of the laws."
— Fourteenth Amendment to the United States Constitution, 1868

"Constitutional rights do not mature and come into being magically only when one attains the state-defined age of maturity. Minors, as well as adults, are protected by the Constitution and possess constitutional rights."
— U.S. District Judge Walker Miller, 2000[1]

"Among kids my age, childhood is the leading cause of stress."
— Lily Tomlin's "Edith Ann"

Perhaps a paternalistic, utilitarian argument can be made that young people are better off without a political voice than with one—despite logical inconsistencies in the adultist position as spelled out in Chapter 5. Of course, we cannot know ahead of time how well children would fare under a fully democratic system that counted their votes along with those of their elders. But we can look at the evidence of how well children are doing under the exclusive regime of adults. When we do so with open eyes and caring hearts, we find cause for deep concern.[2] The political correctness of the child-friendly left—so attentive to issues of race, class, and gender—obscures the distinction between helpful and hurtful forms of adult paternalism. And as we shall see, enfranchising children can actually serve to strengthen families and parental authority.

How Can It Be?

When we awake each morning, looking forward to our daily newspaper over a cup of tea or coffee, headlines shock us with stories of child abuse, such as "Dog Eats Infant; Parents Suspected"[3]; "6-Year-Old Dragged by Stolen Car, Dies," [4] "Parents of Girl Who Starved Get Prison"[5]; "Mom, Girls Die After She Throws Them from Roof"[6]; "Man Who Injected [AIDS] Virus in His Son Gets Life Term,"[7]; "Mom Left Kids Alone Before: Infant's Bathtub Death Followed Repeated Warnings on Neglect"[8]; "Baby Dies After Medical Care Withheld"[9]; "Couple Get Probation for Ditching Disabled Son,"[10] "Couple Plead Guilty to Forcing Daughter to Sleep in Doghouse,"[11]and "When Kids Kill Abusive Parents." [12] In order to sell newspapers and airtime, the media feature such events but treat them as bizarre departures from the norm.

As we get deeper into the news, we learn that children's tragedies go well beyond deviant families with abusive parents, as in "87 Kids Endure Trek of Terror to Flee Rebels,"[13] "73 Million Girls Denied Education"[14]; "19 [Afghan] Children Drown Trying to Flee War"[15]; "India's Famous Carpets Woven by Toiling Children: Youths Bought or Sold into Virtual Slavery"[16]; "Pakistan's Poverty Forces Kids to Work"[17]; "Siege Takes Toll on Sarajevo Children"[18]; "Pollution Scars Silesia's Children: Kids Deformed and Unteachable"[19]; "Romanians Turn Backs on Kids: The Unwanted Live on the Streets, Fill Nation's Orphanages"[20]; "'Appalling Abuse' Cited in Russian Orphanages"[21]; "4 in 10 Russian Children Live in Poverty"[22]; and "Ulster Firebomb Kills Three Children."[23] We shudder, hoping such tragedies are confined to a few backward parts of the world.

In fact, even when we read UNICEF's (1998, 1999, 2000) annual, comprehensive reports on the state of the world's children, we may be tempted to read selectively and conclude that the really bad conditions for children exist in the impoverished Third and Fourth Worlds rather than closer to home.[24] Indeed, children's death rates in the Third World are much higher than those in industrial societies such as Japan, France, Germany, and the United States. Most genital mutilation of girls—but not of boys—occurs in Third World countries whose religions are interpreted by some to justify this traditional practice.[25] Complete abandonment of infant girls occurs in the tens of thousands in China today.[26] Most of the sixty-five ongoing military conflicts in 1999, which killed, maimed, and orphaned children, were occurring in less economically developed parts of the world.[27]

We pity children who live in "undeveloped" places so different from our own. Unfortunately, the record of societies run by the world's most privileged adults also leaves much to be desired. How well cared for are children throughout the world and in the United States?

The Way It Is

In the World

Of the world's 1.2 billion people living in poverty, one-half are children (UNICEF 2000). The relentlessly blinking lights on the world map of The

Hunger Site show when and where "every 3.6 seconds someone dies of hunger; 3/4 of the deaths are children under 5."[28] Because there is plenty of food in the world to feed everyone, UNICEF (1998) calls the worldwide epidemic of child malnutrition "an egregious violation of child rights" (p. 9). Specifically, denying children adequate nutrition by acts of omission or commission violates Articles 6 and 27—the right to life and the right to an adequate standard of living—of the United Nations' 1989 Convention on the Rights of the Child. Every day, over 30,000 children under five—or nearly 12 million every year—die from preventable causes, more than half from the "silent emergency" of malnutrition. The 1998, 1999, and 2000 UNICEF reports document not only juvenile deaths from malnutrition-related causes, but lifelong physical and cognitive impairment suffered by children throughout the world, including average IQ deficits of five points from low birth weight, eight points from lack of breastfeeding, and nine points from iron-deficiency anemia. "The depletion of human intelligence on such a scale—for reasons that are almost entirely preventable—is a profligate, even criminal, waste" (1998: p. 13).

In addition, hundreds of millions of children suffer from blindness, spina bifida, and other diseases as a result of needless deficiencies of iodine, zinc, vitamin A, or vitamin D. "More than 2 billion people—principally women and children—are iron deficient, and the World Health Organization (WHO) has estimated that 51 percent of children under the age of four in developing countries are anaemic" (UNICEF 1998: p. 15). A poignant example is North Korea, whose misguided policies caused widespread famine and where "62 percent of children under age 7 . . . have stunted growth and large numbers face mental development problems."[29]

UNICEF research identifies cultural practices that seriously undermine children's health in many countries, including policies that discourage breast-feeding as well as norms of preferential feeding of males over females and of adults over children. In many cultures "food and liquids are withheld during episodes of diarrhoea in the mistaken belief that doing so will end the diarrhoea. The practice is dangerous because it denies the child the nutrients and water vital for recovery" (1998: p. 28). Elsewhere, newborns suffer low birth weight because pregnant women are denied nutritious foods on the erroneous grounds that eating such foods as fish, meat, and eggs will result in babies too large and difficult to deliver (p. 31). Because infants' immune systems are not yet developed, they are especially susceptible to disease, even when cultural practices are beneficial to their thriving. But "in as many as 35 of the poorest countries 30 to 50 percent of the population may have no access to health services at all" (p. 25).

Adult acts of omission and commission have damaged the immune systems of millions of children worldwide with HIV, a number predicted to rise to between 4 and 5 million in the near future (1998: p. 71). By 2000, a quarter of a million youth worldwide were contracting HIV every month (UNICEF 2000). But as UNICEF (1998) points out, "It is less well known that malnutrition impairs the immune systems of at least 100 million young children and several million pregnant women, none of them infected by HIV" (p. 71). The comparison is ironic: "Unlike the situation with AIDS, the 'cure' for immune deficiency due to malnutrition has been known for centuries: It is achieved by ensuring an adequate dietary intake containing all essential nutrients" (p. 71). Adults' political conflicts and flawed institutions have stymied this cure.

One factor contributing to poor health in children is the forced work performed by hundreds of millions of them worldwide (Kielburger 1998). In 1998, the UN's International Labour Organization (ILO) reported that one-third or more of these working children labor under dangerous and debilitating conditions in jobs such as mining and construction.[30] While UNICEF (2000) estimates that 20 to 40 million children are indentured workers in South Asia, Children Against Underage Servitude and Employment reports that India alone employs 50 million children between the ages of ten and fourteen (not all are indentured). ILO surveys "show that about half of working children age 5 to 14 described their work as stressful, up to 60 percent said they return home exhausted, and up to 80 percent said they had no days off or free time."[31] Fifty to sixty million children aged five to eleven work in hazardous conditions, according to the ILO (UNICEF 2000). Family poverty and child labor help to explain why "nearly one quarter of the world's children between the ages of six to eleven never go to school" (Kielburger 1998: p. 309).

In addition to the forced sweatshop labor of children like Iqbal Masih, detailed in Chapter 5, the sexual enslavement of girls has become increasingly common in many parts of the world. "Selling naive and desperate young women into sexual bondage has become one of the fastest growing criminal enterprises in the robust global economy. . . . Child virgins are in particular demand in these markets because of a fear of AIDS."[32] International experts on child prostitution and pornography conservatively estimate the industry at $4 billion.[33] Marx (1988 [1848]: p. 71) once asked, "Do you charge us [communists] with wanting to stop the exploitation of children by their parents? To this crime we plead guilty." In some ways, this exploitation has worsened since 1848.

The curse of global conflicts hits children hardest of all. "Soldiers used to be the main casualties of war. No longer."[34] Throughout the 1990s, wars and their aftermath have been traumatizing millions of children around the globe.[35] In 1996, for instance, the number of refugees had risen to 43 million, of whom at least half were children. Every year, land mines kill between five and ten thousand children. Despite an international, Nobel Prize–winning movement to ban land mines, the Clinton administration in 1999 sought nearly $50 million from Congress "for a new type of artillery-fired land mine system designed to blow up tanks and people, which would violate an international treaty that the president had pledged to try to sign someday." [36] War and civil strife in Afghanistan have left 28,000 children surviving only "by scavenging through bombed-out buildings, salvaging scraps of metal, unexploded warheads and wood."[37] A quarter century after the Vietnam War ended, it is still killing children: "An old artillery shell exploded at the site of a former U.S. military base in southern Vietnam, killing seven people—including six children—and seriously injuring two others."[38] Between 1988 and 1997, armed conflict killed 2 million children; disabled (maimed, blinded, or brain-damaged) another 4 to 5 million; rendered 12 million homeless, orphaned, or separated from their families; and psychologically traumatized another 10 million. "The pain of Kosovo's children is whispered in troubled silences and shallow smiles. It is shouted in wakeful nights and wet beds. It is realized in play where they yell 'kill' and in drawings whose frequent theme is the violence that visited their villages. 'It isn't fair that my country is always burning,' said Kumrije, 13."[39] Not only are children killed by combatants, but, the UN reports, children around the world are dragooned into armies, an estimated 300,000 in 1999.[40] In the seventeen-year-old war between the Sri Lankan government and Tamil rebels, "children as young as 10 are groomed to be efficient killers, made possible by modern lightweight weapons."[41] Since the fall of the Berlin Wall, wars in Eastern Europe have left 2 million children homeless.[42]

Dramatic events such as plane crashes capture more public attention than the relentless daily tragedy these figures represent for the world's children. But the 35,000 children who die every day, mostly from preventable causes, are "the equivalent of ninety 747 jetliners filled with children crashing every 24 hours."[43] Most of these deaths are directly traceable to policies pursued by adult decisionmakers around the world. In the aftermath of the Persian Gulf War, U.S.-led United Nations economic sanctions against Iraq and its leader, Saddam Hussein, have had little success in changing Saddam's behavior but have killed an estimated 4,500 Iraqi children each month as a result of malnutrition or illness caused by the sanctions.[44]

In the United States

Despite the much greater resources available in the United States, U.S. children suffer grievously from a wide variety of harmful conditions. Hunger, for instance, afflicts more than one-quarter, or 13 million children, in the United States.[45] "Over 20 percent of children in the United States live in poverty, more than double the rate of most other industrialized countries." At the turn of the century, U.S. children remained 50 percent more likely to be in poverty than adults.[46] For African-American children, the figures are more than twice as grim, with almost half living in poverty. Over half the children born in New York City are born in poverty (UNICEF 2000). Even families living above the official poverty line—about $13,000 for a family of three in 1998—must forgo many basics, choosing from among food, clothing, housing, utilities, medical care, insurance, safety, and transportation (UNICEF 1998: pp. 15–16). *"40 percent of American children live in or near poverty,* with incomes below 200 percent of the poverty line."[47] Joint research by Housing America and the Doc4Kids Project has found significant relationships between inadequate housing, including homelessness, and a range of health problems in children, including, asthma, burns, lead poisoning, respiratory and diarrheal infections, and iron deficiency. In the United States, "21,000 children have stunted growth and 120,000 children suffer from anemia because their families must choose between food and rent."[48]

U.S. adults have a spotty record in terms of practices that affect children's health. According to the National Institutes of Health, one-fourth of U.S. children grow up exposed to alcoholism or alcohol abuse.[49] Millions of adults continue to smoke around children despite medical evidence that breathing secondhand smoke is unhealthy, especially for children. For instance, research published in the *New England Journal of Medicine* in 1990 found that "nonsmokers who grew up with two parents who smoked are twice as likely as other nonsmokers to develop lung cancer." Dr. Alfred Munzer, a pulmonary specialist with the American Lung Association, noted that "children are really a captive audience. They're the ideal guinea pig, because they have no way of escaping their parents' smoke."[50] In 1992 the Environmental Protection Agency warned that between 150,000 and 300,000 young children, especially infants, suffer serious respiratory illness because of exposure to adults' secondhand smoke.

A 1998 report in *Archives of Pediatric and Adolescent Medicine* found that "children exposed to secondhand cigarette smoke at home before age 3 are twice as likely to get serious middle-ear infections."[51] Some children, such as seven- and nine-year-olds Kate and Mary Binder, do try to escape their parents' smoke. After their father, a heavy smoker, died of lung cancer, they came to view cigarettes "the way some children think of monsters under the bed. They have thrown their mother's cigarette packs into the trash. In some cases, they have taken each cigarette out of the pack and broken every single one into pieces. They have begged, pleaded and cajoled her to stop. And they have thrown tantrums." Their mother, Jan, has tried to stop smoking but confesses, "I just don't know how."[52] In 1997, tobacco companies began publicly admitting that for decades they had targeted teens as young as thirteen, hoping to addict them to cigarettes and hook them on the companies' own brands.[53]

Exposure to lead-based paints and lead solder in pipes has also seriously compromised the health of young people, by tainting water and soil. In the early 1990s, the U.S. Department of Health and Human Services (HHS) identified lead as "the No. 1 environmental poison for children." Noting that between 3 and 4 million children under age six suffer from lead poisoning, HHS secretary Louis Sullivan charged, "Lead poisoning is entirely preventable, yet it is the most common and societally devastating environmental disease of young children."[54] In 2000, research in Ohio and Pennsylvania found a strong connection between exposure to lead and subsequent juvenile delinquency.[55] According to the EPA, not just lead but widely used pesticides, especially organophosphates, contaminate fruit, vegetables, and baby food consumed by over a million children younger than five every year. As a result of pesticides such as diazinon, malathion, and methyl parathion, these foods contain unsafe doses of toxic chemicals. "Kids should be able to eat a diet rich in fruits and vegetables without risking brain or nerve damage," says Richard Wiles of the Environmental Working Group.[56]

Pesticides, diesel exhaust, and other environmental hazards in poor neighborhoods have contributed to a doubling of the incidence of acute asthma in children in the 1990s, with the death rate from asthma attacks rising almost as steeply. "Asthma is the most common cause of hospitalization among American children, affecting 5 million of them," and a first-of-its-kind study in New York City found the hospitalization rate dramatically higher in poor, predominantly nonwhite neighborhoods.[57] In the case of diesel exhaust, "children appear to be especially vulnerable because they inhale a larger dose of the particles in proportion to their lung size."[58] When the EPA in 1999 banned the highly toxic pesticide methyl parathion, it was the first time the government had used children, rather than the average adult, in developing the risk standards. A given toxic concentration is more harmful to a typical child than to a typical adult.[59] The title of John Wargo's (1998) meticulous study tells the sad story: *Our Children's Toxic Legacy: How Science and Law Fail to Protect Us from Pesticides.*

"The essential powerlessness of children is nowhere more apparent than in the matter of child abuse" (Cohen 1980: p. 1). In the 1990s, survey researchers confirmed what feminist scholars and counseling psychologists had long been saying about the sexual abuse of children, especially girls. "As many as one-fourth of girls [in the United States] are sexually abused before their teenage years end," concluded *The Girls Report,* commissioned by the National Council for Research on Women.[60] In terms of child abuse and neglect more generally, about 1 million cases per year are reported to the U.S. Department of Health and Human Services, including over one thousand child deaths annually, with 80 percent of the perpetrators being the parents. Not just adults' acts of commission but also their acts of omission can harm children. Census Bureau reports throughout the 1990s have shown little improvement in the dismal record of ex-husbands on child support as reported in the early 1990s, when half of them failed to meet their child-support obligations.[61] A quarter failed to make any payments, dropping millions of children below the poverty line. Cliff Johnson, family-support director of the Children's Defense Fund, warned of the "great jeopardy" experienced by children in economically strained families unsupported by ex-husbands.[62] As an alternative, sadly, "the state has not proven itself to be a fit parent where the biological parents have failed" (Cohen 1980: p. 151).

The 1999 Columbine High School massacre underscored once again the exceptionally high level of violent crime, and youth deaths from violent crime, in the United States compared to other countries. For instance, according to the Centers of Disease Control and Prevention, "the gun-related death rate of U.S. children under the age of 15 is nearly 12 times higher than the combined totals of 25 other wealthy, industrialized nations. . . . The homicide rate by all causes for U.S. children is five times that in all those nations combined." A study by the United Nations found that in 1994–1995, 86 percent of the children around the world who were killed by firearms died in the United States. "Broken down per capita, the U.S. rate of firearms deaths is more than triple the next closest nation, Canada." In three of four Asian countries surveyed, there were no reported firearms deaths of children during the same period.[63] "In 1996, the last year for which comparative statistics are available, there were 15 handgun-caused deaths in Japan, 30 in Britain, 106 in Canada—and 9,390 in the United States."[64]

Much of the well-intentioned hoopla concerning the increased incidence of youth-on-youth violence overlooks the fact that the vast majority of violence against young people is committed by adults. FBI statistics show that only 13 percent of violent crime, and only 8 percent of murders, are committed by youth. Three-fourths of young murder victims are killed by adults, and "family violence is the chief killer of children under age 13," as well as of women generally. In short: "The youth culture of violence is the adult culture of violence." The highly publicized killings by students in the first half of 1998 resulted in the deaths of eleven youths and six adults, "fewer kids than are murdered by parents, and fewer adults than are killed by partners, in just two days of household violence in the United States."[65] To put the rate of violence against U.S. children in sobering perspective, we might consider the facts that the nearly 50,000 children killed by guns alone between 1979 and 1991 matched the number of Americans killed in the Vietnam War, and that a child in the United States in the 1990s was fifteen times more likely to be killed by gunfire than a child in politically violent northern Ireland.[66]

Automobile executive and one-time presidential hopeful Lee Iacocca has suggested expanding the concept of child abuse to encompass the fiscal irresponsibility of the current generation of U.S. adults: "We've created a congenital $3 trillion handicap that will be visited on every generation of Americans to come, a bitter legacy for our kids. Adding even another dollar to it should be considered a form of fiscal child abuse."[67] Iacocca may have gotten inspiration from Thomas Jefferson, who once said, "We should consider ourselves unauthorized to saddle posterity with our debts, and morally bound to pay them ourselves."[68] The buoyant U.S. economy of the late 1990s finally enabled the U.S. government to begin to pay down the enormous national debt.

Although many of the problems cited affect adults as well as children, it is widely recognized that they affect children more severely. Contrary to the presumption that benevolent paternalism provides children with unique protections, "life's miseries fall disproportionately on children" (Sulloway 1997: p. 119). Both in the United States and around the world, the single largest severely disadvantaged class is not women, people of color, or impoverished adults; it is children. "More than half the world's refugees are children under 18 years of age."[69] In all countries where young people either want or desperately need to find work, the youth unemployment rate is higher than the adult rate.[70] Marian Wright Edelman, president of the Children's Defense Fund, reports, "American children have become our nation's most frequent victims of poverty, hunger, drug addiction and abuse," adding that "we have one of the highest child poverty rates in the Western industrialized world."[71] According to a national study by the National Victims' Center, two-thirds of the victims of sex crimes are children, and 61 percent of rapes were carried out on children aged sixteen and younger.[72]

Not only are children the largest class of victims, but it is the youngest children who suffer the highest rates of victimization. A study by the Carnegie Corporation found that "the earliest years of a child's life are society's most neglected age group" and that "the life situation for many of the youngest children has deteriorated badly in the last 30 years." The three-year study found that one in three victims of physical abuse is a baby—a "quiet crisis" largely ignored by policymakers. "Our nation's children under 3 and their families are in trouble, and their plight worsens every day. To be sure, the children themselves are not quiet, they are crying out for help. But these sounds rarely become sound bites. Babies seldom make the news. They do not commit crimes, do drugs or drop out of school."[73]

The United States remains the only major industrialized nation in the world that lacks a system of national health insurance or its equivalent.[74] The failure of the Clintons' health initiative in the early 1990s was especially painful to the 40 million impoverished Americans, especially children, whose financial situation left them inadequately protected against medical disaster. The Clinton plan sought in part to address the fact that over 7 million U.S. children in the United States had no access to routine medical care at all, according to a study by the National Association of Children's Hospitals and Related Institutions. "Children are the most affected by the lack of universal medical care in this country," said Ron Pollack, executive director of Families USA, adding that "we'll all be better off if they grow up healthy because we're going to need them to run the country and take care of us."[75]

Underlying U.S. children's vulnerability to health problems, malnutrition, inadequate shelter and clothing, and other conditions affected by economics is the fact that they are 50 percent more likely than adults to be poor.[76] As co-median Lily Tomlin's 1970s fictional child Edith Ann quipped, "Among kids my age, childhood is the leading cause of stress." In the following decade, things got even worse for young people in the United States. The Reagan and Bush administrations imposed harsh cutbacks on programs for the needy, especially children. "Children are poor in extraordinarily large numbers. They are less healthy than their parents. . . . Our political system allowed 2 million children to fall into poverty in the 1980s while the num-ber of billionaires quintupled."[77] The child-friendlier Clinton administration fought Republicans in Congress to stem some of the worsening indicators for children, but poor families and their children benefited very little from the generally robust U.S. economy of the 1990s.[78] The official (and under-estimated) poverty rate for children remains around 20 percent, compared to about 13 percent for the overall U.S. population. Almost half of poor children live in extreme poverty.[79]

The United States is one of only six countries that regularly execute young people for juvenile crimes. One hundred and sixty children have been sentenced to death in the United States since 1973, despite the fact that international human-rights treaties prohibit the execution of children. "The youngest person executed since WWII in the U.S. was George Stin-ney, a 14-year-old black boy who was so small his mask fell off while he was being electrocuted by the state of South Carolina."[80] In early American Puritan settlements, "witchcraft, idolatry, blasphemy, and even rebellious-ness by children all merited the death penalty" (Lind 1996: p. 365). The first child executed in the American colonies was Thomas Graunger of Ply-mouth Colony, Massachusetts, in 1642, for having sex with an animal. Since then, 357 young people have been executed for juvenile crimes, in-cluding 13 since 1976, when the death penalty was reinstated. Governmen-tal executions are the most cold-blooded of killings; they undermine the Judeo-Christian standard that "thou shalt not kill"; they fail to deter crime[81]; and when carried out mistakenly, they are irreversible.[82] Moreover, if the slogan "no taxation without representation" helped to justify the American Revolution, perhaps "no execution without representation" fur-ther calls into question the disfranchisement of youth.[83] The U.S. practice of executing children has been chillingly satirized by cartoonist Ed Stein, who depicted an electric chair with a booster seat.

The widespread and persistent record of children's suffering indicts not only the general social regime of adult paternalism but also governments, elected and run exclusively by adults, that persist in policies harmful to children. The U.S. government is culpable across a wide range of children's issues, especially compared with other capitalist democracies. Economist Sylvia Ann Hewlett has shown that the United States spends less time and money on children than any other country with comparable per capita in-come.[84] Sociologist Stephanie Coontz (1997: p. 175) believes that U.S.

leaders and institutions have a responsibility to make up this difference: "The Economic Policy Institute estimates that it would take $112 billion a year to bring our children's health, nutrition, and education up to the standards that now exist in Europe." More than half of this amount, or $73 billion per year, could be raised by merely taxing the richest 1 percent of Americans at the rate they were taxed at in 1954. The rest could be raised by converting 17 percent of the military budget of $300 billion, or $50 billion, to children's programs. An example of an underfunded program that more than pays for itself is Head Start, which, the Children's Defense Fund calculates, saves three dollars in future costs of teen pregnancy, welfare, and crime for each dollar spent on the three-to-five-year-olds covered.[85]

U.S. public and corporate health authorities have dragged their heels in responding to the Baby Friendly Hospital Initiative launched by UNICEF and the World Health Organization in 1991 to improve hospital protocols in such areas as encouragement of breast-feeding. In the first six years of the initiative, 12,700 hospitals in 114 countries were certified as baby-friendly, compared with a mere dozen U.S. hospitals certified.[86] By 1998 only two nations in the world, the United States and Somalia, had refused to sign the United Nations' 1989 Convention on the Rights of the Child. The U.S. government dislikes the Convention's banning of capital punishment for children, its nonrecognition of a fetus as a child, and other features that might encroach on adult authority. In 1997, Human Rights Watch faulted the Clinton administration for its failure to push for U.S. ratification of the child-rights convention as well as its foot-dragging on other children's issues, including an international ban on land mines.

U.S. leaders often seem oblivious to the effects of their policies on children. In 1997 the government "cut off cash benefits for 95,180 disabled children. . . . The cash benefits, averaging $436 a month for a child, are paid under the Supplemental Security Income program. The children are all from low-income families."[87] A year later, House Republicans, not satisfied with the 1997 cuts, sought additional benefit reductions for tens of thousands more disabled children. Subcommittee chairman Clay Shaw (R-Florida) assured critics that "we're going to do it in a caring, cautious manner."[88]

Paternalism: Benevolent and Misguided

The point is not that adults just don't care about children. Many do, despite a recent national survey showing that "only 20 percent of adults strongly agree that youths are a top priority in their communities"[89]—a finding mirrored in a 1997 national survey by the Search Institute of Minneapolis reporting that only 17 percent of ninth-graders think that adults in their community value youth. Examples of benevolent paternalism abound. Even the U.S. Congress and President Clinton, often at odds, agreed in 1998 to target

3 million deadbeat parents as a part of the government's increased concern for children's suffering. The government expressed concern that teenagers make up a third of the nation's victims of violent crimes, that 2.8 million additional children are abused or neglected annually (including the 1 million officially reported), and that 9 million adolescents aged twelve to seventeen have witnessed serious violence. President Clinton said that it is "time to ask why a bank robber who unintentionally kills an innocent bystander can be charged with felony murder but a repeat child abuser who unintentionally kills a child cannot be."[90]

Both the Gray Panthers and the American Association of Retired Persons, who advocate for senior citizens, have supported health and other benefits for children as well. The Kempe National Center for the Prevention and Treatment of Child Abuse and Neglect and the U.S. Advisory Board on Child Abuse and Neglect have persistently urged the government to take dramatic steps to protect children through social services, public health, criminal justice, and school policies. Children's campaigns in various states seek to increase public awareness and funding of children's needs. The Child Welfare League of America works with agencies that provide foster care and children's residential programs. The nationwide Association of Child Advocates supports programs in the states covering a wide range of children's needs. The national group Hear My Voice advocates for children involved in disputed adoption proceedings. Some children's museums feature exhibits on problems afflicting children, such as the Indianapolis Children's Museum's photographic exhibit "Outside the Dream: Child America in Poverty," intended to build compassion for poor children "from the barrio slums of Los Angeles to the welfare hotels of New York."[91]

Alongside such benevolent paternalism is a great deal of arguably well-intentioned but misguided paternalism. Hitting another person is considered assault and battery—unless the other person is a child. Although many adults hit children out of anger or frustration, many others sincerely believe that hitting or spanking children helps discipline them to become better persons.[92] The best scientific evidence, however, shows just the opposite. The more parents spank, the worse the child's behavior is likely to become. Children who are spanked are subsequently more likely to cheat and lie, become aggressive, bully their peers, get into trouble at school, destroy property, physically abuse their dates and spouses, become depressed, and lag behind their nonspanked peers in cognitive development.[93] Despite such evidence, and despite recommendations against spanking by groups such as the American Medical Association, the American Academy of Pediatrics, the National Association of Social Workers, and the U.S. surgeon general, 94 percent of U.S. parents still spank their four- and five-year-olds. However, in the last generation, the percentage of U.S. adults who believe that spanking is necessary has decreased dramatically, from over 90 percent to just over half in 1999.[94] Though common in much of the world, spanking has been banned in an increasing number of countries. Throughout Scandinavia, as well as in Austria, Italy, Cyprus, Latvia, Croatia, and Israel, spanking is now illegal and may subject a spanking adult to charges of assault.[95] The new Social Democrat–Green coalition government in Germany is considering a ban on spanking, as is the Labour government in England. "The right of children to be reared without violence must be anchored in the law books," the *Cologne Express* quoted the new German family minister, Christine Bergmann, as saying.[96] A ban on corporal punishment is under consideration in more than a dozen additional countries.[97]

A generation of physical disciplining of children has transpired since children's liberationist John Holt (1976) wrote that "we know that many of our most unruly young, in or out of schools, the ones who most fiercely and violently defy all authority, who form gangs and commit crimes, are those who in their early years were most strictly and punitively brought up" (p. 31). Seventy-three-year-old Eda LeShan, a teacher, author, and therapist, writes, "There won't be any headstone to mark my passing, but I keep thinking that if there were, all I'd want it to say is, *Please don't hit your kids. . . . In my work in prisons, I have never met a person convicted of serious crimes who wasn't beaten as a child.*"[98] Irrespective of child-friendly laws in Europe or the United States, children still depend on adults, whether parental or governmental, to protect them legally from being struck by other adults; they themselves have no official say in the matter. Many parents justify spanking by reference to their religious beliefs, and think that government should recognize and authorize this religious practice.

Also reflecting religious influence, legislatures in many of the United States have required girls seeking an abortion to inform both parents, even if they are estranged from a parent or if the parents are divorced. In August 2000, U.S. District Judge Walker Miller struck down a Colorado law requiring that parents be notified before minors have abortions, ruling that women's constitutional abortion rights apply to minor women as well. The U.S. Supreme Court has been deeply divided on this issue. Some religions forbid dancing, and U.S. courts have approved public school bans on students' dancing on the basis of local school authorities' religious view that dancing is sinful or satanic. In an increasingly typical case of secular concern, ten-year-old Shanon Coslett was expelled from her Denver school in 1998 for violating a state "zero-tolerance," antiweapons policy, when, discovering that she had inadvertently brought a steak knife to school in a lunchbox she had borrowed from her mother, she promptly reported the oversight to her teacher. The teacher reported her to the principal, who sent her home. After much outrage by other students and many parents, the traumatized ten-year-old was reinstated at her school. Young people themselves have no political voice in setting or abolishing such policies, whether they relate to abortion, dancing, or weapons.

More dramatically, many children have suffered and, according to a *Pediatrics* study, 140 have died needlessly because their parents' religious beliefs opposed medical treatment.[99] Many of these parents may have wished the best for their children. Courts have been inconsistent in intervening to protect such children, who themselves have no legal right to participate in making, administering, or interpreting laws that might protect them from the death sentence unintentionally passed on them by their zealous parents.

Children have often been deprived of excellent teachers because parents or administrators disapproved of the teacher's style or choice of materials. Such a teacher is Ruth Sherman, whose mostly black third-grade class in the Bushwick neighborhood of Brooklyn loved both her and the books she assigned, including *Nappy Hair,* a story criticizing adult intolerance of the natural hair of black children. The story's author, Carolivia Herron, wrote the book about her own experience as an African-American child. Herron says, "Children understand right away that this book"—acclaimed by educators and critics alike—"is about acceptance and celebration. It pains me that some adults have not gotten there." The adults she is referring to are the African-American parents who drove Sherman, who is white, to resign after threatening her and calling her "cracker" and other racial epithets. Sherman "was caught in the cross hairs of political correctness. Some parents thought a white teacher had no business raising such a culturally sensitive subject."[100] The students had no say in retaining their teacher.

A good example of well-meaning adultism is Neil Postman's (1994) *The Disappearance of Childhood,* intended to save children from capitalism by putting them back in their proper place. In modern times, children are being made to grow up too fast, Postman argues, enticed by television, consumer culture, cosmetics manufacturers, and fashion designers; they should be protected by benevolent adults. His arguments for keeping adults in control and children in the dark illustrate the dangers of kindly adultism. He admits that the regime of adults is characterized by contradiction and hypocrisy. "But," he argues, "the better face of hypocrisy is, after all, a certain social idealism. . . . Childhood, as we ideally think of it, cannot exist without a certain measure of hypocrisy. . . . Surely, hypocrisy in the cause of strengthening child growth is no vice." By the standard of benevolent adultism, hypocrisy becomes a virtue because being truthful with young people will "undermine a child's belief in adult rationality," given "the plain fact that the adult world is filled with ineptitude, strife, and worry." He thinks it unhealthy for children to learn of "the persistent incompetence of political leaders" (pp. 92–93).

Perhaps he had in mind a youngster such as Gro Waeraas, a sixteen-year-old from Bergen, Norway, who commented on World Environment Day in 1990, "They say knowledge is power; well, we have much knowledge, but not any power. We have to rely on the adults to make the decisions that affect our future, and we aren't liking what we are seeing."[101] Or Postman may have envisioned a child such as Illinois seventh-grader Will Boyd, who, observing state legislators screaming at each other during his school trip to the capitol in 1998, reported, "It isn't looking very impressive. They're banging their books and stuff."[102] Postman fears that such experiences might cause children to develop "what may be called adult attitudes—from cynicism to indifference—toward political leaders and toward the political process itself" (1994: pp. 94–95). He commends Moral Majority–supported censorship as protective of children (p. 148).

The "cynicism," or, more accurately, realism, of Free the Children founder and Medal of Freedom winner Craig Kielburger, sixteen, is the best response to Postman. Asked if he would consider "going into politics," Kielburger laughed and replied, "I've met too many politicians. It's a very noble pursuit, but you have to compromise too many of your morals." Having observed firsthand the effects of war in Kosovo and elsewhere, he plans to pursue a Ph.D. in international conflict mediation. His disinterest in running for political office, however, has not stopped him from helping change corporate and governmental policies affecting children when adults had failed to do so.[103]

Ignoring evidence of youthful protests against adultism as well as adults' efforts to maintain it, Postman asserts that it is actually adults who want to abolish childhood, and children who want to maintain it. "Children themselves are a force in preserving childhood. Not a political force, certainly. But a kind of moral force." His evidence for this counterintuitive generalization is scanty and unconvincing. Despite his harsh judgment of adult governance, he prefers to keep government an adult monopoly in which young people are "not a political force" (p. viii).[104] In short, Postman believes that children are better off idealizing, and entrusting their fates to, a political class he admits is hypocritical, irrational, and inept. Far from being oppressive, as charged by children's liberationists Richard Farson (1974) and John Holt (1976), he believes that this paradoxical formula preserves for children their "preferred status" (p. 5) of political dependency.

The illogic of this position is so striking that we need to remind ourselves of the important kernel of truth underlying Postman's paternalism. No doubt the charlatans of corporate capitalism—hawkers of cosmetics, titans of tobacco, purveyors of pornography and violence—exploit young people in the pursuit of profit.[105] And no doubt advertisers and the media pressure young people to "grow up too fast." But the crucial point missed by adultist doomsayers of idyllic childhood is that it is primarily the arbitrary ageist restrictions placed on youth that make acting like an adult seem so attractive, so romantically rebellious. Let us note the cultural contexts, from medieval Europe to traditional Iroquois and Balinese society to modern Zimbabwe and Denmark, in which lesser distinctions between childhood and adulthood have discouraged self-conscious adolescent posturing at "acting grown-up."[106] In such places today, capitalism may still hawk its wares, but it must do so in a bear market for adultophilia.

In *The Sibling Society*, Robert Bly (1997) approvingly cites Postman's position regarding the disappearance of childhood (p. 133), but goes much

further than Postman in hypothesizing—and hyperbolizing—that as paternal authority waned in the late 1950s, "the children soon saw that they had
been put into power," that "by 1980 most high schools were being run by
their own students" (p. 6), and that "the elders are without power" (p. 161).
Beyond anecdotes, which by themselves, Bly concedes, prove nothing, he
gives no systematic evidence for this inflated claim, which would certainly
surprise the young activists against adultism whom we met in Chapter 5.
Contrary to Bly's claim of youth empowerment, today's effete fathers and
harried mothers have handed over far more of their powers to external authorities and institutions than to their sons and daughters. Ingleby shows
"how the state, mediating the psy complex, has infiltrated the very heart of
family dynamics. Professionals maintain power *through* the parent by educating the parent about the professional's worldview. . . . These professionals produce ways of living and thinking consistent with the social order."[107]
In Chapter 7, I return to families' increasing dependence on government,
corporations, and the "helping professions."

As we shall see, U.S. courts start by distinguishing Americans on the
basis of age, but then modify age by an ad hoc incorporation of qualities
such as intelligence, maturity, experience, and responsibility. The rational
criteria lurking beneath the arbitrary one of age are revealed in the adultist
view of juvenile-court judge Lindsay G. Arthur, who regards children as
less than people: "Should children be as equal as people? Certainly not.
They should not have equal liberty: they should have less. Neither should
they have equal protection—they should have more. How much less and
how much more *will depend on the maturity of the particular child at the
particular time*."[108] But why, then, is level of maturity not relevant in the
case of adults as well?

The problem with all systems of benevolent despotism is that the "beneficiaries" have no recourse if the despotic policies in fact hurt them rather
than help them.

"I'd Like to Help You, Son . . .

. . . But you're too young to vote," says the politician in Eddie Cochran's
1958 hit song "Summertime Blues"—and again in Blue Cheer's 1968 version and The Who's 1970 version. Young people's purchases of the record
made all three versions top-thirty hits.[109] The message of the lyric is that
adult politicians will do something for you, but only if there's something
in it for them, like a vote. Being "a kind of moral force" has not protected
children from the ongoing ravages of the adult-controlled world. A number
of observers have noted, somewhat incidentally, that children are harmed
by their political disfranchisement. For instance, U.S. Senator Patrick
Leahy, Democrat from Vermont, has charged, "The Republicans know that

children are not old enough to vote, so they have targeted the school lunch program."[110]

Marian Wright Edelman, president of the Children's Defense Fund, has noted that "politicians love to make speeches about families and children, but when they get back to Washington and budget battles, kids are the last to cross their minds. Kids don't vote."[111] In a 1990 campaign-support solicitation, New York Democratic U.S. senator Daniel Patrick Moynihan called for welfare reform, adding that "its main beneficiaries—children—do not vote." Child-care supporter Mary Anne Moore suggested that "if children could vote, Congress might sit up and take notice. 'But since they can't,' she said angrily, 'they are easily overlooked by politicians—except when they need a campaign picture in a child care center.'"[112] When the Federal Trade Commission proposed in 1979 to ban television commercials aimed at children, notes Gary Ruskin, "Congress prohibited the agency from proposing such rules, and revoked many of the FTC's powers. Children cannot vote or make the large campaign contributions needed to win political power in Washington. They have neither powerful lobbyists nor a powerful political organization. Advertisers do, and in Washington they win."[113]

"Why Don't Our Votes Count!" read the widely published placard of a grade-schooler protesting forced school busing in 1968. "If they could vote, how many babies and toddlers would 'veto' formula feeding and early weaning in favor of extended breast-feeding?" asks La Leche League leader Petra Ulrych.[114] Infants' cries in effect "vote for" mother's milk over formula, she says, noting the ironic fact that scientific studies confirm the visceral, biological wisdom of the young children over the health-risking preference of the formulaic adults. Social ecologist Andrew Males argues that what is really the adult problem is mislabeled as the "youth problem" because "grown-ups vote and kids don't."[115] The founders of the Initiative for Children and Families see themselves as advocating for those who are prevented from voting, especially children.[116] As we shall see, Paul Peterson (1993) makes a strong case that it is children's disfranchisement that best explains the superior benefits government provides to seniors compared with children.

In sum, the evidence is weak for the claim that the adult world takes such good care of children that concerns about their disfranchisement are moot. If empirical evidence fails to support a utilitarian argument for political adultism, what theoretical rationale might there be for breaking up the adult monopoly and giving young people a political voice?

Children's Right to Vote

Democracy's basic rationale for citizens' voting rights rests on the equal consent of the governed, the idea that everyone affected by governmental policy is equally entitled to a say—and, in a formal sense, entitled to an equal say—in shaping that policy or in holding the policymakers accountable.[117] Any group denied the right to vote can expect to find its way of life controlled by those who do enjoy this right. Giving each member of the polity one and only one vote denies any special voting privileges to citizens on the basis of their greater knowledge, rationality, responsibility, experience, selflessness, or intelligence (the KRRESI test). The U.S. Supreme Court's banning of literacy tests for voting confirmed that voting is a citizen's automatic right, not an earned privilege. The primary argument for the 26th Amendment to the U.S. Constitution, which enfranchised eighteen-, nineteen-, and twenty-year-olds in federal elections, was the injustice of drafting them to fight and die in Vietnam while denying them a political say in the policies that were sending them to their deaths. Before the statistical carnage and graphic footage of dead youth became politically irresistible, the Congress of elders had ten times rejected lowering the voting age.[118]

As we have seen, unfortunately, more than distant wars kill young people, and do so on a daily basis. Dozens of U.S. policies—on health care, pollution, land mines, welfare cuts, parental powers, crime, economic and foreign policy, and children's rights themselves—kill children just as surely as Viet Cong bullets did a generation ago. The logic underlying the 26th Amendment remains alive today for citizens younger than eighteen. Enfranchised sixteen- and seventeen-year-olds may have made the difference in the 2000 electoral victory of reformist, prodemocracy forces in Iran— hardly a bastion of democracy.

On what grounds, we might ask, may citizens below the age of eighteen, or below any particular age, be denied the *right* to vote? Democracy is not based on a voting privilege that must be earned by virtuous citizens, by those who can demonstrate some particular level of KRRESI-ness. Rather, it is based on a right to participate in a political process that affects one's well-being. The essence of adultist ideology is the assumption that subadults, those below some chronological age set by self-defined adults, are incapable of voting in an adult way. By some abrupt, mysterious process, on their eighteenth birthday young people purportedly acquire adult voting virtues they formerly lacked.

This rationale for adultist enfranchisement suffers from two fatal flaws. First, many young people are more politically virtuous—more knowledgeable, rational, responsible, experienced, selfless, and intelligent—than many older people. Second, even if they were not, the democratic right to vote is not based on one's virtue but on one's being affected by public policy. No adult is required to demonstrate any political virtue whatsoever. If the ability to vote virtuously is important enough to disfranchise an entire age class, why then is it simultaneously so unimportant that the most ignorant, irrational, irresponsible, inexperienced, selfish, and unintelligent adult is automatically permitted to vote? Clearly, it is the difference in power, not virtue, that explains elders' disfranchisement of youth. Like adults who spank, adults who deny children a political voice teach them that might makes right.

Aristocrats and meritocrats, unlike democrats, can argue logically for the disfranchisement of the politically unvirtuous and unmeritorious. Given their commitment to the rule of the best, or most deserving, these elitists can legitimately argue for a political test to determine which citizens deserve the privilege of voting. But some of these virtuous or meritorious citizens will turn out to be children, and many of the undeserving will be adults. Adultist enfranchisement thus contradicts both democracy and aristo/meritocracy. The aristo/meritocratic form of discrimination, though undemocratic, is not capricious but is based on a consistent principle of virtue or desert. Defenders of democracy, however, cannot logically make this argument on behalf of ageist disfranchisement.[119]

American adults complain of young people's loss of respect for authority. But nothing breeds disrespect for authority more than arbitrary rules and hypocritical practices. Having admitted in 1971 that they had no right to send children to their deaths in Vietnam without allowing them a political voice, adultists ever since have been clawing hard not to slide farther down the slippery slope of democratic logic. Southern aristocrat George Fitzhugh warned of this danger in 1857: "The widows and free negroes begin to vote in some of those States, and they will have to let all colors and sexes and ages vote soon, or give up the glorious principles of human equality and universal emancipation."[120]

Indeed, if children forced to go to war should be able to vote against the military draft, why shouldn't children who are forced to ingest harmful chemical residues have the right to vote for traditional, organic agriculture? Why shouldn't children whose medical benefits are cut have the right to vote for national health insurance? Why shouldn't children who are forced to breathe toxic air caused by adults' driving habits have the right to vote for mass transit? Why shouldn't children whose future is being mortgaged by adults' fiscal irresponsibility have the right to vote for a balanced budget? Why shouldn't children who value their earthly inheritance have the right to vote against adult despoliation of the environment? Why shouldn't children taught to work out their problems without fighting have the right to vote for peace rather than war?

Adultist ideology has no convincing answers to such questions. In the final analysis, it rests its case neither on its logic, which is faulty, nor on its laurels, which are tarnished, but on the power wielded by its adult believers. The continuing triumph of adultism is by fiat of the well-armed faithful. The proper means for redressing this ageist injustice is a national movement to secure a constitutional Amendment 28 removing from Amendment 26 the offensive clause "who are eighteen years of age or older." The highest law of the land would then read: "The right of citizens of the United States to vote shall not be denied or abridged by the United States or by any State on account of age."

It may be instructive to view this proposed amendment in light of the U.S. historical tradition of removing limitations on the right to vote. About every half century since the founding of the republic, an arbitrary disfranchisement has been excised. In the early nineteenth century, the Jacksonian revolution swept away property requirements for white male voters in the states. Amendments 15 (1870) and 19 (1920) prohibited disfranchisement on the basis of race and sex, respectively. The stock arguments against these amendments were virtually identical to the arguments against the amendment to enfranchise minors: namely, the allegation that whites and men (like adults) were politically more knowledgeable, rational, responsible, experienced, selfless, and intelligent than blacks and women (who were like children). The stock arguments against allowing the lower classes to vote were virtually identical to those against allowing blacks, women, and children to vote.[121] In 1971, the eighteen-to-twenty-one-year-old chunk of ageist disfranchisement was abolished. If history continues to repeat itself, it will take antiadultist forces until about 2020 to remove the final remnant of arbitrary disfranchisement.

As of 1999, Kids Voting USA had established voting mechanisms for school children in 16,000 voter precincts in forty states plus the District of Columbia. Involving 5 million students and 200,000 teachers from 6,000 schools, "Kids Voting USA teaches youth . . . the importance of being informed and the responsibilities of voting." Started in 1988 by three Arizona businessmen inspired by a similar system of youth voting in Costa Rica, this private initiative encourages entire families, or school classes, to discuss elections and go to the polls together. Youth votes are counted separately from the official, adult votes. Although the youth votes are not legally binding, in Costa Rica they appear to have influenced subsequent adult voting on such issues as environmental protection. "Kids Voting increases parent voter turnout between 5 and 10 percent." [122] It also reduces the socioeconomic status gap in political awareness and participation, eliminates the traditional gender gap, and doubles newspaper reading among its youthful participants.

Perhaps most important, programs such as Kids Voting USA may suggest to the young participants that their ideas count—and that their votes should count too. "It's created political monsters among Arizona kids," according to Kids Voting president Marilyn Evans. "We couldn't stop them." Thousands of the children initiated political discussions in their homes and pressured their parents to vote.[123]

But, But, But—
The Most Common Lines of Adultist Defense

In conferences across North America and in Europe, as well as on talk radio, I have fielded a wide range of objections to my proposed 28th

Amendment. The following are the most common objections, along with my responses.

1. *The Tiny Tot Objection:* "You have to set the limit at *some age*, after all. How could an infant vote?

On the contrary, there is no need to prohibit anyone, even infants, from voting. A guaranteed right merely ensures that anyone who can and wants to exercise it may do so. A right to do something one is unable to do becomes moot. However, like an elderly or disabled person, a child who wishes to express a political preference may need physical help in doing so. Further, there is no more need to prohibit a very young child from casting a "meaningless" vote than there is to prohibit a clueless or senile adult from casting an equally meaningless vote. Statistically, meaningless votes by children and adults alike will cancel one another out, and not affect the electoral outcome. At the other end of the ageist spectrum, if we were really serious about eliminating meaningless votes, we would need to rescind the franchise from senile senior citizens, such as former President Reagan—a political maelstrom into which even the most ageist of ideologues fear to tread. Incidentally, some states do prohibit the insane from voting, while others do not. For obvious reasons, senior citizens are a tougher constituency to railroad than children or the mentally incompetent.

2. *The Big Family Objection:* "Kids will vote however their parents tell them to, and bloc voting would be unfair."

Since when is bloc voting unfair? Voting conspiracies are not only legal; they are as American as apple pie. They are a highly rational way of increasing the likelihood that the conspiring voters will make a difference. On the other hand, I always ask the Big Family objectors whether they have children, and if so, whether their children always do what they tell them to do, especially when the children can do just the opposite *in guaranteed secrecy*. Secret ballots ensure that children, like adults, will vote exactly how they want to—like my mother, who always voted the way she wanted to (Democratic) and then told my father that she had voted the way he wanted her to (often Republican). As documented in Chapter 5, in some issue areas children as a class hold consistently different political views from adults as a class—evidence that many children do not follow their parents' views.[124] No doubt children on the whole do tend to vote the way their parents want them to, but so do most adults.[125] No one suggests that adults who follow a family tradition in voting should for that reason be disfranchised.

Finally, we should note that according to democracy's criterion of one-person, one-vote political equality, big families *should* have a bigger say than small families. In many cases, the Big Family Objection is at root a Big Family of Color Objection, whereby childless or small-family whites fear they will be electorally swamped by larger black, Latino, or Asian families. "A citadel mentality predominates in which fears of engulfing hoards of unwanted children (all those 'dangerous' HIV-infected and drug-addicted babies) and their irresponsible parents ('impossible' teenage mothers, post-welfare 'losers,' and deadbeat Dads) have coarsened the political culture" (Scheper-Hughes and Sargent 1998: p. 11). Enfranchising children of color would compound white fears of nonwhite fertility and immigration, which are already reducing white electoral dominance in many parts of the United States. But white adults who believe in democracy are just going to have to "get used to it": more people deserve more votes than fewer people. One recourse is for whites to hope that future voters of color will be less racist than whites have been. A better recourse is for them to work actively to reduce racism in U.S. society.

3. *The Manipulated Child Objection:* "Children would be manipulated and harmed by adults seeking their votes."

This objection is related to the Big Family argument but focuses less on the injustice of adults multiplying their votes by bamboozling children than on the harm done to the children themselves. In a sympathetic but critical appraisal of Arendt's objection to the politicization of children as practiced under communism, Elshtain (1997a: p. 120) notes that "children are never *spared* politics" because a "nation's or homeland's life is entangled with personal lives of children everywhere." As Coles (1986: p. 310) had argued earlier, "A nation's politics becomes a child's everyday psychology." As Elshtain warns, "It is not only impossible to shield children entirely from political controversies that engage their parents, it may sometimes be damaging to do so" (1997a: p. 123). She cites children who have benefited from their involvement as "workers, patriots, and protestors" while serving as "apprentice citizens" (p. 125). Arendt tried to separate the private from the political, a dichotomy Elshtain (p. 121) questions: "When children *do* politics *with* their parents, or urge their parents into politics (as nearly every parent of my generation can attest in the matter of environmental concerns, it was the children that compelled recycling, energy-saving, non-smoking in many households), we are in a world that puts pressure on Arendt's categories."[126]

Children are already manipulated and harmed by adults seeking their dollars, their addictive potential, their bodies, their minds, and their loyalty to corporate products. Many children already speak out against these forms of manipulation and organize themselves to take political action against them. Gaining the vote would strengthen their voice in these efforts.

4. *The Unlimited Candy and Recess Objection:* "Children would immaturely and self-destructively vote for unlimited candy, perpetual recess, and other foolish things."

How easily we forget that foolish voting is the inalienable right of all democratic voters—a feature that inspired Ambrose Bierce's (1993 [1911]: p. 54) definition of an "idiot" as a member of "a large and powerful tribe whose influence has always been dominant and controlling." But in fact, the evidence suggests that children, more than adults, would vote for environmental protection, fiscal responsibility, rehabilitation of criminals, mediational alternatives to litigation, better funding of schools and antidrug programs, mass transit, gun control, racial and sexual tolerance, national health insurance, and peaceful solutions to international conflict.[127] Political opponents, especially conservatives, may disagree with these positions, but hardly on the grounds that they are "childish."

Despite these age-based patterns of difference, the ideological diversity among young people, like that among adults, is far greater than the average ideological differences between young people and adults. Said differently, on most issues conservative children will politically align themselves with conservative adults, and liberal children with liberal adults, more readily than young conservatives will ally themselves with young liberals. The adultist fear that children will politically swamp their elders recalls earlier fears that whites would be politically swamped by blacks or that men would be swamped by women, an actual majority. On the contrary, enfranchising an unfairly disfranchised class removes one of its prime incentives for class consciousness. Absent a common adult oppressor, the natural political diversity of young people will more readily emerge.

5. *The Apathetic Youth Objection:* "The evidence suggests that most children wouldn't vote anyway."

So what? Unfortunately, most adults "don't vote anyway," either. Ironically, they decline to exercise the very voting rights they categorically deny the young.[128] Granted, the youngest adults have the lowest voting rates.[129] But their lifelong disfranchisement up to age eighteen is the primary reason for their low voter turnout. Carole Pateman (1970: p. 42) advises, "If we are interested in more extensive political participation than we now have in our society, then it can only be to our benefit to involve people early. . . . Owing to the age barrier, all who come to politics, come to it late." John Dewey puts the matter more generally: "Thinking is secreted in the interstices of habit."[130] Adult society traditionally denies its children political personhood for their first two decades and then hopes for a miraculous, virgin birth of political adulthood and civic responsibility. But why should we expect people who have been told for their entire lives that their opinions don't count suddenly to become active participants in an alien political process?

In any case, this objection is irrelevant, since Amendment 28 would protect the rights of children *who do want to vote.* We can hardly justify disfranchising the politically aware and active on the basis of other people's "apathy." Moreover, "apathy" is a misnomer for powerlessness, implying incorrectly that people, including children, don't care what happens to them. I have yet to meet a person, even a suicidal person, who didn't care what happened to him or her. But I have known many people who felt powerless to use the political system to advance their goals. College students' interest in politics has plummeted by 50 percent since 1968, a trend coinciding with a general disengagement of Americans from the political process.

Only 14 percent of college freshmen say they "frequently discuss politics," down from 30 percent in 1968. Factors cited by many young people include a sense of powerlessness, disgust with national politics, and a PC-based fear of offending their friends.[131]

By contrast, gradual, lifelong engagement in the political process, as experienced by students in the British Summerhill school system, steadily builds a sense of empowerment, or efficacy, in young citizens. At Summerhill (and its varied offshoots) all members of the community, including students, faculty, and staff, have enjoyed the right to participate equally in policymaking. Founder and principal A. S. Neill had one vote, just like the youngest child. Neill (1960: pp. 47–48) reports a revealing case of the private school's nonadultist, democratic process:

> I once brought forth a motion that swearing be abolished by law, and I gave my reason. I had been showing a woman around with her little boy, a prospective pupil. Suddenly from upstairs came a very strong adjective. The mother hastily gathered up her son and went off in a hurry. "Why," I asked at a meeting, "should my income suffer because some fathead swears in front of a prospective parent?" My question was answered by a lad of fourteen. "Neill is talking rot," he said. "Obviously, if this woman was shocked, she didn't believe in Summerhill. Even if she had enrolled her boy, the first time he came home saying damn or hell, she would have taken him out of here." The meeting agreed with him, and my proposal was voted down.[132]

Young people, like all people, learn from their mistakes. If they exercise their votes foolishly—and who hasn't?—perhaps by failing to heed wise advice from their elders, they can learn from their misjudgments. When the schoolchildren at Summerhill discussed their prospective field trips and then voted on whether to go, for instance, to the British Museum or the Surrey countryside, they lived with the consequences of their decisions. If they chose Surrey while failing to heed their elders' warnings that the weather might turn rainy, and consequently ended up rained on, cold, and unhappy, they became more likely to listen to their elders the next time around. Having their voices heard made them more responsive, not less, to the voices of their parents and teachers. Few Summerhill students have grown up to become the politically uninvolved, "apathetic" citizens typical of modern English and U.S. society. Their youthful experience of empowerment taught them a different lesson.

6. *The Dumbing Down Objection:* "Even if many adults are politically childlike, adding actual children to the electorate would even further 'dumb down' our polity."

This objection, while possibly true in the short run—since people require practice to get good at most things—rests on aristocratic rather than democratic grounds. The logical implication would be to develop a "political literacy" test that would identify the "dumbest" electors, both children and adults, and disfranchise them, thus "brightening up" the polity. A valid, reliable, and fairly administered political-knowledge test would be a much better proxy for political virtue and good citizenship than is chronological age. But let there be no doubt: if the political literacy bar were set even moderately high, then the electorate would shrink from a democratic river of mediocrity to an aristocratic rivulet of virtue. And some of the few who passed this embarrassing muster would be children.

7. *The Disappearing Childhood Objection:* "Pressuring children to vote would warp their development by forcing them to grow up too fast."

Despite the weakness of Postman's paternalistic argument, criticized earlier, this objection is at least a plausible one. As Postman and Bly both illustrate, crass commercialism, premature sexualization, and dilatory parenting do indeed foster Vincent Canby's "kidult" pseudoculture that is especially unhealthy for children. These influences are harmful because they substitute a craving for material goods and narcissistic gratification for children's real needs, which are for love, understanding, exploration, acceptance, guidance, nurturing, and discipline. Some careerist or otherwise distracted parents might take the enfranchisement of children as a further excuse for avoiding their parental responsibilities. But then the real problem would not be in our allowing children a political voice but in our depriving them of ourselves as a developmental resource. The best alternative to "kidultism" is not the muting of children and their concerns. Indeed, nothing encourages children to "grow up fast" more than arbitrary ageist restrictions on their opportunities for exploration, assertion, and personal choice. The best alternative is parents, and polities, strong enough to welcome rather than fear the voices of the young.

The single most important insight in the brilliantly practical book *How to Talk So Kids Will Listen and Listen So Kids Will Talk* (Faber and Mazlish 1980) is that children respond best when they feel that their concerns are being heard and are considered important. This feeling nurtures children's own inner resources much better than constant (and thus false) praise or perfunctory agreement with the child's opinions, which is often patronizing, misleading, or both. Similarly, citizens come to respect political leaders who convey real concern about their needs and opinions without patronizing or pandering to them. An enfranchised child, like any enfranchised citizen, is someone whose needs and opinions officially count, even if on occasion they are overruled by the needs and opinions of others. The cynicism Postman wants to forestall in children results not from children knowing too much but from adults delivering too little: too little straight talk, too little of what they promise, too little of the public good and of policy that addresses young people's legitimate concerns.

Postman is right to criticize adults who pressure children to grow up too fast. But neither the social scientists hired by Kids Voting USA nor any other researchers have uncovered evidence that young people's participation in political discussion and ballot-casting has had deleterious effects, comparable to those, for instance, of corporate-hawked nicotine and alcohol, media violence, trash culture, television advertising, credit cards, shopping malls, and parents who promote bigotry or harangue their Little Leaguers to win at all costs. Indeed, evidence of youths' political preferences suggests that children allowed to vote might well favor policies to curtail these truly deleterious influences.

At first blush, the indelibly powerful 1997 Italian film *Life Is Beautiful* might seem to illustrate with ultimate starkness Postman's recipe for benevolent hypocrisy as a protection for vulnerable children against political horror. In the film, the imaginative and loving husband-father of an Italian Jewish family sent to a concentration camp during World War II convinces his young son that their camp experience is actually a game, thereby sparing the little boy its full horror. But since there is no escaping many of the harsh features of the camp, the father makes the camp's Spartan conditions into tactical challenges, and the nasty guards into dramatic characters in the game. If he and his son (segregated from their wife-mother) can outwit these characters and accumulate a thousand points, they will win a brand new military tank to take home with them. When the camp is in fact liberated by allied forces (and the boy is taken out in a U.S. tank!), the boy and his mother survive, and the boy later learns of the sacrifices his martyred father made to save his life and spirit.

The father's fantasy, incorporating both the bad and the good of the adult world, suggests an alternative to Postman's paternalistic hypocrisy as a formula for protecting the young and vulnerable. Children can handle a truth that is both good and bad, if it is appropriately translated for them and if loving and competent adults are reliably available to guide them in finding the good and avoiding the bad.[133] Through heroic efforts, the father was just barely able to pull off this reliable availability. Children can handle eventually learning that Santa Claus and fictionalized camp guards were metaphors for good and bad.[134] Much harder for children to handle is the discovery that those on whom they most depend, especially their parents, cannot be counted on to hear, understand, and attend to their needs.

To survive and thrive, children need love, not perfection. A sanitized world can later turn out to be a very bad joke on them, shaking their confidence in the reliability of authority, good and bad alike. The Resource Center for Youth and Their Allies, an explicit and radical opponent of adultism, makes this point in the pamphlet *Building Relationships:* "The job of adults with young people is not to give them perfect childhoods, not to make sure they never get hurt or are protected from everything and happy all the time. . . . Our fears make us long for perfection. It does not exist. . . . A better picture of our job is that we try to give young people perspective on how inherently smart and powerful they are."[135]

8. *The Slippery Slope of Antiageism Objection:* "If you're going to ignore age when it comes to voting, will you also abolish ages of sexual consent, drinking, driving, and mandatory schooling?"

In brief, the answer is "yes," because age is a poor proxy for sexual vulnerability (some youth are much savvier than many adults), for the ability to drink responsibly (most French, Austrian, and Czech youth drink more responsibly than many U.S. adults), for the ability to drive safely (youth pilots and farm youth have just as good driving records as many adults), and for the need for education (which begins earlier and/or ends later for some people than others). For instance, who is likely to be the better driver, an unusually responsible twelve-year-old who scores a nearly perfect 98 on a valid driver's exam, or an all-too-common, irresponsible thirty-five-year-old who scores a barely passing 70?

The arbitrariness of age as a criterion in these and other areas of U.S. law is reflected both in the inconsistency with which it has been applied by the fifty states and in the common, ad hoc practice by U.S. courts of adjusting age-based legal standards with more relevant criteria such as intelligence, knowledge, maturity, and experience (Guggenheim and Sussman 1985). Though inconsistently, the courts have in effect accepted UNICEF's (2000) official position: "Adolescents, like all children, have the right to be heard and to participate in matters affecting them and in which they have an interest, in accordance with their age and maturity."

At the bottom of the slippery slope of antiageism, we are left with no good rationale for summarily denying children a wide range of legal rights granted adults, including the right to a jury trial, the right to appeal a conviction, the right to an attorney during divorce or custody proceedings, and the right to be heard at an abuse or neglect hearing (Guggenheim and Sussman 1985). But the system of adultist privilege and benevolent paternalism is a two-edged sword, because it is not just young people who need protection from harm and from their own shortcomings. The very kinds of sexual and financial predation from which we want to protect children become perfectly legal when used on adults, even though adults are themselves vulnerable because of naivety, ignorance, incapacity, anxiety, family crisis, psychological dysfunction, financial need, substance addiction, physical disability, or senility. In short, ageism errs not only by encroaching on the rights of children, but by ignoring the needs of adults.

Pioneers of Voting Rights for Children

A. S. Neill is not the only pioneer of voting rights for children. Among the Iroquois, whose governmental system of democratic checks and balances influenced our Founding Fathers, "native children were introduced very early into 'public councils,' a practice which produced young adults 'with a composed and manly air,' who were inspired 'to emulation' and made 'bold and enterprising.'"[136] Richard Farson (1974) and John Holt (1976) advocated equal rights for children, including the right to vote, as did Howard Cohen (1980), though in a more legalistic and somewhat paternalistic way. In the 1980s I began publicly arguing for abolishing all age-based disfranchisement.

In the 1990s, the development of Kids Voting USA coincided with many other initiatives. TBS and CNN founder Ted Turner sponsored the children's program *Captain Planet* on the theme "power is yours."[137] The intentional community Kidstown was formed in California to help children from troubled families, and made a point of ensuring them "an equal part in our democratic process when they reach and maintain a defined level of responsibility."[138] Many of the hundreds of other intentional communities publicized in the three editions of the Fellowship for Intentional Communities' *Communities Directory* (1990, 1996, 2000) also allow their children to participate in communal decisionmaking. The Canada-based Youth Ecology Alliance has campaigned for children's right to vote in public elections. The Boston-based Resource Center for Youth and Their Allies sponsors workshops and publicity campaigns for children's rights, including the right to vote.

In "An Immodest Proposal: Let's Give Children the Vote," Paul Peterson (1993) compares the policy benefits enjoyed by senior citizens with the much worse benefits for children, who are twice as numerous as seniors. He concludes that the reason for this discrepancy is that children do not vote.[139] No matter which of five different estimates is used, "government programs had greater impact on the elderly than on children. . . . The sums available for the would-be poor elderly were 10 times those allocated to programs for children" (p. 20). As a result, during the 1970s and 1980s, seniors' poverty rate fell 56 percent, while that of children rose 50 percent. Noting that "public school officials have campaigned hard and successfully" to restrict young people's educational choices and thus preserve their own educational monopoly, Peterson argues that "if children had the vote, they would probably demand greater choice over the schools they attend" (p. 23). Contrasting the considerable clout of the American Association of Retired Persons and other senior lobbies on behalf of 32 million seniors with the powerlessness of the 65 million U.S. children under eighteen, he concludes: "If children were enfranchised, fundamental public policy changes would certainly follow. Groups representing children would immediately acquire status and power, they would frighten politicians with organized letter-writing campaigns, they would demand a bigger share of the welfare pie, and they would insist that programs for children be redesigned" (p. 23).[140] In line with Peterson's prediction, Domhoff (1998: p. 215) has pointed to the 26th Amendment's enfranchisement of college students as a factor in the defeat of progrowth forces in some college towns such as Santa Cruz, California.

In South Africa, then-president Nelson Mandela made waves by advocating a lowering of the voting age below eighteen.[141] President Clinton himself seemed to be on the cusp of children's political activism, recently advising fifth-graders: "Start to take the responsibilities of citizenship seriously, and find some way, even at the age of 10, to be of service to your community."[142] In return, he, his successors, and the rest of the government could start taking seriously children's right to an official political voice. In fall 2000, Free the Children founder Craig Kielberger, seventeen, spoke in favor of a movement to lower the voting age in Canada to sixteen, noting that young people "are making their voices heard on the street because they can't be heard in the political arena." He suggested, "We should learn from the tobacco companies—hook them while they're young"—and predicted that if more teenagers could vote, "politicans would have to come up with solutions to problems like child poverty."[143]

Conclusion: Adultism and the Generation Gap

Adultism does not strengthen family authority. It undermines it. In the guise of keeping children in their place, adultism eats away at the vital place parents should occupy. That place is a seat of authentic parental guidance, based primarily on powers of loving persuasion and exemplary modeling rather than coercion. Commands of "Do this" and "Don't do that" work just so long as the commanders patrol the deck. When absent, however, the leaders risk disobedience, even mutiny.

By contrast, children whose voices count do not need "liberation" from their parents, because they help shape the family life that nourishes them. They feel little "generation gap" from their elders because they are encouraged to partake of opportunities according to their abilities. Their participation in decisionmaking helps them develop as humans and as citizens. They can learn from elders' wisdom without being forced to act according to elders' prejudices, with all ages benefiting. Only in entropic, zero-sum families is the empowerment of children tantamount to the disempowerment of parents.

Adultists may raise the specter of competence by asking whether children should have equal rights to play with fire, wander into busy streets, and dispose of family finances. But children have no corner on incompetence. The inept, whether younger or older, need restraint from harming themselves and others. Small communities, like families, are better at supplying such restraints than are large, anonymous societies. "As institutions, families are far superior to their alternatives—the state or the corporate world" (Pipher 1996: p. 226). Children, like adults, do best when families and communities nurture them, guide them, and afford them opportunities that match their abilities.

Professional political theory virtually ignores the problem of adultism, both because the theorists are adults and because they are mired in sterile debates between liberal individualism and republican communitarianism. Is "the end of adultism" an issue of the rights of individual children or one of the well-being of families and communities? This question is as fruitless as the question of whether "the individual" is more important than "society." Just as adult individualists (even libertarians) benefit from healthy communities, children need families in order to thrive. But just as societies that disrespect their individual members thereby diminish community and breed rebellion, families that subordinate their children thus undermine their own legitimacy and alienate the young from their elders. Youth voting protects rights while strengthening communities.

By the late 1990s, four-fifths of U.S. adults thought that children had become less respectful of their elders.[144] This generation gap reflects a mutual disrespect generated by adult dominion and its discontents—a system of rule consistent neither with democratic rights nor with community responsibilities. Despite their unhappiness with young people's disrespectful attitudes, these same adults conceded that young people now come from less stable homes than before, have worse role models, grow up in more dangerous neighborhoods, and have worse schools. These concessions seem to justify young people's declining respect for elders. A 1996–1997 national poll by the Search Institute of Minneapolis found that only 17 percent of ninth-graders perceive that adults in their communities value youth, only 23 percent believe that young people are given useful roles in their communities, and only 25 percent judge adults to be positive role models of responsible behavior.

The political economy of consumer capitalism feeds on young people's compensatory desire for the material trappings of adulthood—and thus on adultism—as well as on grown-ups' guilty need to buy off children whom they are too busy to nurture. Advertisers home in on both sides of the coin of narcissistic consumerism. Commodity fetishism stokes the embers of familial resentment: "Media programs and commercials portray children as frivolous and voracious consumers. These images contribute to parental pride in their children's possessions, which announce the affluence of the household, but such images also incite adult resentments toward 'lazy' and 'greedy' offspring" (Scheper-Hughes and Sargent 1998: p. 10).

In addition to corporations' pursuit of profits, progressives' political correctness is implicated in both adultism and family disintegration. Adult progressives act holier than thou as partisans for the disadvantaged, neglecting the adultism that tarnishes their own egalitarianism. Moreover, by defending the right of parents, especially women, to escape the confines of domesticity in order to make it in the "real world" of cash payment, progressive ideology defaults on the needs of children and promotes a wide range of personal and family pathologies. These maladies, in turn, invite the paternal state and its allies in the helping professions to take over the traditional functions of the family and save it from itself.[145]

The left, rather than reexamining its own default on family issues, prefers to ridicule the "family values" posturing of the right as old-fashioned. But the problem with the right-wing embrace of the family is less its old-fashionedness than its two-sidedness. The right, and especially its dysfunctional agent the Republican Party, is divided between economic and social conservatives, between profiteers and zealots. Consequently the American right serves up a mishmash of family-friendly and family-hostile policies that should provide transformational forces with a golden opportunity to capture a traditionally conservative issue. To date, however, conservatives are still winning by default in this arena in which they deserve to get pounded, primarily because far too often there is "nobody at home on the left."

The disempowerment of young people does not empower families; it artificially divides them. Young people are human beings. They should be treated like citizens. They are not the property of either their parents or the state. To treat young people as if they were productive assets is to deny both them and us our humanity. As educator Katia Peterson says, "Kids should be treated as human beings, not human doings."[146] To treat young people with the respect we give citizens is to empower us all. Adultism passes the hurts and errors of one generation on to the next, depriving humans of an enormous resource toward the realization of our potential. "The Lakota word for child, *wakanyeja*, translates literally as 'the child is also holy.'"[147] To accord young people equal dignity with adults strengthens the family as a social and political unit. Chapter 7 takes up the possibility that a progressive program of family empowerment might play a vital role in social transformation.

Notes

1. George Lane and Julia Martinez, "Abortion Notice for Parents Tossed Out," *Denver Post*, August 18, 2000.

2. "Children have not been advantaged by the state's claims to be acting on their behalf. . . . In fact, many paternalistic interventions have not only failed to improve the lives of children but may actually have disadvantaged them. . . . Consequently, grounding claims in child protection simply underscores the need for a coherent account of the rights of children." Katherine Federle, "A Future for the Juvenile Courts?" in Schwartz (1999: p. 35).

3. *Denver Post*, August 11, 1990.

4. Associated Press, February 23, 2000.

5. *Denver Post*, July 25, 1990.

6. *Denver Post*, December 22, 2000.

7. *Miami Herald*, January 9, 1998.

8. Marilyn Robinson, *Denver Post*, February 3, 1999.

9. Nancy Lofholm, *Denver Post*, March 3, 1999.

10. Associated Press, March 3, 2000.

11. Associated Press, December 14, 2000.

12. Anastasia Toufexis, *Time,* November 23, 1992, pp. 60–61.

13. Dean E. Murphy, *Los Angeles Times,* May 27, 2000.

14. John Daniszewski, *Los Angeles Times,* January 20, 1999.

15. Associated Press, September 9, 1999.

16. Edward A. Gargan, *New York Times,* December 27, 1992. "When parents are in fact paid, the going rate for an 8-year-old boy is 1,500 to 2,000 rupees ($50 to $66), a substantial sum for many families."

17. Amir Zia, Associated Press, June 3, 1999.

18. Associated Press, July 12, 1992.

19. Charles T. Powers, *Los Angeles Times,* November 25, 1990.

20. Lori Montgomery, Knight-Ridder News Service, November 30, 1997.

21. Richard C. Paddock, *Los Angeles Times,* December 17, 1998.

22. Doctors of the World, "A Report from the Field," 1998.

23. John-Thor Dahlburg and Marjorie Miller, *Los Angeles Times,* July 13, 1998.

24. "Fourth World" refers to indigenous peoples. See the *Fourth World Bulletin,* published by the Fourth World Center for the Study of Indigenous Law and Politics at the University of Colorado at Denver.

25. Among Western countries, male genital mutilation, or circumcision, is carried out on a routine basis only in the United States. Although the American Academy of Pediatricians recommends against it, 59 percent of U.S. infant boys are still circumcised, down from 80 percent in 1975. "An article in the British Journal of Urology noted that the [infants'] elevated cortisol levels and heart rates associated with neonatal circumcision were 'consistent with torture.'" Claire Martin, "Doctors Less Apt to Circumcise: Pediatrics Association Says Surgery Unnecessary," *Denver Post,* March 1, 1999.

26. Renee Schoof, "Adoptive Parents Flock to China," Associated Press, January 14, 1999.

27. Annual Report of the National Defense Council Foundation, December 29, 1999.

28. <www.thehungersite.com>.

29. Michael Laris, "North Korean Famine Leaves Long-Term Scars," *Washington Post,* February 4, 1999.

30. "Every single day tens of millions of children work in conditions that shock the conscience," President Clinton said in June 1999. James Gerstenzang, "Clinton Seeks Child-Labor Limits," *Los Angeles Times,* June 17, 1999.

31. Associated Press, "1/3 of Working Kids Have Hazardous Job," May 26, 1998.

32. Robert Scheer, "The Shame of Sexual Slavery Haunts the New World Order," *New York Times,* January 15, 1998.

33. "Experts Set Accord to Protect Children," Associated Press, February 5, 2000.

34. Tony Lang, "Children of the World in Need," *Cincinnati Enquirer,* December 22, 1993.

35. Figures on children as war casualties are taken from UNICEF's *Facts and Figures, The Progress of Nations,* and *The State of the World's Children* reports, 1997–2000.

36. "Fund Sought for New Land Mines," *Los Angeles Times,* February 20, 1999.

37. Kathy Gannon, "Afghanistan's Orphans Suffering," Associated Press, February 15, 1999.

38. "Old Shell Explodes, Kills 7 in Vietnam," Associated Press, November 20, 1999.

39. Peter Finn, "Program Helps Wars-Scarred Balkan Kids Deal with Fear," *Washington Post*, February 4, 1999.

40. Alexandra Zavis, "The Youngest Casualties Live On: Children Forced into War Have Few Options," Associated Press, November 18, 1999.

41. "Girl Rebels Killed in Sri Lankan Battle," Associated Press, December 25, 2000.

42. "UNICEF Fears for Kids in E. Europe," Associated Press, November 5, 1999.

43. United States Committee for UNICEF, "Every Child Is Our Child" (New York: United Nations, 1996).

44. Val Phillips, American Friends Service Committee, "A Gesture of Friendship for Infants in Iraq," *Footsteps*, winter 1998; Larry Kaplow, "Sanctions Hurt Iraqi People, not Saddam," Cox News Service, June 16, 1999.

45. Bread for the World Institute, *What Governments Can Do: Seventh Annual Report on the State of World Hunger* (Silver Spring, MD: 1997), p. 8.

46. Katherine Pfleger, "1 in 7 Live in Poverty, Report Says," Associated Press, November 3, 1999.

47. National Center for Children in Poverty, "Young Child Poverty Fact Sheet (July 2000)," at <http://cpmcnet.columbia.edu/dept/nccp/ycpf.html>. Emphasis in the original.

48. Janet Bingham, "Young Placed at Risk: Housing Squeeze Hurts Kids Most," *Denver Post*, April 8, 1999.

49. "One in Four Kids Exposed to Family Alcoholism," Associated Press, December 31, 1999.

50. "Kids Cancer Risk Soars if Parents Smoke," *Denver Post*, September 6, 1990.

51. Steve Sternberg, "Study Links Smoking, Child Ear-Infection Risk," *USA Today*, February 1998.

52. Dirk Johnson, "Smokers Endure a Social Exile," Associated Press, November 1998.

53. John M. Broder, "Tobacco Firm Confesses Sins," *New York Times*, March 21, 1997.

54. Marlene Simons, "Kids' Lead Poisoning Targeted," *Los Angeles Times*, February 22, 1991.

55. "Delinquency, Exposure to Lead Linked," Associated Press, May 16, 2000.

56. Curt Anderson, "Kids May Be Eating Unsafe Food: Agency Warns of Pesticide Danger," Associated Press, January 30, 1998.

57. Holcomb B. Noble, "Study: Poor Kids' Asthma Risk High," *New York Times*, August 27, 1999.

58. Maria Cone, "Industrial Asthma Threat to Many," *Los Angeles Times*, June 18, 1999.

59. Lisa Ramirez, "EPA Outlaws Pesticide, Draws Fire: Ban 'Protects Children,' Agency Says," Knight Ridder News Service, August 3, 1999.

60. Deborah Mathis, "Report: 'Mixed Picture' for Girls," Gannett News Service, June 17, 1998.

61. The minority of noncustodial parents who are mothers do even worse in terms of child support than noncustodial fathers (Hewlett and West 1998; p. 178).

62. Tim Bovee, "Half of Ex-Husbands Shortchange Wives on Support Checks," *USA Today*, October 11, 1991.

63. Michael Booth, "School Tragedy Reflects Gun Use: U.S. Death Rate Leads the World," *Denver Post*, April 25, 1999.

64. Fred Hiatt, "Too Many Guns Around," *International Herald Tribune*, April 26, 1999.

65. Andrew Males, "Who's Really Killing Our Kids?" *Denver Post*, June 7, 1998.

66. "U.S. Kids More Apt to Be Killed Than Those in Northern Ireland," *Denver Post,* January 21, 1994.

67. Lee Iacocca, "Let's End the Poltroonery," *Newsweek,* April 16, 1990, p. 10.

68. Quoted in George F. Will, "A Revolution Writ in Black Ink," *Washington Post,* April 3, 1992.

69. UNICEF, *The Progress of Nations 1997* (New York: UN Division of Communication, 1997), p. 56.

70. Ibid., p. 62.

71. Children's Defense Fund, Washington, D.C., membership letter, June 1994.

72. John C. Ensslin, "67% of Sex Crimes Strike Children," *Rocky Mountain News,* June 27, 1992.

73. Elizabeth Mehren, "Report: Kids Under 3 in 'Quiet Crisis,'" *Los Angeles Times,* April 12, 1994.

74. "If children had the vote, five changes in public policy might well be anticipated. . . . a system of national health insurance would extend to all households the medical benefits now enjoyed by those over age 65." Paul E. Peterson (1993: p. 23).

75. Karen Hosler, "Preventive Care No Luxury for Kids Under Clinton Plan," *Baltimore Sun,* September 19, 1993.

76. Cf. Holly Sklar (1995: p. 12).

77. Anthony Lewis, "We Know the Needs of Our Children, But We're Not Meeting Them," *New York Times,* July 15, 1990.

78. Mary Williams Walsh, "Wealth Gap Grows Steadily," *Los Angeles Times,* January 19, 2000.

79. Deb Riechmann, "War on Poverty Flares up Again: Veterans Recall 35 Years of Programs," Associated Press, July 9, 1999. Because economic basics for families cost about 150 percent of the official poverty rate, the true poverty rate is about half again what the government estimates. Sklar (1995: p. 13).

80. National Coalition to Abolish the Death Penalty, "America's Shame—Killing Kids," <http://www.ncadp.org/fact3.html>.

81. "The dozen states that have chosen not to enact the death penalty since the Supreme Court ruled in 1976 that it was constitutionally permissible have not had higher homicide rates than states with the death penalty. . . . Homicide rates have risen and fallen along roughly symmetrical paths in the states with and without the death penalty, suggesting to many experts that the threat of the death penalty rarely deters criminals." Raymond Bonner and Ford Fessenden, "Doubt Cast on Death Penalty as Deterrent," *New York Times,* September 30, 2000.

82. It is known that more than fifty people have been executed for crimes that, it was later proved, they did not commit. This number is increasing rapidly now that genetic testing has become available. Ibid.

83. Critics of the death penalty have also pointed out the greater likelihood that blacks convicted of murder will be executed than whites convicted of murder. Of the nine girls who have been executed, eight were black and one was Native American. Ibid.

84. Sylvia Ann Hewlett, *When the Bough Breaks: The Cost of Neglecting Our Children* (New York: Basic Books, 1991).

85. See the Children's Defense Fund's annual report *The State of America's Children.*

86. UNICEF (1998: pp. 48–49).

87. Robert Pear, "95,180 Disabled Kids Denied Benefits," *New York Times,* August 15, 1997.

88. Laura Meckler, "Deeper Child-Welfare Cuts Sought," Associated Press, June 7, 1998.

89. Carol Kreck, "Many Urban Teens Feel Isolated, Poll Finds," *Denver Post*, December 10, 1998.

90. Sarah Wyatt, "Clinton Seeks New Child-Abuse Law," Associated Press, December 30, 1998.

91. Madeleine Bonnett, "Update. Museum Exhibits," *Hemispheres*, January 1993, p. 84.

92. A nationwide Yankelovich Survey in 2000 found that "61 percent of the parents condone spanking as a regular form of punishment for young children despite research indicating corporal punishment can be harmful." Associated Press, "Survey: Parents Raising Aggressive, Frustrated Kids," October 5, 2000.

93. Murray A. Straus, "The Benefits of Avoiding Corporal Punishment: New and More Definitive Evidence," updated to December 27, 2000, at <http://www.childrightseducation.org/english/strausarticle.html>. This update of a 1997 article published in *Archives of Pediatric and Adolescent Medicine* summarizes five recent studies that avoid a key methodological problem of earlier studies, which consistently found corporal punishment to correlate with child misbehavior but could not pinpoint the direction of causality (i.e., did spanking kids make them worse, or did worse-behaving kids simply get spanked more often).

94. Ibid.

95. Cf. The Natural Child Project: <www.naturalchild.com/home/>.

96. Associated Press, October 15, 1998.

97. Straus, "The Benefits of Avoiding Corporal Punishment."

98. Eda LeShan, "Please Don't Hit Your Kids: All Children Need Guidance, Applied Controls, and Discipline, But They Should Not Have to Learn Through Fear and Anger," *Mothering: The Magazine of Natural Family Living*, no. 78, spring 1996, pp. 23–24 (emphasis in the original).

99. Nancy Lofholm, "A Matter of Faith, Justice: Is Witholding Care a Crime?" *Denver Post*, March 15, 1999; the *Pediatrics* study is cited in a *Denver Post* editorial of August 6, 2000.

100. Lynette Clemetson, "Caught in the Cross-Fire: A Young Teacher Finds Herself in a Losing Racial Battle with Parents," *Newsweek*, December 14, 1998, pp. 38–39.

101. "Children in Spotlight," *Denver Post*, June 6, 1990.

102. "Perspectives," *Newsweek*, May 4, 1998, p. 25.

103. Having met Bill and Hillary Clinton, Queen Elizabeth, the Dalai Lama, and Mother Theresa, Kielburger was asked what had gone through his mind while he was sharing a podium with such famous people. His reply: "How to get them more involved." He found such luminaries interesting, he commented, "but they're still not the people who impressed me the most." Who impressed him more, wondered Ed Bradley, of *60 Minutes?* The answer: "A lot of the children I met." Giving examples of children who had shown extraordinary concern for other children, he added, "If you took those children and put them in those positions, we would see this world be a truly different place." CBS, *60 Minutes*, October 3, 1999.

104. "In gaining their 'rights' in the form of protection from family work, apprenticeship, and wage labor, modern children may have gained their childhoods but lost considerable power and status." Scheper-Hughes and Sargent (1998: p. 11).

105. "Movie studios, record companies and video game producers are aggressively marketing violent entertainment products to children even as they label the material inappropriate for young audiences, a year-long Federal Trade Commission has found." Christopher Stern, "Violence Marketed to Children, FTC Concludes," *Washington Post*, August 27, 2000.

106. For instance, in the Zambesi Valley of Zimbabwe, "children are accorded positions of dignity and worth in Tonga society. . . . They are valued for themselves and . . . as companions and workers. They are accorded rights and these are upheld

at public forums such as during court cases." Pamela Reynolds, quoted in Scheper-Hughes and Sargent (1998: p. 11).

107. The "psy complex" is defined as "those whose aims are to apply psychological technology . . . to social problems." David Ingleby, quoted in Mary John (1995: p. 123).

108. Lindsay G. Arthur (1973: p. 137), emphasis added.

109. Joel Whitburn, *The Billboard Book of Top 40 Hits* (New York: Billboard Publications, 1985), p. 501.

110. Robert Pear, "Complexity of GOP Plan Fuels School-Lunch Debate," *New York Times,* April 9, 1995.

111. Marian Wright Edelman, "Kids First!" *Mother Jones,* May-June 1991, p. 32.

112. "Angry Moms Ask Congress to Pass Child Care Bill," Knight-Ridder News Service, September 13, 1990.

113. Gary Ruskin, "Why They Whine: How Corporations Prey on Our Children," *Mothering: The Natural Family Living Magazine,* no. 97, November-December 1999, pp. 45–47.

114. Personal conversation, Denver, Colorado, December 5, 1998.

115. Andrew Males, "Who's Really Killing Our Kids?" *Denver Post,* June 7, 1998.

116. Carol Kreck, "Group Pushes Tax to Aid Denver Kids," *Denver Post,* March 29, 1992.

117. "The rush [of identity politics] to eliminate equality from our political idiom and our political aspiration strikes me as daft, for democracy without equality is an impossible proposition." Jean Bethke Elshtain (1998: p. 263).

118. West Virginia Democratic senator Jennings Randolph took pride in his persistence in introducing the 26th Amendment eleven times to a resistant Congress. From a nursing home in 1994, he reminded reporters: "I'm the one who lowered the voting age, you know. I gave 18-year-olds the vote. Now that's a federal act, so I'm proud of that" (Associated Press, May 9, 1998, the day after Randolph's death).

119. Illogic does not stop them from making the argument. See, for instance, Carl Cohen's case for the adult-only franchise, stressing the immaturity and irrationality of young people. Cohen (1971: pp. 41–50).

120. Goerge Fitzhugh, *Cannibals All!,* excerpted in Dolbeare (1998: p. 278).

121. A February 2, 1993, flyer of The Youth Ecology Coalition of British Columbia lists most of the stock arguments against children's voting discussed in this chapter, noting: "All these arguments have been used in the past to keep women, blacks, Asians and other groups from voting. All are based on stereotypes, on ageism."

122. <www.kidsvotingusa.com.>, Kids Voting USA web page, January 2, 1999.

123. Katrine Ames, "The Election Connection: Want to Get Adults to Vote? Send in the Kids," *Newsweek,* October 26, 1992, p. 74.

124. In 1992 in Colorado, for instance, children voting in Kids Voting Colorado preferred Bill Clinton over Bob Dole for president, Tom Strickland over Wayne Allard for the U.S. Senate, and Joe Rogers over Diana DeGette for U.S. House District 1—all three in opposition to Colorado's adult voters. In the first two cases, the children favored the Democrat over the Republican; in the third, they favored a black male Republican over a white female Democrat.

125. Despite some changing trends in voting behavior—notably the lessening importance of party identification—the tendency of children to follow in the political footsteps of their parents, along with a significant minority who do not, has persisted since publication of *The American Voter,* the pioneering study of U.S. voting behavior. Angus Campbell et al., *The American Voter* (New York: Wiley, 1964).

126. Elshtain (1997a) quotes a thirteen-year-old who participated in her first protest at the age of seven: "When the media is saying that our parents forced us into this, it's not true. Many of my friends got our parents into this" (p. 119).

127. See Chapter 5.

128. Perhaps this dismissal is a misapplication of the parental dictum, "If there's a toy you can't share, then just put it away before your friends arrive, and nobody will play with it."

129. Kids Voting USA reports that voters aged eighteen to twenty-four are less than half as likely to vote as older voters. Cf. <www.kidsvotingusa.com>.

130. Quoted in Dolbeare (1998: p. 450).

131. "I don't think our opinion matters in the grand scale of things," said eighteen-year-old Nebraska freshman Jessica Evans, in an opinion shared by many of her college peers. Robert Greene, "Freshman Interest in Politics Hits Low," Associated Press, January 12, 1998; Doyle McManus, "A Generation Lost in Distaste," *Los Angeles Times,* December 28, 1998.

132. A. S. Neill, *Summerhill: A Radical Approach to Child Rearing* (New York: Hart, 1960), pp. 47–48.

133. Accepting guidance is by no means tantamount to waiving one's right to a political voice.

134. In the famous 1897 *New York Sun* editorial "Yes, Virginia, There Is a Santa Claus," Francis P. Church makes clear to adult readers, although not to eight-year-old Virginia O'Hanlon, that he is speaking metaphorically: "Not believe in Santa Claus! You might as well not believe in fairies." Santa Claus, writes Church, "exists as certainly as love and generosity and devotion exist."

135. Jenny Sazama, *Building Relationships* (Boston: The Resource Center for Youth and Their Allies, 1994), p. 21.

136. Donald A. Grinde Jr. and Bruce E. Johansen, *Exemplar of Liberty: Native America and the Evolution of Democracy* (Los Angeles: University of California American Indian Studies Center, 1991), p. 13.

137. J. Sebastian Sinisi, "Turner Delights World Affairs Crowd," *Denver Post,* April 11, 1992.

138. Fellowship for Intentional Community, *1990–91 Directory of Intentional Communities: A Guide to Cooperative Living* (Stelle, Illinois: Communities Publications Cooperative, 1990), p. 196.

139. On ABC's *Politically Incorrect* late-night show, host Bill Maher agreed with Peterson's argument. Responding good-naturedly to three under-eighteen guest panelists who had challenged Maher's adultist assumptions, he said, "If only adults were as smart as you guys," adding that while senior citizens are politically able to "shake their booty, you guys can't vote." August 20, 1999.

140. A medical anomaly might also be reversed: unlike in Europe, "two-thirds of children's livers donated for transplant in the United States went to adults, while about 75 children a year died waiting for new livers." Brenda C. Coleman, "Donated Children's Livers Go to Adults, Study Finds," Associated Press, May 18, 1999.

141. "ANC Media Statement on the Voting Age Controversy," <http://www.anc.org.za/ancdocs/pr/1993/pr0526d.html>.

142. Robert A. Rankin, "Diversity Could Help or Hurt, Clinton Says: President Describes His Vision for Future," Knight-Ridder News Service, April 12, 1997.

143. Allison Lampert, "A Child Leads Them: Activist Kielburger Wants Voting Age Lowered to 16," *Montreal Gazette,* November 17, 2000.

144. Gannett News Service poll of 1,009 U.S. adults, conducted December 11–15, 1997, by Opinion Research Corporation.

145. "The service professions, acting on behalf of the state, intruded into the private domain, helping to replace habit and custom with esoteric techniques for addressing everyday problems, causing a situation of dependence on elites that is antithetical to democracy." Elizabeth Lasch-Quinn, ed., "Introduction" to Christopher Lasch (1997: pp. xii–xiii).

146. Personal conversation, Durango, Colorado, January 23, 1999.

147. Ian Frazier, "On the Rez," *Atlantic Monthly* 284, no. 6, December 1999, p. 55.

7

Family Empowerment in Social Transformation: The Politics of Birthing, Nursing, and Parenting

"To distress is to weaken, and weakening the children weakens the whole family."
                                                                —Benjamin Franklin[1]

"He has endeavored, in every way that he could, to destroy her confidence in her own powers."
                                                —The Seneca Falls Declaration, 1848[2]

"The family, however shakily and imperfectly, helps to keep alive an alternative to the values which dominate the marketplace."
                                                                —Jean Bethke Elshtain[3]

"The issue is not whether we have the money to help America's families but whether we have the values to do so."
                                                —Stephanie Coontz (1997: p. 176)

"Boy, keeping them married sure is going to be hard work."
                                                —Child Cindy, on *The Brady Bunch*

In *Haven in a Heartless World: The Family Besieged,* Christopher Lasch (1977) noted that the very forces driving people to seek familial refuge from the economic war of all against all were invading the family itself. A generation later, things have gotten much worse. "How do you bond with an infant," ask Sylvia Ann Hewlett and Cornell West (1998: p. xii), "if you are constrained to be back at work ten days after birth? How do you enforce a curfew or insist on homework when the sound bites of our culture undercut parental authority in myriad ways? . . . In late-twentieth-century America, parenting had become a countercultural activity of the first order."[4] With half of all marriages ending in divorce, teen suicide and youth violence commonplace, and conflicts between paid work and parenting intensifying, more and more families find themselves besieged and struggling to carry out their vital tasks.

Conservatives fault parental permissiveness and public welfare for weakening the family. Yet they resist family-friendly policies such as paid parental leave and guaranteed day care for single parents because such policies might reduce business profits and redistribute wealth (Hewlett and West 1998: p. 92). In 2000, the Clinton administration's effort to get either Congress or state legislatures to enact government-paid parental leave was defeated by business opposition despite growing popular support. Unlike conservatives, on the other hand, the politically correct left views "family values" as conservative and oppressive, claiming that families today are just different, not worse, and that right-wing family rhetoric is a thinly veiled attack on women's rights (Stacey 1996; Christopher Wolfe 1998). Both sides avoid looking closely at our family origins—in birth, early sustenance, and attachment—and at the way these origins strengthen or weaken the family as a political actor.

Empowered families—and a progressive family-empowerment movement—could challenge corporate America and the paternal state. A strong family comprises far more power than the sum of the powers of its individual members, especially if it links up with other, like-minded families.[5] To achieve this synergistic empowerment while also challenging the family-unfriendly status quo, most families need to consider (1) taking fuller control of their reproduction and child rearing, (2) changing their habits of consumption, (3) building their habits of production, (4) networking with other families, and (5) acting as self-conscious political actors in the public arena.

These five areas of current family default, but potential family empowerment, are linked. Family development along these lines could help curb the institutional predators that feast on America's ailing families, specifically government, business, and the helping professions.[6] Ironically, America's most influential profamily conservative, James Dobson, has threatened to take his millions of followers and jump the Republican ship because it is not conservative enough on such issues as abortion, school prayer, and gay rights (or wrongs). Transformationalists should be quietly cheering him on, not so much for his ship-jumping as for his insistent dictum (and moniker) that we should "Focus on the Family." Radical PC to the contrary notwithstanding, nothing is likely to bear more radical fruit than an insistent focus on our families, which could upset applecarts right and left, indicting both capitalism and "progressive" trends whose focus on individual adult rights ignores the needs of children and the transformative potential of the family itself.[7]

Conservative Fault and Progressive Default on Family Values

Until recently, "family values" had become a red herring of the right, distracting many Americans from the ruin wrought on the family by corporate capitalism, especially in its late-twentieth-century consumerist and narcissistic phase (Lasch 1979). In the last decade, perceptive critics, including liberals, socialists, feminists, communitarians, and religious fundamentalists, have noted the hostility of the profit motive to such family values as stable marriage, economic security, parental love and discipline, respect for authority, wholesome entertainment, clean and safe neighborhoods, community solidarity, children's health, development, and self-esteem, and a proper appreciation for the past and concern for the future (Blankenhorn, Bayme, and Elshtain 1990; Friedan 1997; Lasch 1997; Hewlett and West 1998). Many conservatives continue to tout both strong families and corporate capitalism with little sense of their mutual contradiction. For instance, as David Abalos points out, Presidents Reagan and Bush romanticized the traditional family, yet "also supported economic policies that forced women into the workplace in order to make it possible for the family to survive."[8] The less conservative of the two, Bush, twice vetoed the Parental and Disability Leave Act, in 1990 and 1992. Collectively, U.S. conservatives have trouble choosing between Christian love and capitalist lucre.

Many conservatives have no problem with the activities of Cheryl Idell, who advises corporations, literally, on how to get kids to whine at their parents and nag them to buy advertised products; with George Broussard, whose company markets violent and sexually explicit video games to kids because "it'd be [economic] suicide to make the game unplayable by younger people"; with marketing professor James U. McNeal, who teaches his students that "children are the brightest star in the consumer constellation"; with Kids-R-Us president Mike Searles, who says that "if you own this child at an early age, you can own this child for years to come"; or with General Mills executive Wayne Chilicki, who says, "When it comes to targeting kid consumers, we at General Mills follow the Proctor & Gamble model of 'cradle to grave.' We believe in getting them early and having them for life." Would war-toy and violent-comics maker Todd McFarlane, of McFarlane Toys, "let his own daughters have these toys or comic books? 'Are you kidding?' he says, 'I'm still a dad after five o'clock.'"[9]

It is no coincidence, however, that the left has politically failed to exploit the family contradictions of the right. Many progressives still regard the family as the seat of patriarchal oppression, and the act of family making itself as a regressive step that turns young radicals into middle-aged conservatives. Moreover, left-wing adults who value their individual freedom to "make it" professionally, often regard family commitments as an intolerable inconvenience. Conservative criticisms of the paternal state and helping professions are too quickly dismissed by the left because of their proponents' conservatism. A defense of the family, in many politically correct minds, becomes a defense of privilege and an attack on the rights of women and children, as well as on the benevolent state that would protect women and children from their common, patriarchal oppressor.

It is thus by default that the right, despite its attacks on public programs to strengthen families, remains the ally of family values in the eyes of many. To the extent that people view the left as favoring abortion, day care, women's liberation from domesticity, and disrespect for familial authority, they often succumb to conservatives' hypocritical claim that "we are your family's best friend." The left's politically correct resistance to personal values as a key to social change (Chapter 3) spills over into the issue of family values, and indeed of the family itself.

To Begin at the Beginning: The Politics of Birthing

What does childbirth have to do with politics? Beginnings usually have great consequences for what follows. It should come as no surprise that the politics of our lives closely follows the politics of our births. "Women birth the way they live," Lauri Umansky (1996: p. 66) quotes a California midwife as saying. Mother and obstetrician Christiane Northrup (1994: p. 374) reminds us of a comment by medieval mystic Meister Eckhart: "For all eternity, God lies on a birthing bed, giving birth. The essence of God is birthing." But what may fairly be called the medical-industrial complex has convinced most women that their bodies do not work well enough for them to give birth naturally. It has given us "obstetrics, the manly art of interfering, as opposed to midwifery, the womanly art of supporting" (Goer 1995: p. 351). As an ob/gyn in a cartoon says to one of his patients, "You're in labor? I'm in management" (p. 356).

Remarkably, the PC lens that has faulted the medical profession for excluding women has largely ignored its unnatural acts on women, partly because the "essentialist" view that women are biologically different from men is politically suspect on the left.

Medical obstetricians and manufacturers claim to have supplanted, in a mere half century, the inherited wisdom of natural selection, and especially the natural power of women's bodies. Ignoring the fact that "each woman that's alive today is the product of thirty million years of excellence in childbearing,"[10] the relentless propaganda of medico-technical elites has convinced most Americans—left and right, rich and poor, black and white, men and women, feminists and patriarchs—that without the elites' special expertise and high technology, pregnancy becomes a dangerous illness, and birthing a catastrophe waiting to happen (Jordan 1993; Goer 1995; Umansky 1996; Arms 1996; England 1999). In short, ordinary people are allegedly unable to do the single most important thing evolution has equipped them to do, reproduce themselves—unless, of course, they have the expert help of doctors and nurses equipped with all the most advanced medical technology.

Medicalized Versus Natural Birth

Americans are conditioned to believe not only that they need their children born (1) in a hospital and (2) under the care of an obstetrician, but that birth will go better and be safer if:

3. the mother receives an epidural drug for pain relief,
4. she is subjected to an episiotomy (a cut in her perineum, the area between the vagina and anus) to prevent tearing,
5. she is hooked up to an electronic fetal monitor,
6. her labor either progresses according to a predetermined schedule or, failing that, is induced or enhanced with Pitocin (a drug imitating her own natural oxytocin),
7. she does not eat, is hooked up to an IV, and severely curtails her mobility during labor,
8. she gives birth reclining, usually on her back,
9. the baby is delivered by Caesarian section (C-section) rather than vaginally in the event of a wide variety of conditions that in U.S. hospitals occur in 22 percent of all births, and
10. the birthing process occurs in the ostensibly "sterile" environment of a hospital or allied birthing center.

Few Americans know that for the great majority of births, the available scientific studies either fail to support these protocols or actually contraindicate them (McCutcheon-Rosegg 1984; Bean 1990; Gaskin 1990; Baldwin 1991; Kitzinger 1991; Jordan 1993; Arms 1996; Goer 1995; Griffin 1997; Riordan 1999; England 1999). For instance, in subjecting mothers to the lithotomy (reclining on back) position of giving birth, U.S. doctors ignore its many medical disadvantages. Because it decreases the size of the pelvic outlet, it has "negative effects on the mother's pulmonary ventilation, blood pressure, and cardiac return, which in turn lowers oxygen supply to the fetus." It also "causes contractions to become weaker, less frequent, and more irregular and makes pushing harder because increased force is needed to work against gravity," thus increasing the likelihood of forceps extraction, perineal tearing, and episiotomy (Jordan 1993: p. 85).

Only 8 percent of Dutch mothers are given episiotomies, whereas over 90 percent of first-time mothers in the United States are. Forceps are used in more than half of births in many U.S. hospitals, whereas they are virtually unheard of in Sweden or Holland. Pitocin is used to speed up deliveries in over 80 percent of U.S. births, whereas it is rarely used in many other countries (pp. 77–89). In a study comparing hospital and home births over thirty years, Dr. Neal Devitt concluded: "While the techniques of modern hospital obstetrics have saved the lives of many women and infants from genuine pathologies of birth, the literature of obstetrics in the United States from 1930 to 1960 does not show that healthy women benefited from hospital obstetric care" (Bean 1990: p. 275). Indeed, "the incidence of birth injuries and obstetric mortality was greater in hospitals, probably due to interference in the birth process."

Despite Dr. Grantly Dick-Read's (1974 [1944]) pioneering work *Childbirth Without Fear*, few Americans today are aware of the ways in which the strangeness, artificiality, and authoritarianism of hospitals or attached birthing centers contribute to problems of women in labor.[11] In particular, conditions that relax the mother make birth less difficult than conditions that increase her anxiety and stress, a fact that helps explain why a far higher percentage of women choose natural birth after experiencing artificial birth than choose artificial birth after a natural one. A 1992 survey found that "more than 90 percent of women who have had a homebirth, would give birth at home again. 76 percent of women who have birthed both at home and in the hospital prefer homebirth" (England 1999: p. 58).

The Safety of Natural Homebirth Versus Hospital Birth

Cross-national statistics (Kitzinger 1991; Jordan 1993; Goer 1995) show that planned, drug-free homebirths with qualified midwives are at least as safe as hospital births in terms of infant and maternal mortality and morbidity, and that homebirth outcomes are superior to hospital outcomes in avoidance of unnecessary surgery, reduced infection rates, shorter duration of postpartum pain, and cost.[12] In *Birth in Four Cultures,* Jordan (1993: p. 142) reviews multiple studies and concludes, "The strongest argument that the homebirth movement can (and does) make in the U.S. is the statistical argument which shows that homebirth outcome is in no way inferior to hospital outcome." In Holland, where infant mortality rates are lower than in the United States, 90 percent of births are attended by midwives rather than obstetricians, and almost half occur at home, with another 40 percent taking place in free-standing birth centers. Only 10 percent occur in high-tech hospitals. Planned homebirths, in the United States and elsewhere, include planned transport to a hospital in the event of complications that occur about 5 percent of the time (Sullivan and Weitz 1988; Goer 1995; Lapetino 2000).

U.S. statistics on the safety of planned homebirths with qualified midwives have consistently been impressive. For instance: "In a famous 1977 project, Dr. Lewis Mehl studied birth outcomes from the medical records of 1,146 elective homebirths in the San Francisco area. The results: the perinatal mortality rate among women who elected homebirth was 9.5 per 1,000 births—compared to a rate of 20.3 per 1,000 among California women who gave birth in the hospital." From this large urban study, Dr. Mehl concluded that "the [homebirth] outcomes were better than average and the complications rates lower than expected" (England 1999: pp. 57–58). The largest rural study also confirms the safety of homebirth (Gaskin 1990). In 1,723 births (between 1970 and 1990) managed by midwives at The Farm, a Tennessee spiritual commune of 250, maternal mortality was zero and perinatal mortality was 18 infant deaths, or 10.4 per 1,000, compared to 18 per 1,000 in the United States (in 1980). Only 73 births, or 4.2 percent, required transport to a hospital; only 1.4 percent required C-section; and only 1.5 percent involved anesthesia. Nationwide, 22 percent of hospital births are by C-section, and drugs are used in 80 to 90 percent. As a result, according to Farm attorney, ecologist, and author Albert Bates: "Lately we've had women doctors and gynecologists who come to have their babies with us."[13]

Similar results were obtained in a carefully controlled study of a thousand planned births, five hundred at home with midwives and five hundred in hospitals with obstetricians, in which mothers were matched for age, risk factors, socioeconomic status, and parity (mother's first birth, second birth, etc.). While mortality rates were comparable, morbidity rates were higher in hospital births than in home births (Baldwin 1991). Even within hospitals, doctors have done worse than midwives, both in Holland and in an experimental project in California, in terms of infant mortality. Additional evidence shows that the mere presence of a supportive, though untrained, lay woman, or *doula,* during birth improves birth outcomes in a hospital (Jordan 1993: pp. 63–65).

Despite media portrayals of birth as intolerably agonizing for the mother, women who give birth naturally, without pain medication, typically describe labor as very hard work, with some pain, rather than as nonstop excruciating pain (Bradley 1965; Tanzer 1976; Rothman 1982; Gaskin 1990; Northrup 1994; Goer 1995; Lapetino 2000). They also say that they would not trade the experience of their birthing for anything else in the world. By contrast, drugs administered during labor often interfere with the progress of labor as the mother loses sensation, and they result in lower average Apgar scores of responsiveness in newborns.[14] By slowing labor, they increase the likelihood that the mother will be injected with pitocin to increase her contractions. Ironically, though, Pitocin-induced contractions are more severe and more painful than natural contractions. A cross-cultural study of pain in childbirth found that in cultures that regard childbirth as natural and normal, women perceive and experience giving birth as less painful than in cultures in which it is viewed as an abnormal, medical event.[15]

In the 1960s, Dr. Robert Bradley shocked his fellow obstetricians when he reported the results of thousands of births he had managed drug-free. His colleagues "could scarcely comprehend his announcement" because "most of the physicians had never seen even one unassisted, spontaneous birth" (Bean 1990: p. 79). In 14,000 births Bradley had attended by 1984, 94 percent were unmedicated, "three percent require(d) medication for some medical reason, and three percent require(d) Caesarean surgery" (McCutcheon-Rosegg 1984: p. 9). He rejected not only drugs during pregnancy and childbirth but, in his words, all forms of "meddlesome interference with nature's instinctual conduct (induction of labor, silly 'due dates,' routine IVs, monitoring, etc.)" (p. x). Despite Bradley's excellent statistics and many followers, the American Society of Anesthesiologists reported that in 1997 only one in seven U.S. women remained drug-free during hospital births.

Drug intervention can decrease the mother's pain in the short run, but it also increases the likelihood of vacuum extraction, forceps delivery, and C-section, all of which increase the incidence of maternal and newborn injury and infection (Tanzer 1976; McCutcheon-Rosegg 1984; Bean 1990; Jordan 1993; Goer 1995; England 1999; Riordan 1999). "Epidural labor analgesia puts mothers and infants at risk for a variety of health problems that are not encountered in an unmedicated labor" (Riordan 1999: p. 12). Drugs administered during labor make newborns drowsy, making it harder to initiate nursing. It is perhaps no coincidence that many of the same companies that make drugs and delivery systems, such as Abbott Laboratories and Bristol Myers, also manufacture baby formula that can account for up to half of the company's profits (Baumslag and Michels 1995: p. 171). Not only is an epidural drug likely to increase infant formula use, but formula use in turn increases the incidence of infant sickness treatable by additional drugs manufactured by the companies. By contrast, breast-feeding reduces demand for both infant formula and drugs (Baumslag and Michels 1995; Riordan 1999).

In the United States, between 80 and 90 percent of C-sections are medically unnecessary, and are carried out (1) as a result of previous interventions, (2) for the convenience of doctors (a disproportionate incidence of C-sections occurring around weekends and holidays), and (3) for prospective parents who have planned work schedules, childbirth leaves, and visits by friends and relatives according to often inaccurate and misleading "due dates" "guestimated" by their doctors (Bean 1990; Cohen 1991; Arms 1996; Goer 1995). C-sections increase health risks and sacrifice health benefits for both mother and infant. For instance, not only does C-section increase the mother's risk of death but "many women with precancerous cervical lesions can avoid surgery by giving birth vaginally."[16] Vaginal birth also helps clear mucus that can obstruct the newborn's breathing.

Ironically, refusing food to laboring women as well as unnecessarily limiting their mobility can weaken them and increase their anxiety, thereby interfering with labor and increasing the likelihood of delivery by C-section (Jordan 1993; Goer 1995). Giving birth while reclining, as opposed to squatting on a birthing stool, works against gravity, restricts the size of the vaginal opening, and compresses a major blood vessel, thus restricting blood supply to the baby. The "hygienic" environment of hospitals is far from it, often infecting mother or child with hospital-acquired germs, especially when combined with other interventions such as electronic fetal monitoring and vacuum or forceps extraction of the baby (England and Horowitz 1998). Dr. Northrup (1994: pp. 402–403) laments, "I am deeply saddened by all the unnecessarily medicalized births that occur because women in labor don't trust themselves and aren't surrounded by those who could assist them in this process."

Why Unnatural Birthing Protocols Persist

Obstetrician Don Creezy of the Stanford Medical School observes, "Obstetricians, initially trained in the scientific method, adopt clinical practices, many of which have no scientific basis whatever."[17] If these practices are medically unwarranted, why do they persist? Equally important, what are their consequences for women and their families? In part they persist because, as in other professions, the doctors with the most power over policy are often the ones with the most dated training—and often the ones least familiar with the latest research and most resistant to change. Defense of traditional practices is observed in all cultures, including the subculture of obstetrics and gynecology. "Obstetrics," in the view of medical anthropologist Robbie Davis-Floyd, "is a set of internally consistent rituals designed to reinforce certain core values held by the [obstetrics] culture as a whole."[18]

Traditionalism helps to explain the persistence of unjustified practices but hardly accounts for their rather sudden introduction about fifty years ago, before which time most births occurred at home without drugs. Ulrich (1991) uncovered evidence from the late eighteenth and early nineteenth centuries that indicates surprisingly low mortality and morbidity rates in attended but unmedicalized homebirths. Her Pulitzer Prize–winning book, *A Midwife's Tale: The Life of Martha Ballard, Based on Her Diary, 1785–1812*, records the births midwife Martha Ballard attended: "In almost 1,000 births Martha did not lose a single mother at delivery, and only five of her patients . . . died in the lying in period. Infant deaths were also rare" (p. 170).

From the 1940s on, a key factor changing birthing protocols was both doctors' and patients' rapid conversion to a belief in the beneficence of modern drugs and advanced technology as cure-alls for pain, disease, discomfort, and premature death. The clear success of some drugs, such as polio vaccine, and some technology, such as CAT scans, has led Americans to an unhealthy dependence on both drugs and technology—an overdependence fostered by medical corporations that profit from it.[19] Most Americans, according to Dr. Samuel Preston of the University of Pennsylvania, are unaware of a key fact: "Most of the health advances and resulting declines in mortality rates occurred in the first few decades of the 20th century. This means . . . that they were due to simple changes in hygiene and public health [especially, washing of hands], not to sophisticated medical treatments."[20] By contrast, Goer (1995: p. 351), who supports appropriate obstetrics, estimates that obstetrical interventions "have maimed and killed more women and babies than ever have been saved by their use."

The Myth of Medical Infallibility

The central myth of the medical-industrial complex is the incomparable safety of modern medical practice and the dangers of any alternative to it, including the practice of ordinary people taking primary responsibility for their own health. Ignored in this mythology is the very real danger posed by the medical establishment itself. Behind the medical horror stories that periodically gain national attention is systematic evidence of dangerous practices and conditions in medical care. According to the inspector general of the U.S. Department of Health and Human Services, "18 percent of hospital patients received inappropriate care that could cause injuries or other 'serious adverse events,' like drug overdoses, the mistaken amputation of a leg or surgery on the wrong side of a patient's brain." Yet "hospital inspectors were generally unable to detect substandard care or to identify incompetent doctors because the inspectors 'strive to foster a collegial atmosphere' and do not aggressively scrutinize practices that could threaten patients' lives."[21] In 1999, the National Academy of Sciences reported "stunningly high rates of medical errors." The report said that in hospitals alone "medical errors kill 44,000 to 98,000 people a year. This exceeds the number of people who die annually from highway accidents (about 43,450), breast cancer (42,300), or AIDS (16,500)."[22]

Contrary to claims of sterile conditions, "the rate of infections picked up by patients while they're in the hospital has increased 36 percent since the last count was made in a 1975–80 study." According to the Centers for Disease Control and Prevention, "2 million people a year acquire such infections, and nearly 90,000 die."[23] A contributing factor to the increased incidence and lethality of bacterial infections is the steadily growing resistance of bacteria to antibiotics overprescribed by physicians. "Researchers estimate that half of all antibiotics prescribed by doctors are unnecessary."[24] An *American Journal of Nursing* survey found that "more than two-thirds of nurses don't have time for basic nursing care, like teaching patients how to tend wounds or inject themselves with insulin. More than half are too busy to consult with other members of the patient's health-care team." Of special concern: "A full one-third would not recommend that their family members receive care at the facility where they work."[25]

While nurses are pressed for time, many doctors do not stay current in their specialties and are overly influenced by the solicitations of drug companies. "Studies find doctors frequently fail to prescribe some lifesaving older drugs for their patients with bad hearts and high blood pressure, while overusing newer, less effective medicines." Researchers at Massachusetts General Hospital confirmed earlier studies, finding that "despite scientific studies in medical journals and guidelines issued by expert panels, many doctors simply do not know which medicines are best."[26] A survey of doctors in North Carolina, Ohio, Colorado, and Texas, conducted by United HealthCare, the nation's largest managed-care company, found that many internists and cardiologists "routinely fail to give patients drugs and tests proven to work against conditions ranging from heart disease to diabetes."[27] One reason that "[t]he resistance of diseases to antibiotics threatens to undermine decades of advances in modern medicine," is that doctors overprescribe these drugs.[28] Such findings of doctors' fallibility make it all the more troubling that in a recent study published in the *Journal of the American Medical Association,* "in nine out of 10 decisions made between doctor and patient in routine office visits, the doctor did not allow the patient to make an informed choice."[29]

The United States is unsurpassed in medical technology and in medical care for the wealthy. Unfortunately, it also ranks first in health costs per capita while ranking only thirty-seventh in overall quality of health care, according to the World Health Organization.[30]

The Politics of Birthing

What are the psychological and political consequences of the American way of birthing? Unlike mothers who give birth naturally, those administered drugs during labor often have little clear memory of their labor or delivery (Tanzer 1976; Rothman 1982; Sullivan and Weitz 1988; Lapetino 2000). Drugged mothers often miss out on what many other mothers describe as the most magical and empowering moment of their lives (Bradley 1965; Tanzer 1976; Gaskin 1990; Kitzinger 1991; Northrup 1994; Lapetino 2000). One thing must be remembered, writes eco-feminist midwife Arisika Razak: "As women we experience great physical power in the process of giving birth. Birth is a physical ordeal that serves as a model for all subsequent rites of passage. It is a model for physical, emotional, and spiritual transcendence." It also belies a debilitating stereotype: "As a woman who works with birth, I can truly attest to the strength of women. We are *not* the weaker sex."[31] Research by anthropologist Donald Grayson supports Razak's claim. His study of two winter catastrophes found that "women—protected by body fat and toughened by childbearing—were much more likely than men to survive cold and famine."[32] Obstetrician Christiane Northrup (1994: p. 413), whose experience of giving birth transformed her philosophy of birthing, urges women to reclaim their birth power collectively.

In addition to medical professionals' serious incidence of ignorance and incompetence, feminist critics cite another reason for hospitals' unwarranted birthing practices: doctors' desire to retain control of the birthing process, appropriated from mothers and midwives only in the last hundred years (Jordan 1993; Arms 1996; Umansky 1996). Although this political-psychological explanation may be untrue for particular doctors, much evidence seems to support it generally. For instance, a 2000 study published in the *Journal of the American Medical Association* found that in the 1990s, an increasing number of doctors induced labor several weeks early for their own convenience, despite tripling the risk that such moderately premature babies will die in the first year.[33] Doctors have argued in print that women who desire natural childbirth are on a neurotic power trip—that is, on a trip to reduce doctors' own power.[34] The lithotomy (or reclining) position of birthing, instituted, preferred, and defended by obstetricians, is contraindicated by the law of gravity, common sense, and scientific data. But mom-on-her back, which reduces the size of the pelvic opening and makes parturition more difficult, is more convenient for the doctor and enables the doctor to more easily control the process of delivery (Cohen 1991; Kitzinger 1991; Jordan 1993, Umansky 1996). Feminists also point to longstanding negative views in Euro-American culture regarding the female body, which serve to legitimize high-tech birthing practices that purport to make up for deficiencies in the mother.

The point is not to debunk the many excellent U.S. doctors and hospitals, or the health benefits they confer. Indeed, midwives' associations agree that certain conditions warrant a hospital birth attended by a physician—including a small percentage requiring C-section (Gaskin 1990; Jordan 1993; Lapetino 2000). The point, rather, is to question the inflated claims of medical-industrial-complex propagandists that their way is the only way to proper health maintenance and birthing (Rothman 1982; Sullivan and Weitz 1988; Goer 1995).

Perhaps even more important than the reasons for the American way of birth are its political consequences. "A standard piece of advice contained in doctors' printed hand-outs for first-time mothers is to ignore what they might hear from other women," including midwives (Jordan 1993: p. 56). Many of these midwives have attended far more births than recently certified ob/gyns (Lapetino 2000). This advice is widely followed, and the main political consequence is the disempowerment of the mother, father, and family in the birthing process. Implicitly, these actual givers of life, along with their families, announce ahead of time, "We are incapable of birthing. We need your help and direction. Deliver our child for us." This act of deference in the potentially most magical and powerful time in a family's life not only undermines a treasured ritual of lifelong significance, but sets a pattern for family members of deference to experts and powerful institutions—a pattern that most Americans follow from cradle to grave.

The remembrance of our Birth Days, or days of birthing, instead of reconfirming our powers of loving creation, has become an occasion for honoring the special girl or boy with mass-produced and mass-advertised commodities. Instead of sharing with the child the parents' and perhaps older siblings' fond memories of exactly how, when, and with whom she or he came into the world, parents and guests hover nervously over the frenzied unwrapping to see which corporate products hit a home run and which ones strike out. By contrast, Umanski (1996: p. 58) documents the efforts, from the 1960s on, by birthing traditionalists to reinstitute natural birthing practices "as a way to promote 'family togetherness' and keep the state and its medical missionaries out of the family; a birth was a deeply private happening, meant to bond wife, husband, newborn, and siblings."

"I should have known better than to rely on experts," complained President Kennedy after the Bay of Pigs fiasco. A family whose child comes into the world at home and without medical or pharmaceutical intervention, says "No" to the partisans of power and profit, "No" to advertisers and hucksters, "No" to an unhealthy dependence on experts and authority, "No" to the gratuitous invasion of their private lives and sense of competence. When the family choosing natural homebirth is an entire community, as at

The Farm, a spiritual village of 250 in Tennessee, the political possibilities increase dramatically. The best-selling book *Spiritual Midwifery* (3rd ed. 1990), written by Farm founder Stephen Gaskin's wife, Ina May Gaskin, has helped thousands of families take fuller control of their reproductive process. Midwifery pioneering has also helped inspire many other empowerment efforts by Plenty International, The Farm's nonprofit outreach wing, recognized by the United Nations.

Families that have transformed their practice of birthing often feel inspired to transform other aspects of their lives as well. Natural birth, and the opposition it fuels, can teach its participants valuable lessons about corporate capitalism. They learn that they do not need nearly as many products as they had thought necessary. They discover or develop craft skills to make their own Birth Day presents—of higher quality and duration than commercial ones. They find that even in cities, they can save money and eat better by participating in organic gardening cooperatives. For items they cannot themselves produce, they can network with other families to enjoy bulk savings in a purchasing cooperative. Such families share many values with one another and avoid the expense and risks of commercial day care by sharing cooperative child-care arrangements with other families they know well.

Against the possessive individualism and narcissism of contemporary society, argues Rothman (Umansky 1996: p. 164), "we have motherhood, the physical embodiment of connectedness. We have in every pregnant woman the living proof that individuals do not enter the world as autonomous, atomistic, isolated beings, but begin socially, begin connected." We might add that this connection expands when the family as a whole participates in the process of pregnancy and childbirth. Recent, highly publicized homebirths by celebrities such as supermodel Cindy Crawford and actress Pamela Lee Anderson, along with eco-feminist activism and the legalization of midwifery in many states, have prompted an increasing number of American families to consider the possibility of natural homebirth.[35]

We Are What We Eat: The Politics of Breast-Feeding

Following birth, the patterns of family consumption, production, networking, and political activism become even clearer regarding what we feed our newborns and young children. If we have the health of the mother and child in mind, we breast-feed the newborn and continue to do so for at least a year (according to the American Academy of Pediatrics) and preferably two years (according to the World Health Organization and the Koran) or more. Despite such advisories, supported by scientific evidence, 40 percent of U.S. babies are never breast-fed, less than a third are still breast-feeding at four months, and only one-fifth are breast-feeding after six months—compared with a worldwide average weaning age of three years.[36] In the United States "each year 1.8 million mothers elect not to breast-feed" (Baumslag and Michels 1995: p. 106).

As in the case of childbirth, much of the politically correct left regards breast-feeding as imprisoning women to their biology. The influence of this segment of progressives, including many feminists, has trumped any united progressive critique of the formula industry and its tragic effects on mothers and their children. What difference does breast-feeding make? Why are Americans so inclined to substitute artificial baby foods? And what is the political significance of these choices?

Breast-Feeding Makes a Difference

As reported regularly by the World Health Organization, the International Pediatric Association, UNICEF, the International Confederation of Midwives, the U.S. Surgeon General, and all major medical journals, the scientific jury is in, and it is virtually unanimous: parents—and societies—that deprive their infants of mother's milk are compromising the health of their children while increasing the nonnursing mother's risk of breast, ovarian, and cervical cancer, osteoporosis, and other diseases.[37] By now, even formula companies (mostly owned by pharmaceuticals) have been forced to admit that mother's milk is best, although for decades they have done their best—and continue to try—to entice mothers to buy artificial baby food. Today, only their tactics have changed. Perhaps the most egregious example is the Nestle Corporation, which for decades aggressively marketed its infant formula in Third World countries where babies desperately need human milk's protective antibodies and where polluted water contaminates the formula with which it is mixed. Only a long-term, worldwide consumer boycott persuaded Nestle to curb, though not eliminate, these practices (Baumslag and Michels 1995).

Among dozens of health benefits, breast-fed children suffer fewer food allergies, fewer respiratory infections, fewer ear infections, fewer cases of life-threatening diarrhea, and lower overall infant and child mortality rates. Breast-fed children also enjoy numerous advantages in neurological and intellectual development, including a significant increase in IQ—an average of 8.3 IQ points in one matched study of premature infants[38]—as well as better teeth and stronger jaws. With full-term infants, breast-feeding is correlated with higher IQ, better performance in school, and higher scores on standardized tests, even when researchers control for the effects of parents' age, education, and wealth.[39] "Research results indicate that early breast-feeding offers optimal brain development."[40]

Breast-feeding also provides natural birth control by delaying the nursing mother's ovulation, thereby increasing birth spacing by a year or more, to a minimum of eighteen to twenty-four months. Evolution has ensured that each mammalian species' milk is biochemically tailored to the needs of that species' young, and indeed each mother's milk is uniquely matched to the physiology of her own child, although human milk from a milk bank is superior to any artificial formula. La Leche League's periodically updated manual *The Womanly Art of Breastfeeding* documents the advantages of breast-feeding and explains successful techniques for mothers faced with various problems. UNICEF (1998c: p. 22) summarizes current knowledge on key benefits of breast-feeding to children: "Breastfeeding perfectly combines the three fundamentals of sound nutrition—food, health, and care. . . . Because breastmilk contains all the nutrients, antibodies, hormones, and antioxidants an infant needs to thrive, it plays a pivotal role in promoting the mental and physical development of children."

Studies at the state level within the United States show the same pattern correlating formula feeding with disease and breast-feeding with wellness. In a study comparing four hundred exclusively breast-fed infants with four hundred formula-fed ones, "pharmacy costs for the breast-fed group were one-half what the formula-fed group's were." Of children examined by Women, Infants, and Children program coordinator Debbie Montgomery, "breast-fed kids were less likely to get recurrences of the four common childhood illnesses . . . ear infection, gastrointestinal infection, and upper and lower respiratory infections. For example, 43 percent of the formula-fed children who had one ear infection experienced . . . recurrences, but only 18 percent of the breast-fed babies did."[41]

Some U.S. skeptics of human milk's importance for U.S. children allege that it is only disadvantaged children who significantly benefit from breast-feeding. The evidence shows otherwise: "The finding that protective effects [of breast-feeding] did not differ between income groups challenges the current belief that breastfeeding is beneficial to infants living in poverty or in developing nations but is less important for advantaged babies in industrialized nations."[42] In fact, Sudden Infant Death Syndrome (SIDS) disproportionately kills U.S. infants, and the evidence suggests that lack of breast-feeding and lack of co-sleeping with infants are implicated in the high U.S. SIDS rates: "In situations where mothers breastfeed, do not smoke, and keep their infants next to them for nocturnal sleep, SIDS death rates appear to be extremely low."[43] Pediatrician Allan Cunningham reports that the U.S. SIDS rate is five times higher for formula-fed than breast-fed babies.[44]

In the United States, even for infants who are initially nursed, the typical weaning age of a few weeks or months is radically lower than in most other countries of the world, where weaning typically occurs at two to four years of age. Like failure to initiate nursing, early weaning compromises the health chances of the child. Indeed, "in every culture, there is an increased morbidity when nursing ceases early. In cultures where survival is difficult, the continuation of breastfeeding is a life-and-death issue" (Baumslag and Michels 1996: p. 9). In U.S. subcultures such as that of African

Americans, lower rates of breast-feeding are correlated with a higher incidence of health and developmental problems.[45] Contrary to the common but false belief that the quality of human milk declines greatly after the first six months, "human milk continues to complement and boost the immune system for as long as it is offered."[46]

In *The Politics of Breastfeeding*, Gabrielle Palmer (1993: p. 19) notes the irony of our bottle-feeding culture: "If a multinational company developed a product that was a nutritionally balanced and delicious food, a wonder drug that both prevented and treated disease, cost almost nothing to produce and could be delivered in quantities controlled by consumers' needs, the very announcement of their find would send their shares rocketing to the top of the stock market." Indeed, the ingenious scientists who had developed the product might win a Nobel Prize. But of course we need no scientists or corporations to produce this wonder. "Women have been producing such a miraculous substance, breastmilk, since the beginning of human existence" (p. 19). Why then do so many women themselves ignore it during the period in which it can do its irreplaceable magic?

Why Human Milk Is Replaced with Inferior and Dangerous Substitutes

We might begin with a look at public policy. A 1998 study by the UN's International Labour Organization found that "maternity and nursing benefits given to working mothers in the United States are the least generous in the industrialized world."[47] Unlike the United States, 80 percent of countries provide paid maternity leave, and 80 percent mandate working mothers' right to breaks for nursing. Both reflecting and shaping this governmental policy, the U.S. medical profession after World War II officially treated artificial baby milk as roughly interchangeable with human milk. The advice given my pregnant sister in the early 1980s was not uncommon. Having breast-fed her first child, she was discouraged from nursing by her doctor, who asked, "Why would you want to be a cow?"

By 1990, observers noted an important change: although "targeted heavily by formula companies, and often poorly trained in the practices of breast-feeding, pediatricians have generally supported and responded to the [recent] change [back] from bottle to breast" (Bean 1990: p. 147). Although the medical profession in North America and Britain has indeed been swinging back toward breast-feeding, the effects of the past linger on, with a majority of staff members in pediatric hospitals having no practical training in breast-feeding support, and 69 percent of staff members describing the hospitals' breast-feeding support as poor.[48]

Companies selling formula and drugs have long lobbied doctors, nurses, hospitals, and the general public with not only propaganda but pens, prescription pads, tote bags, and free formula that mothers routinely take home after giving birth. Formula manufacturers contribute millions of dollars every year not only to individual doctors and their hospitals but to the American Academy of Pediatrics, the American College of Obstetrics and Gynecologists, the American Dietetic Association, the National Association of Neonatal Nurses, and the Association of Women's Health, Obstetric, and Neonatal Nurses. When the pediatricians built a new national headquarters, the formula industry picked up $3 million of the tab (Baumslag and Michels 1995: pp. 171–172).

As of 1998, despite overwhelming scientific evidence of the superiority of breast-feeding, only eleven U.S. hospitals had been recognized by the World Health Organization and UNICEF as complying with those organizations' Baby-Friendly Hospital Initiative (BFHI). The BFHI "brought a structured programme to breast-feeding support and, in just six years, has helped transform over 12,700 hospitals in 114 countries into centres of support for good infant feeding" (UNICEF 1998c: p. 48). All but eleven U.S. hospitals have refused to implement one or more of the BFHI's "Ten Steps to Successful Breastfeeding," including (step 3) "Inform all pregnant women about the benefits and management of breast-feeding," (step 6) "Give newborn infants no food or drink other than breastmilk, unless *medically* indicated," and (step 9) "Give no artificial teats or pacifiers . . . to breast-feeding infants" (p. 49).

Not only doctors' foot-dragging in catching up with the scientific studies but political lobbying by formula/pharmaceutical companies continue to discourage government from bringing public health policy into accord with the BFHI. By contrast, in Chile the adoption of the BFHI as a matter of public policy has increased the percentage of infants who are exclusively breast-fed from 4 percent in 1985 to 40 percent in 1996. In Cuba, the BFHI has resulted in a corresponding increase in exclusive breast-feeding rates from 63 percent in 1990 to 98 percent in 1996 (UNICEF 1998c: p. 50). The U.S. government does not even keep such breast-feeding statistics; the only comparable data come from such formula makers as Ross-Abbott Laboratories (Baumslag and Michels 1995: p. 108)!

The American Academy of Pediatrics identifies five key factors as discouraging mothers from breast-feeding: "misinformed physicians, insufficient education, maternal employment at sites lacking facilities and support for nursing moms, lack of broad social support, and aggressive commercial promotion of formula."[49] American cultural attitudes complement U.S. political economy in accounting for low breast-feeding rates. The sexualization of breasts in our culture, unusual across cultures, discourages breast-feeding, especially in public, both from a concern for modesty and as a result of the mistaken belief that nursing causes breasts to sag and become less sexually attractive.[50] Movies, television, advertisements, magazines, and other popular media portray mothers far more often bottle-feeding than nursing.[51] In March 2000, Epinion.com's breast-pump ad, featuring a woman using a breast pump while wearing a blouse that fully concealed her breast, was rejected by several TV stations as "offensive," including stations that had "aired the Oscars telecast, with its ample asset-baring."[52] In December 2000, the Illinois Department of Children and Family Services described a thirty-two-year-old mother's breast as a "sexual organ," depicted her occasional nursing of her six-year-old son as "sexual molestation," and took custody of the boy.[53]

By the mid-1990s, breast-feeding mothers and advocates were strongly pressuring state legislatures to protect mothers' right to breast-feed in public. Beginning in 1993 with Florida, Virginia, and North Carolina, nineteen states by 1999 either had passed or were considering legislation protecting nursing mothers from harassment by businesses or arrest for "indecent exposure." In February 1999, Congress passed a law protecting nursing mothers on federal property. Despite these legal successes, many new mothers today continue to be dissuaded from breast-feeding both by friends or relatives who grew up in the height of the postwar anti-breast-feeding period in the United States, and by their infants' fathers, many of whom feel threatened by the intimate breast-feeding connection between mother and child (Coughlin and Mergler 1999).

Many hospitals, in addition to encouraging the use of drugs during childbirth, separate mothers from newborns for long periods of time, encourage formula feeding as a supplement to nursing, and encourage the use of pacifiers and other artificial nipples. As a result, babies often become nipple-confused, have difficulty latching on, or suck inconsistently. Thus many mothers lose confidence in their ability to breast-feed and succumb to enticements to switch to artificial baby foods. It is likely no coincidence that hospitals built with money from formula companies separate their maternity wards from their nurseries by greater distances than do hospitals built without such subsidies, thus increasing the likelihood that breast-feeding will be supplemented or replaced with formula feeding (Baumslag and Michels 1995: p. 174). Even when inappropriate hospital protocols have caused problems in nursing, almost all mothers and their infants can successfully return to exclusive breast-feeding through the medically recommended minimum of four to six months, followed by gradual introduction of solid foods in combination with slowly decreasing amounts of mother's milk (Mohrbacher and Stock 1997).

In U.S. hospitals, one of BFHI's most frequently violated guidelines is the last one, which is the most obviously political one: Baby-friendly hospitals must "foster the establishment of breastfeeding support groups and refer mothers to them on discharge from the hospital or clinic" (UNICEF 1998: p. 49). This directive, even more obviously than the preceding nine, directly threatens the profits of formula/pharmaceutical companies. La Leche League International, a mother-to-mother breast-feeding support group, has found that virtually all mothers who are solidly committed to breast-feeding can do so successfully. As a La Leche League (LLL) leader, my wife has advised hundreds of mothers who were having trouble with nursing, usually because of inappropriate interventions or unsupportive attitudes by others. Virtually the only cases in which she and other LLL leaders have found breast-feeding to fail have been those in which the mother had become too discouraged to put in the effort to reestablish the nursing relationship. Many women have become erroneously convinced that they "just don't have enough milk" for their babies.[54] The truth is that, with rare exceptions, breast-feeding works as a naturally balanced system of supply and demand: The more the baby drinks, the more the mother produces.

Distinct from these cases are ones in which the mother decides to forgo reestablishing nursing, or establishing it in the first place, because she wants to return to work, school, or some other activity that makes nursing inconvenient or impossible. This situation brings us to the politically charged issue of conflicts between working and mothering, or more accurately and fairly, working and parenting. This issue involves breast-feeding, and will also lead us into our final topic of conflicting styles of parenting.

Empowerment Through Breast-feeding

It is no coincidence that a recent study found that "staff members in [pediatric hospitals'] neonatal units who had midwifery training were significantly more likely to have had training in helping mothers to breast-feed and express milk."[55] Natural birth and natural feeding go hand in hand. By emphasizing women's natural powers as well as their constriction by patriarchy, eco-feminists have helped transcend the sterile "essentialist"-versus-"constructivist" argument about whether gender differences are natural or socially constructed. They are both, of course, and the real question is what the consequences are of these social and biological differences. Lasch (1997), Chira (1998), and others have pointed out the dangers of asserting, with Carol Gilligan and associates, that women are essentially more nurturing, loving, cooperative, and socially connected than men.[56]

But there are also dangers of ignoring women's unique powers, especially childbearing and breast-feeding. To the extent that some feminists have encouraged women to escape the "burden" of breast-feeding and its aura of enslaving women to domesticity, they have unintentionally tipped the balance of power even further away from women and their families to institutional providers.[57] The latter are only too happy to fill the void left when women (often pressured by men) choose vanity and careerism over their own and their babies' health. Such families end up more dependent not only on formula makers to feed their babies but on those same companies in their pharmaceutical guise to help cure babies and their mothers, since formula use compromises the health of mothers and babies (Baumslag and Michels 1995: p. 190). Many large corporations profit from parents' and professionals' denying human milk to children.

The point is not to relegate nursing mothers to the home while fathers continue on their merry workaday way. The point, underscored in Penelope Leach's (1994) book title, is to put *Children First,* at least during their earliest, most formative years. This responsibility should fall on both father and mother. In *Working Fathers,* James A. Levine and Todd Pittinsky (1997) offer "new strategies for balancing work and family." As director of The Fatherhood Project at the Families and Work Institute in New York, Levine argues for a kind of special attention, a sort of affirmative action for working fathers seeking to spend more time with their families. A 2000 study by the Radcliffe Public Policy Center found that "more than 70 percent of men age 21 to 39 would give up some of their pay for more time with their families. . . . In fact, they were more likely than young women to give up pay,"[58] despite other survey findings that two-thirds of women would prefer to give up the daily grind at work to return home.[59] Despite inflated claims of discrimination against childless workers,[60] it is in fact working parents who more typically face employer unfriendliness toward the family needs of employees—even with employers, as I personally experienced, whose official policy is family-friendly.[61]

Breast-feeding should not exclusively burden the mother. Rather, families and ideally a nationwide movement for family empowerment, should insist that employers, educators, and others (1) allow for extended childbirth leave, without prejudice, for one or both parents, and (2) create baby-friendly, nursing-friendly workplaces, places of learning, and other places of social activity (Leach 1994; Chira 1998; Hewlett and West 1998). Pregnancy, childbirth, and breast-feeding create a unique bond between mother and child, as reflected even in physiological measures such as infants' greater sensitivity, in utero and ex utero, to mothers' voices than to fathers' voices. Yet some fathers are better at nurturing children, even infants, than some mothers. In any case, choices about which parent does what work, paid and unpaid, during the earliest years of a child's life should be made jointly by mother and father.

There is a good deal of highly suspect, defensive rationalization on the part of some feminists, against Leach, Lasch, Friedan, and others, to the effect that career women "can have it all"—meaning that they can continue their careers virtually unabated through pregnancy, childbirth, and their children's earliest years without compromising the health or well-being of their children. For instance, nonstop careerist Susan Chira (1998) caricatures Penelope Leach (who also has a career) as "the high priestess of the baby cult" and her prochild stance as ignoring the needs of mothers. A deputy foreign editor of the *New York Times,* Chira seeks to reassure mothers like herself, who do not want to interrupt their careers for even a year or two, that turning most of their infants' care over to others should not be cause for self-doubt, guilt, or shame. She skirts the issue of breast-feeding with a veiled reference to those who cavalierly "pronounce that breast is best" (p. 64). However, the importance she places on getting her infants to sleep through the night ("I had to wait in the bathroom, with the water running, to block out the sounds of crying" [p. 55]) strongly suggests that she either never breast-fed her infants or weaned them very early.[62] Despite approving of Sheila Kitzinger's (1993) belief that mothers should "stay true to what they feel" (p. 63), Chira cites her own stoic refusal to respond to her infants' crying as allowing her more sleep and making her "a more joyous mother" (p. 55).

Chira's contradictory and unconvincing section "Science Weighs In" conveniently ignores the scientific evidence on the health risks to children when parents allow career priorities to trump breast-feeding. This evidence becomes especially relevant when we consider that in the United States (1) "only 13% of the women who return to work full-time shortly after giving birth breast-feed for at least six months, significantly fewer than those who stay at home" (Baumslag and Michels 1995: p. 189), and (2) 58 percent of mothers with preschoolers work outside the home (p. 191).[63]

Mothers who breast-feed, like fathers and mothers who insist on childbirth leave and child-friendly workplaces, declare their independence from corporate America by saying that they, not manufacturers, are most competent to feed their children, and that their children's well-being is more important than corporate profits or their own short-term career goals. "It should come as no surprise that the two biggest producers of infant formula, the United States and Switzerland, are the only two industrialized countries without mandated paid maternity leave" (Baumslag and Michels 1995: p. 200). As more families join forces with the World Health Organization, UNICEF, and the World Alliance for Breastfeeding Action to pressure U.S. hospitals to comply with the Baby Friendly Hospital Initiative, they are potentially setting the stage for united action on a wider range of issues that might help transform U.S. social institutions.

The authors of *Milk, Money, and Madness* sum up the primary advantages of breast-feeding for infants: "Breastfed babies are healthier, better protected from disease, and have a closer and more secure attachment to their mothers than babies who are formula fed" (Baumslag and Michels 1995: p. 192). Disagreeing with feminists is still politically incorrect, and many feminists continue to view breast-feeding as an imposition on women, who (they believe) should be just as free as men to continue their careers unimpeded through childbirth. They may be unaware of the health benefits of breast-feeding for mothers, whose risk of uterine, ovarian, and breast cancer, as well as of urinary-tract infections, hip fractures, and osteoporosis, is significantly decreased by breast-feeding (p. 91). In fact, the longer a woman breast-feeds, the lower her risk for cancer.[64]

Baumslag and Michels (p. 190) show how, in addition to health benefits for mothers and children, breast-feeding helps the nation by releasing scarce medical funds and staff, saving foreign exchange, cutting environmental

waste and pollution, and reducing demand for agricultural and energy resources. They also explain the benefits for employers who provide employees with nursing breaks and day care, including increased employee productivity and loyalty, greater employee satisfaction and cooperativeness,
lower absentee rates, lower turnover, reduced training costs, and fewer demands on employee health benefits. In "Breastfeeding and Empowerment:
Why the Breastfeeding Mother Is Truly an Empowered Woman," Eileen
Lindner stresses many themes that are critical for family empowerment:
self-confidence, resourcefulness, pride in one's own abilities, personal autonomy from outside influence, better budgeting of family resources through
reduced consumerism, enhanced health, connection with loved ones, and living in accordance with natural rhythms and patterns.[65]

This kind of mother's empowerment is not the kind envisioned by the
rigidly authoritarian, fundamentalist-friendly, and capitalist-convenient
"babywise" vision of authors Gary Ezzo and Robert Bucknam. Ezzo and
his wife run Growing Families International, which offers workshops on
topics such as "Growing Kids God's Way."[66] God's way is purportedly to
put infants on a rigid feeding and disciplinary schedule, ignoring their cries
for mother's milk if they don't fit the adults' schedule, and justifying this
"anti-spoiling" regimen with such profound pediatric insight as the allegation that "the Father did not intervene when His Son cried out on the
cross."[67] Never mind that the son was thirty-three years old. Ezzo's point is
to teach youngsters that their elders, not they, are in control. Such youngsters will then be well on track to submit to religious authorities as well as
to the clockwork green of corporate capitalism. Command-and-control parenting, however, ignores evidence that parental reliance on verbal commands and physical discipline typically makes young people less obedient
to parents, not more obedient (Bell 1998). Not only the American Academy
of Pediatrics (AAP) but even many evangelical Christians and others who
favor strict parenting, including Focus on the Family founder James Dobson, fault Ezzo's approach as rigid and dangerous.[68]

Toronto pediatrician and breast-feeding advocate Jack Newman calls
Ezzo's timed-feeding dogma the "babystupid" approach, and attachment-
parenting advocate William Sears calls it the "most dangerous program of
teaching about babies and children that I have seen in my 25 years as a pediatrician."[69] The American Academy of Pediatrics asks: "What's the best
feeding schedule for a breast-fed baby? It's the one he designs himself.
Your baby lets you know when he's hungry."[70] The AAP's advice does not
change for parents who choose bottle-feeding. Sears (1987) pinpoints the
flaw in Ezzo's fundamentalist/capitalist formula for child control: "It teaches
a mother not to listen to the baby's cries," which have evolved by natural
selection over eons of time for good reason. "Eventually what happens is
that the mother loses trust in her instinct. The baby loses trust in the
mother." Studies show that, far from spoiling children and making them

overly dependent, responsive parenting helps them become better organized and more self-disciplined. In cultures that do not have "the 'benefits' of parenting books and professional advisors, mothers carry their infants in slings during the day, share sleep with them at night, allow unrestricted breastfeeding, and give immediate nurturing responses to crying" (p. 13). In the traditional Inuit view, "there must be something wrong with a baby you keep in a box, for a baby belongs on its mother's back."[71]

Although close contact between mother and infant conveys many developmental benefits, studies show that breast-feeding can compensate for separations between mother and child, often resulting from unnecessary narcotics administered during birth (Bell 1998: p. 6). In a culture in which breast-feeding either never starts or ends early, and where social pressures promote detachment parenting, it is not surprising that parents progressively lose contact with their children and "47% of Americans say very few parents really know what their teens are up to."[72] Clearly, the issue of breast-feeding has already raised our final topic, attachment versus detachment parenting and its political consequences.

The Ties That Bind: The Politics of Child Rearing

Close, supportive family relationships early in life make for close, supportive families later in life. Along with strong marriages, attachment parenting (Granju 1999) plays a key role in building families that nurture their members and play participatory roles in the larger community. The priorities of empowered families may run counter to those of corporate advertisers, social-service agencies, and paternal government. The demurral of leftists on the issue of family empowerment reflects the fact that their PC antennae have been more sensitive to the oppressions of the family patriarch than to those of his external surrogates.

Attachment Versus Detachment Parenting

Physically and psychologically, breast-feeding is nature's original, life-or-death attachment between mother and newborn. Artificial baby food and its hawkers have disrupted this attachment for two generations of Americans. Like unnatural childbirth, artificial feeding detaches its participants both from each other and from their natural powers. By doing so, it makes them more dependent on outside providers and helps dissolve the social solidarity of the family. Taken together, technological birth and artificial feeding encourage a detachment style of parenting favored by liberal capitalism, which treats the pseudo-independent, acquisitive individual as the essential unit of society. Such individuals often lack clear personal identities and inner strength, and are in fact deeply dependent on the decisions, purse strings, and approval of others. Monkeys separated from their mothers fail to thrive, and "the distinction of attachment behavior is just as consequential in humans as it is in other primates" (Sulloway 1997: p. 121).

To the voices of early attachment theorists such as Mary Ainsworth and John Bowlby must be added those of contemporaries William and Martha Sears (1993) and Penelope Leach (1994), who urge parents to resist the competitive and atomizing pressures of today's market society. These pressures encourage parents to distance themselves from their children in order to foster early independence as well as their own careers. Ongoing research by Michael Commons and Patrice Miller at the Harvard Medical School confirms the developmental benefits of an attachment style of parenting as well as the harm caused by a detachment style that promotes premature independence of children. "Parents should recognize that having their babies cry unnecessarily harms the baby permanently," says Dr. Commons. "It changes the nervous system so they're sensitive to future trauma."[73] Commons and Miller favor lots of skin-to-skin contact between parents and babies, cosleeping, responsiveness to babies' cries, and nursing on demand. Such attachment parenting, they conclude, strengthens rather than weakens children's eventual independence, self-confidence, and willingness to take appropriate risks.

Related research at the University of Miami School of Medicine's Touch Research Institute has uncovered important health benefits of physical touch, including boosted immune response for HIV patients, increased sociability of autistic children, and better weight gain for premature infants.[74] "Critics of attachment parenting," notes William Sears (1987: p. 13), "argue that it puts the baby in charge and promotes disorganization. Research shows the opposite is true. Attachment parenting not only takes the rigidity out of schedules and respects the individuality of the baby and parents; it also promotes organization within the baby."

Scholars' "longitudinal research. . . . clearly shows that secure attachment at age 1 provides a preview to the child's social and personality development in the years to come." Specifically, it is predictive of curiosity and exploration, enthusiasm, outgoingness, self-direction, popularity, chances of being chosen as a leader, and friendliness.[75] A recent study compared the longitudinal outcomes of the style of attachment parenting typical of La Leche League members with those of a less responsive, more detached style of parenting. The author (Bell 1998: p. 2) concludes that "the grown offspring of women who were members of LLL and adhered to the principles of responsive parenting scored significantly higher on the Quality of Life Questionnaire, reasoned at a significantly higher level on the Defining Issues Test (moral reasoning), and scored higher on the Psychap Inventory (happiness) than the grown offspring parented by women who were not members of nor adhered to LLL principles."

The research on attachment parenting also makes it clear that healthy attachment precludes inappropriate attachment—more like "attackment"—which is smothering, unwanted, uncomfortable, or injurious.[76] As psychologist Mary Pipher (1996: p. 229) suggests, "Good parents try to be available emotionally but not omnipresent in their children's lives."

As clinical psychologists such as Kornberg, Beldoch, Hendin, Stern, and Kovel, and cultural critics of narcissism such as Sennett, Lasch, Jacoby, and Kovel have increasingly noted in the last quarter century, detachment-parented, atomized individuals are at best pseudo-independent. An absence of love and self-love at their cores makes them fragile and highly dependent on external reward, gratification, and validation. These narcissistic personalities typify the later stages of corporate capitalism, which require ever-greater levels of consumption and the minimization of worker-consumers' commitments to family, friends, craft, religion, and community—traditional foes of bottom-line profit maximization. "Thus," says Neil Postman (1994: p. 151), "as parents of both sexes make their way in the world, children become something of a burden."

One consequence of today's entropic war of all against all to work and consume at ever higher levels is the increased pressure that families feel for both parents to work outside the home.[77] Doing so leaves child care in the hands of outside providers, most of whom are underpaid and poorly trained. To the degree that such children feel neglected and unloved, they and their guilty-feeling parents become easy prey for advertisers who tempt them to fill their emotional void with commodities, further fueling the cycle of capitalist consumerism and psychological narcissism.

The heated debate between Penelope Leach and Susan Chira typifies much of the ideological argumentation about attachment versus detachment parenting.[78] Much of this argumentation is needless, since a perusal of works such as Leach's (1994) *Children First,* Chira's (1998) *A Woman's Place,* Lasch's (1997) *Women and the Common Life: Love, Marriage, and Feminism,* and Stephanie Coontz's (1997) *The Way We Really Are: Coming to Terms with America's Changing Families* reveals that all contestants accept the importance of children's initial attachment to, *and* eventual independence from, their parents. In *Beyond Gender: The New Politics of Work and Family,* Betty Friedan (1997: p. 83) attempts to mediate this debate, asserting, "There's been a false polarization between feminism and families." With the notable exception of two decades of work by Lasch (1977, 1979, 1984, 1991, 1995, 1997), what is mostly missing from this debate is its broader political context and its profound political consequences.

Politically, detachment parenting *feeds* corporate capitalism, while attachment parenting *threatens* it. Most of the child-development authorities who push early independence for children have been males with full-time jobs in capitalist societies. Detached parents forgo the close parent-child connection typical of most traditional societies and of all other primates, substituting a wide range of consumer goods that permit them to parent at a distance. These goods include not only manufactured bottles, nipples, and formula (as opposed to breast-feeding), but pacifiers (as opposed to picking up the child and/or breast-feeding), cribs (as opposed to family beds[79]), playpens (as opposed to adult supervision), remote monitoring devices (as opposed to adult supervision), "baby-proofing" devices (as opposed to adult supervision), infant-carrier car seats (as opposed to baby slings and other forms of body-to-body contact), and prefabricated toys (as opposed to playthings discovered or created by the child or parent). A website advertises and displays "The Nanny," a plastic figure that can be attached to a stroller and can hold a bottle in a baby's mouth. It's PC, though, available in black or white!

Even without day care and nannies, corporate America, abetted by child-development authorities who favor early independence of children, has made it possible for parents to "nurture" virtually without touching their children. What these choices do make parents touch is their pocketbooks, on a regular basis. Indeed, the concept of "virtual parenthood" has marketers salivating. Michael Lind (1996: p. 206) writes, "Virtual capitalism thus meets the virtual family in the utopia of the American overclass: Dad will bask in the Caribbean sun sketching out marketing designs on his laptop computer, while Mom keeps an eye on Baby, via satellite, as she flies from New York to Frankfurt to Tokyo."

The Vital Role of Mothers and Fathers

Many attachment-versus-detachment antagonists spend hundreds of pages camouflaging the real issue that divides them: Should mothers work in the cash economy? More precisely, should mothers of very young children work for pay if doing so requires them to leave their children with others? On average, the services that families lose when a stay-at-home parent goes into the cash economy had an annual market value in 1997 of about $36,000.[80] For many two-earner families, this cost means that the net economic gain of the second earner is often negligible, zero, or even negative. Disclaimers aside, this fact suggests that careerism, rather than economic need, is motivating many two-earner families with small children.[81] Parents who temporarily put careers on hold in order to care for their children got a small break in 1999 when the Clinton administration finally acceded to Republicans' politically incorrect proposal of a tax break for stay-at-home parents. The importance of the issue of mothers' work is heightened by the fact that the United States remains one of the few countries in the world without some form of paid maternity leave.

Most public debate on this question gets bogged down in the inconclusive evidence on whether young children given up by their parents for most of the day suffer lasting harm. The lack of longitudinal studies, and the inherent methodological problems of measuring children's well-being, their attachment to parents, their individual strength and resiliency, and confounding variables such as parental sensitivity, have created a field day for antagonists to pick and choose among the studies, or parts of studies, to "prove" their points. On the one hand, we read headlines such as "Kids of Working Mothers Turn Out OK, Study Shows"[82] and "No Harm in Day Care: Study Disputes Earlier Findings,"[83] which seek to assure readers that turning over child care to others is harmless. On the other hand, we read "Lies Parents Tell Themselves About Why They Work"[84] and "The Myth of Quality Time,"[85] which interpret much of the same research in just the opposite way. Taken together, the studies do seem to agree on three points: (1) many children from otherwise nurturing and supportive families can thrive despite spending most of their days in nonparental child care; but (2) more vulnerable children can be harmed by being put in day care; and (3) high-quality day care (about 25 percent) is less likely to harm children than mediocre (25 percent) or poor (50 percent) day care.

Susan Chira (1998), despite admirably documenting the complexities and uncertainties of the existing studies on attachment parenting and working mothers, describes as "the best new study" one that she admits is incomplete and mixed in its findings, but nevertheless finds "immensely reassuring." Despite the ambiguities of the findings, Chira states flatly that "working mothers do not have to fear that they endanger their relationship with their child by working" (pp. 94–98) and that the children are unharmed. Not only is this absolute claim counterintuitive and suspect on its face, but she neglects to mention a widely heralded, large-scale study (Helburn 1995) that had found three-quarters of day-care centers in four different regions of the United States to be substandard, compromising both the safety and the development of the children. This study also found that parents consistently rated the quality of their children's day care as better than it was rated by trained outside observers, suggesting rationalization at work in the minds of parents who want to feel "immensely reassured" about relegating their young children's care to others.

Chira's omission is significant for her own argument, because in justifying mothers' early return to work after childbirth, she explicitly recognizes the importance of parents' finding high-quality child care. In *The Silent Crisis in U.S. Child Care,* Helburn and collaborators (1999) update earlier studies with the most current data on a wide range of serious concerns, including the more than doubling, from 30 percent in 1970 to 64 percent in 1995, of mothers with a preschool child who work outside the home; the continuing low quality of most day care; the low pay, poor training, and high turnover rate of most day-care workers; and the fact that one-third of U.S. children aged five to fourteen are latchkey children. Chira's wishful thinking notwithstanding, "all recent studies indicate that [child-care] services are of mediocre or poor quality and that infants and toddlers received the lowest quality." While more and more infants "are experiencing nonparental care for at least part of the day within two or three months of birth," there is no assurance that this care is being provided "by individuals who truly substitute for the loving and active caring of a devoted parent" (p. 14).

The chilling videotapes made by Columbine High School killers Eric Harris and Dylan Klebold give us further pause to consider. The killers describe their parents as "clueless" about them and their long-brewing murderous plot. Klebold goes back to his early childhood, reminiscing bitterly about his experience at the Foothills Day Care Center, where he hated the "stuck-up" kids he felt hated him. "In private, the Klebolds try to recall every interaction they had with the son they now realize they never knew." Harris resents being perpetually uprooted because of his father's military career, as a result of which he was always having to start over "at the bottom of the ladder." It is not clear whether his sexist sentiments—e.g., "Yes, moms stay home. That's what women are supposed to fucking do"—reflect resentment over his own mother's absence. As the day of the planned slaughter approaches, Harris wishes his parents were out of town "so I didn't have to look at them and bond more." [86] Like the dangerous pediatric virus running rampant in 1999, which doctors suspect may be due to "the rising numbers of babies under six months of age in daycare centers," the Klebold-Harris tapes are less than "immensely reassuring" about the consequences of career-inspired detachment parenting.[87]

The choice is not between enslaving mothers and denying children the care of their parents. Three-quarters of Americans state that "too many children are being raised in day care centers," but less than a third would solve that problem by relegating mothers to traditional roles. Indeed, Americans think that the second-most-important solution to society's problems (after getting tougher on crime) is for fathers to focus more on their families.[88] It could be father, mother, aunt, uncle, grandparent, or a close family friend who fills a vital need by being at home when schoolchildren arrive at an otherwise empty house at the statistically most dangerous time of day for latchkey children, from 3 to 8 P.M. Otherwise, such children face not only loneliness and an increased incidence of depression but a higher likelihood of using drugs or alcohol, having early sex, getting poor grades, and committing crimes.[89]

In some quarters, it has become "patriarchal," "oppressive," and politically incorrect to suggest that mothers would do well to stay at home for even the first year or two of their children's lives. But a long line of research from Mary Ainsworth's studies in the 1970s to the work of Sears, Leach, Bell, and others in the 1990s confirms the value for children of early attachment to their mothers. For instance: "Securely attached children were more cooperative and positive. They were competent and sympathetic with peers, had longer bouts of explorations, and were better able to elicit and accept their mother's help. They had higher scores on developmental and language measures." Moreover, "mothers giving the least time and attention had infants who cried the most when separated, . . . in a healthy attachment the baby initiated separation, not the mother. Securely attached infants did not exhibit behaviors associated with being abandoned." Contra the "baby-wise" mythology of Ezzo and associates, "there was no evidence that those infants held were clingy or spoiled" (Bell 1998: pp. 7–8).

John O'Neill (1994: pp. 47–48), a socialist advocate for children and a critic of postmodern capitalism, renders a harsh verdict on liberal feminism and the men who support it:

> From the standpoint of the child it may be argued that such concepts as "*day* care," "single parent," or "single-parent family" are biased towards the ideological interests of individualizing adults, especially bourgeois feminists . . . [who follow] the standard of the "market family" touted by the double-income person/pair. . . . The apologists of late capitalism promote the emancipation of women as producers and consumers by according to them the right to control their own bodies—aborting not only the foetus but all social relationships that limit the myth of postmodernity.

The most extreme rationalization of parents' neglect of their children, eagerly seized on by "quality time" and day-care advocates, is Judith Rich Harris's theory that parental practices just don't make much difference because children are more influenced by their peers than by their parents.[90] The kernel of truth in this dubious claim is that sufficiently detached parents do indeed turn over the development of their children to peers and other outside influences such as television and advertisers. In other words, Harris begs the question of what kind of parenting allows peer groups to play such a dominant role. The answer to the begged question—detachment parenting—disempowers the family as a political unit. By contrast with Harris's claim, the National Longitudinal Study on Adolescent Health has found that risky teen behavior is best deterred by closeness between teens and their families, by high expectations of the teens by their parents, and by having a parent a home at important times of day.[91]

Unlike apologists for unengaged parents, O'Neill believes that fathers and mothers alike bear responsibility for the neglect of children. Despite the importance of mothers for children's development, it is arbitrary and sexist to place disproportionate responsibility for attachment, nurturing, and indeed "staying at home" on the mother. Research demonstrates the dramatic value of children's attachment to their fathers as well (McLanahan and Sandefur 1994; Popenoe 1996; Coughlin and Mergler 1999): (1) these fathers' children do better in school; (2) their children have higher self-esteem and are more sociable; (3) the strongest predictor of empathy in adults is their fathers' involvement with them as children; (4) "the proportion of single-parent families is the single strongest predictor of violent crime and burglary in any given locale" (Coughlin and Mergler 1999: p. 1); (5) "60% of rapists, 70% of long-term prison inmates, and 72% of adolescent murderers grew up without involved fathers" (p. 1); (6) involved fathers greatly reduce the rate of teen pregnancy in daughters; (7) children who lack two actively involved parents have a greater incidence of emotional problems, suicide, and becoming single parents themselves; (8) children whose mothers never marry are twice as likely to require therapeutic intervention[92]; (9) lacking a father in the home is a stronger predictor of delinquency than is poverty; and (10) children who live apart from their fathers are 4.3 times more likely to smoke as teenagers.

Coontz (1997) and others stress that such alarming correlations are sometimes reduced when statistical controls are exercised for the intervening effects of race, education, or socioeconomic class, and that a talented and dedicated single parent can in some ways make up for the absence of the other parent. Popenoe (1996: p. 56), however, reports (1) that single-parent children "are three times more likely to have a child out of wedlock, 2.5 times more likely to become teen mothers, twice as likely to drop out of high school, and 1.4 times more likely to be idle (out of school and out of work)," and (2) that these "conclusions were reached . . . after adjusting for such income-related variables as race, sex, mother's education, father's education, number of siblings, and place of residence." As William Galston and Elaine Kamarck have noted about the impact of one-parent families on crime: "The relationship is so strong that controlling for family configuration erases the relationship between race and crime and between low income and crime."[93]

Just as it is politically incorrect to discuss racial factors in high crime rates, low breast-feeding rates, and educational achievement, Coontz (1997) and others are concerned not to offend or stereotype single-parent families by stressing their overall worse performance in caring for children than two-parent families. Many of the disadvantages suffered by single-parent children can be traced directly or indirectly to the relative poverty of their families. But Popenoe (1996: pp. 56–58) and others have shown that children's lower economic level accounts for only half of their differential risks. He summarizes a large body of research showing that the children of divorced parents suffer a wide range of problems, partly because family income falls by an average of 30 percent but partly because children get less parenting from both parents after a divorce. Popenoe's colleague Barbara Dafoe Whitehead (1996: p. 7) shows how a "divorce culture" became sufficiently PC that "both Republicans and Democrats avoided the issue of divorce and its [harmful] consequences [for children] as far too politically risky."

Large and sophisticated studies done in the United States, Sweden, and elsewhere confirm the longitudinal clinical research of Judith Wallerstein,[94] showing that children of divorce typically perform more poorly on such assessments as: (1) parents' ratings of hostility toward adults, peer popularity, nightmares, and anxiety; (2) teachers' ratings of school-related behavior and mental health, including dependency, anxiety, aggression, withdrawal, inattention, peer popularity, and self-control; (3) scores in reading, spelling, and math; (4) school performance indices, including grades in reading and math as well as repeating a school grade; (5) physical health ratings; and (6) referral to the school psychologist.[95] David Blankenhorn (Glendon and Blankenhorn 1995: p. 277) summarizes the arguments, counterarguments, and studies thus: "Child well-being is declining. The family is weakening. Case closed."

With world-leading rates of both divorce and out-of-wedlock births,[96] the number of single-parent U.S. households has doubled since the 1970s, making these problems even more alarming. Parents spend 40 percent less time with their children than they did in the 1950s: "The average American teenager watches twenty-two hours of TV per week, while spending five minutes alone with his or her father and twenty minutes alone with his or her mother" (Hewlett and West 1998: p. 149). The 50 percent divorce rate underlying these trends is not surprising when we consider the fact that today's couples spend a daily average of only twenty minutes together.[97] Television has increasingly (1) replaced family conversation with passive viewing, (2) supplanted schoolwork and reading as sources of information, and (3) displaced parents as a source of child care.[98] A steadily increasing family workload combined with isolating forms of entertainment provides a dubious formula for family relationships.[99] For couples who do stay together, however, there are benefits not only for their children but for themselves. Based on cross-cultural and longitudinal studies, University of Chicago sociologist Linda J. Waite concludes that marriage confers economic, psychological, and health benefits on men and women. "There's something about being married that makes people work better," she says. "We're group-living animals, and we're hard-wired to bond."[100]

Family therapists Randy Mergler and Roger Coughlan have established La Pa's, a support network for fathers to help fathers empower themselves and their families.[101] As Friedan (1983) advised women, Mergler and Coughlan advise men to sequence their life plans to accommodate their families and their careers. Rather than urging men to relegate child care to their wives, they encourage fathers to take a break in their careers so they can support their wives in nurturing their young children and building their families. Addressing a common concern of employed fathers, the two therapists (1999) cite a four-decade study showing that "fathers who temporarily get off the career track to pursue family involvement are at the same level of career advancement as their non-involved peers five years later."

Although many husbands resist taking on their fair share of domestic responsibilities, from 1991 to 1996 the number of stay-at-home dads aged twenty-five to fifty-four roughly doubled, to 8.2 percent, and has continued to grow. In addition, many working fathers care for their children while their wives work a different shift.[102] In contrast to feminist criticisms of parental leave mentioned earlier, conservatives criticize paternal leave for a different reason: "For some, any increased use of leave by men threatens to undermine not only traditional gender roles at home, but also the work ethic that supports the United States economy" (Levine and Pittinsky 1997: p. 129).

Not only some feminists but many therapists take a casual-at-best stance on marriage. In "How Therapists Threaten Marriages," family-therapy director William Doherty (1998: p. 165), who inspired the Family Life 1st organization, warns couples about his own profession, saying that they should beware "the prevalence of therapist-assisted marital suicides. We need a consumer awareness movement about the potential hazards of individual or marital therapy to the well-being of a marriage." Gallup polls confirm Wallerstein's (2000) clinical study of families of divorce by showing that U.S. teenagers are twice as likely as adults to think that it is too easy to get a divorce.[103] Studies support the teenagers' view by documenting the many economic, psychological, social, and health advantages for children—and parents—of the parents' getting, and staying, married.[104] Israeli kibbutzim have rethought their traditional daytime "divorce" of children from their parents via the system of communal child rearing. Out of concern over attachment problems between parents and children, most kibbutzim have returned to a reliance on parental child rearing.[105]

Political Implications of Detachment Parenting

Most parties to the "parenting wars" focus almost entirely on how individual children and individual mothers are affected for better or worse. Even more important for my purposes, however, are the ways in which detachment parenting, even if it did not harm children as individuals, weakens the family as a community. Many American families are comprised of individuals who casually use family resources to aid their largely individualistic, extrafamilial activities: "The family becomes the launchpad on the carrier ship, with the real action occurring in the skies around the ship."[106] Such families mesh conveniently with the rationales of corporate capitalism and its allies, the helping professions and paternal state. For the most part, these loosely bonded families provide the U.S. political economy with atomized workers and consumers, uninvolved citizens, and little political flak from the family as a cohesive unit. Unlike families involved with support groups such as midwives' associations, La Leche League, and attachment-parenting networks, families of detached individualists are unlikely to join with other families for common goals, including political goals. Lacking tight-knit emotional bonds, they are unlikely to organize themselves and like-minded families into economic cooperatives, neighborhood improvement associations, community environmental groups, humanitarian social causes, or a broad-based political movement for more humane and family-friendly laws and institutions.

The politically charged question of whether mothers should work for pay serves as a red herring to distract progressives from these bigger issues. Of course mothers should earn income if they want to, and polls show that most do (Coontz 1997; Chira 1998), although many would prefer to stay home when their children are very young and if they felt they didn't need the income. Few mothers or fathers want to work in ways that they know needlessly imperil or disadvantage their children. The choice to bear children brings with it the responsibility to make at least temporary sacrifices for their well-being, especially when they are very young, impressionable, and vulnerable. Some parents, especially single parents and poor parents, need day care or the help of friends and relatives to provide care for their children. But many middle-class and well-to-do parents, including "progressive" ones, are unwilling, even for a year or two, to reduce their discretionary income or slow their career advancement in order to provide optimal nurture for their small children.

By 1995, 55 percent of new mothers were returning to work before their babies turned one year old, up from 31 percent in 1976. The 1995 figure was a whopping 77 percent of college-educated women between the ages of thirty and forty-four.[107] And a recent study found that those best positioned in their jobs to negotiate employer support for their family needs were the least likely to do so.[108] A striking example is Microsoft founder and chairman Bill Gates, who took "several days off" rather than the company's permitted twelve weeks of paternity leave when his wife gave birth to their daughter.[109] By contrast, professional football quarterback Jeff Hostetler sat out the entire 1999 National Football League season to help care for his sick son.

In criticizing the oppressive features of "the feminine mystique," second wave feminist founder Betty Friedan (1983 [1963]), like Emma Goldman before her, was far from debunking marriage or motherhood. Nor did she offer Chira's illusion of women "having it all" at every step of the way. Rather, she encouraged women to make "life plans" whose stages could sequentially accommodate various kinds of paid and unpaid activity, including motherhood. Unlike some feminists today who value career above family and resent family leave,[110] Friedan supported (and supports) maternity leave and even maternity sabbaticals. Far from envisioning "power women" who ape the lifestyles of corporate and professional males, she discouraged women from handicapping themselves and shortchanging society "either by slavishly copying the pattern of man's advance in the professions, or by refusing to compete with man at all" (p. 375). Like Goldman, she warns women against imagining that the road to freedom is to follow men into an oppressive workplace.[111] In the words of women's-poverty authority Diane Dujon, "Women know that we cannot sacrifice our children to meet the needs of the job—that is the true meaning of the work ethic."[112]

More recently, in *Beyond Gender,* Friedan (1997: p. 84) faults some of her feminist friends for saying that women "have been defined too long in terms of family, and we have to think of ourselves first, of women first." In making these kinds of self-centered choices, parents not only disadvantage their children as individuals but also disempower their families as part of a potentially progressive political force for social change. Friedan counters, "As a mother of three and grandmother of six, I'm one feminist who is a passionate believer in the value and the importance of families." She complains that when she advocated reconciling feminism with families, husbands, and motherhood in *The Second Stage* (1981), her views "were bitterly attacked by *Ms.* and other voices of what was becoming 'politically correct' feminism, as if I was betraying the women's movement" (1997: p. 7).

In *What's a Smart Woman Like You Doing at Home?,* stay-at-home moms and authors Linda Burton, Janet Dittmer, and Cheri Loveless (1986: p. 68) argue for an alternative to the housewife of the 1950s and the employed woman of the 1970s: "a mother who has decided to put her family first without putting herself last." They were early critics of the "quality time" rationalization by parents who have no appreciable quantity of time for their children. "Quality time" mythology has fallen out of favor with many U.S. women since 1979, when 66 percent agreed with the statement "It's not the quantity of time you spend with your children—it's the quality." By 1998, that number had fallen to 40 percent.[113]

Julia Grant questions the wisdom of substituting advice from outside experts for on-the-job wisdom of parents.[114] She believes that advice by pediatricians such as T. Berry Brazelton and child psychologists such as Penelope Leach may prove useful if considered in relation to a family's own experience. Indeed, "if parents organized and hired their own experts," Lasch (1979: p. 384) suggested, "things might be different." John Wargo's (1998) pessimistic conclusions in *Our Children's Toxic Legacy: How Science and Law Fail to Protect Us from Pesticides* lead him to advise parents to take up the slack themselves. The close family bonds created by attachment parenting and shared experience can help families detach themselves from an unhealthy dependence on elite directives and bureaucracies, perhaps the single most important step on the road to family empowerment.

A good model of expert help that empowers rather than disempowers mothers and their families is the mother-to-mother breast-feeding-support network of La Leche League. LLL leaders, all of whom have breast-fed their children and been certified under the LLL Leader Applicant certification process, provide information to mothers who request it on how to cope with breast-feeding problems and maximize their chances of breast-feeding success. By giving information rather than advice, however, the LLL leaders encourage mothers to make their own decisions, even about whether or not to breast-feed, based on their own nursing and parenting experience, combined with the additional information they seek and acquire. The LLL philosophy of mothers' empowerment assumes that mothers who are well-informed are the best authorities on their own situations, in part because mothers' instinctual tendency to hold their babies close to them, respond to their crying, and nurse them on demand are validated by the best scientific studies.[115]

There is growing evidence that self-determining families can often deliver better services to their members than outside providers, while they are also empowering their members to help shape the surrounding community. For instance, not only are homebirth outcomes generally superior to hospital outcomes, but home-schooled children score above the national median on standardized tests.[116] Such families are reversing the twentieth-century trend lamented by John O'Neill (1994: p. 49): "Just as the de-skilling of labour weakens its position in the market, so the de-skilling of families in favor of the smart products and ideologies that they consume in the marketplace weakens family authority." These families are re-skilling themselves. Many of them limit their television viewing as inimical to their children's well-being, their family's self-reliance, and their civic engagement, a decision supported by Robert Putnam's analysis of the contribution of television to Americans' declining levels of community involvement over the last forty years.[117]

Families as Political Actors

Mass society, consumerism, and bureaucratic institutions have reduced the self-reliance of citizens and their families. In addition to our learned incompetence in birthing, nourishing, and nurturing, we have come to depend on experts we cannot hold accountable and on machines we cannot make, maintain, or repair. Thus we have come to depend heavily on the political and technical powers-that-be. Political anthropologist James Scott (1998: p. 346) observes this disempowerment under both state socialism and corporate capitalism: "What is perhaps most striking about high-modernist schemes, despite their quite genuine egalitarian and often socialist impulses, is how little confidence they repose in the skills, intelligence, and experience of ordinary people." The National Commission on Civic Renewal recently concluded that Americans are "a nation of spectators." Its report states: "Too many of us have become passive and disengaged; too many of us lack confidence in our capacity to make basic moral and civic judgments, to join our neighbors to do the work of community; to make a difference."[118] Many parents have lost confidence in themselves as authoritative and civic role models for their children.

Mothering Magazine publisher Peggy O'Mara asserts that the low status of parents hurts families across the United States.[119] "The reason that day-care workers are underpaid and thus day care is in such a wretched state," says La Leche League leader Petra Ulrych, "is that there is no respect for the profession day care replaces: namely, parenting."[120] Hewlett and West (1998: pp. 230–258) deplore "America's war against parents" and assert a twenty-three-point Parents' Bill of Rights. Between parents' low status, on the one hand, and such high aspirations, on the other, lies a great deal of agitating and organizing. It is beyond the scope of this book to develop a grand strategy for uniting millions of U.S. families into a national family empowerment movement (FEM) or into a political voice such as a householders' party. But a few comments are in order.

Unlike sectarian "family values," the values underlying this family movement and political party would be inclusive, welcoming not only "traditional families" but empty-nesters, single parents, and indeed single persons, as long as they comprise households that value the love, nurture, respite, and autonomy implied by the phrase "home sweet home." Just as homes without elderly members can support seniors by providing Meals on Wheels, households without children can help youth by supporting strong schools. The FEM would welcome multicultural families, atheist families, gay families, Muslim or Buddhist families, and American Indian extended families, as well as the broad spectrum of Christian and Jewish families familiar to most Americans. Unlike the periodically persecuting authorities of South Dakota and Arizona, the FEM would have room for the communal Hutterites and the polygamous families of fundamentalist Mormons. Unlike some "not in my back yard" neighbors in suburbia, the FEM would embrace communal homes of senior citizens, recovering addicts, or nonviolent youth offenders.[121] And it would welcome the foster homes that provide critical transitions for orphaned, abandoned, abused, and runaway youth. A step in the direction of the FEM was the October 2000 Million Family March in Washington, D.C., called by Louis Farrakhan, who emphasized that government must be made more family-friendly.[122]

The U.S. Census Bureau records U.S. families moving at a rate of once every five years. "Although about 43 million people moved in 1993, or 16.7 percent of the population, almost as big a share—15.3 percent—had lived in the same house for more than 20 years."[123] This mixture of mobility and stability can enrich yet anchor family empowerment in neighborhoods. Family-activity networks of schools, labor unions, and neighborhood-watch programs can create bonds of trust and reciprocity among families.[124] Community gardening projects, consumer cooperatives, and neighborhood recycling and clean-up projects can also make friends and political allies of otherwise anonymous residents. Youth athletic leagues, cultural centers, performing groups, and places of worship provide additional sources of neighborly connection. Nationwide, family-based neighborhood activism is making the kind of difference my South Denver neighbors recently made when their decade-long efforts finally succeeded in persuading the Environmental Protection Agency to remove the Shattuck Superfund toxic waste site from our neighborhood. Locally based family networking gives families an incentive to stay in their neighborhoods.

Joshua Karliner (1997), in *The Corporate Planet,* and David Korten (1999), in *The Post-Corporate World,* give a wealth of current examples of grassroots activism that could strengthen, and be strengthened by, a family empowerment movement. In *The Activist's Handbook,* Randy Shaw (1996) offers a primer of strategies and tactics such a movement could successfully use. More engagement in local activism would likely increase parents' sense of political efficacy and might erase the current 12 percent deficit they suffer in voting rates when compared with nonparents.[125]

Giving young people a voice, as advocated in Chapters 5 and 6, strengthens rather than undermines family empowerment. It brings youth into the fold rather than driving them into the streets and shopping malls. An emotionally attached child is not a politically voiceless child. A young person respected becomes a young person respectful. To respect is not to coddle and is sometimes to discipline, but it is always to listen, respond, and communicate. Communicating is hard when couples spend only twenty minutes a day together, parents spend 40 percent less time with their children than in the 1950s, and fathers talk with their children less than thirty minutes per week (Pipher 1998: p. 231).

Children have a right to time with their parents, and that time can strengthen the family. The United Nations (1989) officially recognized the vital connection between children's rights and family empowerment in its 1989 International Convention on the Rights of the Child, which reads in part: "The family, as the fundamental group of society and the natural environment for the growth and well-being of all its members and particularly children, should be afforded the necessary protection and assistance so that it can fully assume its responsibilities within the community." The official motto of Kids Voting USA is "Bringing children and parents together as active citizens for today and tomorrow."

Above all, the hoped-for FEM must distance itself from superficially liberatory but deeply entropic advice "to reject the view of the family as a unit, or as a homogeneous actor with common objectives" and to regard it instead as "a locus of gender, class, and political struggle" (Rubin and Hartmann, in Bowles and Gintis 1987: pp. 107–108). Women and children have struggled, will struggle, and must struggle against patriarchal oppression. But if in the aftermath of this struggle no one replaces errant fathers or makes good their proper role, families will falter and individual patriarchs will give way to the patrimonial state and paternal helpers. To dissolve the unity of families is to render their living remnants unto Caesar. By contrast, profamily feminists believe that "connecting [family] relationships to a vibrant sense of responsibility would engage wide circles of people, including even public-policy makers and voters, who would need to consider what social and economic structures are necessary to permit continuous, caring human relationships especially responsive to those most dependent on such care."126

Robert Putnam makes a strong evidentiary case that television viewing is the principal cause of Americans' dramatic drop in civic engagement since 1960, isolating people from one another, weakening social trust, and reducing membership in civic organizations.127 Television's replacement of reading helps to account for the 1999 finding that "one-third of high school seniors lacked a basic grasp of the principles of American government and that fully three-quarters were not proficient in civics."128 By contrast, family empowerment can help rebuild communities and organize citizens to demand that government serve their needs rather than elite interests. In a survey of parents' political views, Hewlett and West (1998: p. 225) found that parents overwhelmingly favor the creation of a lobbying organization for parents along the lines of the American Association for Retired Persons. In a book about how families can survive and thrive, Mary Pipher (1996: p. 230) advises, "To be strong the family must build walls that give the family definition, identity and power." But those walls against intrusion must also include doors of opportunity: "The cure for cynicism, depression and narcissism is social action. Action solves two problems. It makes communities better and it gives people a sense of meaning and purpose" (p. 251).

Conclusion: Born to Rebel?

A groundbreaking, twenty-five-year study by Frank J. Sulloway (1997) might be mistaken to challenge my argument for family empowerment. In *Born to Rebel: Birth Order, Family Dynamics, and Creative Lives,* Sulloway argues that families with more than one child are typically a seedbed of political conflict as authority-friendly firstborns defend their turf against more rebellious later-borns. This evolution-based tendency for firstborns to be more conservative and later-borns to be more radical can be reversed by other systematic influences, including age spacing, gender, parental ideology, temperament, child-parent conflict, and social environment. With adequate data on eight key variables, a person's likelihood of becoming generally conservative or rebellious can be correctly predicted 90 percent of the time.

Transcending political correctness, Sulloway shows that revolutions, whether political, religious, or scientific, typically divide families along birth-order and related intrafamilial lines, rather than, for instance, uniting proletarian families against bourgeois families, as Marx predicted. Sulloway also rejects Freud's theory of an inherent Oedipus complex whereby children wish to kill their same-sex parent. "Childhood," writes Sulloway, "is about maximizing parental investment, not reducing it by half" (1996: p. 146).

At first blush, Sulloway's conclusions might seem to render hopelessly utopian any notion of empowered families helping to transform society along progressive lines. If sibling conflict so strongly predicts intrafamilial ideological differences, what hope do progressives have of rallying united and empowered families to progressive causes? But twentieth-century egalitarianism, combined with modern psychology, has already inclined many parents to rectify the inequalities imposed by birth order. Indeed, unlike families in earlier cultures where firstborns were heavily favored, many parents today compensate for firstborns' advantages in size, skill, and experience by actively favoring—acting affirmatively to level the playing field for—younger children. Most of Sulloway's sample of rebels and conservatives precede the twentieth century and such equalizing influences.

Rather than mooting the notion of family empowerment for social transformation, Sulloway actually provides valuable lessons for progressive parents. In particular, close and loving attachments between parents and all their offspring can help reduce siblings' anxieties about getting their fair share of parental time and resources. Sulloway shows that firstborns tend to be more defensive than later-borns, protecting their valuable turf against interloping siblings. This defensive conservatism is bound to be greater when parental investment is more distant and tentative, as recommended by detachment theorists, who believe that early independence better prepares children for the competitive world of modern market society.

On the other hand, parents strongly bonded to their children are well-positioned to help redirect the rebellious tendencies of later-borns away from their oldest sibling and onto external forces that promote artificial scarcity by preaching the gospel of power, wealth, and status as the keys to personal fulfillment. Jane Humphries writes, "Rather than promoting individualism, the mutual dependence of the family could well stimulate the social dimension of human development and, in turn, community and class ties" (Elshtain 1982: p. 218). But to ensure that parents have enough love and energy to go around, they cannot afford to sell too much of themselves to the market and its consumerist and careerist enticements. Resisting these influences reduces the incidence of progressive parents' practicing what they preach against, and helps to secure the love and respect of their children. It then becomes more likely that "a radical tradition could be preserved within the family during times of oppression and perpetuated intergenerationally" (p. 219).

Sulloway's findings offer rich insights for parents who wish to minimize unhealthy sibling rivalry and maximize family solidarity. If anything can resolve sibling struggles based on evolutionary survival concerns, it is an early childhood rich in love, security, and parental presence and support. We do not require a definitive study to surmise that strong bonds between parents and children are more likely than weak ones to provide such a childhood. Strongly bonded families can help build a family-friendlier and more humane society by joining with other families in addressing the crisis of faltering democracy. As Theodore Norton (Elshtain 1982: p. 268) argues, "It is when millions of families, representing the human interest in regeneration, confront civil society and the state with a bill of accounts that they can become factors in a positive resolution of the crisis."

Notes

1. Quoted in Dolbeare (1998: p. 34).
2. "Declaration of Sentiments," Seneca Falls, New York, in Lyman Tower Sargent, ed., *Political Thought in the United States: A Documentary History* (New York: New York University Press, 1997), p. 233.
3. Jean Bethke Elshtain, "Feminists Against the Family," *The Nation,* November 17, 1979, p. 500.
4. Two years earlier, Mary Pipher (1996: p. 225) had written, "Good parents are what Ellen Goodman called counterculture; they counter the culture with deeper, richer values."
5. Despite this chapter's focus on families with children, most of the arguments made for family empowerment apply to childless families as well.
6. Cf. Lasch (1977) and Carlson (1998).
7. "The political establishment can be as hostile [to parents] as the media. In recent years government has pulled the rug from under adults raising children, because neither the right nor the left of our political culture values or supports the work that parents do." Hewlett and West (1998: pp. 31–32).
8. David T. Abalos, *The Latino Family and the Politics of Transformation* (Westport, CT: Praeger, 1993), p. xiii.
9. Gary Ruskin, "Why They Whine: How Corporations Prey on Our Children," *Mothering: The Natural Family Living Magazine,* no. 97, November-December 1999, pp. 41–43.
10. Cory Lie-Nielsen, "Something's Wrong Here," *Special Delivery* 18, no. 1, winter 1994–1995, p. 12.
11. In the United States, "in-hospital alternative birthing centers are no improvement over the labor and delivery room in regard to issues of territory and decision-making power" (Jordan 1993: p. 141).
12. Our two homebirths, in 1993 and 1995, cost $1,400 and $1,600 total, including a birthing class for my wife and me, and all birthing supplies—about one-quarter the cost of a typical hospital birth. The seventeen lengthy prenatal and postnatal visits with our midwives, per pregnancy, and the midwives' (two plus an apprentice) steady presence for an average of twelve hours surrounding each birth, more than tripled the time we would have gotten from medical personnel at Kaiser-Permanente, our health-care provider.
13. Albert Bates, "The Farm, USA," in Jillian Conrad, ed., *Eco-Villages and Sustainable Communities* (Findhorn, Scotland: Findhorn Press, 1996), p. 21.
14. The Apgar score measures the newborn's heart rate, respiratory effort, muscle tone, reflex irritability, and color.
15. Janice M. Morse and Carolyn Park, "Differences in Cultural Expectations of the Perceived Painfulness of Childbirth," in Karen L. Michaelson, ed., *Childbirth in America: Anthropological Perspectives* (South Hadley, MA: Bergin and Harvey, 1988), pp. 121–129.
16. According to Dr. David Ahdoot of the University of California at Irvine, "The chances of the lesion regressing if you have a vaginal delivery are 33 times

greater than for C-sections." Katherine Bouma, "Labor May Help Halt Cervical Cancer," *Orlando Sentinel,* February 1998.

17. Foreword to Goer (1995: p. x).

18. Quoted in Goer (1995: p. 350).

19. Recent studies comparing nonprofit with for-profit hospitals and HMOs conclude that the profit motive increases health costs and compromises health outcomes for patients, especially by deemphasizing preventive care. David A Himmelstein et al., "Quality of Care in Investor-Owned Versus Not-for-Profit HMOs," *Journal of the American Medical Association* 282, no. 2, July 14, 1999, pp. 159–163; Elaine M. Silverman et al., "The Association Between For-Profit Hospital Ownership and Increased Medicare Spending," *New England Journal of Medicine* 341, no. 6, pp. 420–426.

20. Gina Kolata, "Health Care Let Population Surge," *New York Times,* January 7, 1997.

21. Robert Pear, "Hospital Inspectors Too Friendly to Uncover Problems," *New York Times,* July 21, 1999.

22. Robert Pear, "Malpractice Kills Tens of Thousands," *New York Times,* November 30, 1999.

23. "Hospital Patient Infections Rise 36%," *USA Today,* March 11, 1998.

24. Denise Grady, "Antibiotics Spawn More 'Superbugs,'" *New York Times,* December 28, 2000.

25. Barry Adams, "Protecting Our Patients: Nurses Should Be Free to Speak out Against Dangerous Practices—It Could Save Your Life," *Newsweek,* November 16, 1998, p. 17. Adams is an IV-infusion nurse.

26. Daniel Q. Haney, "Doctors Ignoring Older, Better Heart Drugs, Studies Say," Associated Press, March 21, 1998.

27. "Survey Documents Doctors' Mistakes," Associated Press, July 9, 1998.

28. The World Health Organization and the U.S. Centers for Disease Control and Prevention issued a joint warning to doctors in June 2000. Erin Chan, "Diseases Resisting Antibiotics: Drugs Often Misused, Overused, Report Says," *Chicago Tribune,* June 13, 2000.

29. Brenda C. Coleman, "9 in 10 Doctors Fail to Inform Patients Fully," Associated Press, December 22, 1999.

30. Robert Cooke, "U.S. Ranked 37th for Health Care," *Newsday,* June 21, 2000.

31. Arisika Razak, "Toward a Womanist Analysis of Birth," in Irene Diamond and Gloria Feman Orenstein, eds., *Reweaving the World: The Emergence of Ecofeminism* (San Francisco: Sierra Club Books, 1990), p. 169.

32. Susan Gilmore, "In Tough Going, Women Survive," *Seattle Times,* May 29, 1996.

33. Lindsey Tanner, "Death Risk Found Higher for Slightly Premature Babies," Associated Press, August 16, 2000.

34. For instance, Dr. Waldo Fielding said, "Psychiatrists do not as yet agree on precisely what it is the disturbed woman seeks in 'Natural Childbirth.' Some say it is proof of femininity; others, oddly enough, say that it is power or psychic masculinity they are after." Tanzer (1976: p. 85).

35. As of 1999, direct-entry midwifery was clearly illegal in ten states, effectively prevented in seven, legally unclear in five, legal and regulated in sixteen, and legal and unregulated in thirteen.

36. American Academy of Pediatrics report (1999). The mammals closest to humans in relative brain size—primates, whales, and dolphins—wean at a human-equivalent age of between two-and-a-half and seven years. See Dettwyler (1995:

p. 39). The surgeon general's November 2000 report found 29 percent of mothers still nursing after six months, with black mothers still lagging at 19 percent. Lauran Neergaard, "Black Moms Not Breast-Feeding Enough, Study Says," Associated Press, November 7, 2000. Mothers who start nursing were 64 percent in the most recent report. In the 1990s, the breast-feeding trend was up.

37. A good summary of the health advantages of breast-feeding for children is Cunningham (1995). Good sources for scientific updates on breast-feeding research are Jay Gordon, M.D., and La Leche League's *Breastfeeding Abstracts*.

38. A. Lucas et al., "Breast Milk and Subsequent Intelligence Quotient in Children Born Preterm," *Lancet,* no. 339, 1992, pp. 261–264. The study found that the IQ boost came from the human milk itself, not from the act of nursing.

39. L.J. Horwood and D. M. Fergusson, "Breastfeeding and Later Cognitive and Academic Outcomes," *Pediatrics,* no. 101, 1998, p. e9; J. Raisler, C. Alexander, and P. O'Campo, "Breastfeeding and Infant Illness: A Dose-Response Relationship?" *American Journal of Public Health* 89, no. 1, 1999, pp. 25–30.

40. R. Uauy and I. De Andraca, "Human Milk and Breastfeeding for Optimal Mental Development," *Journal of Nutrition,* no. 125, 1995, p. 2278.

41. Diane Eicher, "Breast-Feeding Program Dealt a Blow," *Denver Post,* January 29, 1996.

42. *Breastfeeding Abstracts* 18, no. 4, May 1999 (abstract of Raisler and O'Campo, "Breastfeeding and Infant Illness" cited above), p. 31.

43. McKenna and Bernshaw (1995: p. 266). McKenna, Peggy O'Mara, and Penelope Leach, among other scholars, have refuted a recent study that (a) purported to show the dangers of cosleeping but (b) failed to compare the reported deaths of cosleeping infants with crib-death rates.

44. Cunningham 1995.

45. S. M. Bass and M. W. Groer, "Relationship of Breastfeeding and Formula-Feeding Practices with Infant Health Outcomes in an Urban Poor Population," *Journal of Perinatal and Neonatal Nursing* 11, 1997, pp. 1–9. Laura Meckler, "Health Inequities Divide Blacks, Whites: Rates of Death, Disease Follow Racial Lines," Associated Press, December 31, 1998. Neergaard, "Black Moms."

46. American Academy of Pediatrics, cited in Lisa Marasco, *Common Breastfeeding Myths* (Schaumburg, IL: La Leche League International, 1998), p. 6.

47. Kirstin Downey Grimsley, "U.S. Less Generous with New Mothers," *Washington Post,* February 16, 1998.

48. M. Pantazi, M. C. Jaeger, and M. Lawson, "Staff Support for Mothers to Provide Breast Milk in Pediatric Hospitals and Neonatal Units," *Journal of Human Lactation* 14, no. 4, 1998, pp. 291–296.

49. Claire Martin, "Breastfeeding as Public Policy," *Denver Post,* March 7, 1999.

50. It is pregnancy, not nursing, that changes breast shape. See Dettwyler (1995b).

51. Keynote address and slide show by Dr. Jack Newman at the Colorado/Wyoming La Leche League 1999 Health Professional Seminar and Area Conference, Colorado Springs, Colorado, November 7, 1999.

52. "Stations Reject Breast-Pump Ads," *Denver Post,* March 30, 2000.

53. Sue Ellen Christian and Julie Deardorff, "Illinois Seizes 6-Year-Old Still Being Breastfed," *Chicago Tribune,* December 11, 2000.

54. Quandt 1995.

55. *Breastfeeding Abstracts* 18, no. 4, May 1999 (abstract of Pantazi, Jaeger, and Lawson, "Staff Support for Mothers" cited in note 48 above), p. 31.

56. Carol Gilligan, *In a Different Voice* (Cambridge: Harvard University Press, 1982); Lyn Mikel Brown and Carol Gilligan, *Meeting at the Crossroads* (Cambridge: Harvard University Press, 1992).

57. Unlike European feminist groups, U.S. feminists have generally avoided calling for better maternity leave, on the assumption that such calls, if successful, would encourage women to resume traditional domestic roles (Baumslag and Michels 1995: p. 199). Pateman (1988: p. 227) notes that too many feminists today still see equality "as a matter of women acting like men." She warns: "For feminists to argue for the elimination of nature, biology, sex in favour of the 'individual,' is to play the modern patriarchal game and to join in a much wider onslaught on nature within and beyond the boundaries of civil societies" (p. 226). *Sex in the City* author Candace Bushnell's take on feminism "is that it gives women the freedom and the right to be the way men are. 'Why do we have to be perfect?' she wonders. 'Women can be just as evil as men.'" Jennifer Weiner, "'Sex and City' Author Knows Single Lifestyle," Knight Ridder News Service, October 11, 2000.

58. Stephanie Armour, "Dads Make 'Revolutionary Shift' to Home: More Taking Care of Kids, Cutting Office Hours, Even Quitting," *USA Today,* June 18, 2000.

59. Maureen Dowd, "Rescue Me, Please," *New York Times,* June 8, 2000.

60. It is employers' desire to maximize profits, not the family needs of working parents, that converts workplace benefits into a zero-sum game that pits employed parents against childless employees.

61. When I opted to trade in six months of accumulated sick leave in 1995 to help my wife care for our infant and toddler, my officially family-friendly employer balked. The University of Colorado's legal counsel advised resistant administrators that they had better honor the policy, contained in an unambiguous single paragraph, which has since been changed to several pages of incomprehensible legalese. To my knowledge I was the first and am still the only faculty member, male or female, on my campus to use the university's parental-leave policy.

62. Evidence is mounting that "letting babies cry it out" harms them, physically and permanently. Yale psychiatrist Dr. Kyle Pruett pinpoints the key to this harm: "If you don't pick up a baby when he is crying, you can build up his levels of stress and distress." "Survey: Parents Raising Aggressive, Frustrated Kids," Associated Press, October 10, 2000.

63. Employment of mothers with babies less than a year old increased from 31 percent in 1976 to 59 percent in 1998. Tamar Lewin, "Working Parents: 2-Income Families Now the Norm," *New York Times,* October 24, 2000.

64. Micozzi 1995.

65. Paper given at the Colorado/Wyoming La Leche League 1999 Health Professional and Area Conference, Colorado Springs, Colorado, November 7, 1999.

66. Ezzo has published Christian and secular versions of his put-the-baby-in-its-place approach.

67. Quoted by Claire Martin, "Time to Eat: Controversial Book Advocates Training Babies to Live by the Clock," *Denver Post,* September 14, 1997.

68. According to the AAP, "scheduled feedings designed by parents may put babies at risk for poor weight gain and dehydration." Hanna Rosin, "Is 'Babywise' Parenting Foolish?" *Washington Post,* March 1, 1999.

69. Jack Newman, "Breastfeeding Myths," keynote address, Colorado/Wyoming La Leche League 1999 Health Professional Seminar and Area Conference, Colorado Springs, Colorado, November 7, 1999; William Sears, 1996 ABC television interview, quoted in Martin, "Time to Eat."

70. American Academy of Pediatrics, "Caring for Your Baby and Young Child: Birth to Age 5," in Martin, "Time to Eat."

71. James Houston, *The White Dawn: An Eskimo Saga* (New York: Harcourt Brace Jovanovich, 1971), p. 211.

72. *Newsweek,* "The Secret Life of Teens," May 10, 1999, p. 59.

73. <http://www.naturalchild.com/research/harvard_attention.html>, July 7, 1999.

74. Tom McNichol, "The Power of Touch," *USA Weekend,* February 6–8, 1998, p. 22.

75. Kathleen Berger and Ross Thompson, *The Developing Person Through the Life Span,* 3rd ed. (New York: Worth, 1994), pp. 187–190.

76. Russell A. Isabella and Jay Belsky, "Interactional Synchrony and the Origins of Infant-Mother Attachment: A Replication Study," *Child Development* 62, 1991, pp. 373–384.

77. "While Labor Department statistics show two-thirds of mothers of preschool children working outside the home, Public Agenda found that 70 percent of parents of children age 5 or younger believe it best for one parent to be at home with them; 60 percent doubt that even a top-notch day-care center is a close equivalent of a stay-at-home parent; 63 percent worry about physical or sexual abuse in day-care centers; and 78 percent say the best alternative to parent care is to rely on grandparents or other close relatives." William Raspberry, "Necessary Compromises," *Washington Post,* September 9, 2000.

78. Critics of attachment do not necessarily accept the "detachment" label I assign them.

79. Statistically, family beds, typical in non-Western cultures, are associated with a reduced risk of Sudden Infant Death Syndrome, or SIDS (Thevenin 1987; Sears 1995).

80. Barbara Wylan Sefton, "The Market Value of the Stay-at-Home Mother," *Mothering: The Natural Family Living Magazine,* no. 86, January-February 1998, pp. 26–29. The 1995 United Nations Fourth World Conference on Women, in Beijing, recommended that at-home, unpaid work be counted in the Gross National Products of nations.

81. "One in five children ages 6 to 12 are regularly left without adult supervision after school. . . . more affluent, nonminority workers reported leaving children home alone even if they worked 9–5 jobs." Anjetta McQueen, "Many Children Are Home Alone," Associated Press, September 11, 2000.

82. Paul Recer, Associated Press, March 1, 1999. "The results of this rigorous study are much more mixed than the misleading headline conveys." See Elizabeth Harvey, "Short-Term and Long-Term Effects of Early Parental Employment on Children of the National Longitudinal Survey of Youth," *Developmental Psychology* 35, no. 2, 1999, pp. 445–459.

83. Barbara Vobejda, *Washington Post,* April 21, 1996. A 1999 study by the National Institute of Child Health and Human Development reached the opposite conclusion: that "the mother-child relationship often takes a hit when babies are cared for by someone other than Mom." Amy Dickinson, "The Mother Load: A New Study of Day Care Will Make Many Moms Guilty for Using It. But They Shouldn't," *Time,* November 15, 1999, p. 120.

84. Shannon Brownlee and Matthew Miller, *U.S. News & World Report,* May 12, 1997, pp. 58–64.

85. Ibid., pp. 62–69.

86. Cf. *Time* magazine's exclusive story on the tapes, <www.Time.com>, December 13, 1999.

87. Holcomb B. Noble, "Contagious Pediatric Virus Running Rampant," *New York Times,* December 14, 1999.

88. Times Mirror Surveys, *The People, the Press, and Politics: The New Political Landscape* (Washington, DC: Times Mirror Center, 1995).

89. Jane Gross, "'Dangerous Hours for Kids a Growing Dilemma: After-School Care Solutions Few," *New York Times,* May 26, 1998. "Who wants to go home to an empty house?" asks Pam Carrano, who runs the after-school Homework Club for children of affluent working parents. "It goes against nature. Kids this age are social

creatures." Many of the children she cares for "complain that their mothers are inattentive after a long day of work and their fathers do not get home until bedtime."

90. Judith Rich Harris, *The Nurture Assumption* (New York: Free Press, 1998). Wendy Williams identifies the cop-out afforded by Harris. "Frustrated and overworked parents may take solace in the message that they cannot control how their kids turn out, but years of research show that this simply isn't so. . . . Unfortunately, the Harris phenomenon illustrates Americans' tendency to be uncritical consumers of messages that get us off the hook." Wendy Williams, "Do Parents Really Matter? Scholars Need to Explain What Research Really Shows," *Chronicle of Higher Education* 45, no. 16, pp. B6–7.

91. Susan Gilbert, "Study Stresses Family Role," *New York Times,* September 10, 1997.

92. "About a quarter of all family groups with children are mother headed (for blacks, more than half), which is almost double the 11.5 percent figure in 1970" (Popenoe 1996: p. 54).

93. Quoted in Christina Hoff Sommers, "The War Against Boys," *The Atlantic Monthly* 285, no. 5, May 2000, p. 73.

94. Judith Wallerstein, *The Unexpected Legacy of Divorce* (New York: Hyperion, 2000).

95. See McLanahan and Sandefur (1994) and Richard Weissbourd, "Distancing Dad: How Society Keeps Fathers Away from Their Children," *The American Prospect* 11, no. 2, December 6, 1999, p. 32.

96. A half million of these occur annually to unwed teenagers alone (Hewlett and West 1998: p. 162).

97. Brenda Turner, "Culture Crash," USA Weekend, April 26–28, 1996, p. 4. Mary Pipher (1996) stresses the "junk values" that prey on America's weakened families and especially their vulnerable children.

98. When the American Academy of Pediatrics recommended in 1999 that parents keep children's rooms "electronic-media-free," television program distributor Kenn Viselman revealingly retorted, "It's a bunch of malarkey. I don't think this takes into account how parents raise their children anymore. . . . Parents use TV in three ways—as an educator, a treat and a babysitter. That's not going to change, and this report is not going to change it." David Bauder, "TV Ban for Infants Called 'Malarkey,'" Associated Press, August 5, 1999; see also Barbara Vobejda, "Kids See Free Time Fade Away," *Washington Post,* November 9, 1998.

99. Barry Bluestone and Stephen Rose, "Overworked and Underemployed," *The American Prospect,* no. 31, March–April 1997, pp. 58–69.

100. Natalie Angier, "Marriage Maxim Adjusted: Genders Benefit in Different Ways, Researchers Say," *New York Times,* July 8, 1998.

101. Cf. <www.lapas.org>.

102. Shellenbarger (1999); Rick Marin, "At-Home Dads Find They Aren't Alone," *New York Times,* January 2, 2000.

103. Cited by Galston (1997: p. 157).

104. A good summary of the studies is Waite (1998: pp. 247–255).

105. See the chapter "Collective Education and Attachment Problems Between Children and Their Parents," in Werner Folling and Maria Folling-Albers, eds., *The Transformation of Collective Education in the Kibbutz* (Frankfurt am Main: Peter Lang, 1999).

106. William Doherty, author of *Take Back Your Kids* (2000), quoted in Ross Werland, "Take Back Kids, Experts Warn," *Chicago Tribune,* March 1, 2000.

107. Faye Fiore, "New Moms Going Back to Work Earlier," *Los Angeles Times,* November 26, 1997.

108. Hertz (1999: p. 19).

109. Levine and Pittinsky (1997: p. 128).

110. "In general, 'family-friendly' policies, like 'family values,' can push us back," writes Barbara Bergmann in "Watch Out for 'Family Friendly' Policies," *Dollars and Sense: What's Left in Economics,* no. 215, January-February 1998, pp. 10–11. Jane Kiser, on the other hand, writes that most women "desperately want work-family benefits." Whereas Bergmann sees too much family-friendliness in the workplace, Kiser and most other women see too little. Jane Kiser, "Behind the Scenes at a 'Family Friendly' Workplace," *Dollars and Sense: What's Left in Economics* 215, January-February 1998, pp. 19–21.

111. In "The Tragedy of Women's Emancipation," Goldman (1910) wrote, "As to the great mass of working girls and women, how much independence is gained if the narrowness and lack of freedom of the home is exchanged for the narrowness and lack of freedom of the factory, sweatshop, department store, or office?" Quoted in Dolbeare (1998: p. 378).

112. Diane Dujon, "The Ethics of Work," *Dollars and Sense: What's Left in Economics,* no. 215, January-February 1998, p. 26.

113. *Update: Women* surveys cited in "Now the Word Is Balance," *USA Weekend,* October 23-25, 1998, p. 5.

114. Julia Grant, *Raising Baby by the Book: The Education of American Mothers* (New Haven, CT: Yale University Press, 1998).

115. See Robert Hotz's summary of recent studies, "Baby Brain Needs Mom's Love," *Los Angeles Times,* October 28, 1997.

116. Jay Mathews, "Kids Taught at Home Test Higher," *Washington Post,* March 25, 1999.

117. Robert D. Putnam, "The Strange Disappearance of Civic America," *The American Prospect* 24, winter 1996, pp. 34–48.

118. <www.puaf.umd.edu/civic renewal>.

119. Keynote address, "Love Is a Necklace of Moments," La Leche League Colorado/Wyoming Health Professional Seminar and Area Conference, Colorado Springs, Colorado, November 6, 1999.

120. Personal communication, November 17, 1998.

121. Despite the widespread sentiment of "Not In My Back Yard" toward such group homes, there is no convincing evidence that they increase crime rates or lower property values.

122. Bob Dart and Kavita Kumar, "Mellow and Prayerful, Families Crowd Mall," Cox News Service, October 17, 2000. Christopher Lasch (1997: p. 183) warned that friends of families should "have nothing to do with the official search for a national policy on families. What the family needs is a policy on officials, designed to keep them in their place."

123. Randolph E. Schmid, "Americans Average 1 Move Every 5 Years," Associate Press, October 29, 1998.

124. The union reform movement Teamsters for a Democratic Union, for instance, encourages spouses to join the union and participate in its outreach activities: "This inclusion of family participation in TDU affairs is inseparable from its political ideology of union democracy" (Tillman and Cummings 1999: p. 226).

125. Ruy Teixeira report, cited in Hewlett and West (1998: p. 228).

126. Minow and Shanley (1997: p. 102).

127. Viewing of TV news and public-affairs programs appears to be an exception to Putnam's generalization. See Pippa Norris, "Does Television Erode Social Capital? A Reply to Putnam," *PS: Political Science and Politics* XXIX, no. 3, September 1996, pp. 474–480.

128. E. J. Dionne, "Why the Culture Needs Civics Classes," *Washington Post,* November 27, 1999.

8

Missing Synergies in Ecology, Crime, and Political Economy

"Growth for the sake of growth is the ideology of the cancer cell."
—Edward Abbey[1]

"A thing is right when it tends to preserve the integrity, stability, and beauty of the biotic community. It is wrong when it tends otherwise."
—Aldo Leopold[2]

". . . the criminal's best plan is to tell the truth as far as he can. . . . If only fate had granted him remorse."
—Fcodor Dostoevsky[3]

"I hope that we shall crush in its birth the aristocracy of our moneyed corporations, which dare already to challenge our government to a trial of strength and bid defiance to the laws of our country."
—Thomas Jefferson, 1814[4]

"Private property is a creature of society, and is subject to the calls of that society."
—Benjamin Franklin, 1783[5]

Blushing Green While Selling Out to Growth

Political correctness squanders the natural advantage that progressives should enjoy in their battle against the increasingly unpopular, oppressive features of corporate capitalism. We have seen how left-wing political correctness can perversely serve the status quo in the areas of affirmative action, values, ageism, and family empowerment. Political correctness can also obscure key linkages among different problem areas and thus lead to disparate "solutions" that in fact undermine one another and miss potential problem-solving synergies. Those with transformative hopes of protecting the environment, reducing crime, and ensuring that social wealth and power serve the common good often ignore the relationships among ecology, crime, and political economy, given their PC tendencies.

255

The left charges that the right is willing to sacrifice the environment in the pursuit of mindless growth, obscene profits, and conspicuous consumption. Strong charges—but, alas, things are much worse ecologically than even the left would have us believe.

What's Wrong with the Ecosystem

According to the National Academy of Sciences, "17,000 plants and animals become extinct every year, compared with something like 20 a year before man roamed the earth." Since 1975, of the 1,520 species listed as endangered or threatened in the United States, only eleven have been designated "recovered" while seven have perished. While 9 percent of endangered species have improved, 80 percent have worsened.[6] According to the Worldwatch Institute: "Almost every ecological indicator shows a world on the decline." Worldwatch president Lester Brown calls "the scale and the urgency of the challenges . . . unprecedented."[7] As Worldwatch's *State of the World 1998* (1998) notes with irony, "The twentieth century has been extraordinarily successful for the human species—perhaps too successful. As our population has grown from 1 billion to 6 billion and the economy has exploded to more than 20 times its size in 1900, we have overwhelmed the natural systems from which we emerged and created the dangerous illusion that we no longer depend on a healthy environment" (p. xviii). Enthusiasts of growth, charges economist Herman Daly, have forgotten that the economy "is a subsystem of a finite and nongrowing eco-system."[8]

Extinction threatens one-ninth of bird species, one-quarter of mammals, one-third of fish, and almost half of primates (Worldwatch Institute 2000). Of the tropical rainforest on which the earth depends for its oxygen supply, we are seeing "some of the world's most diverse tropical forests . . . going up in smoke" (Worldwatch Institute 1998: p. xvii) and "16 million hectares of forest . . . now being cleared of trees each year, . . . equivalent to twice the entire land area of Nigeria" (p. xviii). Many countries, including Mauritania, Ethiopia, and Haiti, have sacrificed almost all of their forests in search of firewood. Such destruction is related to the global output of goods and services, which "grew from just under $5 trillion in 1950 to more than $29 trillion in 1997, a nearly sixfold expansion. From 1990 to 1997, it grew by $5 trillion—matching the growth from the beginning of civilization to 1950" (p. 3). This growth puts accelerating pressure on the earth's resources and sustainability: "From 1950 to 1997, the use of lumber tripled, that of paper increased sixfold, the fish catch increased nearly fivefold, grain consumption nearly tripled, fossil fuel burning nearly quadrupled, and air and water pollutants multiplied severalfold" (pp. 3–4).

"Polls show the global public becoming more worried about environmental problems every year" (Worldwatch Institute 1999: p. 183), cued by telltale signs such as rising prices of fresh fish whose stocks are in trouble, such as Atlantic swordfish, Pacific perch, Caribbean redfish, and New Zealand orange roughy. Overfishing has pushed fisheries around the world to capacity or beyond, endangering many species such as North Sea cod, herring, and sole. "Ocean stocks of cod, haddock, and flounder—staples of the fishery—have collapsed."[9] Having produced over 40 million kilograms of fish as recently as 1960, "the Aral Sea is now dead" (Worldwatch Institute 2000: p. 4). "Scientists have warned that they have found unacceptably high levels of toxic industrial chemicals [especially dioxin] in the [European] region's seafood."[10] Not only species' survival but agriculture suffer from abuse of water resources. "As water use has tripled since mid-century, it has led to massive overpumping. Water tables are falling on every continent," including in the southern Great Plains and the southwestern United States (Worldwatch Institute 1998: p. 5). As a result, many areas traditionally self-sufficient in grain production have been forced to import grain. "To import one ton of grain is to import 1,000 tons of water" (p. 7). For instance, in North Africa and the Middle East, the grain and other commodities now imported each year require water use in the countries of origin equivalent to the annual flow of the Nile River.

Overuse of water now means that for much of each year, some of the world's largest rivers, including the Colorado River and China's Yellow River, run dry before they reach the sea. "Rivers running dry not only deprive key species of spawning opportunities, they also rob fisheries of nutrients" (p. 8). Chemical fertilizers used in agriculture have overloaded rivers and damaged a third of U.S. coastal areas with surplus nitrogen, causing excess algae growth that has depleted fisheries, killed Florida manatees, and sacrificed coral reefs and sea grasses.[11] The loss of half of the world's original forests in the last century has exacerbated both aquifer depletion and soil erosion by increasing runoff. The loss of forests threatens the world's oxygen supply and increases the level of carbon dioxide, thus hastening global warming (p. 8). With each of the 1998, 1999, and 2000 winters setting new records as the hottest ever, global warming is accelerating, with potentially dire consequences of coastal flooding, increased severity of storms, desertification, reduced harvests, and higher food prices.[12] The earth's average temperature has increased almost a full degree Fahrenheit in only thirty years (Worldwatch Institute 2000). "As fossil fuel use has increased nearly fivefold since 1980, carbon emissions have far exceeded nature's capacity to fix carbon dioxide (CO_2). As a result, atmospheric concentrations of CO_2 have climbed to the highest level in 150,000 years" (Worldwatch Institute 1998: p. 10).

Contrary to claims of industrial apologists who, unlike atmospheric scientists, discount global warming, the fifteen warmest years since record keeping began in 1866 have occurred since 1979 (Worldwatch Institute 2000). "The North Pole is melting. The thick ice that has for ages covered the Arctic Ocean at the pole has turned to water, recent visitors there reported.

'There was a sense of alarm,'" said Harvard oceanographer James Mc-
Carthy. "Global warming was real, and we were seeing its effects for the
first time that far north."[13] In a related matter, scientists have concluded
that the hole in the ozone layer over the Arctic will not soon recover from
the combined effect of atmospheric pollutants and a colder stratosphere.
The greenhouse gases that cause global warming thereby also lower stratos-
pheric temperatures. The recent Arctic and Antarctic ozone holes permit
cancer-causing ultraviolet radiation to reach the earth.[14] "New evidence
shows man-made pollution has 'contributed substantially' to global warming and the earth is likely to get a lot hotter than previously predicted, a
United Nations–sponsored panel of hundreds of scientists has found."[15]

In addition to CO_2, toxic gases from cars and industrial plants, especially carbon monoxide and oxides of sulfur and nitrogen, have polluted the
air and caused not only widespread sickness but millions of unnecessary
deaths every year. The Tata Energy Research Institute estimates that in
India alone, in 1997 "the combination of indoor and outdoor air pollution
was causing 2.5 million premature deaths a year" (Worldwatch Institute
1998: p. 11). In its *State of the Air 2000* report, the American Lung Association warned that over 130 million Americans could be at risk because of
dangerously high smog levels, especially in cities such as Los Angeles,
Phoenix, Houston, Atlanta, and Washington, D.C. When the Environmental Protection Agency enacted stricter ozone controls in 1997, industry got
the court to block enforcement. Water pollution also continues to worsen
with the expansion of the fossil-fuel-driven global economy. For example,
50,000 miles of China's rivers are classified as not even suitable for irrigation. In much of China, staple foods such as rice and cabbage are laced with
harmful heavy metals such as lead, chromium, and cadmium.

No individual statistic is as frightening as the combined, unforeseeable
effects of our misbehavior on the world's ecosystems as a whole. It is upsetting enough to learn that "in semiarid regions of Mexico, 68 percent of
native and endemic species have disappeared" (Worldwatch Institute 1998:
p. 11) and that every year Mexico loses over 1.5 million acres, or 1.2 percent, of its forests. Of much greater concern, however, is the rippling, or
domino, effect such losses can cause locally, regionally, and globally: "As
various life forms disappear, they affect the entire ecosystem and particularly the basic services provided by nature, such as pollination, seed dis-
persal, insect control, and nutrient cycling. This loss of species is weakening the web of life, and if it continues, it could tear huge gaps in its fabric,
leading to irreversible changes in the earth's ecosystem." Bio-ecologists
Paul and Anne Ehrlich suggest that modernity's extinction crisis may be as
severe as the event that destroyed the dinosaurs: "All organisms are working
parts of ecosystems that provide indispensable and mostly irreplaceable free
'services' that support the human economy. These services include controlling the mixture of gases in the atmosphere, generating and maintaining

soils, recycling nutrients critical to agriculture, supplying fresh water, controlling nearly all crop pests, providing food from the sea and the land, pollinating many crops, and maintaining a vast genetic 'library.'"[16] Underlying the relentless eco-disruption is an ideology and global political economy in which, as Robert Kuttner (1997) charges, "everything is for sale."

Like the civic decay of modern cities, the accelerating global degradation might be less alarming if it were sustainable, but it is not (Scott 1998: p. 348). "Global economic trends during the 1990s were remarkably bullish, but environmental trends were disastrous" (Worldwatch Institute 2000: p. 8). Unfortunately, "the ideology of growth knows no geographic boundaries. It has permeated every corner of the planet" (Worldwatch Institute 1998: p. 4). As ranger and ecology writer Edward Abbey warned, "Growth for the sake of growth is the ideology of the cancer cell." The dangers red-flagged by early critics of growth—such as naturalist John Muir, forest manager Aldo Leopold, social ecologist Murray Bookchin, biologist Rachel Carson, philosopher Herbert Marcuse, Club of Rome economists, and eco-feminist Carolyn Merchant—may soon be irreversible.

What's Wrong with Eco-Politics

When science provides overwhelming evidence that human habits are destroying the earth, we might expect the voices of change to speak loudly and consistently, both from soapboxes and in the trenches, on behalf of slowing, halting, and finally reversing a growth process that the earth cannot tolerate. But a lethal potion of shortsightedness and political correctness has instead produced a dismaying blend of cacophony and silence, what *Democracy and Nature: The International Journal of Politics and Ecology* calls "the present ideological confusion in the Left and the Green movements." We need to examine why many progressives think that "the Green movement, despite the growing ecological crisis, has lost almost all of its radical potential."[17]

For most of the twentieth century, *ecologically correct* was not *politically correct*. Progressives have been ecologically compromised both by their ties to organized labor and their admiration of socialist models in Europe and Asia. When environmental education and protection threaten to close factories, workers carry bumper stickers that read, "If you're hungry and out of work, eat an environmentalist." Domhoff (1998: p. 61) observes that a local growth coalition, typically dominated by business interests and favored by progrowth newspapers, "sometimes includes a useful junior partner—the unions of the building trades . . . which are often on the side of the growth coalition against neighborhood groups, environmentalists, and university faculty, staff, and students." Nationally, the United Auto Workers has joined automobile, oil, and coal companies in lobbying the government to lower and postpone clean air standards. In addition to labor's historical "unwelcome mat" for women and ethnic minorities, "even more hostility was expressed toward the environmental movement because it was seen as a threat to jobs" (p. 303).

Beyond union ties, leftists who were impressed by the egalitarian social-welfare policies and productive prowess of the Soviet Bloc and communist China have been tempted to overlook these countries' miserable environmental records. "Socialism would conquer nature; it would build everything—dams, steel mills, skyscrapers—bigger than under capitalism; it would usher societies into the realm of order and reason. But nature fought back. The worst ecological disaster in Europe today is the area where Czechoslovakia, East Germany, and Poland meet." Like corporate capitalism, state socialism equated bigger with better. "'Bigger' turned out to apply also to mistakes: After the massive irrigation of Ukraine, the yield per hectare dropped as the soil became poisoned with salt" (Przeworski 1991: p. 121). Seven out of the world's ten most polluted cities are in China.[18] When, under socialism, people ate better and got better medical care and housing, partisans of the left excused socialism's environmental incorrectness in the interests of political correctness.

In the last decade, this twin legacy has waned with the collapse of the Soviet Bloc regimes and the rise of environmentalism among rank-and-file unionists (Tillman and Cummings 1999). Especially important has been the development of the green movement and green parties with their explicit efforts to connect the plight of workers with the plight of the planet. The Social Democrat–Green coalition that replaced Helmut Kohl's Christian Democrats in Germany in 1998 has agreed to dramatically raise taxes on energy use (while reducing them on wages) and to shut down all of Germany's nuclear power plants, reflecting a dramatic greening of the pro-growth Social Democrats. But legacies die hard, especially when economic growth boosts ordinary citizens and when strict ecology would require even the working class to tighten its belt. When push comes to shove, most progressives remain more sensitive to loud pleas of partisans than to silent sufferings of nature. Never mind that the wronged planet will strike back at all humans if we keep pushing it beyond its carrying capacity.

Despite environmentalist hounding by their children (Temple 1993), adult progressives have caved in to the dictates of growth.[19] Under attack from conservatives for tree hugging, whale loving, and business bashing, leftists overestimate their environmentalist credentials while ignoring their own complicity in the ongoing ecocide. The reassurance that "we're more ecological than our opponents" may be factually and politically correct, but it helps to rationalize consumerist lifestyles that remain firmly entrenched on the left. A plethora of pseudo-green companies has sprung up to capture the market of left-leaning consumers who want to give lip service to environmentalism: "Kevin Hartley, vice-president of Green Mountain Energy Resources, describes deregulation as an opportunity for consumers to support the environment without changing their lifestyles. 'It can be done from your couch. . . . Reduction of eco-guilt. That's really what we're selling.'"[20] Corporate investment in fossil fuels combined with low demand for alternative energy by pale green couch potatoes has held renewable energy to a meager 2 percent of the U.S. energy budget. The small percentage of progressives who live communally and ecologically stands out as a telling exception to left-wing consumerism and could serve as ecological Jiminy Cricket to the pale green Pinocchio.[21]

The point is not a simple-minded opposition to tactical compromise on growth versus the environment. Indeed, the German Greens have had to compromise with their Social Democratic partners on the issue of timing the closure of nuclear power plants. The point, rather, is that political and personal considerations have impeded the development of any clear and compelling ecological vision among progressives in the United States. The left's historical attraction to grand-systemic explanations works against the kind of self-critical introspection that might lead progressives to examine how well their own lifestyles accord with their ideologies. Ignoring the psychological and cultural forces operating in our daily lives makes it easy to project consumerism onto our enemies while failing to notice it in ourselves.

The left's hit-or-miss approach to environmental protection is mired in arguments about trade-offs between Growth Project X and Environmental Cost Y. Faber (1998) argues that an overreliance on the technical expertise and professional status of compromise-prone environmental elites, inside and outside government, can dampen grass-roots activism. Virtually no mainstream U.S. politicians run for office on an antigrowth or reverse-growth platform, despite polling evidence that a growing majority of Americans reject the more-is-better ideology and, unlike in the 1970s and 1980s, say they are willing to pay more in order to pollute less (Kay 1998). Al Gore, one of the greenest of U.S. politicians, expresses the collective view of the politician genus he represents: "There is no higher priority for government than jobs and strong, sustainable growth."[22] His 1999–2000 campaign for the presidency notably stressed growth while slighting eco-sustainability.

The left has failed to put sustained heat on progrowth politicians whose constituents value environmental protection. Despite valuable work in ecological economics by Lappe (1994), Benton (1996), Daly (1996), Karliner (1997), James O'Connor (1998), Worldwatch (2000), and others, what is missing in the trenches of progressive politics is a clear and compelling vision of how to run a healthy economy without despoiling the earth. Nothing like the democratic vision, the Marxist program, or the ideology of equal rights has yet captured the collective imagination of the friends of the earth—a progressive default that benefits the forces of plunder. Many left radicals and socialists, especially males, view environmentalism as a liberal hang-up clouding the more central issue of how to liberate the disadvantaged from oppression.[23] They correctly attribute such wrongs as environmental racism and unsafe workplaces to the profit motive of corporations and to government's complicity in corporate profiteering. But they have not anchored any solutions they propose in a broader vision of an ecologically sustainable economy. Rather, the radical vision typically advocates putting the oppressed in power and trusting them to make the right decisions for society and the planet. Much of the left remains allergic to "utopian" speculation about how the future ought to look, socially or ecologically.

Just as adult progressives fail to ask whether children should have standing in the corridors of power, until 1972 none had thought to ask the question "Should Trees Have Standing?", a landmark essay by legal philosopher Christopher D. Stone. Stone proposed that society should "give legal rights to forests, oceans, rivers and other so-called 'natural objects' in the environment—indeed, to the natural environment as a whole" (Nash 1989: p. 128). Not only Supreme Court Justice William O. Douglas, in an influential dissenting opinion, but also many lower courts have answered Stone's startling question in the affirmative, granting legal standing in the 1970s to a polluted river, a marsh, a brook, a beach, a species, and a tree. The species was the palila, a small Hawaiian bird threatened by livestock grazing. In 1979, with the help of the Sierra Club and the Audubon Society, "for the first time in American legal history a non-human became a plaintiff in court. Moreover, the bird won!" A federal court gave Hawaii two years to eliminate livestock grazing on Mauna Kea (p. 177).

Around the world today, it is encouraging to see some of the Marxian and post-Marxian left now embracing ecology and reaching out to the green movement, as reflected in Australia's *Green Left Weekly* and its affiliated resistance centers in large cities, New Zealand's *GATT Watchdog* and *Native Forest Action,* England's *Red Pepper* and *The New Internationalist,* Canada's *Alternatives Magazine* and *Sustainable Times,* and the United States' *Synthesis/Regeneration: A Magazine of Green Social Thought, Capitalism, Nature, Socialism,* the Institute for Social Ecology, and *Democracy and Nature: The International Journal of Politics and Ecology.* Thoughtful experimentation in ecological political economy is being carried out by the Global Ecovillage Network and the Ecovillage Network of the Americas.[24] These cutting-edge initiatives in bridging the leftism-ecology gap face a daunting task in transforming the thought and practice of radicals, socialists, and post-Marxian progressives, as well as of environmentalists. The tendency of all PC to close off debate has relegated the question of whether progressives may not be ecological enough to a few advocacy groups, including the American Indian Movement, as well as environmental "extremists" such as philosophers Peter Singer and Tom Regan,[25] People for the Ethical Treatment of Animals, and the Animal Liberation Front, whose limited focus narrows their political appeal. Compared to conservatives, progressives do blush green, but their lives favor consumerism, and they share no clear vision of an ecologically sustainable economy for the future.

Disadvantaged Criminals as Victims of Oppression

In the United States, neither the right nor the left has an adequate analysis of or solution to crime. U.S. politicians greet the release of the FBI's official crime report with the same fervor as the French greet the release of the current vintage of Nouveau Beaujolais. Their passion about crime reflects a hope that they can put a spin on the statistics that will cast themselves in a favorable light. As reported crimes rose steadily from 1955 to 1980, few officials took responsibility for failing to carry out effective anticrime policies. But as the aging of the baby-boomer generation has thinned the ranks of the most crime-prone age group, all sorts of politicians are taking credit for the recent drop in reported crimes. "With the murder rate down by more than 25 percent since I took office," bragged President Clinton in 1998, "Americans are safer today than they have been in many years." The Democratic president cited his support for putting more officers on the street and getting more guns off the street. Majority Republicans in Congress stressed the budgetary incentives they had given to states that lengthen prison sentences for violent offenders. Mayors and police chiefs such as St. Louis's Clarence Harmon (former police chief and current mayor) claimed that local policies such as community policing have keyed the recent crime-fighting success.[26] Unlike the opportunistic politicians they rightly criticize, most progressives treat crime with a studied indifference, partly for reasons of political correctness.

Who Cares About Crime?

Most Americans do. By any measure, crime is a serious problem in the United States. Nine out of ten Americans say that crime is a serious problem, and eight out of ten say it is one of the nation's biggest problems. Most people think that crime is worse in other neighborhoods than in their own, but two out of five do not feel very safe at home. Recent crime reductions, if real, have a long way to go in reversing the overall trend of the last four decades, during which crime has increased dramatically.

> In 1955 forty-six robberies occurred annually per 100,000 in the population; today the rate is more than 270—a sixfold increase. Rape rates have more than tripled. Murder per capita has more than doubled. The aggravated-assault rate has increased more than sixfold. Overall, taking into account both urban and rural areas, the major crime rate is more than four times what it was four decades ago.[27]

Until 1994, when teenage homicides began to decline, the post-1980 decrease in adult murder rates was matched by increases in youth homicides. Reports of domestic and child abuse have increased, and by late 1998, over half of U.S. women report having been physically assaulted at some time in their lives, and almost one in five has been raped.[28] By the late 1990s, about one-quarter of American families were "touched by crime" each year, down from one in three in 1975.

University of Chicago economist Steven Levitt and Stanford law professor John Donahue contend that high abortion rates among single, young, poor, and minority mothers may explain half of the overall crime drop in the United States from 1991 to 1997. For this suggestion, reports liberal journalist and legal scholar Susan Estrich, the authors have been called racist and "have been forced to defend their right as scholars to report what they learn, even if everyone finds it politically incorrect."[29] Noting that "40 percent of all African-American men between 18 and 25 are in prison, on parole or on probation," she calls it common sense that Levitt and Donahue found a tie between the high abortion rates in the 1970s of a group of mothers whose children are statistically most likely to commit crimes and a comparable drop in crime rates twenty years later. She writes that it has become "racist" to point out "correlations between race and anti-social behavior, or low test scores, or school failure even when those correlations are true."

Zero-tolerance policies in cities such as New York, long-term imprisonment for habitual offenders in states such as California and Colorado, and community policing in many cities across the country have all coincided with the aging of the boomers and may have contributed to the last few years' decrease in reported crimes. In addition, however, the worsening clearance rates for reported crimes may have discouraged more Americans from reporting crimes. "The national clearance rate for homicide, which was 93 percent in 1955, has steadily declined to 67 percent. That for rape has declined from 79 to 52 percent, and that for burglary from 32 to 14 percent." Even more disturbing to many law-abiding citizens are the short sentences served by convicted criminals: "the median time served by those actually sentenced to state prison ranges from 5.5 years for murder to 2.2 years for kidnapping to 1.4 years for arson."[30] Since 1945, the time served for all crimes except rape has been cut in half, from about two years to about one year.[31]

Survey research reveals that "the *victimization rate* is many times higher than the official crime rate. The number of forcible rapes is three to five times greater than the number reported to police, the number of unreported burglaries is three times greater, and the number of robberies is over twice that of the reported rate" (Dye 1999: pp. 295–296, emphasis in the original). Most crimes are not reported to the police, and increases or decreases in the reporting rate may give an inaccurate impression of actual crime trends.[32] In addition, police departments in Los Angeles, Philadelphia, and elsewhere have been known to "shave" their crime numbers in order to make departmental anticrime efforts look more successful than they actually are. Indeed, in summer 2000, just as the Justice Department was reporting a 10 percent decrease in U.S. violent crimes for 1999, a city audit uncovered 37,000 major crimes that had gone unreported in 1998 in Philadelphia alone.[33]

In 1999 the Milton S. Eisenhower Foundation issued a report warning against complacency over recent decreases in reported crimes.[34] The report attributed most of the recent decrease to an unusually prosperous economy rather than crime-fighting strategies or any improvement in the underlying conditions that breed crime, including the "vast and shameful inequality in income, wealth and opportunity." It noted that more than a quarter of U.S. children live in poverty and that U.S. violent-crime rates exceed those of almost all other industrialized nations. Between 1969 and 1998, violent crime in large U.S. cities increased by half. "From this longer, and deeper, perspective," the report concluded, "it is painfully clear that, when it comes to violence, we remain a society in deep trouble."

Gun-control advocates attribute the mid-1990s drop in gun-related deaths to tougher gun-control laws, whereas law-and-order proponents point to tougher gun-enforcement policy.[35] John Lott's (1998) *More Guns, Less Crime,* a time-series, county-by-county, multiple-regression analysis of crime rates, credits the deterrent effect of new laws allowing citizens to carry concealed weapons, for reducing violent crime rates. The partially improving crime picture of the last few years may be about to reverse itself. As of the year 2000, notes James Q. Wilson, there were a million more people between the ages of fourteen and seventeen than there were six years ago. Half of this extra million are male, and it is likely that "six percent of them will become high-rate, repeat offenders—30,000 more muggers, killers, and thieves" than in the early 1990s.[36] In fact, in 1999 some violent crime rates began to rise again in several large cities, including Boston, Houston, New York, San Antonio, and San Diego.[37] In the first half of 2000, "some of the country's biggest cities—often a harbinger of criminal trends—saw significant upturns in murder and less serious types of crime, including Los Angeles, Boston, Dallas, New Orleans, and Philadelphia."[38]

Nightly-news paranoia aside, the fact remains that crimes are far more likely to occur in the United States today than forty years ago and that U.S. crime rates, especially of violent crime, are some of the highest in the world. "Victimization surveys . . . appear to confirm that the United States is the most crime-ridden of the advanced nations of the world" (Dye 1999: p. 300). The U.S. murder rate is about twice that of Canada or France, four times that of Spain or Switzerland, five times that of Norway or England, and eight times that of Japan. Almost one in every twenty Americans is behind bars, compared to one in every two hundred Japanese.[39]

Crime According to the PC Right and the PC Left

According to the PC right, crime is basically caused by criminals, individuals who freely choose to break the rules and harm others. "People who commit crimes are people like us who have chosen to do bad things," says law professor Paul H. Robinson.[40] Some conservatives qualify the "free" will of offenders by allowing that dysfunctional families and even bad neighborhoods may contribute to criminal choices. James Q. Wilson, for instance, cites "neglectful, immature, or incompetent parenting" and "entire communities . . . dominated by a culture of fatherless boys preying on innocent persons and exploiting immature girls" as important influences on offenders.[41] Other conservatives account for criminality with a "rotten apple" theory, according to which natural flaws incline a minority of people from birth toward deviant behavior. These rotten apples need to be culled, and the public protected from them by decisive measures such as long-term confinement and the death penalty. Modern-day Hobbesians such as Chief Justice William Rehnquist suggest a third variant of conservative criminology, whereby a selfish and short-sighted human nature makes all human beings potential law-breakers, a danger properly met by an authoritarian state whose police presence can frighten us into obedience.[42]

All of these conservative theories reject social injustice or disadvantage as an important cause of crime. Their proponents point out that most socially disadvantaged people go on to become law-abiding citizens. The stock conservative solution to crime is a crackdown plus an ideology that (1) exhorts parents and neighbors to become more responsible but also (2) demands that those who have suffered misdirection as children shape up as adults—or ship out to jail.

By contrast, individual responsibility takes a backseat in PC progressive views of crime. Whereas conservatives blame individuals, the left blames the system. If society bears no responsibility for crime, asks the left, why then are Americans so much more inclined to lawbreaking than citizens of other countries? Why are members of groups suffering from high unemployment rates or racial discrimination more likely to break the law than others?[43] Clearly, social conditions and institutions contribute to crime. Therefore, to reduce crime we must change society. The liberal solution is to change specific leaders and policies, which can ameliorate such crime-breeding conditions as unemployment, poor education, drug addiction, and run-down neighborhoods.[44] The radical solution is to transform corporate capitalism into something less alienating and unjust. Neither liberal nor radical version says much about the role of individual responsibility in reducing crime.

In fairness to liberals, although they lack transformative solutions, at least they (like conservatives) try to do something in the here and now to protect innocent citizens from criminal predation. Radicals and socialists, on the other hand, pronounce that crime will go away when capitalism collapses; in the meantime, ordinary citizens will have to fend for themselves. Many leftists resist reforms such as job-training programs as serving to prop up an unjust system and promote false consciousness about the benevolence of reform. Some radicals also reconstrue ordinary street crimes such as arson, theft, and assault as acts of political protest and liberation, and their perpetrators as righteous heroes. This reconstruction is especially likely in the case of urban riots following acts of police brutality. Both liberals and radicals excuse a great deal of thuggery on the basis of imagined political heroism as well as the real disadvantages suffered earlier in life by many of the lawbreakers.

The point is not, with conservatives, to deny that social disadvantage promotes crime; it does. The point is to ask whether the disadvantaged have any responsibilities at all toward nonparties—innocent bystanders—to their oppression. Even asking this question has become difficult for progressives who fear being labeled "sell-out," "racist," or "classist" by other progressives sensitive to the racial and class composition of offenders. If a legal police crackdown nets a disproportionate percentage of criminals of color (a politically incorrect–sounding phrase), that fact alone is enough for some leftists to label the operation racist—even if persons of color are disproportionately more likely to commit crimes, as the radical analysis indicates they should be.[45] PC pressures have discouraged the left from blaming ethnic minorities for crime. Liberals and radicals, including "critical race theorists," view criminals of color as victimized by the racial dynamics of class society, perhaps as much so as the victims of the crimes, who are themselves disproportionately people of color. Indeed, "criminologists are loath to speak openly on race and crime for fear of being misunderstood or labeled racist."[46]

In short, so long as effective anticrime programs net high percentages of ethnic minorities and poor people, the PC left is inclined to demur. This "softness on crime" benefits the right by putting progressives at odds with at least four of their natural constituencies: women, the physically disadvantaged, seniors, and youth, all of whom are particularly vulnerable to crime. A hands-off, exculpatory stance toward muggers, rapists, purse-snatchers, and con men does not sit well with advocates of groups disproportionately injured by such crimes. Political correctness thus serves to disunite the people as a whole by exonerating criminals.

Leftist leaders assume, incorrectly, that most residents in communities of color oppose law and order and sympathize with "oppressed" criminals of color. Most of these leftists do not live in nonwhite neighborhoods. Most of my neighbors in Latino and black neighborhoods I have lived in obeyed the law and resented those who did not. What they resented most about the police was neglect rather than abuse.[47] Black intellectuals Glenn Loury and Shelby Steele speak for the majority of inner-city residents when they assess dual responsibility to offenders and society for crime: "We do not want our advocacy of black responsibility to represent a general absolution from responsibility for the larger society. Why doesn't America keep the peace in inner cities?"[48]

Despite a substantial incidence of racist police brutality and unfair targeting of ethnic minorities in the United States,[49] a far greater problem in U.S. minority neighborhoods is law enforcement's casual, laissez-faire attitude.[50] Citizen patrols by groups such as the Blackstone Rangers and the Guardian Angels—"vigilantes" to police—have helped take up the slack in many cities. In West Palm Beach, Florida, churchgoing former bodyguard Samuel Mohammed, charged with arson, testified that "he set fire to an abandoned crack house because police ignored crime in his mostly black neighborhood."[51] Typical of police neglect was the response of police to a burglary at my former home in North Park Hill, Denver, which was and is about 90 percent black. My two adjacent neighbors, both African American, observed three teen-aged burglars in the act (two black and one white) and called the police. The burglars having escaped, I happened to arrive at my house at about the same time as the police. The officers' attitude was indifferent at best. "What do you expect, living in this neighborhood?" one asked me. "I expect you to investigate the crime," I replied, asking that they bring in their lab truck to take fingerprints. They doubted that getting fingerprints would make any difference, but reluctantly agreed. My African-American neighbors were interested to see Denver's finest give a white resident of their neighborhood the same shoddy service they were used to. A fingerprint on a Seven Up bottle from my refrigerator led to the arrest of one of the burglars (the white one).

Community-policing advocates George Kelling and Catherine Coles (1996: p. 254) reject the crime theories and solutions of the PC left and right. "Neither the programs of the right nor left offer much promise," they say. The right advocates more prisons and prison time, and the left advocates social justice. "In the meantime, children are in peril, citizens cannot protect themselves or their property, a generation of African-American male youths is near to being lost to death and imprisonment, and the quality of life of all citizens has been diminished." And meanwhile, both white-collar and street crimes remain profitable while fostering anxiety about crime and skepticism toward the criminal-justice system. If society-as-criminal and offender-as-criminal will not take Dostoevsky's advice to take responsibility for their respective roles in crime, neither will be able to repent and help restore our troubled communities.

Progressive Allergies to Markets and Leaders

Encouraging both criminal and ecocidal lifestyles is the corporate-capitalist political economy. Unfortunately, as in the cases of ecology and crime, progressives seem unable to agree on either a convincing critique or a practical alternative to the political and economic powers-that-be. And once again, political correctness is implicated in the problem.

Progressive political economy is a shambles. The collapse of state socialism, along with "the crisis of the kibbutz," has left radicals somewhere between disarray and despair. Despite provocative work by progressive scholars such as Adam Przeworski (1991), Herman Daly (1996), James O'Connor (1998), and kibbutz economists,[52] no theory to explain, criticize, and replace corporate-capitalist development has captured and united activists for change. Progressives seem uncertain (1) how much of socialism to abandon, (2) how much of market economics to embrace, (3) whether to try to transplant Scandinavian social democracy to the United States, and, if not, (4) what transformational alternative might work best in this country. This challenge is, of course, not itself a result of political correctness but arises from the manifest flaws of the three existing models, identified in earlier chapters. PC, however, is stifling progressive responses to the challenge, because most left-wing activists are ideologically allergic to markets, to leadership, and to recognizing the vital importance of both in any system of power and production. Since markets and leaders are permanent facts of life that will not defer to wishful thinking or the strictures of PC, this allergy has bred an ideological myopia that threatens to derail programs of social transformation. "In my own utopian vision," writes *The Nation*'s European correspondent Daniel Singer, "there will be no market and no private capital."[53] Singer presumably thinks his clarion call for socialism still has resonance on the left.

Roots of Anti-Economics and Anti-Politics

Political scientists have noted left activists' distrust of markets.[54] Once again, the socialist legacy is implicated both in the allergy and in its contribution to the present strategic vacuum. Part of "the root problem in the failure of Marxism as politics," according to Domhoff (1998: p. 313), lies in its idea of "the economic market as inherently exploitative combine[d] with the belief that 'bourgeois freedoms' are a thin veil for repression of the working class." Marx and Engels envisioned "the Communistic abolition of buying and selling" and predicted that transferring ownership and control to the working class would eliminate oppression and the need for a coercive state.[55] The communist ideal was thus one that vanquished both markets and leaders while expecting citizens to voluntarily contribute according to their abilities while receiving only according to their needs. William Greider (1997: p. 416), a critic of corporate capitalism, calls this Marxist solution "a fatal misunderstanding of economics as well as human nature."

As economics proved less determining and human nature less cooperative than predicted, Marxists revised their theories while claiming to remain true to Marx. They split into bitterly quarreling factions, each claiming political correctness. As Marxist regimes hardened rather than withered away, and socialist economies evolved toward capitalism rather than communism, the very notion of a politically correct socialist vision has shriveled. "Today, as market-oriented reforms sweep the countries that have experienced 'socialism on earth,' this vision is no longer credible" (Przeworski 1991: p. 100). These problems leave the left ambivalent both about markets (Ollman 1998) and "about problems of organization and leadership" (Flacks 1988: p. 235).

The debate among socialists Schweickart, Lawler, Ticktin, and Ollman (in Ollman 1998) about market socialism epitomizes the ideological vacuum on the left. The parties to this debate disagree about such fundamentals as whether the market has redeeming social value, whether money is a convenience or an evil, whether China is an encouraging example of market socialism (or an example of market socialism at all), what Marx really thought about public versus cooperative ownership, whether the source of oppression in capitalism is economic competition or outside ownership, and what lessons can be learned from the collapse of state socialism. The point is not that discussion of these issues should be foreclosed in search of premature consensus. On the contrary, the traditional unwillingness of Marxists—lest they be dubbed "revisionist"—to grapple openly with these questions helps to explain why the discussion has progressed so little after a century and a half of Marxism. In the wake of the socialist collapse, green parties also "are not yet fully clarified on this critical [economic] question: views extend from rejection of markets and private ownership by some to an eager embracing of free enterprise by others" (Rensenbrink 1999: p. 18)—and everything in between.

Markets and Leaders: Get Used to Them

Attempts to suppress market forces merely drive them underground, as reflected in state socialism's vigorous black and gray markets, which "supply, in a thousand ways, what the formal economy fails to supply" (Scott 1998: p. 261). Supply and demand will operate, despite state ownership of business. State planners require weights—i.e., prices—for inputs and outputs; lacking the automatic weights given by competitive pricing, they essentially ad lib after the fact. "This is why socialist economies are not in fact planned," concludes Przeworski (1991: p. 118). Or in Zaleski's more literal formulation: "In every command economy, we witness an innumerable quantity of plans, in perpetual evolution, which are definitively coordinated only ex post facto, after they are put into effect."[56] Scott (1998: p. 351) adds, "Collectivized command economies virtually everywhere have limped along thanks to the often desperate improvisations of an informal economy wholly outside the schemata."

Economically, most Soviet citizens fared better under state ownership than they had under the czarist regime overthrown by the Bolsheviks. But two new generations of Soviet citizens who had not suffered under the czars and felt no sense of ownership of the Bolshevik revolution, became frustrated by the lack of consumer goods and cynical about the state's arbitrariness and corruption. "On the one hand," reports Przeworski (1991: pp. 119–120), "over the long term the aggregate rates of growth of the socialist countries have matched those of the most rapidly developing capitalist economies." On the other hand, the income inequalities that were always present under socialism grew considerably, and social welfare worsened as corruption and inefficiency mounted in the final two decades of the Soviet Bloc regimes.The disillusioned socialist Milovan Djilas (1957) wrote convincingly of *The New Class* of privileged socialist bureaucrats, later described in great detail by sympathetic socialist critics Michael Albert and Robin Hahnel (1981) as "the coordinator class." Indeed, a notorious double standard developed by which high-ranking officials enjoyed a much higher standard of living than ordinary citizens. The leaders enjoyed personal limousines, country villas, a wide range of consumer goods, and even basic medical care unavailable to most socialist citizens (Przeworski 1991: p. 120). For decades, the politically correct line of communist parties held that the socialist remnants of class society—thriving self-interest as well as differential pay, power, and status under proletarian dictatorship— were but a temporary phase in the inevitable march toward stateless, egalitarian communism.

With significant local adjustments, the Soviet story holds true for the communist systems of Eastern and Central Europe as well as for China, North Korea, Vietnam, and Cuba, although "communism" itself has not yet officially ended in the last four countries. If, contrary to Ronald Reagan's claims, capitalism did not defeat communism, it has at least outlasted it despite predating it by more than a century. What do the critics of capitalism make of this Marxist-socialist debacle? Everything and nothing, apparently. That is to say, every disillusioned socialist faction seems to have its own interpretation of what went wrong, but few consensual lessons have emerged to guide progressives toward a society that might avoid the common pitfalls of bureaucratic socialism and corporate capitalism. These pitfalls include their shared features of ecocidal economies, crime-ridden polities, depressingly materialistic cultures, and costly penchants for armaments, war, and imperialism.

Granted, the complexities of causal inference and the inherent difficulty of political strategizing explain part of today's radical doldrums. But so does political correctness. Progressives seem unwilling to put on the table for serious discussion the discomfiting possibility that they and Marx were wrong all along about the desirability and possibility of banishing markets and authority from the good society. In the face-to-face indigenous, traditional, or intentional communities admired by Marx and Engels, bad neighbors faced indifference or retribution when they later found themselves in need. Good neighbors, on the other hand, could expect future reciprocation of their own thoughtful acts. Voila!—communist cooperation. But such reciprocal, as opposed to pure, altruism is the only kind of altruism society can regularly count on from most people most of the time. And it can work well on a relatively equal and unforced basis—i.e., communistically—only when its participants know one another well.

Erasmus (1985) shows that as societies increase in size and anonymity, differential pay and legal enforcement universally replace informal social incentives to ensure that the personal goods pursued by individuals also promote the common good. In modern society, we all depend on the efforts of countless other people whom we have no way of holding directly accountable to us. So we leave it to employers and the market to pay them selectively, and the sheriff to arrest or protect them, according to good or bad behavior that we ourselves cannot directly observe. Labor markets and law enforcement thus become permanent fixtures, not transitional phases, in modern society. Erasmus exposed the inefficiencies of collective production in Communist China and the Soviet Union, where, for instance, individual farmers were exhorted to maximum production for the state without being rewarded in proportion to their efforts compared to those of their comrades. "For almost any crop one can name," writes political anthropologist James Scott (1998: p. 189), "with the possible exception of sugarcane, smallholders have been able historically to out-compete larger units of production."[57]

Virtually alone among Western social scientists, Erasmus predicted the demise of the Soviet and Chinese systems of political economy well before glasnost, perestroika, and the market reforms of post-Maoist China had gotten under way. He showed in minute detail why the daily incentives for good behavior were failing to bring it forth among proletarians and vanguards alike. With allowances for exceptional individuals, the Marxist hope for "fight-self" behavior among socialist citizens, including Cuba's touted "New Socialist Man," has generally faded all across the socialist horizon. Still politically communist, China is straining to avoid the political chaos of the former Soviet Union, while finally seeing its growth rate "greatly leap forward," not by Maoist collectivization but by post-Maoist privatization of farming and small business, accompanied by market incentives for increased productivity of state-owned firms.[58]

There has been no dearth of state authority in China and the former Soviet Bloc countries. But the harsh, undemocratic quality of communist leadership, on top of the utopian anarchy originally envisioned by Marx and Engels, has made strong leadership itself suspect in progressive circles. Not only Marxian groups such as the U.S. Socialist Party, the Socialist Workers Party, the Revolutionary Communist Party, and the National Caucus of Labor Committees, but also today's green parties have reflected this skepticism. For many years, the German Greens annually rotated their parliamentarians out of office, replacing them with other Greens. They ended this practice on the grounds that it was wasting Green M.P.s' valuable experience. Many Greens, however, still view the change as an unjustified compromise with Green egalitarian principles.

Some U.S. green activists have criticized their own green groups for a similar aversion to effective leadership, a hyper-egalitarianism that produces endless discussions and fruitless nitpicking (Rensenbrink 1999: pp. 35–38). More generally, while left activists continue to criticize capitalist elites in government and business, they offer few guidelines on how they themselves would lead in a transformed society of the future. Maine's Green Party candidate for the 2000 U.S. Senate, John Rensenbrink (1999: p. 21), urges progressives to surmount the antipolitical tradition of the Marxian, socialist, and populist left: "Governing can now be seen for what it is: a natural activity." He believes that the Green Party's vital emphasis on personal values and ecological consciousness must not come at the expense of political-economic responsibility: "Transformation means overcoming the fear of money and the fear of power" (p. 40).

Some progressives argue that the growing economic inefficiency and political collapse of Soviet-style socialism reflected the ills of authoritarian governance rather than the unworkability of socialism. Indeed, the possibility of democratic socialism needs to become part of a wide-ranging discussion about the lessons of the state-socialist demise. But so does an exploration of economic democracy as an alternative to capitalism and socialism. The most promising alternative to capitalism may not be the communist anarchy envisioned by Marx. Before Marx, progressive U.S. founders such as Franklin, Jefferson, and Paine warned against big government and big business while championing popular government and economic democracy.

The Crime of Ecocide Rooted in Corporate Capitalism

Human activities that pollute the air, foul the water, and poison the earth comprise a toxic assault on other human beings and the biosphere. Such behavior is no less an assault—though a different kind of assault—than if I punch you in the face or poison your drink. More typically, however, progressives talk about trade-offs between economic growth and environmental protection, trying to persuade people that a particular growth benefit is outweighed by a particular environmental risk or cost.[59] Unlike earlier, more militant approaches, "the new pragmatism extends even to environmental groups. . . . With better knowledge about what is most endangered and what costs attach to what problems, a grove of ancient redwoods, say, can be balanced against an even rarer grove of oaks in determining which should be protected."[60] This approach is comparable to weighing the costs of getting punched in the face against the possible benefits, such as greater alertness, a better understanding of one's pain threshold, and appropriate guilt for having offended the assaulter or for being a bad person.

The ongoing despoliation of the planet, accelerated by such pragmatism, enjoys the advantage of being the status quo and therefore of being presumptively justified, though perhaps imperfect and "costly." The challenge for transformationalists is to get people to see ecocidal activities in a provocatively new and unacceptable light. Scientific evidence that we are killing the planet while harming innocent people is strong, growing, and increasingly available to the public. Worldwatch Institute notes, "Polls show the global public becoming more worried about environmental problems every year."[61] An even more important voice is that of nature itself, which "now insists on fundamental change in our economic, social, and political arrangements" (Rensenbrink 1999: p. 51). If we do not listen to nature's wounded voice, we will suffer dire consequences.

People readily understand the profit motive as the primary basis for ecologically harmful production, and profit-driven advertising as a key contributor to environmentally harmful consumption. Many Americans are also aware of the widespread incidence of white-collar crime, some of it directly ecological in nature. It does not take a genius to grasp a basic connection among corporate-capitalist political economy, crime, and environmental degradation. Yet something is getting in the way both of understanding these linkages and of developing transformational alternatives. Part of that something is the PC tendencies we identified earlier. These tendencies create ambivalence and confusion among progressives about the wrongness of crime, the seriousness of environmental destruction, and the key role of markets and leaders in confronting these wrongs.

The Conservative Implications of Social Determinism

A fundamental contradiction of Marxism was its theoretical claim that communist revolution was inevitable, combined with its moral exhortation of workers to revolutionary action. Most workers did not join up, perhaps wondering why personal sacrifice was necessary for something that was inevitable in any case. Since revolution is a dirty and dangerous business, any excuse to sit one out can prove irresistible. But the inevitability of revolution depends on workers' not sitting it out. In practice, of course, Marxists selectively ignored their claim of inevitability while urging workers to take history into their own hands. "WORKERS OF THE WORLD, UNITE!" concluded *The Communist Manifesto.*

The certainty of Marxist predictions was based on the belief that people's behavior is determined by their relationship to the means of production. Exceptions were tacitly allowed for individuals such as Marx and Engels (and later Mao Zedong, Ho Chi Minh, Fidel Castro, Che Guevara, and other leaders), who rose above their bourgeois origins to become revolutionaries. But most capitalists could not help but pursue profits and wealth so single-mindedly that they would eventually seal their own fate. And once the intensifying exploitation by capitalism helped workers overcome their false consciousness of self-blame, they could not help but unite as the oppressed class to overthrow their capitalist oppressors.

Individual capitalists could hardly be faulted for exploiting their workers, because in theory they were forced by their class position to play out their class role, which was to extract maximum "surplus value," or profit, from their workers. Similarly, the criminal class, or "lumpenproletariat," could hardly be blamed for its antisocial acts, because its members were compelled to criminality by their loser status in the capitalist war of all against all. Only the developing structural contradictions of capitalism, not individual choices responsibly made, could transform petty criminals into partisans of proletarian revolution. Marxists had a keen eye for the conservative implications of the opposite view, the notion that people make all of their choices freely and therefore bear responsibility for them. This view exonerates society for people's sufferings, undermining any justice-based argument for revolution. But Marxists have overlooked the subtly conservative implications of their own view, a socio-environmental determinism that today, ironically, serves an apologistic purpose for capitalists and criminals alike.

We have seen that progressives are reluctant to fault criminals of color or the poor for their offenses, even for crimes against the innocent. But social determinism aborts the left's finding fault with *any criminals,* white or black, rich or poor, capitalist or socialist, calculating or impulsive. Social conditions and flawed institutions "made them do it." In popular culture, "them" has come to include not only black men who rape black women, youth gangs who attack each other and innocent bystanders with equal abandon, and working-class parents who beat their children, but also middle-aged suburbanites who abuse their elderly parents, white-collar con men who defraud the gullible, corporate executives who steal billions from the public by insider trading, and politicians who get elected by illegal campaign financing and then stock their larders with bribes once they are in office. As more and more such crimes have come to light, cynicism has replaced outrage among many Americans (Blankenship 1993; Simon and Hagen 1999). Little wonder that for more than a decade national polls have tracked a growing public disdain for both U.S. institutions and professionals in business, law, government, and medicine.

Progressives enamored of social determinism play into this pervasive cynicism, in effect approving it and removing any grounds for criticizing antisocial behavior. Radicals who selectively depart from determinism to blame corporate criminals for their immorality, but return to determinism to exonerate lumpenproletarians for *their* immorality, understandably meet with skepticism from people they are trying to persuade. PC breeds such contradictions by discouraging its proponents from examining their own arguments. Moreover, these PC radicals have given up their grounds for morally criticizing—as opposed to scientifically explaining—corporate production and popular consumption that harm the environment. In short, determinism weakens transformative critiques by letting people off the hook for the very kind of behavior any good society needs to condemn.

By criticizing overly deterministic left-wing explanations, we do not retreat to free-will rationalization for the status quo. The injustices of corporate capitalism, like the inefficiencies of bureaucratic socialism, greatly increase the likelihood of criminal and ecocidal behavior. People who have been wronged, more readily mistreat others and more irresponsibly exploit nature. Both institutions and individuals bear partial responsibility for the good things and bad things that happen in life, for acts of love and heroism as well as for acts of malice and cowardice, for instituting slavery and for dismantling it, for driving species to the brink of extinction and for struggling to bring them back.

Leaders, Laws, and Stewardship

Stewardship of the earth will not occur without strong leadership that considers ecocide a crime and that uses public institutions to instill ecological values. Many green activists and Green Party members of European governments have cited Ernest Callenbach's 1975 utopian novel *Ecotopia,* along with economist E. F. Schumacher's 1973 treatise *Small Is Beautiful: Economics as if People Mattered,* as the two works that most inspired their own ecological awareness and impelled them to political action. Callenbach's novel portrays an ecological utopia of the near future that has come about by virtue of the Pacific Northwest's secession from the United States. Like other utopian novels that play by their own rules, *Ecotopia* has offended some PC progressives. Callenbach was criticized by feminists for the "war games" among Ecotopian males, intended to work off excess testosterone with minimum harm. He was criticized by multiculturalists for "Soul City," a semiseparatist black community portrayed as more consumerist than most of Ecotopia on the grounds that blacks had been more materially deprived than whites. And socialists disliked the large role Callenbach allowed private enterprise to play in the ecological society of the future.

The most compelling features of Ecotopian society are its ecological innovations in the areas of renewable energy, alternative transportation, and systemic recycling, all of which reflected Callenbach's own expertise. Less convincing were Ecotopia's patchwork economy, occasionally arbitrary laws, and unimaginative political system, hardly distinguishable in many respects from the U.S. system it had replaced. But perhaps most troubling from a transformational viewpoint was a feature ignored by most of Callenbach's critics but vital to the concerns of this chapter: the elimination of any system of public education. Unlike doctrinaire socialists, Callenbach incorporated a good deal of private ownership into his fictional utopia, including the ownership of all schools by their teachers. The curricula of these cooperative schools emphasize children's hands-on learning in nature, and thus accord well with the Ecotopian system as a whole. But what is to ensure the continuation of the ecological slant of these curricula? Ecotopian schools rise and fall with their market popularity. When student enrollments and tuition fail to pay adequate salaries to the teacher-owners, the schools must either adapt or shut down. A troubling truth is that future generations, who did not make the revolution they are benefiting from, notoriously lack revolutionaries' zeal for the founding ideals—in this case an ideal of stewardship.

Complicating this problem is the fact that Callenbach admirably allows dissent into his utopia, and the dissenters are numerous and active. With no system-wide socialization process in place by which public schools might foster ecological values and practices in the young, what is to keep pro-growthers from using their civil and political liberties to entice future generations away from the ethic of stewardship toward a renewed ethic of growth and consumerism? A trend toward consumerism would pressure Ecotopia's completely private schools, always competing for students, to shift their curricula away from the untrendy ecology favored by elders toward the "excitingly new and better" direction of mass consumerism so familiar today.

The "threshold" feature of environmental assaults increases this danger and calls for a concerted public response. That is, unlike punches in the face, most toxic acts become measurably harmful to other humans and the ecosytem only after they reach a critical mass, or threshold, in combination with many similar acts by others. Just as isolated individuals can rationalize political inactivity by arguing that their single vote won't affect an election, they may also convince themselves that their single act of pollution won't hurt anything. My driving to work will not worsen your emphysema, I might assert. Or, our town's plastics factory will not much deplete the natural resources available to other communities. Or even, our bio-region's use of chemical fertilizers and pesticides will not substantially degrade the water supply for downstream users in other bio-regions. Indeed, unless uniformly enforced laws control such activities, individual producers and consumers have a competitive incentive to cheat on the common good—Garrett Hardin's (1968) famous "tragedy of the commons." That is to say, my company will suffer in the market if my competitors cut costs by polluting while I do not. My reputation as a conspicuous consumer will suffer if I fail to keep up with my consumerist neighbors, the Joneses.

The value of markets is the freedom of choice they provide us to choose our work and to select from a wide variety of goods and services whose producers have an incentive to increase quality while lowering prices. The danger of such freedoms is the harm they can do if we use them to assault, enslave, or kill other human beings, to abuse our children, to defraud our neighbors, to corrupt government, to squander or monopolize scarce resources, to poison the earth, or to upset the balance of nature. There is no legitimate market in violence, slavery, corruption, or ecocide (Kuttner 1997). Small, tight-knit communities routinely prevent such abuses by daily informal encouragements to goodness and sanctions on badness. In large societies where we can never know most of our compatriots—as heroes or villains, slackards or salt of the earth—we need strong, accountable leaders and laws to ensure that we optimize our freedoms by appropriately limiting them (Erasmus 1985). Limiting libertine excess by "legislating morality" does not instantly transform citizens' souls, but—like the public schools Callenbach shuns—it can slowly but surely shape their character. Being made to attend school and work alongside blacks did not quickly erase white bigotry. But over two generations, it has accustomed blacks and whites to one another, thus chipping away at the ignorance and stereotypes that undergird racism.

Similarly, schools that educate us, and laws that require us, to protect our earthly paradise help us build a basis for the stewardly community of the future, a practical utopia to which our children are already better attuned than we. Erasmus (1985: chapter 10) asks whether, in envisioning ecological resocialization, we are not programming our young as pawns on a new chessboard of political correctness. We could be, but we need not be. Citizenship training from an early age need not be a "brave new world" of mind-numbing behavioral engineering. Unlike ants, humans require culture and therefore socialization. There is no such thing as a natural person, unwarped by socialization. Just as every law is a legislation of morality—decreeing X as right and Y as wrong—every childbirth is a commitment to child rearing, by someone. If we are not that someone, then someone else will do it for us. The way we rear our children marks them with our values whether or not we so intend.[62] We can nurture in them both ecological values and critical thinking, even toward the stewardly values we instill.

Political Economy
When Ecology Is Right and Crime Is Wrong

Only a dramatically democratized system of political economy can provide strong, accountable leadership that protects the environment while greatly reducing crime, including environmental crime. Criminals strike at the ecosystem, and they strike at the job site.[63] Political correctness is helping to silence voices and stymie minds that might otherwise be addressing vital links among ecology, crime, and political economy. Too many progressives have literally bought into the demon of unlimited growth. Too many left-wing activists have gone soft on crime. Too many transformational souls remain bollixed up with aversion to free markets and strong leaders.

Part of this transformational confusion can be laid at the feet of the perverse genius of corporate capitalism. "Liberal" capitalism is in fact both radical and conservative, a uniquely moving target that is hard to hit. On the radical side, firms must grow and innovate to survive, an imperative that impels them to provide society with new goods, services, opportunities, and lifestyles. Anything that interferes with the relentless engine of growth, innovation, profit maximization, and market control must be eliminated or transformed, including cultural traditions, family structure, religious values, and the natural world. On the conservative side, companies seek to maintain the rules of property accumulation and class structure that allow them to profit off the work of laborers and the wants of consumers—rules, moreover, that give owners of capital (acquired by hook or crook) advantages in securing their market dominance and political influence. Through campaign contributions, lobbying, and direct participation in government, corporate decisionmakers act to preserve their powerful and privileged roles in society.

In effect, capitalism's market winners tell society, "Look at all we do for you. Look at what you would lack if not for us. We have earned our position in society, and you have benefited from it as well. In fact, anyone can aspire to our eminence, and with hard work and a bit of luck, you can make it too. Since the system allows workers and consumers free choice, and voters the right to change the rules if they don't like them, we end up getting what we collectively want and deserve. If there is an enemy in all of this, it is all of us and our freely made choices." Though flawed, this argument is plausible in some respects, and to the degree it persuades its natural opponents, it seduces them into a war of all against all that divides and conquers them.

Who are the natural opponents of the capitalist rationale? Marx would begin with the workers whose labor creates the profits expropriated by owners (whose at-risk capital was produced by previous workers). The second natural enemy of capitalism is those whose abilities make them uncompetitive in the market economy, as a result of biological or developmental disadvantages, social injustice based on factors such as race and gender, and bad luck. A third enemy is those who value family, religion, tradition, community, or the earth more than goods and services, self-serving liberties, and wealth per se. In today's advanced, corporate phase of capitalism, we might add small-business owners to the list of opponents, since they suffer greatly in competition with large corporations, experiencing business-failure rates of about 50 percent after one year and 90 percent after five years.[64]

How does corporate capitalism survive when its natural opponents comprise the majority, who could theoretically use the democratic process to transform the capitalist system? Marx replied that capitalists' economic dominance allows them informally to control both the government and the socialization process that shapes people's beliefs. This process, Marx argued, produces a "false consciousness" whereby ordinary people accept the ideas of the ruling class and blame themselves or bad luck for their failures. To win the battle of minds, progressives have always had to convince people of the fallacies of the status quo. The essential argument of this book is that while these fallacies are becoming more evident, left-wing political correctness is undermining the progressive case and playing into the hands of conservatives.

We have seen how politically correct affirmative action has created new injustices that distract us from the basic injustice of capitalism and divide the working and middle classes along racial and gender lines. We have explored the PC limitations on fostering synergistic values as a second Invisible Hand of transformation. We have also seen how politically correct adultism creates a generation gap between progressives and their children, and how politically correct careerism and bureaucratic paternalism weaken families as a force for social change.

Here we note the ways in which political correctness has obscured a transformational dynamic linking the three areas of ecology, crime, and political economy. As long as progressives soft-pedal the urgency of ecology and crime, including ecological crime, the political economy of corporate capitalism, which systematically fosters both crime and ecocide, will escape the scrutiny it deserves. But in giving capitalism its proper attention and blame, we err if we wish away markets and leaders simply because they have been historically hijacked and abused by corporate capitalists and state socialists. Lowi (1979) has shown how the U.S. political economy of "interest group liberalism" discourages politicians from offending constituents by taking clear stands and writing just laws. Ironically, progressives have developed the same tendency by avoiding proposals that, while ruffling PC feathers, could help unseat capitalist political economy as the reigning ideology of the twenty-first century.

In the sections that follow, I propose that progressives shed their PC shackles and put on the table for discussion three principles, regarding ecology, crime, and political economy, as core principles (among others) for the transformation of U.S. society. As in Chapter 6, I propose to amend the U.S. Constitution to reflect the fundamental quality of the proposed changes. By no means, however, do I wish to discourage activists from pursuing these principles at state or local levels, or in the form of changes in statutory law as opposed to constitutional law.

Constitutional Protection of the Environment

The United States of America must cease its toxic assault on the earth and its living forms, including humans of this and subsequent generations. Accordingly, I propose the following amendment to the U.S. Constitution:

Amendment 29: Within ten years of the adoption of this amendment, all human activities that poison the earth or its inhabitants, upset the balance of nature, or threaten the earth's sustainability, except in self-defense, are prohibited.[65]

In *A Sand County Almanac* (1949), Aldo Leopold wrote, "A thing is right when it tends to preserve the integrity, stability, and beauty of the biotic community. It is wrong when it tends otherwise."[66] In one swift stroke, Amendment 29 philosophically nixes industrial civilization's relentless assault on the environment and the health of its inhabitants. It also recognizes the impossibility of transforming the economy overnight, giving businesses, government, and consumers a ten-year period to comply with the law by shifting to ecologically appropriate technologies and products. And it gives government time to develop statutory law and regulations defining the key terms "poison," "balance of nature," and "self-defense."

Lest we reject this proposal out of hand as "utopian," let us recall the dramatic greening of citizens' attitudes around the world, while noting that even some corporate and governmental elites have been calling for dramatic environmental measures over the last decade. For instance, in 1991 Pehr Gyllenhammar, president of Volvo AB, recommended a radical yet commonsensical proposal that U.S. automakers are silently fearing: the banning of private cars from big cities to curb air pollution, matched by major investments in public transportation. In 1997, Toyota became the first automaker to mass-produce a low-polluting hybrid vehicle, incorporating an electric motor with a gas engine, resulting in a doubling of energy efficiency to sixty-six miles per gallon. In 1999, ARCO's CEO, Mike Bowlin, conceded that "we've embarked on the beginning of the Last Days of the Age of Oil" and recommended a transition to a renewable, hydrogen-based economy (Worldwatch Institute 2000: p. 12). Two months later, Shell Oil and Daimler-Chrysler announced joint plans to make Iceland the world's first hydrogen-based economy. By 2000, ecological demand by home buyers has enticed large-scale developers such as Canada-based Carma to require their contractors to build environmentally friendly "green" homes.

In 2001 the U.S. Postal Service plans to begin using hundreds of virtually pollution-free, electrically powered vehicles in California and Washington, D.C. The United States and China have officially incorporated ecologism into their forest-management philosophies. In the 1990s, California passed a half dozen sweeping pollution-reduction standards, including one in 1999 that effectively cut almost in half, by twenty-one tons daily, the pollution emitted by seventeen categories of products, from furniture cleaners to insecticides to nail-polish removers. In March 2000, the Environmental Protection Agency issued tougher standards on pollutants emitted by mechanized garden tools, thereby reducing chemical air pollution by 350,000 tons annually by 2007. In May 2000, Britain's Prince Charles elicited a firestorm of defensive reaction from industry and its scientific allies when he urged scientists to try to understand and protect nature rather than transform it for ill-conceived human ends. In December 2000, 122 countries signed a treaty banning twelve highly toxic chemicals, including chlordane, DDT, PCBs, and dioxin.

At the base of most ecology-friendly positions taken by elites is not so much elite vision as relentless pressure from the environmental movements of millions of ordinary citizens, documented in daily newspapers and in works by Sheffer, Gottlieb, Sale, Dowie, and Faber. In *The Struggle for Ecological Democracy: Environmental Justice Movements in the United States,* Faber (1998) shows the links between profiteering, environmental racism and classism, and growing popular struggles for environmental and workplace justice. The dramatic changes called for by Amendment 29 require new alliances among labor, environmentalists, and ethnic groups—including the U.S.-Mexico, cross-border union alliances described by Nissen and by Alexander and Gilmore (Tillman and Cummings 1999).

For two decades, the evidence has mounted that organic farming and gardening can avoid toxic insecticides and chemical fertilizers while operating at a profit. By 2000, European organic farming had overcome its reputation as "the pastime of crackpots and idealists" and grown to $7.3 billion per year.[67] Organic farmers in North America and elsewhere added another $8.3 billion a year. Since the 1970s, organic farmers have expanded from operating commercially in only 3 countries to 130.[68] In the United States, natural-products sales almost tripled to $17 billion between 1993 and 1998 "and are expected to rise to nearly $30 billion by the end of [2000], according to SPINS, a San Francisco-based research company that tracks natural product sales."[69]

Local practices that natural gardeners such as Helen and Scott Nearing (1989) and natural farmers such as Ralph and Rita Engelkin (1981) have long exemplified are now going global. Denmark, which has imposed a blanket ban on the construction of coal-fired power plants, recycles half its waste and is on track to expand its share of electricity generated by wind power from the current 7 percent to 50 percent by 2030.[70] Worldwide generation of wind and solar power is rapidly increasing. The potential of wind-generated electricity, now a $3 billion industry, is dramatized by the fact that wind turbines envisioned for North Dakota, South Dakota, and Texas could alone generate all U.S. needs for electricity (Worldwatch Institute 2000: p. 18). With electrical output up by 39 percent in 1999, the wind-turbine industry is growing faster than the personal-computer industry and almost as fast as cellular phones.[71] In 2000, the World Bank committed $200 million to solar-powered projects in India, Egypt, Morocco, and Mexico.

Worldwatch Institute (1998, 1999, 2000) reports have documented dozens of examples of the viability of sustainable practices when people, including leaders, have the requisite political will. Since 1980, trash recycling has more than tripled to around 30 percent in the United States, which still lags behind Japan and Western Europe.[72] "An estimated 6,000 [U.S.] communities have curbside recycling programs, and more than 60 million tons of paper, glass, metal, and compost . . . are diverted from landfills each year." In addition: "New rules have cut sulfur dioxide emissions from power plants in half and dramatically curbed acid rain. Since 1988, industrial emissions of toxic chemicals have dropped 42 percent."[73] In 2000, Green Party candidates Ralph Nader and Winona LaDuke cited both the continuing ecocidal dangers and growing examples of eco-progress in their appeals to prospective voters.

Let us examine the logic of Amendment 29 as well as some challenges it entails. The simple but powerful rationale for an ecology amendment to the U.S. Constitution is that it is immoral and self-destructive to foul our common nest: the earth, its inhabitants, and our shared ecology. The best science says that we are destroying the earth, making it toxic and uninhabitable for future generations. Alternative technologies and energy sources are available that permit us to have enjoyable, if more modest, standards of living while sustaining the earth. Like people around the world, the general U.S. populace, and especially young people, express steadily increasing support for laws protecting the environment, even laws that raise taxes and restrict freedoms. In the November 1998 elections, "Americans again showed their environmental bent. Corporate hog farmers were ordered to clean up their stink in South Dakota and Colorado, while in Montana, the people told mining companies that they cannot use cyanide in gold mines, thereby halting new projects on the Blackfoot River, famed as a fly fishing mecca. . . . In California, people believe . . . that using steel-jawed leg traps to kill muskrats and other varmints is inhumane."[74] In the 2000 presidential election, the Democratic Party felt the heat of former Democrats voting for the Green Party, with Nader votes appearing to cost Democrat Al Gore several states and thereby the election. It is possible that the Democrats, while continuing their move to the center on selected social and economic issues, may reach out more to Greens on ecological issues. The earth needs humans to become stewards, and more and more people are doing so. Any transformational alternative to capitalism must address the ecological crisis of our times.

Let us acknowledge some challenges of Amendment 29. First, something it shares with much of the U.S. Constitution—and any constitution—is its generality, requiring the statutory specifications mentioned earlier. But the terms needing operational definition in the ecology amendment are no more general than the "general welfare" Congress may provide, the "necessary and proper" laws it can make, the "good behavior" required of judges, the "unreasonable searches and seizures" prohibited of government, the "just compensation" due property owners whose property is taken for public use, the "excessive bail" and "cruel and unusual punishments" government may not use, and the "due process of law" all citizens are guaranteed by the Constitution. Generality should not be confused with vagueness. The intent of Amendment 29 is clear: to preserve our health and environment by giving them priority over unlimited growth, wealth, and consumption.

A complication of the ecology amendment is the need to set guidelines limiting individual acts that do not by themselves poison the environment but do so when combined with the acts of others. What is needed is to supplement regulatory standards by using the market to transform today's misguided "pollution rights" into transferable rights to engage in acts that collectively avoid the threshold level beyond which they would poison the earth and harm others. Rather than arguing that a certain amount of environmental damage is worth the economic benefits, as pale greens do today, the law would allow potentially toxic acts, such as smoking or driving, only up to the point beyond which they would collectively harm the environment or its inhabitants.

Might the "self-defense" loophole undermine the intent of the entire amendment? This loophole is intended to allow individuals and society to cope with a few worst-case scenarios that I hope will never occur. For instance, if the AIDS virus were to prove impossible to control in any way other than extermination, courts might rule that the human species has the self-defense right to "upset the balance of nature" by driving this virus to extinction. Or if a nation were threatened by a hostile power, and the only feasible defense involved environmentally harmful weapons, the Supreme Court might rule that such weapons were constitutional as long as this threat persisted. Neither evolutionary hardwiring nor cosmic morality condemns any species to suicide on the grounds of some greater good.

Is a ten-year transitional period enough to allow the massive technological conversions and changes in consumption patterns that would be necessary to satisfy the new law? The truth is that nobody knows for sure. Most of the necessary nontoxic technologies and renewable resources are already available, though in currently deficient supply because of government's and industry's heavy subsidy of toxic technologies and nonrenewable resources (Worldwatch Institute 2000). Unlike our growth-manic elites, a populace pressuring legislatures to ratify the amendment would presumably be even readier to fall in line with the law's requirements than today's populace. Foresightful companies and agencies would begin the transition long before the law requiring them to do so took effect. More important than chronological prescience is putting the proposal and the timing on the table for discussion.

Political correctness has helped keep fundamental ecological proposals in the closet. But is a change this disruptive of the political-economic status quo at all realistic even to consider? Perhaps not, but we will never know unless we seriously consider it and propagandize for it. If one result of a national debate over Amendment 29 were an extension of the transition period to fifteen or even twenty years, so be it. The radical but commonsensical point is to stop poisoning and depleting the environment *as soon as possible*. Skeptics often forget that many givens of today were the "unrealistically utopian" proposals of yesterday, including independence of the American colonies, the abolition of slavery, women's right to vote, the right of working people to organize in the workplace, Social Security for seniors, and legal protection of endangered species. In retrospect, these "wild-eyed proposals," like the change from ecocide to stewardship, seem like common sense.

We simply do not know what standard of living is ultimately possible in an ecologically sustainable economy. We do know that billions of people worldwide, and 100 million Americans today, live at dramatically lower standards of living than the U.S. median, not to mention the even higher, upper-middle-class standard that skeptics of steady-state economics deem minimally necessary to prevent civil disorder. Put differently, the protagonists of growth, including most politicians, argue that the very concept of a stable and sustainable, rather than a perpetually increasing, standard of living is politically explosive and untenable. But green electoral successes in the United States are beginning to put mainstream politicians on notice.[75] Just as capitalism itself requires perpetual growth, Americans are assumed to be so addicted to consumerism that they perpetually crave more, more, and more. This assumption has never been tested and remains an article of faith. We do know that despite all the pandering of advertisers, more than a quarter of Americans choose to limit their incomes in order to improve the quality of their personal and family lives (Korten 1999: pp. 219–220).

Allowing free markets to operate, though not ecocidally, will ensure an entrepreneurial dynamic of innovation as newcomers rush in to fill the void of appropriate technology and renewable resources left by corporations that give up the ghost rather than retool for the sustainable economy of the future. For companies that fulfill their dire threats of economic shutdown if they must meet stringent environmental standards, many new businesses will be able to break out the champagne of opportunity. The evidence suggests that the outcome will be more mixed than corporate alarmists would have us believe. By 2000, the global market for pollution-control and other environmental technologies exceeded $500 billion, more than the arms and aerospace industries combined and almost as much as the chemical industry (Worldwatch Institute 1998, 1999, 2000). Is the utopia of sustainability impractical? So far, the major investors in renewable energy, especially solar technology, are companies such as Exxon, Texaco, and Shell—hardly tree huggers or Gaia gurus.

Constitutional Protection of Citizens Against Crime

The U.S. system of criminal justice fails to protect citizens by adequately deterring crime, sequestering dangerous offenders, or rehabilitating criminals. Accordingly, I propose the following amendment to the U.S. Constitution:

> Amendment 30: In criminal justice, first offenses merit major public investment in rehabilitating offenders and restoring their communities; repeated offenses call for long-term confinement. Mitigating and aggravating

factors—biological, psychological, developmental, and socio-environmental—may alter these guidelines appropriately.

Amendment 30 targets both white-collar and street crime, and may
therefore offend politically correct partisans of the left and right. "Reports of
corporations producing unsafe products, maintaining unsafe working conditions, engaging in fraud, price fixing, and even homicide are a fact of life in
the 1990s."[76] Those knowledgeable about the incidence and costs of white-
collar crime may fall into the PC trap we have identified earlier. Simon and
Hagan (1999) report disapprovingly that according to the corporate-owned
mass media, "violent (street) crime constitutes the 'real' crime problem in
the United States. Never mind that white-collar criminality costs Americans
over forty times what violent crime does and costs at least four times as
many lives" (p. 22). Regarding that portion of white-collar crime that is
committed by corporations, they note: "Corporate crime takes at least five
times as many lives as street crime [and] costs at least six times more
money" (p. 41). These experts and others document a strong and revealing
case against the stereotype of street criminals as our greatest threat.

However, they begin to undermine their own critique when they imply
that street crime itself is not much of a problem. "In California, a 'three-
strike' felon was sentenced to life in prison for stealing a pizza," they say,
disapprovingly (p. 22). But they don't tell us whether the prior offenses involved a bag of burgers and a chocolate pie or murder and rape. They
would probably object to the "two (or three) strikes and you're out" implication of Amendment 30. In discussing the tobacco industry's crimes—and
heinous offenses they are—Simon and Hagan complain that these cancer titans are aided not only by their immense resources but also by "a heavily advertised and reinforced cultural notion of individual responsibility [of smok-
ers]," which the authors reject, claiming that this notion, "taken for granted
in the United States, is not believed by most of the world's cultures" (p. 27).
The latter claim, unsupported by any evidence, would surprise many cultural
anthropologists and comparative criminologists, for in most cultures individuals are indeed held responsible for their criminal acts.[77]

Simon and Hagan also rue the anticrime success of Mothers Against
Drunk Driving (MADD), "given credibility by mainstream media and politicians because the group fixed the responsibility for drunk driving (which is
responsible for half of the deaths from vehicle accidents) at the individual
level" (1999: p. 27). The authors' lenient view of street felons and drunk driv-
ers contrasts sharply with the moralistic scorn they heap on elite criminals
throughout their treatise. While I may share their feelings about white-collar
offenders, a posture that goes easy on street criminals but not white-collar
ones not only reflects a selective use of structural causality—can't they all
say the system made them do it?—but also irks ordinary citizens harmed by
both kinds of crime. This split attitude is common not only among scholars
of white-collar crime but among activists on the left.

Social transformation must be both an individual and a systemic process, especially any transformation intended to accord dignity to individuals based on their ability to choose right from wrong, and to determine their own way of living. State socialism was based on the premise that common ownership would promote a personal ethic of serving the common good. In communist societies such as Czechoslovakia, however, a common aphorism regarding the prevalence of employee embezzlement from the state employer was: "He who does not steal from the state, steals from his family." Czech workers were especially apt to embezzle materials they could use to fix up their own residences or weekend cottages. No doubt many Czechs and Russians, like embezzling employees in capitalist countries, rationalized that the entire system was corrupt. Indeed, Amendment 30 assumes that both society and offenders share responsibility for crime, at least for crimes that are uncommon in other societies. Let us examine the rehabilitative and incarcerative aspects of this approach to criminal justice, the first of which would offend the PC right and the second of which would irk the PC left.

Rehabilitation for first-time offenders. Under Chairman Mao, Communist China enjoyed a low incidence of crime and a recidivism rate of less than 5 percent, largely attributable to the approach specified in Amendment 30.[78] Under the Maoist regime, local governments and communities invested heavily in the rehabilitation of first-time offenders, convening family, friends, employers, teachers, and others familiar with the offender to determine what conditions, problems, and attitudes had given rise to antisocial behavior. The emphasis was on helping offenders to understand the roots of their antisocial acts and to take responsibility for preventing repeat offenses. Even allowing for statistical underreporting, China's recidivism rate of less than 5 percent contrasts sharply with the U.S. rate of about 70 percent. By contrast, the Chinese attitude toward second offenders was, "We invested a lot in you. You blew it. Society must protect itself from you." The deterrent effects of stiff penalties, including long-term imprisonment and, for heinous crimes, the death penalty, seem to have complemented rehabilitation in minimizing recidivism.[79]

Yet the U.S. left and right seem equally impervious to the success of Chinese criminal justice and its implications for reforming the U.S. system. The right regards rehabilitation as a coddling of criminals, who should be made to pay and suffer for the harm they caused others. The left believes that a policy of "three strikes and you're out"—let alone a mere two strikes—is harsh and unreasonable, given the social disadvantages previously suffered by most street criminals, who are disproportionately ethnic minorities and the poor. In practice, U.S. radicals and socialists have had almost as little to say about rehabilitation as conservatives, inclined as they are to believe that rehabilitating the society by replacing capitalism is the only rehabilitation that counts in the long run. Removal of social disadvantages through structural transformation, they imply, will moot both rehabilitation and incarceration. In the meantime, we should lock our doors and hope for the best.

In theory, most radicals accept the logic whereby offenders are less likely to repeat if they get psychological counseling, treatment for substance abuse, education, job training, and postconfinement job guarantees. But they show little enthusiasm for such programs, regarding them as liberal props for the system. Liberals, on the other hand, seem unaware that as helpful as these programs may be in reducing recidivism, they do little to reduce entropic capitalism's systematic production of crime and other social pathologies in the first place. Even with reduced recidivism, the totality of first offenses alone will continue to injure millions of Americans every year. And reformed criminals may shift from crime to new pathologies of choice, such as exploiting friends, manipulating clients, and free-riding on community resources—actions which, while not illegal, still hurt others and harm the common good.

By making excuses, even if partly valid, for criminals who prey on the innocent, progressives lose credibility in the eyes of law-abiding citizens, thereby delivering voters, sympathy, and ideological allies to law-and-order conservatives and the Republican Party. Socialist economists Bowles and Gintis (1987) remind us of an unintended consequence of Marx's classic view opposing individual responsibility, expressed in *Capital,* volume 1: "My standpoint, from which the development of the economic formation of society is viewed as a process of natural history, can less than any other make the individual responsible for relations whose creature he remains." Wrongdoers of every ilk are thus creatures of their society. Not only does this structural-determinist view exonerate street criminals, but, as Bowles and Gintis point out, "the bureaucrat and the patriarch alike are shielded from criticism" (p. 19). Radical behavioral engineers such as B. F. Skinner might applaud this determinist leap "beyond freedom and dignity," but ordinary citizens are repelled.[80]

Long-term incarceration for second offenders. There is a perverse, unintended kind of "justice" in the leniency of most U.S. courts toward serial offenders. Since U.S. prisons do little to rehabilitate inmates, and in effect teach them new criminal skills, it would be far less fair than in China to throw away the key on recidivists. In effect, the system tacitly recognizes an element of injustice in punishing poor people, especially for property crimes against the privileged, in a highly stratified class society that stacks the deck against the poor. Common sense suggests greater blame for wealthy white-collar criminals such as Ivan Boesky or Michael Milken than for Sharon Ramsey, a desperate laid-off single mother with no previous criminal record, who robbed a bank of $1,300 to help care for her two small children, one of whom suffered from cystic fibrosis.[81] Even a nonviolent burglar selling stolen goods to feed a cocaine habit seems less reprehensible than the Ford executives who sold Pintos with defective gas tanks after calculating that it would be cheaper to pay off incinerated victims of fiery crashes than to recall the cars and fix the tanks.[82] Even law-abiding citizens might sympathize with an underpaid and mistreated employee who embezzles from a greedy boss.

However, during the 1990s, the FBI reported that street criminals were harming about 14 million innocent Americans every year, disproportionately victimizing the young, the poor, and people of color. Holding criminals accountable for their actions is not, as the PC criminology of postmodernists might have it, merely a matter of using "violence as an instrument of the state to control supposed social enemies of a supposedly law-abiding citizenry."[83] Rather, incarceration protects the innocent from further victimization. The fact that one-third of jailed criminals in the United States are *not* reincarcerated suggests that, even without extensive rehabilitation programs, imprisonment not only protects society while the offenders are behind bars but deters a large minority of them from future offenses. Just as victimizers of the innocent bear some responsibility for their acts, responsibility for the two-thirds who repeat falls partly in the lap of a social system that generates some of the world's highest crime rates and then declines to rehabilitate most of the perpetrators while they are in custody. The proper justification for long-term imprisonment of repeat offenders is not retribution but self-defense, the right of society to defend itself against attack. "An eye for an eye" policies that fail to compensate victims, rehabilitate offenders, or deter future offenders may feel good to those seeking revenge but end up increasing societal myopia. "Perhaps the most damaging effect of the retributive paradigm on the juvenile justice system has been its tendency to make nonpunitive 'alternative sanctions' appear weak."[84]

While transformationalists work to eliminate systemic disadvantage based on race and class, along with its predictable criminal consequences, they must resist PC pressures to excuse ordinary criminality that harms innocent people. Such behavior is wrong, is inexcusable, and if condoned creates a field day for conservatives. But as society continues to embody widespread injustice, what position should progressives take toward civil disobedience, eco-sabotage, and other authentically political crimes? Radicals in the 1960s and 1970s sympathized with the antipolice "Off the Pig!" slogan of the Black Panther Party, acts of robbery and sabotage by the Weather Underground, and illegal sit-ins by antiwar protesters. Today, progressives seem uncertain how to respond to such political tactics. What stance should they take, for instance, toward the eco-sabotage carried out in recent years by the Earth Liberation Front (ELF) in Vail, Colorado, as well as in Washington State, Michigan, Indiana, Minnesota, and Long Island, New York? ELF attacked the Vail resort's properties on behalf of the threatened lynx, while destroying Boise Cascade's regional headquarters in Washington on behalf of overharvested forests.

Any attempt to settle the question of when and how it is justifiable to break an unjust law is beyond the scope of this book. But it is worth noting the relevance of the question for a critique of political correctness. PC among political activists discourages an open discussion of ideologically sensitive issues. The purpose of this book is to explore the ways in which such limitations can unintentionally undermine efforts to bring about a better society and a better world. Tunnel vision can set back any political cause, whether progressive or conservative, pacifist or militarist. Dramatic acts such as arson tend to provoke one-sided responses, and one-sidedness can damage the side one is on. At the very least, supporters or opponents of Amendment 30, with its assumption that "crime has both individual and social dimensions of responsibility,"[85] might think through the challenges posed by the distinction between strict law-and-order and a higher justice. Unjust laws can create a "choice of evils" self-defense for forceful resistance reminiscent of Malcolm X's oft-repeated dictum "Be peaceful, be courteous, obey the law, respect everyone, but if someone puts his hand on you, send him to the cemetery."

Who is to blame? As the *Wall Street Journal* began documenting in 1995, juries are increasingly taking the law into their own hands. By acts of "jury nullification," jurors in criminal trials are taking it upon themselves to balance individual guilt with societal responsibility by finding defendants not guilty of offenses the jurors believe the accused actually committed. By thus "nullifying" an unjust law or a prospective punishment they view as excessive, the jurors are suggesting that in some cases society bears a greater responsibility for the offense than the individual perpetrator. Just as white juries in the South routinely acquitted whites accused of crimes against blacks, evidence is mounting today that many black jurors are siding "with African-American defendants against a mostly white-dominated justice system." This trend reflects the fact that "66% of blacks believe the criminal-justice system is racist, compared with 37% of whites," a disparity that "inevitably affects deliberations."[86] The highly publicized O. J. Simpson murder trial reflects just the tip of an iceberg.

We should note the difference between a politically correct activist who resists condemning crimes committed by a poor person or person of color, and a black juror trying to weigh whose fault is greater, the black defendant's or that of the society which had unjustly limited the defendant's options in life. The first person is trying to avoid grappling with politically sticky issues. The second is struggling to minimize injustice in a no-win situation presented by a guilty offender in a culpable society. "Jurors living in dangerous urban areas, recognizing a need to be armed in self-defense, are known to be particularly reluctant to convict for gun possession. Indeed, in the Bronx, 75% of such cases end in acquittals."[87] Yet predominantly black and Latino jurors struggle hard with the facts of such cases.

In the same courthouse in Los Angeles where O. J. Simpson was being tried for murder, twenty-two-year-old Byron Carter was acquitted of a gun-possession charge that would have sent him to prison for life under California's three-strikes-and-you're-out law. "After the verdict, several black jurors talked openly about the illogic of sending another young black man away to spend his life in jail for what they considered the 'victimless' crime of possessing a .22-caliber handgun." This argument ultimately convinced a jury of five blacks, three Latinos, two whites, and especially two Asian Americans who had initially held out for conviction. "Was this jury prepared to defy the law? Not quite, says black juror Troy Richardson. The thought of voting to acquit regardless of the evidence 'did enter my mind,' says Mr. Richardson, 'but I decided if the evidence says he's guilty, I'm going to send him away.'"[88]

Applying lessons from elsewhere. Just as an open discussion of the issues raised by ecology Amendment 29 might entail a revision of the ten-year timetable, a similar discussion of crime Amendment 30 might suggest a "three strikes" or even "four strikes" approach, depending on the seriousness of the crime and other circumstances, rather than a blanket "two strikes" rule more typical in Maoist China. It is worth noting that China's post-Maoist market reforms, like those in post-Soviet Russia, have greatly increased crime rates and undermined the confidence of both officials and citizens in the government's traditional communist approach to crime prevention. These changes serve as a warning that legal systems depend on their socioeconomic and cultural context. In any case, no foreign import, including a system of criminal justice, can be transplanted to a different cultural milieu without appropriate adaptation. This point brings us back to the transformational perspective that underlies our exploration of political correctness throughout the book.

Liberal forms of rehabilitation, or "corrections," have some merit, according to a more conservative skeptic, James Q. Wilson, but "collectively, the best estimate of the crime-reduction value of these programs is quite modest, something of the order of 5 or 10 percent." Mark Lipsey's meta-analysis of many smaller studies suggests "modest positive effects" of rehabilitation.[89] Robert Martinson's analysis of rehabilitative efforts in the 1950s and 1960s "give us very little reason to hope that we have in fact found a sure way of reducing recidivism through rehabilitation."[90] But liberal corrections, like conservative retributions, must work within the limitations of winner-take-all, entropic capitalism, much as the equal-opportunity goal of affirmative action may change the demography of winners and losers but accepts the legitimacy of the struggle for conquest. The limited success of liberal rehabilitation programs raises the question of what changes in U.S. society might make the rehabilitative power of Maoist criminal justice more workable in the U.S. context.

Restorative justice. In an article on juvenile courts, Bazemore and Umbreit contrast an innovative and increasingly popular, alternative form of "restorative justice" with the current system. "Neither punitive nor lenient in its focus, restorative justice gauges success in sanctioning not by how much punishment was inflicted or treatment provided but by how much reparation, resolution, and reintegration was achieved."[91] This approach, inspired by indigenous practices among peoples such as the Maori, treats crimes as relational events, connecting perpetrator to both the specific victim(s) and the larger community. A serious rift in this relationship made the criminal act possible. The offender needs to take responsibility for the offense and, as much as possible, repair the damage done to the victim and the community. This reparation is more likely to succeed if the community is involved in the compensatory and curative aspects of the judicial process. Following the model of many traditional societies, a curative shaming and restorative process can help reintegrate the offender into the community. Unlike the fate that did not grant remorse to Dostoevsky's criminal Raskolnikov, a community can give offenders a chance to make amends.

Bazemore (in Karp 1998: pp. 327–329) summarizes four common models of restorative justice practiced from Australia and New Zealand to Canada, Vermont, and Europe: Family Group Conferences with family and community members; five-person Reparative Boards of local citizens; an indigenous, consensual process of Circle Sentencing; and trained Victim-Offender Mediators. Face-to-face communication between offender and victim can be helpful in these processes.[92] Less formal and less adversarial rituals such as dialogue, victim-offender mediation, home visits, victim-awareness education, and counseling by peers and elders can complement formal programs of treatment for substance abuse, psychological therapy, schooling, job training, and community service.

In addition to holding offenders individually responsible, restorative justice "acknowledges and builds on group and community responsibility for crime."[93] Studies of the effectiveness of these essentially rehabilitative approaches are encouraging.[94] Unlike the case of traditional "corrections," what is rehabilitated by restorative justice is not only the offender but the fabric of connection—of understanding, trust, and support—among offender, victim, and community. Michigan juvenile-court judge George Economy stresses that early intervention is prevention: "Where we as a society are making a tragic mistake is that we are building punk prisons and jails when we should be taking those millions of dollars early on when programs can make a difference."[95] Countering the simplistic get-tough approach favored by many politicians, the nation's police chiefs overwhelmingly favor Head Start, parent coaching, and after-school programs for youths, whose contribution to crime occurs especially between 3 and 8 P.M., when 7 million of them go unsupervised.[96]

Prosecutor David Lerman sees crimes as community opportunities—as "fuel" for community strengthening. While recognizing social injustice as a key cause of crime, he faults politically correct progressives who have attended more to the needs and rights of offenders than to those of victims. He favors restorative justice for relying on informal social controls, "the strongest and healthiest way to prevent crime." Restorative justice, he believes, "opens the door for understanding the human consequences of crimes, and thus, for building human relationships. This is naturally empowering."[97] New community-justice networks based on restorative justice can make traditional programs such as Big Brothers and Big Sisters even more effective. A study of these mentoring programs in eight cities found dramatic results: "for ten- to fifteen-year-olds—a prime time for young people to start using drugs—there was on average a 40 percent reduction in first-time drug use among those who had mentors. For black males, the reduction was 72 percent" (Friedan 1997: p. 107).

A dramatic experiment in rehabilitative, restorative justice is taking place in the Albuquerque area, where sentencing judges James Abeita and Michael Martinez are toiling in the fields alongside youthful offenders in a jail diversion program that turns criminals into communal farmers for the Isleta Indian Pueblo. "It would be too easy for me to just assign them their community service and never follow through," explains Judge Abeita. "I'm supporting them by serving as a model of hard work and of what they can achieve in life. It also gives me a valuable opportunity to communicate and share with them. They teach me, and I teach them."[98]

Although restorative justice seems to be a promising alternative to traditional, retributive justice, long-term and cross-cultural studies will be needed to test its effectiveness in rehabilitating offenders and preventing crime. "We have all sorts of evidence that victims, offenders and their respective supporters find restorative justice rituals satisfying and just," comments Ted Wachtel, "but we have yet to conclusively demonstrate that any restorative justice ritual significantly reduces re-offense rates or otherwise prevents crime."[99]

Can local communities and neighborhoods in the United States become cohesive enough to play the vital role in rehabilitation and restoration that they played in China? Perhaps not easily, but the transformations we have explored earlier in the book may help point the way in criminal justice as well:

1. A shift away from the competitive ethic of equal opportunity for all toward a "compatriotic" ethic of fullness of opportunity for each, could help communities nurture diversity rather than interpersonal and inter-group envy.
2. If families, schools, and mass media promote synergistic values rather than entropic ones, fewer young people and adults will feel themselves losers, desperate to even the score.
3. If young people are treated in a less arbitrary and demeaning manner by their elders, they will be less likely to resent, and more likely to identify with, authority and societal rules.

4. If families act to build closer relationships among their members and join with other families to defend family interests against commercial and institutional encroachment, children are more likely to have their needs met and less likely to fall into patterns of social pathology.
5. If law and policy require us to recognize our connection with nature, we are more likely to honor our connection with one another. Natural and social ecology are mutually synergistic.

In *Fixing Broken Windows,* Kelling and Coles (1997) make a strong case for community policing, community prosecution, and "zero-tolerance" policies on minor crimes such as tagging buildings, littering, loitering, public noise and other nuisances, prostitution, petty drug-dealing, and extortion by "squeegee men." They emphasize the value of citizens' involvement in combating crime, noting that "the current 1.5 million-agent private security industry in the United States now dwarf[s] public police forces, which number approximately half a million" (p. 239). They argue that "atomistic, self-protective moves by citizens help to erode the quality of urban life, for when locked behind closed doors, individuals abandon their basic civic obligations" (p. 249).

In city after city, from Somerville, Massachusetts, to New Haven, Connecticut, New York City, New Orleans, Austin, Baltimore, San Francisco, and Seattle, a track record was established during the 1990s. A growing "acceptance of responsibility by citizens is not trivial: experience after experience has demonstrated that while police might be able to *retake* a neighborhood from aggressive drug dealers, police could not *hold* a neighborhood without significant commitment and actual assistance from private citizens" (p. 248). In her 1961 classic *The Death and Life of Great American Cities,* Jane Jacobs stresses that "the public peace—the sidewalk and street peace—of cities . . . is kept by an intricate, almost unconscious network of voluntary controls and standards among the people themselves, and enforced by the people themselves."[100] The reduction in reported crimes in the 1990s may be partly attributable to the new communitarian approaches to criminal justice. In 1999, both violent and property crimes were down 7 percent, although the opposite was true in some areas. Factors cited by criminologists to account for crime decreases include new anticrime measures, a booming economy, the continued aging of the baby boomers and hollowing out of the most crime-prone age cohorts, and the decreased market for crack cocaine.

Gerald Caiden, of the University of Southern California, warns that police departments, as noted earlier, may be doctoring their data in order to get better report cards. But criminologist James Allen Fox calls the drop in reported crimes "astounding" and hypothesizes a "reverse contagion effect," according to which "lawfulness is becoming the norm, and it's contagious.

Cities around the country are investing in crime programs as never before. Rather than hiding behind double-locked doors, citizens are getting involved in their communities."[101] A dramatic example was taking place even as the 1999 FBI report on crime was coming out. In Detroit, in response to a string of eight rapes of schoolgirls, students boycotted classes to pressure the city into responding, and "Detroit's mayor mobilized tens of thousands of parents, police officers, city workers and neighbors to patrol the streets to make it safe for schoolchildren."[102] The rapes stopped.

In the final section of this chapter, I examine a constitutional amendment addressing U.S. political economy which might strengthen local communities and help them play a decisive role in both criminal and environmental rehabilitation. In the strong words of David Mitchell, chief judge of Baltimore County's juvenile court, "It is of no value for the court to work miracles in rehabilitation if there are no opportunities for the child in the community. Until we deal with the environment in which they live, whatever we do in the courts is irrelevant."[103]

An Economy of the People, by the People, and for the People

A key reason why residents have allowed so much crime and environmental degradation to occur in their communities is that they lack a sense of ownership in them. Modern market society is nothing if not atomizing. In addition to the two communitarian movements discussed in Chapter 4, many specific programs have arisen in urban neighborhoods to counteract this sense of dispossession. These initiatives include Neighborhood Watch to control crime, community gardens to beautify landscapes and replace corporate food production, watchdog groups that use zoning and neighborly vigilance to guard against harmful growth schemes, and "privatopias," or walled communities with restrictive covenants to protect property values and a shared lifestyle.[104]

The Effect of Absentee Owners

Absentee ownership of local farms, businesses, and residences contributes to feelings of isolation of citizens from their local community. While exercising control over decisions of profound importance to local communities, outside owners lack the incentives of local residents to minimize crime, safeguard community resources, maintain local properties, and protect the local environment. As Greider (1997: p. 441) puts it, "factory owners are less likely to dump their toxic wastes in the river if they have to drink the water. Absentee investors wish to maximize the return on their capital assets, but a community of investors also has to defend the well-being of where they live." Employees of absentee owners also lack the profit-making incentives of worker-owners. Wage earners have an incentive to work as little and receive as much as possible, a mentality that mirrors the owner's incentive to pay workers as little for as much work as possible. The wage-earner's attitude hurts company productivity and profits, while the owner's attitude both hurts workers and, writ large, provides capitalism's perpetual contradiction between overproduction and underconsumption (workers paid little can spend little). In *Going Local: Creating Self-Reliant Communities in a Global Age,* Schuman (1998) urges citizens to fight global capitalism's "race to the bottom" by mechanisms of democratic localism, including local investment, community corporations, import substitution, and the elimination of corporate subsidies.

Not only does outside ownership of business compromise the quality of life of communities; it is also the primary reason for the extremes of wealth and poverty under capitalism. It is not individual hard work that produces an economy with a handful of billionaires overlaying several thousand multimillionaires at the top, 50 million poor people on the bottom, and a few hundred top corporate executives making most of the key decisions affecting the economic well-being of 260 million Americans (Domhoff 1998). Nobody gets super-rich simply by working hard. The road to great wealth in a capitalist economy is paved with other peoples' hard work and one's own entitlement to the fruits of their labor. In *The Power Elite,* C. Wright Mills (1956: pp. 110–111) calculated that for a corporate executive "on a salary of two or three hundred thousand a year, even forgetting taxes, and living like a miser in a board shack, it has been mathematically impossible to save up a great American fortune." On the other hand, "if you had bought only $9,900 worth of General Motors stock in 1913, and, rather than use your judgment, had gone into a coma—allowing the proceeds to pile up in General Motors—then, in 1953, you would have about $7 million"—or $50 million in today's dollars. To take an even more dramatic, current example: Superstar Michael Jordan would have to play basketball at his 1999 salary of $35 million for 2,302 years in order to accumulate the $72 billion of Microsoft stock owned by Bill Gates, whose wealth exceeds that of half of the U.S. populace combined.[105]

In other words, the way to get rich is not to work hard but to appropriate the output of those who do work hard. Not only do corporate owners enrich themselves by others' labor, but the legal fiction of the limited-liability corporate "person" they own protects them from individual responsibility for any irresponsibility on the part of that "person." A corporation, says *The Devil's Dictionary,* is "an ingenious device for obtaining individual profit without individual responsibility" (Bierce 1911: p. 9). Moreover, the engine of capitalist accumulation is far from promoting the delightful economic and cultural diversity we would expect from a truly free-market economy of small entrepreneurs. On the contrary, "large-scale capitalism is just as much an agency of homogenization, uniformity, grids, and heroic simplification as the state is" (Scott 1998: p. 8). Profit maximization, combined with advanced technology and market control, promotes routinization of work and commodification of output. Variety comes more as fads and planned obsolescence than in the form of creative and sustained diversity.

Outside ownership of corporate stocks also corrupts the political process by biasing stock-owning public officials in ways that may corrupt the public good. "After they are sworn into office this week, the congressional class of 2001, mostly upper middle class, faces vote counts that could affect their stock holdings, from high-tech companies to health insurance firms."[106] In "Private Property Versus Markets: Democratic and Communitarian Critiques of Capitalism," Claudio Katz (1997) makes a persuasive case for the democratic critique of capitalism. Economic democracy "differentiates markets from capitalist ownership, inculpating only the latter" (p. 277). He argues, "Capitalist ownership, not the market, constitutes the morally compromised aspect of the modern economy" (p. 278). Katz credits free markets for their liberating aspects while faulting capitalist rules of property accumulation: "Liberal theory establishes a valid connection between markets and liberty. Capitalist ownership relations are another matter" (p. 283). Greider (1997: pp. 418–439) agrees with Katz's recommendation that "democratic alternatives to capitalism envision supplementing or replacing financial markets with public processes of generating and allocating funds for new investment" (Katz 1997: p. 283). By contrast, a free market in goods and labor promotes personal freedom and can be made consistent with democracy. In fact, Katz points out, capitalist ownership removes the workplace from the freedoms characteristic of the marketplace, requiring workers to take orders from the owner rather than allowing them to make free economic choices based on their own interests. In short: "Capitalism's moral failure is not rooted in the operation of these markets [in goods and labor] but in its characteristic property regime" (p. 283). Katz credits earlier democratic critics of capitalist ownership, including Walzer (1983), for pinpointing outside ownership, not free markets, as the main source of gross inequality.

However, unlike the economic democracy envisioned by Katz (1997) and his precursors, who "endorse a 'neutral state,' that is, one which does not deliberately rank different conceptions of the good," the democratic political economy I recommend begins with society's commitment to synergistic values (Chapter 4). Without this prior commitment to a second Invisible Hand of synergy, the benefits of Smith's original Invisible Hand of free markets are greatly reduced, and one of Walzer and Katz's key claims is falsified, namely, that "once its boundaries are appropriately drawn, the marketplace, traditional and modern, ceases to present a moral dilemma" (p. 288). Unlike Walzer and Katz, I believe that even with minimum economic welfare and other "key social goods" provided outside the market, the pervasive entropic behavior of amoral profiteers, financial manipulators, "ad men" and other legal con men, and those zealous to best their neighbors remains deeply problematical.

By attacking private ownership and free markets, socialists have not only missed the magical ingredient of capitalist accumulation—nonworker ownership—but also unnecessarily restricted economic freedoms and forfeited the efficiencies of free markets. In general, homeowners take better care of their property than renters, sole proprietors and business partners work more diligently than wage laborers, and parents invest more energy and love in their own children than do nannies or day-care centers. American family farmers have always been more productive than collective farmers under socialism (Erasmus 1985; Scott 1998). These comparisons suggest that at least some forms of private ownership are superior to public ownership. Market competition increases this superiority with the incentives automatically provided by supply and demand.

Capitalist Rationalizations

Nothing inherent in free markets decrees rules of accumulation that give nonworkers the fruits of someone else's labor. Just as arbitrary rules of socialism prohibit private ownership of business, arbitrary rules of capitalism grant owners of capital the privilege of appropriating those fruits. Capitalist ideologues offer unconvincing rationalizations for this system of expropriation of workers by owners. Let us review these arguments before offering a system that avoids the arbitrariness and injustices of both socialism and capitalism.

1. *"Most businesses would not exist if capitalists had not been willing to risk their capital by investing in the business."* This justification begs the question of where the capitalists' wealth originally came from. Whether a particular capital stock was inherited, stolen, or "earned," the answer is almost always that it came from *previous* expropriations of the fruits of previous workers' labor. We should recall Marx's dictum that originally it is not capitalism that creates alienation, but alienation that creates capitalism. Marx meant that prior to some initial alienation of the product of workers' labor by others, any surplus value, or profit, could not become capital for a separate capital-*ist,* or owner separate from the workers. So long as the workers themselves owned, managed, and appropriated any surplus they had created, there was no separate capitalist owner of the surplus or profit, and thus there could be no class of capitalists who accumulated wealth created by the labor of others.

Marx revealed the initial and ongoing expropriation of workers as a scam, explainable by some combination of the greed of the expropriator, the gullibility of the expropriated, and unequal power relations that make the act of expropriation less than voluntary. Historically, if I was the ex-propriator-become-capitalist, my superior power may have been based on arms ("Give me the surplus or I'll shoot you"), religion ("God has decreed you turn this over to me"), charisma ("I inspire; therefore, I own"), persua-sion ("I deserve the surplus because I am the most important worker" [see below]), patriarchy ("I, the head of the clan, deserve the surplus"), or any of a myriad of other historical circumstances. Once such expropriations are legitimized, the system becomes self-justifying by virtue of the capitalist's claiming the right to the product of "his" workers' labor because it is he who is risking "his" capital.

2. *"The capitalist deserves the surplus, or profit, because as entrepre-neur he is the genius behind the business, the most important of the work-ers."* Some business owners, like Mills's man-in-a-coma, are not workers at all. Owners who are also workers are not necessarily the most important workers. Even if an owner is also the most important worker, it does not follow that he is entitled to all of the surplus. Even by an Aristotelian (or socialist) rather than a communist (or Christian) concept of justice—that is, to each according to contribution—all productive workers should be re-warded according to their marginal productivity. If, for instance, the entre-preneur's contribution in a forty-person firm is twice as important as that of the manager, whose contribution is twice that of each of eight assistant managers, whose per capita contributions are five times those of the re-maining thirty factory workers, the net profit should be divided up as fol-lows: 20 percent to the owner, 10 percent to the manager, 5 percent to each of the eight assistant managers, and 1 percent to each of the thirty factory workers. If profits were in fact shared on the basis of marginal productivity, or merit, market economies would still generate class societies, but the dif-ferences between rich and poor would be far less extreme. Bill Gates might still be a multimillionaire, but he would not be an eighty-billionaire. Even the lowest-paid workers would be able to provide a healthy and dignified sustenance for their families.

3. *"The unprecedented growth and wealth of capitalist societies bene-fits the whole, and would not be possible without the existing incentives to capitalists."* This utilitarian argument is tantamount to excusing an injustice by saying that the happiness afforded to those who benefit from the injus-tice (by higher incomes) outweighs the unhappiness of those treated un-justly (the workers). Similar arguments have sought to justify slavery, pa-triarchy, ageism, and other oppressive regimes. Capitalism's success has also dangerously compromised living systems around the globe. Evidence that capitalist owners, as distinct from worker-owners, are essential to ro-bust economic growth is at best mixed (Przeworski 1991). Many worker-owned and -managed businesses (like consumer cooperatives), produce healthy net earnings (or savings), are long-lived, and are well-liked by their members (Zwerdling 1984).

The Mondragon system of worker cooperatives in northern Spain is a complex, $10 billion-plus operation that includes FAGOR, the largest home-appliance manufacturer in Spain (Hoover 1992). In the United States, Recreational Equipment Inc., a consumer-owned cooperative, is the world's largest recreational-equipment retailer, having expanded in fifty years from a single store in Seattle to fifty stores across the United States in 2000. Before Yugoslavia, with its "market socialist" economy, imploded in long-simmering ethnic conflict, many of the Yugoslav worker-owned and self-managed firms compared favorably to similar enterprises owned by capitalists in the United States and by the state in Soviet Bloc countries.[107] Like other privileged elites throughout history, capitalists promote themselves as essential to society but lack compelling evidence for their claim.

4. *"Most workers prefer to receive a wage and avoid the responsibilities of ownership."* What evidence there is belies most of this claim. For instance, a poll by Hart Associates in 1976 found that two-thirds of U.S. workers would prefer to work for a worker-owned firm as opposed to one owned by outside investors or the government. Since most worker-owned cooperatives are managed by administrators democratically elected by the workers, it may well be true that most workers prefer to delegate the responsibilities of day-to-day management of their companies. But this possibility is no more an argument against worker-owned companies than citizens' preference for representative government is an argument against democracy. Just as most people prefer hiring a professional plumber, auto mechanic, or language teacher, rather than trying to fix their own leaky pipes, overhaul their car engines, or teach themselves a foreign language, most workers may prefer to focus on their own specialties and leave management to others. Although delegating responsibility involves risk, so does a refusal to delegate, and the risk of delegation can be minimized by vigorous democratic mechanisms for holding decisionmakers accountable. Excessive delegation, with little popular oversight, is based on poor habits and faulty institutionalization; it is not decreed by an immutable iron law of oligarchy. As noted in the chapters on adultism, arbitrary age restrictions on young people's participation in decisionmaking contribute to so-called apathy in adults. Children who are encouraged to participate in the decisions that affect them, as in Summerhill schools, seldom grow up to become passive, disaffected nonparticipants in community affairs.

The Alternative of Economic Democracy

These considerations suggest an economic alternative to socialism and capitalism, to ownership and control by state bureaucrats or corporate capitalists. This alternative is *economic democracy,* a system of ownership and control that leaves economic power in the hands of ordinary workers and citizens. All modern economies combine, and should combine, public and private ownership. The principle of economic democracy should apply equally to the public and private sectors. Public enterprises would be owned by the citizens and controlled by them or their elected representatives. Private enterprises would be owned by their workers and controlled by them or their elected representatives. Wage and salary differentials would be democratically determined in both public and private enterprises. Economic activities that poison the earth, upset its natural balance, or threaten its sustainability would be prohibited under Amendment 29. Net profits of private enterprises would be determined by their market success. As Wilson, Skocpol, and others advocate, all citizens should be guaranteed a dignified level of sustenance. In return, all able citizens should be required to work for an equal period of time over the course of their lives, say thirty years, and all citizens seeking to work would be guaranteed work in the public sector. Citizens willing to forgo the societal income guarantee would have no work obligation, casting their fortunes with the free market. Children, the disabled, and the retired would receive the guaranteed sustenance without any work obligation.

Greider (1997: p. 435) points out that, until recently, worker ownership was politically incorrect on the left, especially in labor unions: "Labor's doubts largely dissipated during the last two decades, however, as unions experienced the withering losses in jobs, wages, and bargaining power." Even now, the still-prevalent regime of business-friendly unionism takes for granted the basic split between work and ownership. But, as prodemocracy union reformers are now arguing (Tillman and Cummings 1999), the traditional rationale for democratic government applies logically and equally to economic affairs: Those affected by political or economic decisions *have a right* to participate in the decisionmaking or to delegate the decisionmaking to authorities fully accountable to them. All of the essential features of economic democracy listed above merit eventual inclusion in the U.S. Constitution. My proposed Amendment 31 is a first step in that direction:

> Amendment 31: Within ten years of adoption of this amendment, ownership of all private enterprises shall be transferred to their workers on the basis of one worker, one share, one vote. Government shall extend credit to help employees purchase their companies. Assets currently held in nonemployee ownership, including banks, may be reinvested in public credit unions, whose assets may be lent to individuals or employee-owned businesses.

Greider (1997), Katz (1997), Korten (1999), and others have proposed roughly such a system, and Korten points out that, according to the National Center for Employee Ownership, 15,000 U.S. companies already have some degree of employee ownership. The system of economic democracy embodied in this amendment, and the related amendments that should follow it, incorporates the best of capitalism and the best of socialism while avoiding the most obvious flaws of both. Businesses will still compete on the open market. Workers and consumers will have a great deal of choice. The needy will be provided for. Profits will flow to those who truly created them. Those who work harder, exhibit more talent, and produce more desirable goods or services will earn more than those who do not. Economic reward and personal advancement will primarily be a function of work rather than ownership. Wealth differentials will not be so great as to convert easily into power differentials that allow a wealthy power elite to control government.

This proposed system of economic democracy violates many sacred cows of capitalist and socialist ideologues. It will irk much of the politically correct left and right—a sign that it may have something valuable to offer, beginning with a vigorous discussion of its own merits.

As with the ecology and crime amendments, the economic-democracy amendment requires statutory law to give its key terms operational definition and to set up public and private mechanisms to implement it. During the inherently difficult ten-year transition from capitalism to economic democracy, the wealthiest individuals and most powerful economic elites must learn to swallow the bitter pill of economic justice.[108] Some interesting issues (and my tentative positions) would need to be addressed, such as (1) whether part-time workers should be full-share or pro-rata co-owners of their business (I say pro rata); (2) whether new workers should go through a period of apprenticeship before they become co-owners (I say yes); and (3) whether workers should be permitted to waive their right to co-ownership (I say yes). How might new laws of inheritance reflect citizens' beliefs in (a) the injustice of today's massive fortunes, but perhaps (b) the right of children to inherit some of their parents' wealth but no ownership rights in a business? What should the public sector own, produce, manage, plan, and regulate? Nationwide, publicly owned utilities today provide energy at lower prices than investor-owned utilities, and nonprofit hospitals and HMOs provide cheaper and better health care than for-profit ones.[109] Would worker-owned, self-managed, for-profit businesses close these gaps?

Ideological claims of left, right, and others notwithstanding, no one can say for sure what standard of living is possible under an ecologically responsible system of economic democracy. Przeworski (1991: p. 129) summarizes the theoretical arguments and empirical evidence of Elster, Moene, Putterman, and others regarding the fairness, efficiency, productivity, and employment advantages of cooperative versus capitalist firms. "In the end," he concludes, "market socialism [economic democracy] does appear attractive on distributional grounds. Even if we cannot exactly anticipate its effects on employment, investment, and labor productivity, a combination of cooperatives with markets would be superior to capitalism in equalizing income distribution." This superiority stems from workers' right to ownership: "The distribution of income . . . will be more egalitarian than under capitalism, since employees receive the entire net income of the firm."

In amending the Constitution in the direction of ecological steward-ship, sustainability, and economic democracy, we must be willing to con-front the possibility of a lower living standard for privileged, and perhaps even for most, Americans. On the other hand, if economic democracy does slow or reverse the engine of growth, so much the better for the nation's and world's ecology. In other words, it may be that the economic-democ-racy amendment will make it easier to adhere to the ecology amendment. Conversely, by nixing the profitable but ecocidal projects so popular with outside-investor–owned companies whose executives live far from the en-vironmental damage they cause, the ecology amendment may make the economic-democracy amendment more palatable. In effect, many corporate owners and managers may decide that companies prohibited from external-izing their environmental costs might as well be sold to their employees. Maximum profits, not modest, reasonable, or sustainable ones, are the name of the game under corporate capitalism.

A democratic political economy is also likely to reduce crime, because capitalism's features of extreme wealth and poverty, envy by the "have-nots" directed at the "haves," artificial unemployment, inadequate incomes, poor housing, inferior schools, substandard health care, environmental de-struction, and resentment over injustice all contribute to crime and related social pathologies such as drug addiction, alcoholism, domestic violence, broken homes, teen pregnancy, academic failure, and urban blight. For most of the twentieth century, state socialists claimed they could cure these ills of the market economy by replacing it with public ownership and "the new socialist man." But their record is not encouraging, and their approach has been rejected by their own peoples and by many of their leaders as well. Experiments in economic democracy have shown that it can work, even in the generally hostile environments of corporate capitalism and state social-ism. Economic democracy could become a core part of the more general "strong democracy" envisioned by Barber (1984), including the teledemoc-racy advocated by Becker and Slaton (2000). It is time to give economic democracy a chance to thrive in its own environment.

Notes

1. Speech given in Denver, Colorado, November 25, 1988.
2. Aldo Leopold, *A Sand Country Almanac* (Oxford: Oxford University Press), excerpted in Andrew Dobson, ed., *A Green Reader* (San Francisco: Mercury House, 1991), p. 238.
3. *Crime and Punishment* (New York: Norton, 1964), p. 333.
4. People's Bicentennial Commission, *Voices of the American Revolution* (New York: Bantam, 1974), p. 154.
5. Ibid., p. 152.
6. M. Campbell and J. Spivak, "Endangered Species Act Marked by Progress, Loss," Knight-Ridder News, July 27, 1997.

7. Robert Braile, "Report: Earth's in Bad Shape," *Boston Globe,* January 16, 2000.

8. Herman Daly, quoted in Scott (1998: p. 351).

9. Charles J. Hanley, "Staple Fish Stocks Worldwide Are Collapsing," Associated Press, July 27, 1997.

10. Marlise Simons, "Europe Now Has a Beef with Bad Fish," *New York Times,* December 17, 2000.

11. H. Josef Hebert, "Runoff Wreaking Marine Havoc," Associated Press, April 5, 2000.

12. William K. Stevens, "Winter Warmest Yet for U.S.," *New York Times,* March 11, 2000.

13. John Wilford, "North Pole Visitors Find No Ice," *New York Times,* August 19, 2000.

14. "Arctic Ozone Hole Proves Stubborn," Associated Press, December 17, 2000.

15. H. Josef Herbert, "World to Get Much Warmer, Study Finds," Associated Press, October 26, 2000.

16. Paul and Anne Ehrlich, *The Population Explosion* (New York: Simon and Schuster, 1990), p. 40.

17. "Our Aims," editorial, *Democracy and Nature: The International Journal of Politics and Ecology* 8, 1996, p. vi.

18. Sam Howe Verhovek, "A Day Revolving Around Revewal," *New York Times,* April 9, 2000.

19. Of course, as parents increasingly use television and shopping malls as baby-sitters, and substitute consumer goods for parental love and attention, young consumers themselves partake in eco-plunder.

20. John Entine, "The Green Power Hustle: 'Clean' Energy's Dirty Little Secret," *Utne Reader* 90, November-December 1998, p. 17.

21. For hundreds of eco-communities, see the Fellowship for Intentional Communities' (2000) *Communities Directory.*

22. Albert Gore, "Finding a Third Way: Cleaner Cars and a Stronger Economy," *Newsweek,* November 23, 1998, p. 58.

23. Not only eco-feminists but radical women are more likely to identify with nature than are radical men. Rosemary Radford Ruether argues that "we cannot criticize the hierarchy of male over female without ultimately criticizing the hierarchy of human over nature." *Sexism and God-Talk: Toward a Feminist Theology* (Boston: 1983), p. 73. "Almost every feminist writer noted the parallels between the 'rape' of the 'virgin' land and abuse of women" (Nash 1989: p. 145).

24. See the eco-activism websites and website links at <www.thefarm.org/lifestyle/akb> and <www.gaia.org/international/projects/csareviewgroup/>.

25. Tom Regan and Peter Singer, eds., *Animal Rights and Human Obligations* (Englewood Cliffs, NJ: 1976).

26. FBI figures for 1997, cited in M. Sniffen, "U.S. Crime Continues to Decline," Associated Press, November 23, 1998.

27. Paul H. Robinson, in Sullivan and Victor (1996: p. 34).

28. U.S. government–commissioned nationwide survey by the Center for Policy Research, November 17, 1998. <http://www.ncadv.org/publicpolicy/vawasummary.htm>.

29. Susan Estrich, "Women Know Best," *Los Angeles Times,* August 13, 1999.

30. Robinson, in Sullivan and Victor (1996: p. 35).

31. James Q. Wilson, "What to Do About Crime," *Commentary* 98, no. 3, September 1994, pp. 25–34. Average time served for rape has remained steady.

32. Cheryl Russell, in Sullivan and Victor (1996: p. 56).

33. "Philly Cops Shaving Crime Numbers," Associated Press, September 15, 2000.

34. Eric Lichtblau, "America 'In Trouble,' Violence Panel Warns," *Los Angeles Times,* December 6, 1999.

35. "Deaths by Gunfire Drop to Lowest Levels Since 1960s," Associated Press, November 19, 1999.

36. Wilson, "What to Do About Crime."

37. Pam Bullock, "Cities See Light After Years of Blight," *New York Times,* May 29, 2000.

38. Eric Lichtblau, "The Crime-Drop Party Is Over: FBI Reports Incidents Are Rising in Major Cities," *Los Angeles Times,* December 19, 2000.

39. Crime rates can vary even more dramatically within countries. Violent crime rates in Miami, Florida, the most dangerous city in the United States, are thirty-two times higher than in Wasau, Wisconsin, the safest city in the United States (Federal Bureau of Investigation, *Crime in the United States 1993* [Washington, DC: Federal Bureau of Investigation, 1994]). Such variations strengthen the leftist emphasis on social environment as an important cause of crime.

40. "Moral Credibility and Crime," in Sullivan and Victor (1996: p. 36).

41. Wilson, "What to Do About Crime."

42. Sidney Blumenthal, "How Rehnquist Came Down in Hobbes Versus Locke," *Washington Post National Weekly Edition,* October 6, 1986, p. 23.

43. Alfred Blumstein, "Violence by Young People," in Sullivan and Victor (1995: pp. 158–164).

44. For instance, Irving Spergel, University of Chicago professor and head of the Gang Research and Technical Assistance Group, says, "The single best predictor of kids avoiding or getting out of gangs is finding legitimate employment." "Gangs, Crime Studied," *New York Times,* November 23, 1998.

45. For instance, fourteen- to seventeen-year-old black males are eight times more likely to be arrested for murder than fourteen- to seventeen-year-old white males; nonwhite adults are seven times more likely to be arrested for murder than white adults (FBI's *Supplementary Homicide Reports,* cited by Blumstein in Sullivan and Victor [1995: pp. 158–164]).

46. R. J. Sampson and William J. Wilson, "Toward a Theory of Race, Crime, and Urban Inequality," in Karp (1998: p. 98).

47. See Kelling and Coles (1996: pp. 1–2).

48. Glenn C. Loury and Shelby Steele, "A New Black Vanguard," cited in Kelling and Coles (1996: p. 246).

49. Dramatized in March 2000 by revelations of racial-profiling policies by police in metropolitan Chicago.

50. Elizabeth Gleick, "The Crooked Blue Line," *Time,* September 11, 1995, pp. 38–42; Kelling and Coles (1996); Karp (1998).

51. Tom Wells, "House Burned 'for Neighbors,'" Associated Press, July 26, 1996.

52. See the periodical *Kibbutz Trends,* published in Israel by scholars who live in kibbutz communities.

53. Daniel Singer, "A Realistic Utopia for the Millennium," *Tikkun* 4, no. 5, September-October 1999, p. 28.

54. Richard J. Ellis and Fred Thompson, "Culture and the Environment in the Pacific Northwest," *American Political Science Review* 91, no. 4, December 1997, p. 892.

55. Karl Marx, *The Communist Manifesto* (New York: Norton, 1988 [1848]), p. 69.

56. Edward Zaleski, *La Planification Stalinienne: Croissance et Fluctuations* (Paris: Economica, 1984), p. 615.

57. Scott overlooks the highly productive religious and communal Hutterite farming colonies of North America.

58. In the late 1990s, managers of state enterprises resisted further market reforms, and growth slowed. But in early 2000: "Faced with a foundering economy that demands 'urgent solutions,' China on Tuesday gave one of its strongest endorsements ever to private enterprise, announcing that all obstacles to the development of the private sector should be scrapped." John Pomfre, "China Pushes Private Enterprise," *Washington Post,* January 5, 2000.

59. A good example of this trade-off mentality is Chertow and Esty's (1997) *Thinking Ecologically.*

60. Geneva Overholser, "Greens' Next Path," *Washington Post,* October 31, 1998.

61. Worldwatch Institute (1999: p. 183); see also Kay (1998), as well as Korten (1999: pp. 217–218), on environmental attitudes.

62. See Robert Wheeler Lane, *Beyond the Schoolhouse Gate: Free Speech and the Inculcation of Values* (Philadelphia: Temple University Press, 1995).

63. Job-site killings have become a serious concern of workers all across the economy. Rene Sanchez, "Job-Site Killings Complex: Companies Battle Frightful Rampages," *Washington Post,* November 13, 1999.

64. The *Wall Street Journal* regularly updates this statistic.

65. In 1979, law professor David F. Favre proposed an amendment that would accord all wildlife "the right to a natural life" and would guarantee animals "due process of law prior to any deprivation of their life, liberty, or habitat" (quoted in Nash 1989: p. 133). The animals would be represented in court by human advocates. Favre's amendment also recognized a human self-defense right that could trump animal rights. American Indian activist Winona La Duke has proposed a "Seventh Generation" amendment based on the traditional Iroquois requirement that policymakers consider the effects of proposed policies on the next seven generations.

66. Quoted in Andrew Dobson, ed., *The Green Reader* (San Francisco: Mercury House, 1991), p. 238.

67. Paul Ames, "More European Farmers Growing the Organic Way," Associated Press, December 31, 1999.

68. Worldwatch Institute at <www.worldwatch.org>.

69. Heidi B. Perlman, "Health Food a Natural Fit: Markets Answer Consumer Demand for Organics," Associated Press, August 3, 2000.

70. Warren Hoge, "Power in Denmark Blowing in the Wind," *New York Times,* December 15, 1999.

71 Worldwatch Institute at <www.worldwatch.org>.

72. Erin Kelly, "Recycling Up, But So Is Garbage," Gannett News Service, March 27, 2000.

73. Mark Jaffe, "Earth Day Still Holds Relevance: But Severity of Problems Provokes Renewed Debate," Knight Ridder News Service, April 22, 2000.

74. William Booth, "Voters Keep Taking More Initiatives," *Washington Post,* November 6, 1998.

75. For instance, since 1996 Greens have held a majority or near-majority in Arcata, California, instituting bike lanes, domestic-partner legislation, licensing for medical marijuana, and town meetings. Zachary Coile, "You Say You Want a Revolution," *San Francisco Examiner,* April 18, 1999. In March 1999, Audie Bock became the first Green elected to a state legislative seat, in California, where thirty-two Greens currently hold nonpartisan local offices. Bock won despite being outspent 20-1 by her well-known and politically connected Democratic opponent,

Elihu Harris. Rich DelVecchio, "East Bay Vote Caught Everyone by Surprise," *San Francisco Chronicle*, April 1, 1999. Nationally, by 1999 sixty-four Greens had been elected in fifteen states. Rensenbrink (1999: pp. 195–199) chronicles additional impressive Green Party showings in recent elections.

76. Simpson, Harris, and Mattson (1995: p. 115).

77. See, for instance, Jean Buxton, "The Mandari of the Southern Sudan," in Ronald Cohen and John Middleton, eds., *Comparative Political Systems* (Garden City, NY: Natural History Press, 1967), p. 232.

78. Robert Elegant, "Everyone Can Be Reformed: Why the Chinese Stop Crime Better Than We Do," *Rocky Mountain News: Parade Magazine*, October 30, 1988, pp. 4–7.

79. I would replace the death penalty with life imprisonment.

80. B. F. Skinner, *Walden Two* (New York: Macmillan, 1948), and *Beyond Freedom and Dignity* (New York: Knopf, 1971).

81. Howard Pankratz, "Mom Allegedly Robbed Bank to Feed Kids," *Denver Post*, April 20, 1991.

82. Mark Dowie, "Pinto Madness," *Mother Jones*, September-October 1977, pp. 18–32.

83. Hal Pepinsky, "Geometric Forms of Violence," in Dragan Milovanovic, ed., *Chaos, Criminality, and Social Justice: The New Orderly (Dis)Order* (Westport, CT: Praeger, 1997), p. 97.

84. Bazemore and Umbright, quoted in Sullivan and Victor (1996: p. 136).

85. Ibid., p. 138.

86. Benjamin A. Holden, Laurie P. Cohen, and Eleena de Lisser, "Race Seems to Play an Increasing Role in Many Jury Verdicts," *Wall Street Journal*, October 4, 1995.

87. Ibid.

88. Ibid.

89. Wilson, "What to Do About Crime," pp. 25–34.

90. Robert Martinson, quoted in Sullivan and Victor (1996: p. 34).

91. In Sullivan and Victor (1996: p. 139).

92. John Braithwaite, *Crime, Shame and Reintegration* (New York: Cambridge University Press, 1989).

93. Bazemore and Umbreit, in Sullivan and Victor (1996: p. 140).

94. Anne Schneider, ed., *Guide to Juvenile Restitution* (Washington, DC: U.S. Department of Justice, Office of Juvenile Justice and Delinquency Prevention, 1985); Anne Schneider, "Restitution and Recidivism Rates of Juvenile Offenders: Results from Four Experimental Studies," *Criminology*, no. 24, 1986, pp. 533–552; Jeff Butts and Howard Snyder, *Restitution and Juvenile Recidivism* (Pittsburgh: National Center for Juvenile Justice, 1991); Mark Umbreit and Robert Coates, "Cross-Site Analysis of Victim-Offender Mediation in Four States," *Crime and Delinquency*, no. 39, 1993, pp. 565–585.

95. Nedra Pickler, "Schools May Be Kids' Saving Place," Associated Press, March 5, 2000.

96. Fight Crime: Invest in Kids Survey, October 1999. <http://www.fight-crime.org/reports/schoolbiol.htm>.

97. David Lerman, "Restoring Justice," *Tikkun* 14, no. 5, September-October 1999, pp. 13–15.

98. Iliana Limon, "Work Pairs Judges with Sentenced Kids," *Albuquerque Journal*, October 6, 2000.

99. Ted Wachtel, "Restorative Justice in Everyday Life: Beyond the Formal Ritual," paper presented at the "Reshaping Australian Institutions Conference: Restorative Justice and Civil Society," Australian National University, Canberra, February 16–18, 1999.

100. Jane Jacobs, *The Death and Life of Great American Cities* (New York: Vintage Books, 1961), quoted in Scott (1998: p. 135).

101. Nick Anderson, "Serious Crimes in U.S. Drop 10%," *Los Angeles Times,* November 22, 1999.

102. Robyn Meredith, "Detroit Mobilizes After Rapes," *New York Times,* November 24, 1999.

103. J. David Hawkins, "Controlling Crime Before It Happens: Risk-Focused Prevention," *National Institute of Justice Journal,* August 1995, pp. 10–18, quoted in Sullivan and Victor (1996: p. 165).

104. Evan McKenzie, *Privatopia* (New Haven, CT: Yale University Press, 1994).

105. Jim Campen, "How Rich Is Bill?" *Dollars and Sense: What's Left in Economics* 227, January-February 2000, p. 9.

106. Jonathan D. Salant, "New Congress' Stock Holdings May Affect Votes," Associated Press, January 2, 2001.

107. "We can thus conclude that the economy of Yugoslavia under the participatory system has performed remarkably well, unsurpassed in a significant manner by any economy in the world, and about equal to the economy of the top two or three countries." Jaroslav Vanek, *The Participatory Economy* (Ithaca: Cornell University Press, 1971), p. 49.

108. Concern over potential reactionary efforts—legal and illegal—by capitalists and their allies is far from paranoid. Economic democrats should take note of the long-standing U.S. pattern of economic and military intervention against democratic and socialist regimes that have threatened the interests of U.S. corporations. The history of corporate brutality against U.S. workers seeking to organize is written in blood.

109. The study cited in Chapter 7 found that nonprofit HMOs outperformed for-profit HMOs in all fourteen areas measured, such as prenatal care, infant immunization, and breast-cancer screening.

9

Conclusion:
Ideology as Friend and Foe of Transformation

"One person with a belief is a social power equal to ninety-nine who have only interests."

—John Stuart Mill[1]

"Those who profess to favor freedom, and yet deprecate agitation, are men who want crops without plowing up the ground."

—Frederick Douglass[2]

"A map of the world that does not include utopia is not even worth glancing at."

—Oscar Wilde[3]

The focus of this book is on national transformation, but we must not ignore the global dimension of U.S. problems and any workable solutions to them. David Roodman writes, "So far, the world order emerging is one almost no one wants."[4] This unwanted new world order of global capitalism ravages the earth, encourages criminal behavior, and undermines democracy in governance and economics. The exceptions to Roodman's generalization are the local, national, and international elites who profit from global capitalism and its associated entropic disorders.

These elites run private economies that are richer and more powerful than most nation-states. "Fifty-two of the top 100 economies around the world are transnational companies rather than nation-states." For instance: "Mitsubishi is bigger than Indonesia (the Earth's fourth most populous country), General Motors is larger than either Denmark or Norway, Daimler-Chrysler now outstrips South Africa and Saudi Arabia, and Siemen's yearly income is greater than Ireland's or Chile's." These absentee-owned corporations' wealth is staggering. "Indeed, the combined annual revenues of the biggest 200 corporations is greater than those of 182 nation-states which, in turn, are responsible for the livelihood of over four-fifths of humanity on the planet."[5]

Putting our own nation's entropic house in order is a critical part of joining with other peoples to put the global house in order. This book focuses on the national and subnational parts of the solution. For global aspects of the solution, I recommend Greider (1997), Korten (1999), and the annual editions of the Worldwatch Institute's *State of the World* and *Vital Signs.*

A critique of political correctness should not be taken as a debunking of ideology—or, for that matter, of its close relative utopia. The dangers of ideological zeal and dogmatism do not warrant a retreat to armchair philosophy. It is the ideology of activists, not the philosophy of thinkers, that changes the world. Of course, philosophers influence ideologues. Plato's allegory of the cave prodded the wise to risk themselves in order to enlighten the ignorant, and to do so by becoming politically active. For Plato, pure knowledge was the very Idea of the Good but was also an enchantress that could entice the wise to shirk their political responsibilities. To bring about a better world, we must risk the opposite danger, a dogma that can seduce us into misguided action. For some time now, political correctness has encouraged a dogmatism that has misguided this country's progressive forces.

More powerful than a mere belief or a mere interest is a deep-seated belief inspired by an abiding interest. An ideology is a philosophy that is interest-based, action-oriented, and consciously shared by political allies. Interests, activism, and alliances all promote political correctness. Stakeholders in the ideology dislike trespassers on their holdings. Activists invested in their commitments do not like them threatened. Dissent among allies may connote treachery to the cause. But because the real world of politics is always changing, even true believers need to change with it. Like all living things, ideologies that stagnate eventually die. Ideologies that might improve the world, but instead die by neglect, dishonor their martyred activists—activists such as Nigerian playwright Ken Saro-Wiwa, who, executed in 1995 for fighting oppression in his native Nigeria, spoke eight final words before he was hanged: "Lord take my soul, but the struggle continues." The struggle for a better world must always continue.

We have seen evidence of progressive attitudes that are self-defeating in the areas of affirmative action, values, adultism, family empowerment, ecology, crime, and political economy. When passion motivates us to act but threatens to undermine our cause, we may be tempted—or advised—to "chill out." But chilling out is fatal to social transformation. Coolness kills commitment. As a rap poet in the movie *Slam* recites, "Lack of ideology/ Periodically/ Destroys us/ Psychologically." The poet Robert Bly (1996: p. 167) writes, "Anger vitalizes people; it also temporarily narrows the range of vision."

The genius of the true agent of change is the ability to combine a passion for the good with an inner harmony and self-restraint. In practice, few activists achieve this ideal balance. Consequently, fellow ideologues need to balance one another out. The charismatic rabble-rouser needs the efficient organizer. The rational planner needs the intuitive troubleshooter. The tender-minded needs the tough-minded, and the impulsive needs the contemplative. Fired by passion, an ideological movement must achieve a unity of opposites, or it will probably achieve very little at all.[6] As Ralph Nader once remarked, "The nth factor is the fire in the belly. That's what makes the difference. . . . Never underestimate the metabolism of an ideological drive."[7]

Agents of social change need to build a dynamic unity enriched by diversity. It is by silencing and stifling diversity that political correctness stunts change. Complex analyses of social and political reality may cast doubt on simple diagnoses and comforting solutions. A partisan of affirmative action may not want to hear of its injustices. A champion of labor unions does not like to learn of their racism, sexism, or antienvironmentalism. Liberators of women from domesticity may resist hearing that careerist parents on the fast track are neglecting their children. Critics of capitalism may have trouble seeing the advantages of markets. Progressives may resist truths about family values if they hear them from the Christian right. Socialists enamored of economic growth may ignore evidence that the planet has reached its carrying capacity.

These politically correct tendencies empty the intellectual reserves of movements for social change. Ironically, in situations in which there really is a single correct, or most productive, analysis of a problem, political correctness will *decrease* the likelihood of finding it. PC does so by constricting our field of vision. In achieving feel-good conformity, politically correct activists may avoid anxiety but only by sacrificing truth and lowering their chances for success. The point is not that activists should shun all certainty, because decisive action requires at least temporary closure. The point is to avoid both premature closure in the vital phases of exploring, analyzing, and strategizing, and permanent closure that prevents realistic assessment and self-correction. Transformationalists need to know, for instance, why so many young black men run afoul of the law and injure themselves and innocent others in the process. But if the only explanations they are willing to entertain are institutional racism and police brutality, they do no service to the young black men or to the cause of social transformation.

Regarding constricted vision, are the proposals for change advocated in this book little more than a thinly veiled form of neo-PC? Those who agree with them could certainly do so in a politically correct manner, refusing to hear discordant evidence or voices. My intention, however, is to get these ideas out of the closet and onto the table for serious discussion. I do confess to having a vision of the future based on these proposals: a vision of U.S. communities some decades down the road when citizens enjoy fuller opportunities to reach their unique potentials, when synergistic values have made inroads into the all-American pursuit of winning at all costs, when young people enjoy equal rights with their elders and families are empowered political actors, when desecrating the planet is no longer acceptable, when most offenders are rehabilitated and the fabric of their communities restored, and when our economic needs are met by a democratic economy controlled by ordinary working people.

Inhabited by human beings, this and related utopias would be far from perfect. But they might be as much better than the present as the present is better than "the good old days" when it was glorious to dispossess native peoples, rich white men owned slaves, women and poor men could not vote, and children had no rights. To conceive of dreams for a much better life as utopias of perfection is to marginalize them as quaint and irrelevant curiosities. Such straw theories are easy to debunk and serve to justify an oppressive status quo.

Oscar Wilde explained why he believed that "a map of the world that does not include utopia is not even worth glancing at." The reason was that such a map "leaves out the one country at which humanity is always landing. And when humanity lands there, it looks out, and seeing a better country, sets sail. Progress is the realisation of utopias." I will resist the temptation to draw a detailed picture of the "practical utopia" that I envision for the United States sometime later in this century. Such a picture would be only one man's opinion of an alternative future.

The better society that our children and grandchildren deserve must be the continuing work of concerned and engaged citizens and their progeny for seven generations and beyond. If this book prompts the reader to think and talk about ideas that deserve a fuller hearing than they have had, it will have served its purpose.

Notes

1. John Stuart Mill, *Considerations on Representative Government* (London: J. M. Dent, 1972 [1861]), p. 183.

2. Frederick Douglass, speech given August 4, 1857.

3. Oscar Wilde, "The Soul of Man Under Socialism," in *Selected Essays and Poems* (London: Penguin, 1954 [1891]), p. 34.

4. David Malin Roodman, "Building a Sustainable Society," in Worldwatch Institute (1999: p. 171).

5. Tony Clarke, "Twilight of the Corporation," *The Ecologist,* May-June 1999, quoted in Gary Ruskin, "Why They Whine: How Corporations Prey on Our Children," *Mothering: The Natural Family Living Magazine,* no. 97, November-December 1999, p. 42.

6. A noted communitarian observer reflects this balance when, on the one hand, she warns against a corruption of the educational process by "stultifying dogmas of left- and right-wing ideologues, who abandon reality and assault life with their rigid, abstract chimeras," but, on the other, she joins Vaclav Havel in embracing "the stout of heart who know there are things worth fighting for in a world of paradox, ambiguity, and irony." Jean Bethke Elshtain (1998: p. 268).

7. Greg Phillips, "Politics and Culture at the Grass Roots," *Princeton Alumni Weekly,* January 22, 1992, p. 10.

Glossary

Adultism (1) Politically, an ageist system of allocating rights and responsibilities by a self-defining class of adults. (2) Philosophically, belief in such a system

Ageism The allocation of rights and responsibilities on the basis of age

Attachment parenting A philosophy and practice of child rearing that emphasizes close, loving relationships between parents and children as the key to strong families and healthy, happy children, often associated with concepts of children's rights; as opposed to detachment parenting

Authoritarianism (1) In politics, a system of governance in which a minority rules and its power exceeds its accountability; as opposed to democracy. (2) Psychologically, a disposition to defer to authority rather than thinking and acting independently

Capitalism An economic system based on acquisitive individualism, market competition, private ownership of the means of production, and justice defined as "To each according to ownership and work"

Careerism A disposition to allow career priorities to trump other considerations, especially family ones

Communism A system of political economy in which the major means of production are publicly owned, state coercion has ceased, and justice is defined as "To each according to need, from each according to ability"

Conservatism (1) Generically, a preference for the status quo, especially for the existing distribution of wealth, status, and power and institutional framework of society. (2) In the United States today, general opposition to increased government *economic* intervention and redistribution of wealth, but support for government *moral* intervention in such matters as sex, abortion, drug use, flag honoring, and school prayer as well as *armed* intervention in crime control and international conflict. (3) Classically, a preference for strong government to secure people and property, preserve tradition, and control the ill effects of human nature.

313

Corporate capitalism   An advanced stage of capitalism in which wealth and public decisionmaking are increasingly centralized and controlled by large, limited-liability, for-profit, and often multinational corporations

Corporation   A form of capitalist business ownership that creates a legal corporate "person," thereby limiting the personal liability of its individual owners—a status historically granted by public bodies on the condition that it promote the public good

Democracy   A political system of one-person, one-vote, majority rule in which power and accountability are equal—that is, in which those over whom power is exercised, effectively control policymakers; as opposed to authoritarianism

Detachment parenting   A philosophy and practice of child rearing that emphasizes early independence of children as the best preparation for their entry into the competitive rigors of market society, often associated with concepts of parents' rights; as opposed to attachment parenting

Ecocide   Poisoning, depletion, or destruction of the natural environment

Ecologism   A philosophy that regards the earth as a holistic, natural ecosystem in which the human members should steward rather than exploit nature; holistic and deep environmentalism

Egalitarianism   A philosophy (a) of treating people as if they were equal in certain respects, especially basic needs and dignity, and (b) of belief that institutions should foster such treatment

Elitism   In politics, a system of rule by the specially qualified

Entropy   Culturally, society's loss of collective value (fulfillment, happiness, success) resulting from citizens' pursuit of zero-sum, "win-lose," competitive values; as opposed to synergy

Environmentalism   A philosophy of protecting the natural environment from human encroachment, and especially from pollution, depletion, damage to species, and ecological imbalance

Extremism   (1) Politically, a disposition to take positions much different from the current norm. (2) In common parlance, any position extremely different from one's own and presumptively senseless and unbalanced; as opposed to moderation

Fascism   An authoritarian political economy with strong, centralized governmental control but private ownership of the means of production, as represented during the 1930s and 1940s by Fascist Italy under Mussolini and Nazi Germany under Hitler

Feminism   A philosophy that women should enjoy equal rights and privileges with men; as opposed to patriarchalism

Gaia, Gaea   The earth personified as a goddess or a living being

Green philosophy   A philosophy that favors ecology, economic sustainability, social responsibility, decentralization, feminism, multicultural diversity, grassroots democracy, global awareness, and nonviolent social change; typically espoused by green activists or members of a Green Party

Ideology   A philosophy that is interest-based, action-oriented, and consciously shared among allies; as distinct from pure, abstract, or "armchair" philosophy

Leftist   In the U.S. context, one who generally favors changing society in the direction of greater equality, protection of civil rights and liberties, government intervention on behalf of the disadvantaged, including a social safety net to provide for people's basic needs, protection of the natural environment, and greater engagement of ordinary citizens in the political process; as opposed to rightist

Liberalism   (1) In the U.S. context, a philosophy of achieving the goals of the left by gradual reform of laws and policies. (2) Classically, one who favors a small government that protects the rights of individuals to life, liberty, property, and the pursuit of happiness

Medical-industrial complex   The interdependent system of medical professionals and hospitals, as well as the corporations that sell technology, goods, and services to health-care providers and consumers

Moderate   (1) Politically, one who is averse to straying from the current norm. (2) In common parlance, one who is sensible and balanced; as opposed to extremist

Modernism   A philosophy favoring modern technology and expertise, economic growth, empirical science, rational control, exploitation of nature, and universal norms favorable to such a system

Multiculturalism   A philosophy of respect for a wide variety of historically marginalized cultures and groups, especially indigenous peoples, ethnic minorities, women, and the sexually unconventional

Patriarchy   A system of superior rights and prerogatives for men over women

Philosophy   An interrelated set of beliefs about how things are and how they should be

Political Correctness   (1) In the contemporary U.S. context, an ideological narrowing, intolerance, and silencing of dissent, commonly attributed to the left by the right. (2) In a historical context, as used by socialists, adherence to the political approach currently judged best for advancing the goals of socialism or communism

Political economy   The interdependent system of power and wealth in society—as exemplified by interest-group lobbying and campaign financing of elections or by expressions such as "office politics" and "in Washington, money talks"

Politics   The allocation and use of power and accountability in society and its institutions, including government

Postmodernism   A philosophy that criticizes modernism, asserts the social construction of reality and morality, and typically embraces multiculturalism

Progressive   A liberal or radical leftist

Radicalism   In the U.S. context, a philosophy of achieving the goals of the left or right by fundamental, dramatic change in social institutions

Reactionary   One who favors returning to an earlier status quo

Revolutionary   A radical who favors the use of violence for political ends

Rightist   A conservative or reactionary; as opposed to leftist

Socialism   An economic system based on cooperation, social planning, public ownership of the means of production, and justice defined as "To each according to need and work"

Synergy   Culturally, society's gain of collective value (fulfillment, happiness, success) resulting from citizens' pursuit of positive-sum, "win-win," noncompetitive values; as opposed to entropy

Transformationalism   A philosophy favoring peaceful but fundamental change in personal consciousness, shared values, and social institutions

Utopia   (1) A relatively detailed vision of a much better, though not necessarily perfect, society. (2) Such a society. (3) In common parlance, an unrealistically ideal system, "pie in the sky"

Bibliography

Adorno, T. W., E. Frenkel-Brunswick, D. J. Levinson, and R. N. Sanford. 1950. *The Authoritarian Personality* (New York: Wiley).

Albert, Michael, and Robin Hahnel. 1981. *Socialism, Today and Tomorrow* (Boston: South End).

———. 1983. "Participatory Planning," in Steve R. Shalom, ed., *Socialist Visions* (Boston: South End), pp. 247–274.

Ariès, Philippe. 1962. *Centuries of Childhood: A Social History of Family Life*, trans. Robert Baldick (NewYork: Vintage).

Arms, Suzanne. 1996. *Immaculate Deception*, 2nd ed. (Berkeley: Celestial Arts).

Arthur, Lindsay G. 1973. "Should Children Be as Equal as People?" in Albert E. Wilkerson, ed., *The Rights of Children* (Philadelphia: Temple University Press), p. 137.

Aufderheide, Patricia, ed. 1992. *Beyond PC: Towards a Politics of Understanding* (St. Paul, MN: Gray Wolf).

Baldwin, Rahima. 1991. *Special Delivery* (Berkeley: Celestial Arts).

Barber, Benjamin. 1984. *Strong Democracy* (Berkeley: University of California Press).

Baumslag, Naomi, and Dia Michels. 1995. *Milk, Money, and Madness: The Culture and Politics of Breastfeeding* (Westport, CT: Bergin and Garvey).

Bean, Constance. 1990. *Methods of Childbirth* (New York: William Morrow).

Becker, Ted, and Christa Slaton. 2000. *The Future of Teledemocracy* (Westport, CT: Praeger).

Bell, Steven. 1998. "Long Term Effects of Responsive Parenting," paper presented at Berry College, Mt. Berry, GA.

Benton, Ted, ed. 1996. *The Greening of Marxism* (New York: Guilford).

Bergmann, Barbara. 1996. *In Defense of Affirmative Action* (New York: Basic Books).

Bierbaum, Martin. 1983. "A View from the Northeast," in Steve R. Shalom, ed., *Socialist Visions* (Boston: South End), pp. 91–94.

Bierce, Ambrose. 1993 [1911]. *The Devil's Dictionary* (New York: Dover).

Blankenhorn, David, Steven Bayme, and Jean Bethke Elshtain, eds. 1990. *Rebuilding the Nest: A New Commitment to the American Family* (Milwaukee: Family Service America).

Blankenship, Michael B., ed. 1995. *Understanding Corporate Criminality* (New York: Garland).

Blocker, H. Gene, and Elizabeth H. Smith. 1980. *John Rawls' Theory of Social Justice: An Introduction* (Athens: Ohio University Press).

Bly, Robert. 1992. *Iron John: A Book About Men* (New York: Vintage).
———. 1997. *The Sibling Society* (New York: Vintage).
Bowles, Samuel, and Herbert Gintis. 1987. *Democracy and Capitalism* (New York: Basic Books).
Boyer Commission. 1996. *Reinventing Undergraduate Education* (Washington, DC: Boyer Commission).
Bradley, Robert A. 1965. *Husband-Coached Childbirth* (New York: Harper & Row).
Brecher, Jeremy. 1983. "Socialism Is What You Make It," in Steve R. Shalom, ed., *Socialist Visions* (Boston: South End), pp. 164–174.
Brown, Tony. 1995. *Black Lies, White Lies* (New York: William Morrow).
Burnham, Walter Dean, ed. 1995. *The American Prospect Reader in American Politics* (Chatham, NJ: Chatham House).
Burton, Linda, Janet Dittman, and Cheri Loveless. 1986. *What's a Smart Woman Like You Doing at Home?* (Vienna, VA: Mothers at Home).
Bybee, Keith. 1999. "Political Science, Legal Realism, and the Dilemmas of Modern Constitutional Law," paper given at the annual meeting of the American Political Science Association, Atlanta, September 2–5.
Callenbach, Ernest. 1975. *Ecotopia* (Berkeley: Banyan Tree).
Carlson, Allan. 1998. "The State's Assault on the Family," in Christopher Wolfe, ed., *The Family, Civil Society, and the State* (Lanham, MD: Rowman and Littlefield), pp. 39–49.
Carter, Stephen L. 1991. *Reflections of an Affirmative Action Baby* (New York: Basic Books).
Cary, Eve, Alan H. Levine, and Janet Price. 1997. *The Rights of Students* (New York: Penguin).
Chavez, Linda. 1994. "Just Say Latino," in Nicolaus Mills, ed., *Debating Affirmative Action* (New York: Delta), pp. 174–179.
Chertow, Marian R., and Daniel C. Esty, eds. 1997. *Thinking Ecologically: The Next Generation of Environmental Policy* (New Haven, CT: Yale University Press).
Chira, Susan. 1998. *A Mother's Place: Taking the Debate About Working Mothers Beyond Guilt and Shame* (New York: HarperCollins).
Chivian, Eric, Michael McNally, Howard Hu, and Andrew Haines. 1993. *Critical Condition: Human Health and the Environment* (Cambridge, MA: MIT Press/Physicians for Social Responsibility).
Cohen, Carl. 1971. *Democracy* (Athens: University of Georgia Press).
———. 1995. *Naked Racial Preference: The Case Against Affirmative Action* (Lanham, MD: Madison Books).
Cohen, Howard. 1980. *Equal Rights for Children* (Totowa, NJ: Littlefield, Adams).
Cohen, Nancy Wainer. 1991. *Open Season* (Westport, CT: Bergin and Garvey).
Coles, Robert. 1986. *The Political Life of Children* (Boston: Atlantic Monthly Press).
Coontz, Stephanie. 1997. *The Way We Really Are: Coming to Terms with America's Changing Families* (New York: Basic Books).
Coughlan, Roger, and Randy Mergler. 1999. "Impact of Fatherhood on the Parenting Couple," paper given at the Colorado/Wyoming La Leche League 1999 Health Professional Seminar and Area Conference, Colorado Springs, Colorado, November 6.
Covey, Stephen R. 1994. *The 7 Habits of Highly Effective People* (New York: Franklin Covey).
———. 1997. *The 7 Habits of Highly Effective Families* (New York: Franklin Covey).
Croly, Herbert. 1998 [1909]. *The Promise of American Life*, excerpted in Kenneth M. Dolbeare, ed., *American Political Thought* (Chatham, NJ: Chatham House), pp. 412–426.

Csikszentmihalyi, Mihaly. 1991. *Flow: The Psychology of Optimal Experience* (New York: Harper).

Cummings, Michael S. 1975. "Dogmatism, Ideology, and Political Behavior," doctoral dissertation, Stanford University.

———. 1989. "Taking Liberties with John Stuart Mill in Utopia," in Cummings and Smith, eds., *Utopian Studies II* (Lanham, MD: Society for Utopian Studies and University Press of America), pp. 136–144.

———. 1998. "America's Communal Utopias," review essay on *America's Communal Utopias* by Donald Pitzer, ed. In *Utopian Studies* 9, no. 1, pp. 191–206.

Cummings, Michael S., and Nicholas Smith. 1989. *Utopian Studies II* (Lanham, MD: Society for Utopian Studies and University Press of America).

Cunningham, Allan S. 1995. "Breastfeeding: Adaptive Behavior for Child Health and Longevity," in Patricia Stuart-Macadam and Katherine Dettwyler, eds., *Breastfeeding: Biocultural Perspectives* (Hawthorne, NY: Aldine de Gruyter), pp. 243–264.

Curry, George E., ed. 1996. *The Affirmative Action Debate* (Reading, MA: Addison-Wesley).

Daly, Herman E. 1996. *Beyond Growth: The Economics of Sustainable Development* (Boston: Beacon).

Daly, Herman E., and John B. Cobb Jr. 1994. *For the Common Good* (Boston: Beacon).

Davies, James C. 1986. "Roots of Political Behavior," in Margaret G. Hermann, ed., *Political Psychology* (San Francisco: Jossey-Bass), pp. 39–61.

Davis, Mike. 1999. *Ecology of Fear* (New York: Vintage).

Derber, Charles. 1996. *The Wilding of America: How Greed and Violence Are Eroding Our National Character* (New York: St. Martin's).

Dettwyler, Katherine A. 1995a. "A Time to Wean: The Homonid Blueprint for the Natural Age of Weaning in Modern Human Populations," in Patricia Stuart-Macadam and Katherine A. Dettwyler, eds., *Breastfeeding: Biocultural Perspectives* (Hawthorne, NY: Aldine de Gruyter), pp. 39–73.

———. 1995b. "Beauty and the Breast: The Cultural Context of Breastfeeding in the United States," in Stuart-Macadam and Dettwyler, eds., *Breastfeeding: Biocultural Perspectives* (Hawthorne, NY: Aldine de Gruyter), pp. 167–215.

Dick-Read, Grantly. 1974 [1944]. *Childbirth Without Fear: The Principles and Practices of Natural Childbirth* (New York: Harper and Row).

Dinh, Viet D. 1994. "Multiracial Affirmative Action," in Nicolaus Mills, ed., *Debating Affirmative Action* (New York: Delta), pp. 280–289.

Dobson, Andrew, ed. 1991. *The Green Reader: Essays Toward a Sustainable Society* (San Francisco: Mercury House).

Doherty, William J. 1998. "How Therapists Threaten Marriages," in Amitai Etzioni, ed., *The Essential Communitarian Reader* (Lanham, MD: Rowman and Littlefield), pp. 157–166.

Dolbeare, Kenneth M., ed. 1998. *American Political Thought*, 4th ed. (Chatham, NJ: Chatham House).

Domhoff, G. William. 1998. *Who Rules America? Power and Politics in the Year 2000*, 3rd ed. (Mountain View, CA: Mayfield).

Dye, Thomas. 1999. *Power and Society*, 8th ed. (Fort Worth: Harcourt Brace).

Elshtain, Jean Bethke. 1982. *The Family in Political Thought* (Amherst: University of Massachusetts Press).

———. 1997a. "Political Children," in Mary Lyndon Shanley and Uma Narayan, eds., *Reconstructing Political Theory: Feminist Perspectives* (University Park: University of Pennsylvania Press), pp. 109–127.

———. 1997b. *Real Politics: At the Center of Everyday Life* (Baltimore: Johns Hopkins University Press).

———. 1998. "Democracy and the Politics of Difference," in Amatai Etzioni, ed., *The Essential Communitarian Reader* (Lanham, MD: Rowman and Littlefield), pp. 259–268.

Engelkin, Ralph, and Rita Engelkin. 1981. *The Art of Natural Farming and Gardening* (Greeley, IA: Barrington Hall).

England, Pam. 1999. "There's No Place Like Home: The Advantages—and Joys— of Giving Birth Where You Live," *Mothering: The Natural Family Living Magazine,* no. 94, May-June, pp. 57–58.

England, Pam, and R. Horowitz. 1998. *Birthing from Within: An Extraordinary Guide to Childbirth Preparation* (Palm Harbor, FL: Pantera Press).

Erasmus, Charles J. 1985. *In Search of the Common Good: Utopian Experiments Past and Future,* 2nd ed. (New York: Free Press).

Etzioni, Amitai, 1996. *The New Golden Rule: Community and Morality in a Democratic Society* (New York: Basic Books).

———. ed. 1998. *The Essential Communitarian Reader* (Lanham, MD: Rowman and Littlefield).

Ezorsky, Gertrude. 1991. *Racism and Justice: The Case for Affirmative Action* (Ithaca: Cornell University Press).

Faber, Adele, and Elaine Mazlish. 1980. *How to Talk So Kids Will Listen and Listen So Kids Will Talk* (New York: Avon Books).

Faber, Daniel, ed. 1998. *The Struggle for Ecological Democracy: Environmental Justice Movements in the United States* (New York: Guilford).

Faludi, Susan. 1991. *Backlash: The Undeclared War Against American Women* (New York: Crown).

———. 1999. *Stiffed: The Betrayal of the American Man* (New York: Morrow).

Farson, Richard. 1974. *Birthrights* (New York: Macmillan).

Fellowship for Intentional Communities, "Political Activism in Community," *Communities: The Journal of Cooperative Living,* no. 100, fall 1998, pp. 1–80.

———. 2000. *Communities Directory,* 3rd ed. (Rutledge, MO: Fellowship for Intentional Communities).

Filipovic, Zlata. 1994. *Zlata's Diary: A Child's Life in Sarajevo* (New York: Penguin).

Flacks, Richard. 1988. *Making History: The American Left and the American Mind* (New York: Columbia University Press).

Fox-Genovese, Elizabeth. 1991. *Feminism Without Illusions: A Critique of Individualism* (Durham: University of North Carolina Press).

Franklin, Bob, ed. 1986. *The Rights of Children* (Oxford: Basil Blackwell).

Freud, Sigmund. 1961 [1927]. *The Future of an Illusion,* trans. James Strachey (New York: Norton).

Friedan, Betty. 1983 [1963]. *The Feminine Mystique* (New York: Dell).

———. 1997. *Beyond Gender: The New Politics of Work and Family,* ed. Brigid O'Farrell (Washington, DC: Woodrow Wilson Center Press).

Galston, William. 1997. "A Progressive Family Policy for the Twenty-First Century," in Will Marshall, ed., *Building the Bridge: 10 Big Ideas to Transform America* (Lanham, MD: Rowman and Littlefield), pp. 149–162.

Gaskin, Ina May. 1990. *Spiritual Midwifery,* 3rd ed. (Summertown, TN: The Book Publishing Company).

Geneen, Harold. 1997. *The Synergy Myth* (New York: St. Martin's).

Geoghegan, Vince. 1989. "The Golden Age and Its Return in the Marxism of the Second International," in Cummings and Smith (1989), pp. 60–68.

Giddens, Anthony. 1998. *The Third Way: The Renewal of Social Democracy* (Malden, MA: Blackwell).

Glendon, Mary Ann. 1991. *Rights Talk: The Impoverishment of Political Discourse* (New York: Free Press).

Glendon, Mary Ann, and David Blankenhorn, eds. 1995. *Seedbeds of Virtue: Sources of Competence, Character, and Citizenship in American Society* (Lanham, MD: Madison Books).

Goble, Frank G. 1970. *The Third Force: The Psychology of Abraham Maslow* (New York: Pocket Books).

Goer, Henci. 1995. *Obstetric Myths Versus Research Realities: A Guide to the Medical Literature* (Westport, CT: Bergin and Garvey).

Granju, Katie Allison. 1999. *Attachment Parenting* (Riverside, NJ: Simon and Schuster).

Greenberg, Stanley B., and Theda Skocpol, eds. 1997. *The New Majority: Toward a New Progressive Politics* (New Haven, CT: Yale University Press).

Greider, William. 1997. *One World, Ready or Not: The Manic Logic of Global Capitalism* (New York: Simon & Schuster).

Griffin, Nancy. 1997. "The Epidural Express: Real Reasons Not to Jump Aboard," *Mothering: The Magazine of Natural Family Living* 82, spring, pp. 46–55.

Guggenheim, Martin, and Alan Sussman. 1985. *The Rights of Young People* (New York: Bantam/ACLU).

Hardin, Garrett. 1968. "The Tragedy of the Commons," *Science*, no. 168, pp. 1243–1248.

Harrington, Michael. 1992. *Socialism, Past and Future* (New York: Mentor).

Harris, Luke Charles, and Uma Narayan. 1994. "Affirmative Action and the Myth of Preferential Treatment," *Harvard BlackLetter Journal*, vol. II, pp. 1–35.

Harvey, Elizabeth. 1999. "Short-Term and Long-Term Effects of Early Parental Employment on Children of the National Longitudinal Survey of Youth," *Developmental Psychology* 35, no. 2, pp. 445–459.

Hayden, Dolores. 1983. "Rejoinder," in Steve R. Shalom, ed., *Socialist Visions* (Boston: South End), pp. 95–97.

Helburn Suzanne, ed. 1995. *Cost, Quality and Child Outcomes in Child Care Centers* (Denver: University of Colorado at Denver).

———. 1999. *The Silent Crisis in U.S. Child Care*, special edition of *Annals of the American Academy of Political and Social Science*, vol. 563, May.

Helmbold, Lois R., and Amber Hollibaugh. 1983. "The Family in Socialist America," in Steve R. Shalom, ed., *Socialist Visions* (Boston: South End), pp. 191–222.

Herrnstein, Richard J., and Charles Murray. 1994. *The Bell Curve: Intelligence and Class Structure in America* (New York: Free Press).

Hertz, Rosanna. 1999. "Working to Place Family at the Center of Life: Dual-Earner and Single-Parent Strategies," in Marcie Pitt-Catsouphes and Bradley K. Googins, eds., *The Evolving World of Work and Family*, special edition of *The Annals of the Academy of Political and Social Sciences* 562, March, pp. 16–31.

Hewlett, Sylvia Ann, and Cornel West. 1998. *The War Against Parents* (Boston: Houghton Mifflin).

Holt, John. 1976. *Escape from Childhood* (New York: Ballantine).

hooks, bell. 1995. *Killing Rage: Ending Racism* (New York: Henry Holt).

Hoover, Kenneth. 1992. "Mondragon's Answers to Utopia's Problems," *Utopian Studies* 3, no. 2, pp. 1–20.

Hunter, Dale, Anne Bailey, and Bill Taylor. 1997. *Co-operacy: A New Way of Being at Work* (Auckland, New Zealand: Tandem).

Jacobs, Jane. 1961. *The Death and Life of Great American Cities* (New York: Vintage).

John, Mary. 1995. "Children's Rights in a Free-Market Culture," in Sharon Stephens, ed., *Children and the Politics of Culture* (Princeton: Princeton University Press), pp. 105–137.

Johnson, Cathy M. 1994. "Who Speaks for Children? Representation in the Policy Process," paper given at the meetings of the American Political Science Association, New York, September 1–4.

Jordan, Brigitte. 1993. *Childbirth in Four Cultures,* 4th ed. (Prospect Heights, IL: Waveland).

Karliner, Joshua. 1997. *The Corporate Planet: Ecology and Politics in the Age of Globalization* (San Francisco: Sierra Club Books).

Karp, David R. 1998. *Community Justice: An Emerging Field* (New York: Rowman and Littlefield).

Katz, Claudio. 1997. "Private Property Versus Markets: Democratic and Communitarian Critiques of Capitalism," *American Political Science Review* 91, no. 2, pp. 277–289.

Kay, Alan F. 1998. *Locating Consensus for Democracy: A Ten-Year U.S. Experiment* (St. Augustine, FL: Americans Talk Issues).

Kelling, George L., and Catherine M. Coles. 1997. *Fixing Broken Windows: Restoring Order and Reducing Crime in Our Communities* (New York: Simon & Schuster).

Kessler-Harris, Alice. 1994. "Feminism and Affirmative Action," in Nicolaus Mills, ed., *Debating Affirmative Action* (New York: Delta), pp. 68–79.

Kielburger, Craig. 1999. *Free the Children: A Young Man's Personal Crusade Against Child Labor* (New York: HarperCollins).

Kitwood, Tom. 1978. "'Science' and 'Utopia' in the Marxist Tradition," *Alternative Futures* 1, no. 2, pp. 24–46.

Kitzinger, Sheila. 1991. *Homebirth* (New York: Dorling Kindersley).

Korten, David C. 1999. *The Post-Corporate World: Life After Capitalism* (San Francisco and West Hartford, CT: Berrett-Koehler Publishers and Kumarian Press).

Kozeny, Geoph. 1998. "Compassion and Political Correctness," *Communities: Journal of Cooperative Living,* no. 100, fall, pp. 79–80.

Kuttner, Robert. 1997. *Everything for Sale: The Virtues and Limits of Markets* (New York: Knopf).

Laing, R. D., *The Politics of the Family* (New York: Vintage, 1972).

Lane, Robert. 1991. *The Market Experience* (New York: Cambridge University Press).

Lapetino, Jan. 2000. President, Colorado Midwives Association, personal interview, Denver, Colorado, January 31.

Lappe, Frances Moore. 1994. *The Quickening of America: Rebuilding Our Nation, Remaking Our Lives* (San Francisco: Jossey-Bass).

Lasch, Christopher. 1977. *Haven in a Heartless World: The Family Besieged* (New York: Basic Books).

———. 1979. *The Culture of Narcissism: American Life in an Age of Diminished Expectations* (New York: Norton).

———. 1984. *The Minimal Self: Psychic Survival in Troubled Times* (New York: Norton).

———. 1991. *The True and Only Heaven: Progress and Its Critics* (New York: Norton).

———. 1995. *The Revolt of the Elites and the Betrayal of Democracy* (New York: Norton).

———. 1997. *Women and the Common Life: Love, Marriage, and Feminism* (New York: Norton).

Lawler, James. 1998. "Marx as Market Socialist," in Bertell Ollman, ed., *Market Socialism: The Debate Among Socialists* (New York: Routledge), pp. 23–52.

Leach, Penelope. 1994. *Children First* (New York: Knopf).

Lee, Martha. 1995. *Earth First!* (Syracuse: Syracuse University Press).

Lerner, Michael. 1996. *The Politics of Meaning* (Reading, MA: Addison-Wesley).

Levine, James A., and Todd Pittinsky. 1997. *Working Fathers: New Strategies for Balancing Work and Family* (San Diego: Harcourt Brace).

Lind, Michael. 1996. *The Next American Nation* (New York: Free Press).

Lott, John. 1998. *More Guns, Less Crime* (Chicago: University of Chicago Press).

Loury, Glenn C. 1996. "Performing Without a Net," in George E. Curry, ed., *The Affirmative Action Debate* (Reading, MA: Addison-Wesley), pp. 49–64.

Lowi, Theodore J. 1979. *The End of Liberalism*, 2nd ed. (New York: Norton).

Lynch, Frederick R. 1991. *Invisible Victims: While Males and the Crisis of Affirmative Action* (New York: Praeger).

Malman, Jessica. 1996. "Race-Exclusive Scholarships for Undergraduate Education," in Carol M. Swain, ed., *Race Versus Class: The New Affirmative Action Debate* (Lanham, MD: University Press of America), pp. 143–184.

Mansbridge, Jane J., ed. 1990. *Beyond Self-Interest* (Chicago: University of Chicago Press).

Mao Zedong. 1927, 1953. *On the Rectification of Incorrect Ideas in the Party* (Peking: Foreign Language Press).

———. 1956. "Criticism, Self-Criticism, and Transformation," in *Collected Works of Mao Zedong* (Beijing: PRC).

Marable, Manning. 1995. *Beyond Black and White* (New York: Verso).

———. 1996. "Staying on the Path to Racial Equality," in George E. Curry, ed., *The Affirmative Action Debate* (Reading, MA: Addison-Wesley), pp. 3–15.

Marshall, Will, ed. 1997. *Building the Bridge: 10 Big Ideas to Transform America* (New York: Rowman and Littlefield).

Marx, Karl. 1988 [1848]. *The Communist Manifesto* (New York: Norton).

Maslow, Abraham. 1943. "A Theory of Motivation," *Psychological Review* 50, pp. 370–396.

———. 1954. *Motivation and Personality* (New York: Harper & Row).

———. 1964. "Synergy in the Society and in the Individual," *Journal of Individual Psychology* 20, pp. 153–164.

McCutcheon-Rosegg, Susan. 1984. *Natural Childbirth the Bradley Way* (New York: Dutton).

McKenna, James J., and Nicole J. Bernshaw. 1995. "Breastfeeding and Infant-Parent Co-Sleeping as Adaptive Strategies: Are They Protection Against SIDS?" in Patricia Stuart-Macadam and Katherine Dettwyler, eds., *Breastfeeding: Biocultural Perspectives* (Hawthorne, NY: Aldine de Gruyter), pp. 265–303.

McLanahan, Sara, and Gary Sandefur. 1994. *Growing Up with a Single Parent* (Cambridge: Harvard University Press).

Merchant, Carolyn. 1989. *Ecological Revolutions* (Chapel Hill: University of North Carolina Press).

Micozzi, Marc S. 1995. "Breast Cancer, Reproductive Biology, and Breastfeeding," in Patricia Stuart-Macadam and Katherine Dettwyler, eds., *Breastfeeding: Biocultural Perspectives* (Hawthorne, NY: Aldine de Gruyter), pp. 347–384.

Milbrath, Lester. 1984. *Environmentalists: Vanguard for a New Society* (Albany: SUNY Press).

Mill, John Stuart. 1985 [1859]. *On Liberty* (New York: Penguin).

Mills, C. Wright. 1956. *The Power Elite* (New York: Oxford University Press).

Mills, Nicolaus, ed. 1994. *Debating Affirmative Action* (New York: Dell).

Minow, Martha, and Mary Lyndon Shanley. 1997. "Revisioning the Family: Relational Rights and Responsibilities," in Mary Lyndon Shanley and Uma Narayan, eds., *Reconstructing Political Theory: Feminist Perspectives* (University Park: Pennsylvania University Press), pp. 84–108.

Mohr, Wanda, Richard J. Gelles, and Ira M. Scwartz. 1999. "Shackled in the Land of Liberty: No Rights for Children," in *Will the Juvenile Court System Survive?*, special edition of *The Annals of the American Academy of Political and Social Sciences* 564, July, pp. 37–55.

Mohrbacher, Nancy, and Julie Stock. 1997. *The Breastfeeding Answer Book* (Schaumburg, IL: La Leche League International).

Mort, Jo-ann, ed. 1998. *Not Your Father's Movement: Inside the AFL-CIO* (New York: Verso).

Murray, Charles. 1994. "Affirmative Racism," in Nicolaus Mills, ed., *Debating Affirmative Action* (New York: Delta), pp. 191–208.

Nader, Ralph. 1997. "An Evening with Ralph Nader," talk given at the annual meeting of the American Political Science Association, Washington, D.C., August 30.

Nagle, John D. 1998. *Confessions from the Left* (New York: Peter Lang).

Nash, Roderick. 1989. *The Rights of Nature: A History of Environmental Ethics* (Madison: University of Wisconsin Press).

National Academy of Public Administration. 1994. *The Environment Goes to Market: The Implementation of Economic Incentives for Pollution Control* (Washington, DC: Georgetown University Press).

National Conference of Christians and Jews. 1994. *Taking America's Pulse: The National Conference Survey on Inter-group Relations* (Washington, DC: LH Research).

Nearing, Helen, and Scott Nearing. 1989. *The Good Life* (New York: Schocken).

Neill, A. S. 1960. *Summerhill: A Radical Approach to Child Rearing* (New York: Hart).

Njeri, Itabari. 1993. "Sushi and Grits: Ethnic Identity and Conflict in a Newly Multicultural America," in Gerald Early, ed., *Lure and Loathing: Essays on Race, Identity and the Ambivalence of Assimilation* (New York: Penguin).

Northrup, Christiane. 1994. *Women's Bodies, Women's Wisdom* (New York: Bantam).

Norton, Eleanor Holmes. 1996. "Affirmative Action in the Workplace," in George E. Curry, ed., *The Affirmative Action Debate* (Reading, MA: Addison-Wesley), pp. 39–48.

Norwood, Ken, and Kathleen Smith. 1995. *Rebuilding Community in America: Housing for Ecological Living, Personal Empowerment, and the New Extended Family* (Berkeley: Shared Living Resource Center).

Noyes, John Humphrey. 1876. *Mutual Criticism* (Oneida, NY: Office of the American Socialist).

O'Connor, James. 1998. *Natural Causes: Essays in Ecological Marxism* (New York: Guilford).

O'Connor, Martin, ed. 1994. *Is Capitalism Sustainable? Political Economy and the Politics of Ecology* (New York: Guilford).

Okin, Susan Moller. 1989. *Justice, Gender, and the Family* (New York: Basic Books).

Ollman, Bertell, ed. 1998. *Market Socialism: The Debate Among Socialists* (London: Routledge).

O'Neill, John. 1994. *The Missing Child in Liberal Theory* (Toronto: University of Toronto Press).

Ophuls, William. 1997. *Requiem for Modern Politics* (Boulder, CO: Westview).

Palmer, Gabrielle. 1993. *The Politics of Breastfeeding* (London: Pandora).

Pateman, Carole. 1970. *Participation and Democratic Theory* (Cambridge: Cambridge University Press).

———. 1988. *The Sexual Contract* (Stanford: Stanford University Press).

Peterson, Paul E. 1993. "An Immodest Proposal: Let's Give Children the Vote," *Brookings Review*, winter, pp. 18–23.

———. 1995. *Classifying by Race* (Princeton, NJ: Princeton University Press).

Pipher, Mary. 1996. *The Shelter of Each Other: Rebuilding Our Families* (New York: Ballantine).

Pitt-Catsouphes, Marcie, and Bradley K. Googins, eds. 1999. *The Evolving World of Work and Family,* special edition of *The Annals of the Academy of Political and Social Sciences* 562, March.

Pitzer, Donald. 1998. *America's Communal Utopias* (Chapel Hill: University of North Carolina Press).

Popenoe, David. 1996. *Life Without Father* (New York: Free Press).

Poot, Robert, and Michael Rogin, eds. 1998. *Race and Representation: Affirmative Action* (New York: Zone Books).

Postman, Neil. 1994 [1982]. *The Disappearance of Childhood* (New York: Vintage).

Przeworski, Adam. 1991. *Democracy and the Market* (Cambridge: Cambridge University Press).

Putnam, Robert D. 1996. "The Strange Disappearance of Civic America," *The American Prospect* 24, winter, pp. 34–48.

Quandt, Sarah A. 1995. "Sociocultural Aspects of the Lactation Process," in Patricia Stuart-Macadam and Katherine Dettwyler, eds., *Breastfeeding: Biocultural Perspectives* (Hawthorne, NY: Aldine de Gruyter), pp. 127–143.

Rawls, John. 1971. *A Theory of Justice* (Cambridge: Harvard University Press).

———. 1993. *Political Liberalism* (New York: Columbia University Press).

Rensenbrink, John. 1992. *The Greens and the Politics of Transformation* (San Pedro, CA: R. and E. Miles).

———. 1999. *Against All Odds: The Green Transformation of American Politics* (Raymond, ME: Leopold).

Riordan, Jan. 1999. "Epidurals and Breastfeeding," *Breastfeeding Abstracts* 19, no. 2, November, pp. 11–12.

Roberts, Lisa. 1997. *How to Raise a Family and a Career Under One Roof: A Parent's Guide to Home Business* (Moon Township, PA: Bookhaven).

Rorty, Richard. 1998. *Achieving Our Country: Leftist Thought in Twentieth-Century America* (Cambridge, MA: Harvard University Press).

Rothman, Barbara Katz. 1982. *Giving Birth: Alternatives in Childbirth* (New York: Penguin).

Ruddick, Sara. 1995. *Maternal Thinking: Toward a Politics of Peace* (Boston: Beacon).

Scheper-Hughes, Nancy, and Carolyn Sargent. 1998. *Small Wars: The Cultural Politics of Childhood* (Berkeley: University of California Press).

Schuman, Michael. 1998. *Going Local: Creating Self-Reliant Communities in a Global Age* (Florence, KY: Taylor and Francis-Routledge).

Schwartz, Ira M. 1999. *Will the Juvenile Court System Survive?*, special edition of *The Annals of the American Academy of Political and Social Science* 564, July.

Schweickart, David. 1998. "Market Socialism: A Defense," in Bertell Ollman, ed., *Market Socialism: The Debate Among Socialists* (New York: Routledge), pp. 7–22.

Scott, James. 1998. *Seeing Like a State: Why Certain Schemes to Improve the Human Condition Have Failed* (New Haven: Yale University Press).

Sears, William. 1987. *Growing Together* (Schaumburg, IL: La Leche League International).

———. 1995. *Sudden Infant Death Syndrome* (Boston: Little, Brown).

Sears, William, and Martha Sears. 1993. *The Baby Book* (Boston: Little Brown).

Seo, Danny. 1997. *Generation React: Activism for Beginners* (New York: Ballantine).

Shalom, Steve Rosskamm, ed. 1983. *Socialist Visions* (Boston: South End).

Shanley, Mary Lyndon, and Uma Narayan, eds. 1997. *Reconstructing Political Theory: Feminist Perspectives* (University Park: University of Pennsylvania Press).

Shaw, Randy. 1996. *The Activist's Handbook: A Primer for the 1990s and Beyond* (Berkeley: University of California Press).

Shellenbarger, Sue. 1999. *Work and Family* (New York: Ballantine).

Simon, David R., and Frank E. Hagan. 1999. *White-Collar Deviance* (Needham Heights, MA: Allyn & Bacon).

Simpson, Sally S., Anthony R. Harris, and Brian A. Mattson. 1995. "Measuring Corporate Crime," in Michael B. Blankenship, ed., *Understanding Corporate Criminality* (New York: Garland), pp. 115–140.

Sirianni, Carmen. 1983. "The Council Model of Decentralized Planning: A Critical Analysis," in Steve R. Shalom, ed., *Socialist Visions* (Boston: South End), pp. 279–286.

Sklar, Holly. 1995. *Chaos or Community?* (Boston: South End).

Skocpol, Theda. 1994. "The Choice," in Nicolaus Mills, ed., *Debating Affirmative Action* (New York: Delta), pp. 290–299.

Skrentny, John. 1996. *The Ironies of Affirmative Action* (Chicago: University of Chicago Press).

Small, Meredith. 1998. *Our Babies, Ourselves: How Biology and Culture Shape the Way We Parent* (New York: Anchor).

Smith, Adam. 1759, 1897. "The Theory of Moral Sentiments," in L. A. Selby-Bigge, ed., *British Moralists* (Oxford: Oxford University Press), pp. 257–277.

———. 1776, 1937. *The Wealth of Nations* (New York: Modern Library).

Sniderman, Paul, and Thomas Piazza. 1993. *The Scar of Race* (Cambridge, MA: Harvard University Press).

Sniderman, Paul, and Edward Carmines. 1997. "Reaching Beyond Race," *PS: Political Science and Politics* 30, no. 3, September, pp. 466–471.

South End Press Collective, ed. 1998. *Talking About a Revolution: Interviews with Manning Marable, Winona LaDuke, Michael Albert, Howard Zinn, bell hooks, Urvashi Vaid, Peter Kwong, Noam Chomsky, Barbara Ehrenreich* (Cambridge: South End).

Sowell, Thomas. 1994. *Race and Culture: A World View* (New York: Basic Books).

Stacey, Judith. 1996. *In the Name of the Family: Rethinking Family Values in the Postmodern Age* (Boston: Beacon).

Steele, Shelby. 1990. *The Content of Our Character: A New Vision of Race in America* (New York: HarperCollins).

Stephens, Sharon, ed. 1995. *Children and the Politics of Culture* (Princeton, NJ: Princeton University Press).

Stuart-Macadam, Patricia, and Katherine A. Dettwyler, eds. 1995. *Breastfeeding: Biocultural Perspectives* (New York: Aldine de Gruyter).

Sullivan, Deborah A., and Rose Weitz. 1988. *Labor Pains: Modern Midwives and Homebirth* (New Haven, CT: Yale University Press).

Sullivan, John J., and Joseph L. Victor, eds. 1996. *Criminal Justice 96/97* (Guilford, CT: Dushkin).

Sulloway, Frank J. 1997. *Born to Rebel: Birth Order, Family Dynamics, and Creative Lives* (New York: Random House).

Swain, Carol M. 1996. *Race Versus Class: The New Affirmative Action Debate* (Lanham, MD: University Press of America).

Sweet, Martin. 1999. "The Supreme Court, Affirmative Action, and the Evidence," paper given at the annual meeting of the American Political Science Association, Atlanta, September 2–5.

Tanzer, Deborah. 1976. *Why Natural Childbirth: a Psychologist's Report on the Benefits to Mothers, Fathers, and Babies* (New York: Schocken).

Temple, Lannis. 1993. *Dear World: How Children Around the World Feel About Our Environment* (New York: Random House).

Terkel, Studs. 1993. *Race: How Blacks and Whites Think and Feel About the American Obsession* (New York: Anchor Books).

Thernstrom, Stephan, and Abigail Thernstrom. 1997. *America in Black and White: One Nation, Indivisible* (New York: Simon & Schuster).

Thevenin, Tine. 1987. *The Family Bed: An Age Old Concept in Child Rearing* (Minneapolis: Tine Thevenin).

Thomas, Clarence. 1994. "Affirmative Action Goals and Timetables: Too Tough? Not Tough Enough!" in Nicolaus Mills, ed., *Debating Affirmative Action* (New York: Delta), pp. 290-299.

Ticktin, Hillel. 1988. "The Problem Is Market Socialism," in Bertell Ollman, ed., *Market Socialism: The Debate Among Socialists* (New York: Routledge), pp. 55-80.

Tillman, Ray M., and Michael S. Cummings. 1999. *The Transformation of U.S. Unions: Voices, Visions, and Strategies from the Grassroots* (Boulder, CO: Lynne Rienner Publishers).

Ulrich, Laurel Thatcher. 1991. *A Midwife's Tale: The Life of Martha Ballard, Based on her Diary, 1785-1812* (New York: Vintage).

Umansky, Lauri. 1996. *Motherhood Reconceived: Feminism and the Legacies of the Sixties* (New York: New York University Press).

UNICEF. 1998a. *Kids Helping Kids: Teacher's Guide* (New York: United Nations).

———. 1998b. *The Progress of Nations* (New York: United Nations).

———. 1998c. *The State of the World's Children 1998* (New York: United Nations).

———. 1999. *The State of the World's Children 1999* (New York: United Nations).

———. 2000. *The State of the World's Children 2000*, <www.unicef.org/sowc00>.

United Nations. 1989. *International Convention on the Rights of the Child* (New York: United Nations).

Vittorini, Nancy. 2000. *Everyday Heroes* (New York: Continuum).

Waite, Linda. 1998. "Social Science Finds: 'Marriage Matters,'" in Amitai Etzioni, ed., *The Essential Communitarian Reader* (Lanham, MD: Rowman and Littlefield), pp. 247-255.

Walzer, Michael. 1983. *Spheres of Justice* (New York: Basic Books).

Ward, Jule DeJager. 2000. *La Leche League: At the Crossroads of Medicine, Feminism, and Religion* (Chapel Hill: University of North Carolina Press).

Wargo, John. 1998. *Our Children's Toxic Legacy: How Science and Law Fail to Protect Us from Pesticides*, 2nd ed. (New Haven, CT: Yale University Press).

West, Cornel. 1993. *Race Matters* (New York: Vintage).

———. 1994. "Equality and Identity," in Nicolaus Mills, ed., *Debating Affirmative Action* (New York: Delta), pp. 83-88.

Whitehead, Barbara Dafoe. 1996. *The Divorce Culture* (New York: Vintage).

Wilkerson, Albert E., ed. 1973. *The Rights of Children* (Philadelphia: Temple University Press).

Wilson, John K. 1995. *The Myth of Political Correctness* (Durham: University of North Carolina Press).

Wilson, William Julius. 1987. *The Truly Disadvantaged: The Inner City, the Underclass, and Public Policy* (Chicago: University of Chicago Press).

———. 1994. "Race-Neutral Programs and the Democratic Coalition," in Nicolaus Mills, ed., *Debating Affirmative Action* (New York: Delta) pp. 159-173.

Wolfe, Alan. 1996. *Marginalized in the Middle* (Chicago: University of Chicago Press).

Wolfe, Christopher, ed. 1998. *The Family, Civil Society, and the State* (Lanham, MD: Rowman and Littlefield).

Woodson, Robert L. 1996. "Personal Responsibility," in George E. Curry, ed., *The Affirmative Action Debate* (Reading, MA: Addison-Wesley), pp. 111-120.

Woolpert, Stephen, Christa Daryl Slaton, and Edward W. Schwerin, eds. 1998. *Transformational Politics: Theory, Study, and Practice* (Albany: SUNY Press).

Wootan, George, and Sarah Verney. 1992. *Take Charge of Your Child's Health* (New York: Crown).

Worldwatch Institute. 1998, 1999, 2000. *State of the World.* Lester Brown, Christopher Flavin, and Hilary French, series eds. (New York: Norton/Worldwatch).

———. 1998, 1999. *Vital Signs.* Lester Brown, Christopher Flavin, and Hilary French, series eds. (New York: Norton/Worldwatch).

Zwerdling, Daniel. 1984. *Workplace Democracy* (New York: Harper & Row).

Index

About the Book

Why does the right dominate debates on crime, family values, and economic freedom? Why does the left defend such arbitrary and divisive aspects of affirmative action, while equivocating on questions of ecology and political empowerment for young people? The answer, Cummings believes, is that too many progressives have avoided politically sensitive issues, condemning themselves to intellectual atrophy and political ineffectiveness.

Cummings clearly is not an advocate for the "self-serving, hypocritical right." But he contends that the left handicaps itself with political correctness, and that frank analysis of taboo topics requires us to move beyond the traditional dichotomy of left and right. With passion and rigor, he argues for a transformation of U.S. culture and institutions that will enable individuals to pursue their vital interests without impinging on the rights of others and undermining the public good.

Michael Cummings is chair of the Political Science Department at the University of Colorado at Denver, and co-editor of *The Transformation of U.S. Unions: Voices, Visions, and Strategies from the Grassroots*.